THE JEWISH ORIGINS OF CULTURAL PLURALISM

THE MODERN JEWISH EXPERIENCE
Paula Hyman and Deborah Dash Moore, editors

The Jewish Origins of Cultural Pluralism

The Menorah Association and American Diversity

DANIEL GREENE

INDIANA UNIVERSITY PRESS

Bloomington and Indianapolis

This book is a publication of

Indiana University Press
601 North Morton Street
Bloomington, Indiana 47404-3797 USA

www.iupress.indiana.edu

Telephone orders   800-842-6796
Fax orders   812-855-7931
Orders by e-mail   iuporder@indiana.edu

∞ The paper used in this publication meets the minimum requirements of the American National Standard for Information Sciences—Permanence of Paper for Printed Library Materials, ANSI Z39.48-1992.

Manufactured in the United States of America

Library of Congress Cataloging-in-Publication Data

Greene, Daniel.
The Jewish origins of cultural pluralism : the Menorah Association and American diversity / Daniel Greene.
p. cm. — (The modern Jewish experience)
Includes bibliographical references and index.
ISBN 978-0-253-35614-7 (cl : alk. paper) — ISBN 978-0-253-22334-0 (pbk. : alk. paper) 1. Harvard Menorah Society (Cambridge, Mass.)—History—20th century. 2. Intercollegiate Menorah Association (New York, N.Y.)—History—20th century. 3. Menorah Association (New York, N.Y.)—History—20th century. 4. Jewish college students—Massachusetts—Cambridge—Societies, etc. 5. Jewish college students—United States—Societies, etc. 6. Jews—United States—Identity. 7. Jews—Cultural assimilation—United States. 8. Jews—United States—Intellectual life—20th century. 9. Cultural pluralism—United States—History—20th century. I. Title.
LB3613.J4.G74 2011

378.1'98282960973—dc22

2010038265

1 2 3 4 5   16 15 14 13 12 11

For Lisa

CONTENTS

ACKNOWLEDGMENTS

I have incurred many debts while writing this book, and it is a pleasure for me to acknowledge them here.

I finished this project while directing the Dr. William M. Scholl Center for American History and Culture at the Newberry Library in Chicago. The Newberry is a vibrant and challenging intellectual community for fellows and staff alike. I thank both David Spadafora and James Grossman for supporting this project, and for encouraging Newberry staff to pursue our own intellectual interests. The Newberry's institutional support for this book has been critical.

Fellowship support has made my research and writing possible. The Posen Foundation generously endowed my postdoctoral year in Judaic Studies at the University of Miami. A Visiting Fellowship from the Simon Dubnow Institute for Jewish History and Culture at Leipzig University afforded me time to write. I thank Dan Diner and Tobias Brinkmann for bringing me to Leipzig. At the dissertation stage, I received a Mellon Foundation–University of Chicago Dissertation-Year Fellowship and a Dissertation Research and Teaching Fellowship from the Social Sciences Division at the University of Chicago. A Starkoff Fellowship from the Jacob Rader Marcus Center of the American Jewish Archives in Cincinnati supported my research. Two Freehling Travel Grants and an Arthur Mann Pre-Dissertation Travel Grant from the University of Chicago's History Department defrayed costs of research trips to Cincinnati and Cambridge, Massachusetts.

I conducted much of the research for this book at the Jacob Rader Marcus Center of the American Jewish Archives. Dr. Gary Zola welcomed me there enthusiastically. Kevin Proffitt took an interest in my work and pointed me to many sources that I otherwise might not have found. Elise Neinaber and Camille Servizzi have answered research requests from near and far over many years. Kevin and Camille were especially generous with support for photographic research at the end of this project. I also benefited from many conversations at the AJA with Fred Krome, the former editor of the *American Jewish Archives Journal*.

At the Harvard University Archives, I received assistance from Robin McElheny, Brian A. Sullivan, Michelle Gachette, Kyle Carey, and Melanie M. Halloran. Josh Segal conducted last-minute photographic research for me at Harvard.

Some portions of this book first appeared as articles in scholarly journals. Selections from my article "'Israel! What a Wonderful People!': Elliot Cohen's Critique of Modern American Jewry, 1924–1927," *American Jewish Archives Journal* 55:1 (2003), have been reprinted by permission of the Jacob Rader Marcus Center of the American Jewish Archives. Sections of my article "A Chosen People in a Pluralist Nation: Horace Kallen and the Jewish American Experience," *Religion and American Culture* 16:2 (2006), are reprinted here with permission. Parts of my article, "Reuben Cohen Comes of Age: American Jewish Youth and the Lived Experience of Cultural Pluralism in the 1920s," *American Jewish History* 95:2 (June 2009), are included in chapter 6, and appear here with permission.

I have had many homes while writing this book. This project began at the University of Chicago, where my dissertation committee members offered support, guidance, and generous criticism. Kathleen Neils Conzen, Leora Auslander, Paul Mendes-Flohr, and James Grossman all took an active interest in my work and in my development as a historian. Other graduate school professors, including Michael Berkowitz, Mae M. Ngai, Peter Novick, Salim Yaqub, and the late Mark Krupnick provided useful criticism. Amy Dru Stanley has been one of my toughest critics from the start, and I thank her for that.

I have been fortunate to have a number of colleagues who read parts of the manuscript as I revised it for publication. At the University of Miami, I benefited from productive discussions with Kaylin Goldstein, Ranen Omer-Sherman, Jennifer Ratner-Rosenhagen, and Jeffrey Shoulson. Avinoam Patt, a colleague at the U.S. Holocaust Memorial Museum, read chapter drafts and made useful comments.

Although many people have commented on my work in various forms at conferences and elsewhere, I want to acknowledge Eric L. Goldstein, Tony Michels, Riv-Ellen Prell, and Marc Lee Raphael for critical readings that helped me better understand this project. David A. Hollinger has encouraged my work and challenged my ideas at many points along the way. Timothy Gilfoyle carefully read the entire manuscript at a late stage and provided helpful suggestions. Elliott Gorn must be sick of cultural pluralism by now, having read so many versions of these chapters and discussed this project so many times (between innings, of course).

It is a privilege to work with Indiana University Press on this project, and to be included in The Modern Jewish Experience series edited by Deborah Dash Moore and Paula Hyman. Through Indiana, I received generous criticism from two anonymous readers. Janet Rabinowitch's editorial insight helped me to shape the book. Anne Roecklein and Nancy Lila Lightfoot guided me through the publication process. Eric Schramm provided careful copyediting. John Bealle compiled the index.

I am fortunate that Deborah Dash Moore decided to include this book in her co-edited series. Deborah has unselfishly devoted her time to reading and supporting my work. I learned throughout this process what many others already know: Deborah is not only a great scholar but also a wonderful mentor.

My parents, Alan and Carol, taught me to be inquisitive, to think critically, and to love reading. I have had many teachers; they have been the best. My brother, Richard, has read drafts of multiple versions of this book. He always offers insightful criticism and keen suggestions.

Solomon and Bella both were born while I worked on this book, and Solomon is now old enough to ask when he can finally read what I have been writing all these years. Not yet, but maybe someday. They are my constant sources of joy and always remind me what really matters.

I have no words to express my many debts to Lisa Meyerowitz; she, more than anyone, makes everything possible. This book is dedicated to her.

THE JEWISH ORIGINS OF CULTURAL PLURALISM

Introduction

"Kultur Klux Klan or Cultural Pluralism"

In his 1924 essay "Culture and the Ku Klux Klan," philosopher Horace M. Kallen described a nation in crisis.[1] He wrote that the American body politic was enmeshed in a "widespread hysterical taking of stock" over "the stuff and form of the American being."[2] This hysterical taking of stock accounted for the proliferation of Americanization programs, nativist movements, and even the Ku Klux Klan's terrorist tactics intended to ensure white Protestant hegemony in the United States.[3] Kallen countered this hysteria with the idea for which he is best remembered: cultural pluralism. He invoked pluralism to show that the health of a democratic society depended on its commitment to cultural diversity. As Kallen declared, "The alternative before Americans is Kultur Klux Klan or Cultural Pluralism."[4]

Kallen believed that cultural pluralism not only was *possible* within a democracy, but that it *defined* a healthy democracy. Cultural homogeneity, in contrast, stifled citizens' creativity and limited a society's potential for development. Being American was not singular or restrictive, Kallen insisted. It depended on "manyness, variety, [and] differentiation."[5] In many of his earlier publications, Kallen had portrayed the United States as a "federation or commonwealth of national cultures."[6] He frequently employed musical metaphors to illustrate cultural pluralism, describing the nation as an orchestra in which each cultural group played its own instrument in harmony, although not in unison, with others.

"Culture and the Ku Klux Klan" marked the first time Kallen used the term "cultural pluralism," but pluralism had roots in his writings and his experiences long prior to 1924. This idea even dated well before Kallen's often-cited 1915 *Nation* magazine article "Democracy Versus the Melting

Pot," where he reacted vehemently against both nativists and champions of the melting pot metaphor.[7] Since his days as a Harvard undergraduate from 1900 to 1903, Kallen had been developing the ideas foundational to cultural pluralism.[8] Throughout his distinguished academic career that included helping to found the New School for Social Research in New York City, Kallen rarely would stray far from the topic. Although he published on subjects as varied as consumerism, environmentalism, and adult education, Kallen is best remembered for his work on pluralism.[9]

Yet the history of cultural pluralism often has been told in abstract terms, relegated to the realm of ideas divorced from lived experience. Like all universalistic philosophies, however, cultural pluralism was articulated from a particular point of view. Intellectual concepts are not distant from the people who conceive of them; in this case, cultural pluralism was a tool of introspection for a group of Jewish intellectuals who shared concerns about the future of Jewish culture. In this book, I examine the specific social and cultural milieu from which pluralism emerged, namely that of a cohort of Jewish intellectuals who faced particular pressures and challenges as they sought to integrate themselves into the academy and the literary world. This context is essential to understanding the origins of cultural pluralism in the twentieth century. For one, restoring specificity to the history of cultural pluralism returns Jewishness to a narrative in which it too often has become invisible. Jewish culture mattered profoundly to Kallen and his peers. Indeed, this group of Jewish intellectuals primarily intended cultural pluralism to make space for a thriving Jewish culture in the United States.

The cohort of Jewish intellectuals at the center of this book first gathered at Harvard College just after the turn of the century. In 1906, Kallen chaired the first meeting of a student club that became known as the Harvard Menorah Society. Between the 1910s and the 1930s, the society, eventually known as the Intercollegiate Menorah Association (IMA), spread to approximately eighty campuses across the nation. In 1915, the founders of the IMA began to publish an influential magazine of opinion, the *Menorah Journal*. The thinkers and writers associated with IMA and the *Menorah Journal* were particularly well suited to articulate a pluralistic understanding of American society at this time, for they were seeking in their own lives to develop a vibrant Jewish cultural renaissance in an American setting. They worked on two fronts, arguing for an inclusive definition of American national identity to the larger American public while promoting a cultural definition of Jewish identity to Jewish students and readers. Their nearly thirty-year effort to forge a Jewish cultural renaissance within a pluralist nation had broad implications and lasting significance. Indeed,

Horace M. Kallen.
*Courtesy of the Jacob Rader Marcus Center of the American Jewish
Archives. Photograph by Nicholas Haz.*

a close reading of this cohort's efforts reveals that their ideas and experiences, and even the very vocabulary they originated and relied upon, remain central to contemporary understandings of both Jewish identity and American diversity.[10]

The founders of the IMA embarked on a bold project to remake Jewish life by fashioning Jewish culture in the image of the scholarly world they had come to admire. They sought to preserve Jewish distinctiveness by better synthesizing it with mainstream American political and intellectual thought. Their goals were cerebral but they tried to accomplish them with at least a nod to the practical, forming the Intercollegiate Menorah Association, exporting the model to universities across the nation, and publishing a high-quality journal of opinion that included political and cultural criticism, poetry and literature, reviews, and visual art. During its heyday, the IMA and the *Menorah Journal* formed a vanguard in terms of social integration and participation in the academy.

As students and professors at the nation's most elite colleges, the actors at the center of this narrative enjoyed access to institutions that their parents would not have imagined; in their young adulthood, they founded and edited publications that shaped public opinion. Their position as simultaneous outsiders and insiders in American cultural life allowed them to test the meanings and limits of group difference in America in specific and important ways. Their ideas about Jewish identity and cultural difference developed at a critical moment of transition, during which racial and religious definitions of Jewish identity were under siege, and in an environment where what it meant to be an American also was being contested vigorously. The men discussed here embarked on two interrelated and strategic projects: they promoted Jewish humanities as the foundation of a modern Jewish identity and they championed cultural diversity as the essence of democracy. In other words, they simultaneously sought to refigure Jewish identity and American identity for a modern age. Their history thus is one of culture making and nation making.

With only a few exceptions, the individuals at the center of the IMA were Jewish men. They operated in milieus—especially academia and the literary world of New York City—that had been dominated not only by men but by Christian men.[11] Though the Jewish men discussed in this book gained access to elite educational and literary worlds at the beginning of the twentieth century, it was less common for their female contemporaries to do the same. IMA activities thrived at some women's colleges and women joined Menorah circles at coed schools, but they were never the group's prime movers. Moreover, there simply were many fewer Jewish women than Jewish men, and many fewer Jewish women than Protestant women, attending colleges during the 1910s and 1920s. This is not to say that women do not have a history of advancing cultural pluralism. As historian Diana Selig argues in her recent study of the cultural gifts movement, "Men dominated the ranks of social scientists but many of those who took the lead in implementing their ideas were women."[12] Perhaps even more tellingly, neither the social scientists and literary crowd examined here nor the educational professionals whom Selig studies made gender central to their claims about pluralism and ethnic diversity. Yet, although the actors central to this book rarely addressed gender directly, there is a way in which they sought to redefine Jewish masculinity in their generation, moving Jewish men's space from the synagogue and religious school—the realms their fathers knew— to the editorial office and campus quad.

During the 1910s and 1920s, most Jews in America were not yet thinking in the same terms as the founders of the IMA, nor were most Jews feeling the same pressures to explain themselves to the broader American world. The individuals discussed in this book might not be the first that leap to the popular imagination when picturing Jews in New York City and other urban centers during the first decades of the twentieth century. Their primary affiliations were not religious, but academic. Though most were not wealthy, they had some means and more opportunities than many of their peers. They were not labor activists or union oriented in any way. Although their base of operations was within walking distance of Manhattan's Lower East Side, the needle trade shops might as well have been worlds away. Moreover, the IMA cohort spilled a lot of ink criticizing other American Jews for focusing on material gain rather than intellectual pursuits. This criticism, however, should in no way be interpreted as self-hatred on the part of the Menorah Association's founders. Although they were passionately (and sometimes offensively) critical of fellow Jews, there remains a real difference between Jewish self-hatred and criticism. The IMA crowd cherished Jewish culture passionately, even as they set restrictive boundaries on its proper expressions.[13]

Even their sense of their own Jewish heritage was not simple. Most of the individuals discussed here were children of eastern European Jewish immigrants. In seeking to integrate themselves into an academic-oriented world, for reasons that become clear in this book, they adopted German intellectual traditions that most could not rightly claim from their own family genealogy. The Menorah Association derived inspiration in this realm from the *Verein für Cultur und Wissenschaft der Juden* (Society for Culture and Science of the Jews), a group of Jewish intellectuals in Germany who, beginning in the 1810s, advocated scientific study of Jewish history, culture, and religion.[14] The regularity with which Menorah Association leaders described their scholarly activities as "scientific" and their frequent acknowledgment of *Wissenschaft des Judentums* (the scientific study of Judaism) pioneer Leopold Zunz and his contemporaries signal that they understood their project as a continuation of that initiated by German Jews one hundred years before them.

The IMA's vision for a Jewish cultural renaissance in the United States grew, as well, out of the context of the Haskalah (Jewish enlightenment), though the IMA's founders were less bound in their rhetoric to Haskalah than they were to *Wissenschaft des Judentums*. Nonetheless, the IMA's efforts remained indebted to those European Jews of the nineteenth century who, in Shmuel Feiner's words, "embarked on a conscious, deliberate course to change their cultural environment."[15] Haskalah's emphasis on secular Jewish culture and education, on history as constitutive of identity, and on Hebrew language all echo loudly in the Menorah Association's philosophy.[16] Like many intellectuals at the center of the Haskalah movement, those at the center of the IMA sought to reform Jewish culture and conceived of their work within a context of Enlightenment thought, both Jewish and gentile.

None of the IMA's initiatives would have been possible either had the association's founders not considered themselves inheritors of the opportunities provided by the emancipation of Jews throughout Europe. Jews in the United States, of course, secured legal and political status without enduring the same processes of gradual emancipation that occurred across Europe beginning in the eighteenth century. Yet most of the actors at the center of this book could not claim ancestors in the United States further back than one generation, if that. Their self-conception included a familial history of emancipation that they, or their parents, carried with them during the migration to the United States.[17]

For those individuals who coalesced around the Menorah Association, attending college became a launching point for a highly intellectual movement that depended on the foundation of cultural pluralism. By embracing pluralism, they made it possible to fashion new Jewish selves based on Jewish culture. Their understanding of their Jewish selfhood would emerge out of an anxious quest to find a point of fixity in Jewish identity. Even while we acknowledge all that made this cohort of Jewish intellectuals unrepresentative of American Jews during the 1910s and 1920s, we must recognize that they struggled with a tension between the desire for acceptance and the commitment to difference that has come to define the American Jewish experience of the twentieth century. Like so many American Jews who came after them, the young men at the center of this book passionately searched for a way to fashion themselves as both American and Jewish, without apology or contradiction. In doing so, they ultimately sought to broaden what constituted true Americanness and constrict what constituted appropriate Jewishness.

Neither the IMA nor cultural pluralism became wildly popular during the interwar period. Yet it would do this history an injustice to dismiss it for lack of popularity. The shortcomings of the IMA during its relatively brief history should not cloud the long-term significance of its influence on Jewish culture and identity in the United States. Cultural pluralism, moreover, is an idea that has evolved over many decades. Kallen's ideas about cultural pluralism did not immediately capture the American or the Jewish imagination, but, dressed in a different garb, they became extremely influential for understanding ethnic diversity writ large. By the 1970s, cultural pluralism gained widespread attention, and, as I show here, it has implications that are crucially important for understanding the emergence of multiculturalism in the United States.

Pluralism emerged alongside two contentious and related debates: a universal debate about the meaning of American identity and a particular debate about the proper expression of Jewish identity within America. First, pluralism rejected the argument that cultural groups had to abandon their cultural particularity in order to become Americans. Second, and much less frequently acknowledged by historians, it sought a way to make space for Jews in the United States to articulate a new form of Jewish identity that would allow them to fully enter into the American polity and yet still self-identify as Jewish. Although Kallen and his peers claimed that cultural pluralism applied to all European immigrants in the United States, one simply cannot disregard the fact that the Jewish case dominated their writings on pluralism.[18] Even as he entered into wide-reaching debates about the meaning of American identity and cultural difference with Louis Brandeis, John Dewey, and Randolph Bourne, Kallen remained focused on Jewish culture.

Perhaps these specific concerns about the future of American Jewish culture help to explain the most troubling blind spot of those intellectuals who guided the IMA. The pluralist logic of the Menorah Association paid no heed to similar questions being considered by African American contemporaries. In proposing that dual identities need not mean contradictory loyalties, for example, Kallen ignored fellow Harvard graduate W. E. B.

Du Bois. In 1897, just a decade before Kallen began to publish on pluralism, Du Bois famously asked, "What, after all, am I? Am I an American or am I a Negro? Can I be both? Or is it my duty to cease to be a Negro as soon as possible and be an American?"[19]

Kallen's failure to acknowledge the similarity of his concerns and those of Du Bois is even more glaring considering that Harvard philosopher William James was a dominant intellectual influence on both these Harvard men.[20] The questions central to Du Bois's "double consciousness" and Kallen's "cultural pluralism" were not identical, but the similarities are strong enough to wonder why Kallen did not write about or correspond with Du Bois. Of course, Du Bois was black and Kallen was white.[21] As I discuss in the book's epilogue, when Kallen looked back to his collegiate years at the end of his life, he claimed to be quite aware of his white privilege as he formulated pluralism. For our purposes here, the absence of blacks in the pluralist model reveals both how central Jewish culture was to pluralism and how the Jewish intellectuals who articulated pluralism also sought to set the boundaries of inclusion in national culture. There is no doubt that Du Bois was more of an outsider than Kallen. Perhaps, then, Kallen had little to gain by recognizing Du Bois.

Kallen's blind spot was even more glaring in the case of his contemporary Alain Locke, the first African American Rhodes Scholar and one of the primary voices of the New Negro Movement, or Harlem Renaissance. While a graduate student at Harvard, Kallen worked as a teaching assistant in a class on Greek philosophy taught by George Santayana. Locke, then an undergraduate, enrolled in the class. Only many years later, in 1955, would Kallen claim that Locke was present when Kallen first used the term "cultural pluralism" in that very class.[22] Their association also moved beyond Harvard Yard. In 1907, Kallen and Locke both spent the year studying at Oxford, where they occasionally socialized with each other.[23] Their essays and speeches from this era, as one scholar recently has shown, share similar phrases and metaphors, as well as a concern about how cultural groups could remain independent while integrating into American society.[24]

In addition to sharing institutional affiliations, Locke and Kallen struggled with similar questions about the boundaries of cultural difference. Locke's effort to promote African American arts and culture resembled the IMA's desired renaissance of Jewish culture that Kallen championed his entire life. In fact, both the temporal and ideological parallels between Locke's and Kallen's thought—and thus between the Harlem Renaissance and the Menorah movement—were striking. Locke's 1925 edited collection

The New Negro appeared just one year after Kallen coined "cultural pluralism" in print. Locke dedicated his book to "the younger generation," in the hope that it would liberate young blacks from feelings of cultural inferiority, just as the IMA hoped that an elite cohort of Jewish youth would. Kallen rarely wrote as eloquently as Locke, or with such a clear notion that pluralism should provide a path to cosmopolitan cooperation. Many critics seized on this as well as many other perceived shortcomings in Kallen's pluralist logic. Yet the majority of critics were white, too, and conceived of a pluralist nation of immigrants descended from Europeans. It is in this realm that pluralism differs most obviously from multiculturalism.

Although not alone in his positions, Kallen argued against prevailing assumptions about both American identity and Jewish identity. His challenges were many, on both the American side and the Jewish side. He formulated cultural pluralism even as tirades against "hyphenated Americanism" and for "100 percent Americanism" pervaded political discourse. In fact, his passionate advocacy for pluralism coincided with a period of the most intense antisemitic fervor in U.S. history, from the early 1910s to the early 1930s.[25] He also recast Jewish identity as cultural rather than religious against the grain of the increasingly influential Reform movement in Judaism.[26] Moreover, Kallen had to figure out how to reconcile the long-held idea that Jews were chosen singularly by God over all other groups with his vision of the United States as a pluralist nation.[27] Defending pluralism in the face of these many countervailing trends proved no small challenge.

Exploring the social and cultural origins of pluralism reveals an important example of the way that Jews responded to their unique vantage point in America. Of course, to imagine a unified group of Jews in America during the early twentieth century (or ever) is to immediately go awry. While many new immigrant Jews of the early twentieth century concerned themselves with basic economic survival, the founders of the IMA already had the luxury to consider the importance and potential outcomes of their acceptance into American institutions that were closed to their parents' generation, and that remained closed to many of their peers. Still, like all Jewish immigrants, those who attended elite colleges at the opening of the twentieth century did not have a homeland to return to in Europe. They (or their parents) had fled from economic hardship and from persecution that sometimes became violent. Consequently, there was almost no circular migration pattern for Jews, as there was for so many other immigrant groups in the United States.[28] Jewish immigrants and their children needed to make their peace with America, and they knew it. This reality may help to explain why Jews remained at the forefront of articulating theories of difference in America and took a lead in combating visions of the nation that labeled cultural diversity as un-American.

The activities of the individuals chronicled here were not without risk. Indeed, it required some measure of courage for a group of young Jewish men at Harvard, the bastion of America's Protestant elite, to gather in 1906 to promote Jewish culture. It took a bit of audacity for them to then propose new ways for the nation's many peoples to understand cultural and ethnic diversity. This daring was no doubt made possible in part by Jews' particular relationship to modernity. Pluralism was developing just as social theorist Thorstein Veblen wrote the following about young Jews in Europe: "Intellectually he is likely to become an alien; spiritually he is more than likely to remain a Jew."[29] Although Veblen's claim referred to emancipated European Jews, his point also applied to those young Jews in the United States who sought ways to become active contributors to America's cultural landscape without casting off their Jewishness. Many of the intellectuals who embraced pluralism may have felt alienated from modern American culture, but only to an extent. In the words of historian Andrew Heinze, these thinkers were "intensely *in* modern society but not completely *of* it" and were therefore able to create "novel critiques of the status quo."[30] They were just enough outside the mainstream to see alternate possibilities but not so removed that they could not imagine their inclusion in the pantheon of American culture.

A history of the Menorah Association and cultural pluralism therefore raises a question: Was pluralism a "Jewish idea"? Whatever might be meant by such a term, those who were most influential in shaping pluralism undoubtedly hoped to convince a skeptical nation of the potential for synthesis between American Anglo culture and Jewish culture.[31] Addressing this specific challenge became a primary concern for the key players in the Menorah Association's history. Historian David Biale convincingly argues that we must recognize that Jews "not only adapted to America but also played central roles in shaping the definitions of their adopted country."[32] Surely, the history of cultural pluralism in the early twentieth century demonstrates this point.

In exploring the Jewish dimensions of pluralism, I build upon work by historians Andrew Heinze and David A. Hollinger, both of whom argue for an expansive notion of a "Jewish" point of view. Pluralism did not matter to all Jews in America during the 1910s and 1920s, or even to very many of them. Yet for those who relied on the idea, their Jewish background was more than significant. It was formative.[33]

Still, though many of the writers here thought first of the Jewish case, the question of Jews' Americanization (sometimes called the "Jewish problem" in the parlance of the day) had implications for the spectrum of white ethnic groups in America.[34] The efforts of the actors central to this book are best understood when situated within a much larger group of political scientists, sociologists, philosophers, and other social scientists who were seeking to explain the meanings of religious, racial, and cultural diversity.[35] The debates surrounding the specific case of Jewish Americanization at the opening of the twentieth century ultimately provided much of the language and many of the metaphors that shaped America's discourse about diversity throughout the century. This language emerged within a climate of broad concern about how the nation would best address the cultural and political challenges posed by its increasing diversity.

Even as Kallen formulated the language of cultural pluralism, numerous competing models for addressing American diversity already had emerged. The dominant metaphor of the era was the melting pot, which in its very cultural history demonstrated the tensions between Jewish particularity and American universalism during the modern era. The metaphor resurfaced in American political and popular discourse following the 1908 staging of Israel Zangwill's play *The Melting Pot*.[36] Opening-night attendees Theodore Roosevelt and Jane Addams championed the work.[37] The melodrama featured a marriage between two Russian immigrants—one Jewish and one gentile—who overcame seemingly insurmountable differences because their experiences as immigrants in the United States effectively erased their pasts. Though the idea of the melting pot powerfully influenced the discourse on cultural difference, it did not corner the market entirely.[38]

If the melting pot was assumed by most to mean that the nation would somehow absorb and mix together immigrant group cultures to form a new "American" culture, a less accepting model of cultural diversity would later be labeled "Anglo-conformity." Here, the assumption was that America's culture was an Anglo culture from the days of the Puritans and that becoming American meant conforming to Anglo norms.[39] At an even further extreme was nativism. Nativists claimed that some immigrant and nonwhite groups simply were unmeltable and therefore should be excluded altogether from the American political and cultural spheres.[40] The boundaries between these competing theories of Americanization were not always clear. Writers and critics often conflated aspects of the melting pot and Anglo-conformity during this era. What unified the two ideas (and perhaps even led to the frequent confusion between them) was that neither allowed for the possibility that immigrants and their descendants could continue to foster their own cultures while becoming acculturated into the American polity.

Kallen and his peers thought of cultural pluralism as an alternative to the melting pot. But pluralism was not solely reactive. For American Jews specifically, it represented a necessary precursor for fostering a renaissance based on cultural activities for youth, arts and letters, and political criticism. In explaining his distaste for the melting pot metaphor, Kallen often wrote about the challenges posed by diversity in the early twentieth century that the nation's founders never anticipated in the late eighteenth century. Kallen's primary objection to the melting pot was that he considered it antidemocratic. Even as the melting pot metaphor dominated popular understandings of what it meant to be an American, and even as "hyphenated American" became the epithet used to described immigrants who held dual (read: competing and potentially dangerous) loyalties, Kallen had the courage to declare in 1915, "Democracy is hyphenation."[41] This bold, three-word summary of Kallen's ideology effectively asked Americans to reconsider the meaning of democracy for a new century.

This book begins on American college campuses, focusing on the Menorah Association's efforts to promote Jewish humanities among students and faculty. During the interwar period, Jewish educators, religious leaders, and intellectuals viewed college campuses as the front lines for combating assimilation. Although the many writers I discuss here did not always agree on the meaning of "assimilation" (or its frequent companion, "acculturation"), most understood that assimilating meant abandoning Jewish identity and culture.[42] Almost from the moment that a significant number of Jewish students arrived on campuses, Jewish observers across the spectrum of religious and cultural organizations expressed concerns that attendance at secular colleges provided students with the possibility of casting off Jewish identity. The Menorah Association was founded to address this new reality. Its leaders sought to provide students with opportunities to develop Jewish cultural interests and to convince them that Jewish history and culture were worthy of their attention. This task on campuses represented in microcosm the challenges faced by American Jews across the nation during this era—refiguring Jewish identity in ways that would be interpreted as modern and relevant.

The narrative then moves off college campus to examine the long evolution of cultural pluralism in Kallen's thought from 1900 to 1924. The intense disagreements over pluralism set up the remainder of the book, which examines the influence of pluralism in three realms: the movement for an integrated study of Jewish humanities on American campuses, the writing of an integrated Jewish history, and the development of a literature in which pluralism was embodied in idealized Jewish protagonists.

The central location for these new models of historiography, criticism, and fiction was the *Menorah Journal,* which soon after its 1915 founding became the leading journal of Jewish opinion in the English language. The journal's editors and frequent contributors, especially Henry Hurwitz, Elliot Cohen, Harry Wolfson, and Marvin Lowenthal, published acerbic critiques of what they viewed as the vacuity of interwar American Jewish cultural life, focusing their sights on excessive materialism, anti-intellectualism, and Reform rabbis. Within the journal's pages, historians Cecil Roth and Salo Baron conceived of new methods for writing Jewish history. During the 1920s, the *Menorah Journal* introduced readers to a cohort of influential young fiction writers, essayists, and critics, including Meyer Levin, Lionel Trilling, Ludwig Lewisohn, and Anzia Yezierska. Much of the fiction in the *Menorah Journal* focused on the experiences of Jewish college students and young adults. Like the contemporary nonfiction published in the journal, fictional works found their solution to the Jewish problem in pluralism.

A short epilogue reflects on the history of the Menorah Association and considers pluralism's contemporary resonance. Today, popular liberal discourse has come to define America as a "nation of peoples" and to take as given that ethnic identity is "unmeltable." This book explains that there is a contested history to these assumptions by focusing on a cohort who gave a vocabulary and voice to one important model for imagining American diversity. Understanding pluralism's social and cultural origins during the early twentieth century remains vital for those interested not only in American Jewish history but also in the seemingly continuous debate about what it means to be an American.

1

The Harvard Menorah Society and the Menorah Idea

Harvard students had many extracurricular activities to choose from on Thursday, October 25, 1906. Some turned their attention to the Charles River, where afternoon crew races pitted teams organized by dormitories against each other. Faculty and students in the medical school and psychology department were invited to a lecture on "The Classical Symptoms of Hysteria." At Phillips Brooks House, Francis Greenwood Peabody, dean of the Divinity School, compared university education in Germany and the United States.[1] And, across Harvard Yard that evening, sixteen Jewish students packed into a small dormitory room in Grays Hall to consider whether they should form a Jewish club.[2] Founding clubs was common behavior at Harvard. As Samuel Morison, Harvard class of 1908, later recalled, "Clubs of a new sort sprang up like mushrooms" all over Harvard between the Civil War and World War I.[3] Harvard students could choose to affiliate with a number of political and cultural clubs, including the Harvard Men's League for Women's Suffrage, the Single Tax Club, and the Anarchists Group. French, German, Spanish, and Italian cultural clubs also thrived by 1906.

Although the students who founded this new Jewish club emulated other Harvard students, they were atypical. Jews had a very limited history as students at America's most famous university prior to the twentieth century. More, these young men differed from Harvard's few previous Jewish students, most of whom traced their ancestry back to Germanic lands. Morison had recalled that German Jews "were easily absorbed into the social pattern" at Harvard prior to the turn of the century.[4] But the Jewish students who gathered in the fall of 1906 were different. Most of the students who showed up to the meeting that autumn evening were children of immigrants who had come from Russia or Poland, rather than from Germany; some of the students themselves had immigrated at a young age. Many of them had attended Boston public schools. Now in their late teens and early twenties, they found themselves students at the training ground for the nation's Protestant elite. This transition from households headed by immigrant parents to dormitories on Harvard Yard within one single generation was remarkable for its time. Perhaps they would not be as "easily absorbed" as the few German Jews who had attended Harvard previously.

Founding a Jewish club revealed that easy absorption was no longer the desired goal for some students. These Jewish students, a still small but increasingly noticeable presence at Harvard by 1906, instead began to discuss how to promote Jewish culture within a college environment. They envisioned that their new club would encourage Jewish students at Harvard—and eventually at other campuses as well—to take pride in being Jewish rather than to be so "easily absorbed."

By the time these sixteen students gathered in Grays Hall that October evening, many American Jewish community leaders of the era had expressed deep ambivalence about their presence at Harvard, and more generally about Jewish students' presence at secular colleges and universities. Attending an elite American university, though undoubtedly an impressive accomplishment by this group of young men, demonstrated the possibility of Jewish students' assimilation into the mainstream. Even in the face of persistent antisemitism at Harvard, these students embodied the possibility of an astonishingly rapid integration of a small group of Jews into the American elite. Jewish communal and religious leaders who recognized that college attendance might speed the process of assimilation wondered how Jewish college students would express their Jewish identity over both the short and long term. They began as early as 1906 to ask whether the newfound opportunities enjoyed by Jewish students would incite them to change, or even to abandon, their self-understanding as Jewish.

The founding members of this Jewish club, which by November 1906 would name itself the Harvard Menorah Society, were well aware of their contemporaries' concerns about the continuity of Jewish identity among Jewish college students. They came together to promote a new solution to this very challenge. By the club's second meeting on November 1, 1906, its members announced that the best way to nurture a meaningful Jewish identity was "to foster the study of Jewish History and Culture."[5] This blueprint of using the humanities to encourage students to embrace Jewish identity represented a profound shift for its time. In their quest to redefine themselves as modern Jews, Harvard Menorah Society members chose not to emphasize religion as the cornerstone of Jewish identity. These young men instead embraced Hebraism, which they understood as an identity grounded in scholarly study of Jewish history and culture. Religion was not altogether absent. These young men conceived of religion as one component, although not the required essence, of a broadly fashioned Jewish identity. Rather than viewing the college experience as one in which Jewish students should downplay either private or public identification as Jewish, the Harvard Menorah Society's philosophy rested squarely on the premise that particular cultures, in this case Hebraic culture, should be studied and celebrated.

These Jewish students conceived of themselves as inheritors of both Jewish and American traditions. Indeed, Harvard Menorah Society members drew their inspiration for Hebraism from both scholarly study of the Jewish humanities and from the tenets of American Pragmatism, the philosophy closely linked to Harvard professor William James. In 1906, James was advising a dissertation in philosophy by Horace Kallen, who championed the Harvard Menorah Society from its very beginnings and remained the group's intellectual guide through the next fifty years.[6] Kallen drew on both Hebraism and Pragmatism in his early speeches and publications. A close reading of Kallen's works on Hebraism during this early period reveals that the seeds of the theory that in 1924 he would name "cultural pluralism" already were present. Moreover, the early evolution of his thinking regarding the role of particular cultural groups in a political democracy depended in large part on his association with the Menorah Society and its desire to promote Jewish culture. What emerged for Kallen and for his cohort in the Menorah Society during these early years was a notion that Hebraism could provide the solution to the dilemma of how to be two things—Jewish and American—at once.

Jewish Students at American Colleges

American universities expanded rapidly as eastern European Jewish immigrants flooded into the United States around the turn of the twentieth century. Between 1881 and 1924, when the U.S. Congress passed restrictive immigration laws, more than two million Jewish immigrants entered the United States.[7] During this span, the Jewish population in America increased from 250,000 (less than 1 percent of the total U.S. population) to nearly four million (more than 3 percent of the total U.S. population).[8] Beginning a decade before and continuing for two decades after this spike in immigration, or roughly between 1870 and 1944, the number of colleges in the United States increased fivefold, and student enrollment tripled. In 1900, one of every forty-two college-age youths in the United States was enrolled in a higher educational institution; by 1934, that number soared to one of every fifteen.[9] The boom in college attendance was both enabled by and helped to foster America's modernization; many young Jewish men and women would take great advantage of this rapid expansion in American higher education almost from the moment it began.[10]

During the first decades of the twentieth century, Jewish immigrants attended colleges in significant numbers, and the children of immigrants enrolled at an even higher rate than their parents. Between 1900 and 1909, 19 percent of college-age Jews in the United States attended higher educational institutions; by the mid-1920s, even as the number of Jews entering the country slowed due to Congress's restrictive measures on immigration, the percentage of college-age Jews enrolled increased to 42 percent.[11] During an era when most college students attended schools close to home, university expansion was particularly pronounced in the northeastern United States, where Jewish immigrants concentrated most heavily.

Increased Jewish college enrollment was not unique to the United States. During the 1930s, according to historian Yuri Sleskine, "one-third of all Soviet Jews of college age (19 to 24 years old) were college students," about six to eight times the rate among the Soviet population as a whole.[12] Jewish students also were overrepresented in central Europe. By the 1890s, Jews made up close to half the student body at the German university of Prague and nearly one-third of all students at the University of Vienna. Indeed, so many Jews attended European universities that "Albert Einstein is said to have remarked that it was as though the Israelites had spent the past two millennia of the exile preparing for their university entrance exams."[13]

The vast increase in Jewish college attendance in the United States, which followed the European trend by about twenty years, meant increased access to institutions that formerly were populated almost entirely by Christians. Indeed, until the turn of the twentieth century in America, most universities were unmistakably Protestant. "The intellectual and moral climate was heavily tinged with Calvinism," sociologist Stephen Steinberg writes, "and the main purpose of college education was understood to be the cultivation of mental and moral discipline."[14] Activities at many colleges included compulsory chapel services. Harvard was an exception, having abolished compulsory chapel attendance in 1886. Chapel remained compulsory at Yale until the 1925–26 academic year. At Princeton, juniors and seniors were excused from chapel in 1935, but freshmen and sophomores' presence was required for another thirty years.[15]

Until the 1870s, Harvard remained unmistakably Protestant, like its peers. Harvard underwent a shift, however, during Charles W. Eliot's forty-year presidency, from 1869 until 1909. Eliot, born in 1834 and raised in a well-off Boston family, graduated from Harvard in 1853. In 1858, he became an assistant professor of mathematics and chemistry. Following short stints studying abroad and teaching at the Massachusetts Institute of Technology, Eliot took the helm as Harvard's president. Eliot was without peer in higher education. He transformed Harvard from a small college with professional schools to a modern research university. "But to say that he was the most renowned figure in American higher education," as Jerome Karabel writes, "is to vastly understate his importance, for his influence went well beyond the academy." Eliot's impact on American society both within and beyond the academy was so great that Theodore Roosevelt dubbed him the "First Citizen of the Republic."[16]

As president of Harvard, Eliot led the modernizing trend in education in universities, promoting the scientific study of religions, rather than re-quiring students to enroll in courses on moral philosophy.[17] Other schools followed. Educational reformers did not reject religion altogether; indeed, many still hoped that scientific consideration of religion would stimulate religious commitment among college students.[18] Despite these efforts, a num-ber of college students, including Jewish students, became increasingly in-different to expressions or even study of religion.

President Eliot's tolerance of religious difference on campus allowed for diversity in the student body that Harvard had never experienced. During his tenure at Harvard, the Jewish student population, which previously had been all but nonexistent, became quite noticeable. It might be hard to over-estimate how shocking the presence of so many Jewish students must have been at Harvard in 1906. Consider that sixteen Jewish students attended the October 1906 inaugural meeting of the Harvard Menorah Society; then, compare that with the fact that, when Harvard celebrated its 250th anni-versary in 1886, it counted perhaps twelve Jewish students among its all-time total alumni.[19]

Both the boom in Jewish students' attendance at universities and the general phenomenon of university expansion in the United States can be well demonstrated in Eliot's own history as a Harvard student and, eventu-ally, as its leader. When Eliot graduated from Harvard in 1854, there were, according to his recollection, no Jewish students in the population of 320

Charles W. Eliot, 1910.
Harvard University Archives, HUP Eliot, Charles W. (39).

undergraduates. By the time President Eliot retired, 60 of Harvard's 2,200 undergraduates were Jewish.[20] Only ten years later, in 1916, almost four hundred Jewish students composed 10 percent of Harvard's total student body.[21] By the early 1920s, the Jewish population at Harvard would rise to more than 20 percent of the total student body.[22]

The increase in the Jewish student population at Harvard and other elite schools prior to the 1920s was made possible in part by the changing nature of college admission policies. Before the 1910s, competition to enroll at even the most elite colleges was not especially intense. Schools guaranteed admission to high school graduates who stood before the president (or some other representative) and passed an entrance examination. Admissions officers and college applications did not yet exist.[23] Tuition cost, although difficult for many families to afford, was not as prohibitive an obstacle to higher education as it would become later in the century.[24]

These relatively open admissions procedures allowed Jewish students to enroll at some of the nation's most elite schools. By the 1910s, however, some administrators began to worry about what came to be known as a "Jewish invasion" of American universities.[25] As we see in greater detail in chapter 2, administrators and faculty at both Columbia and Harvard, where the increase in Jewish student population was most pronounced, realized that admissions policies based solely on scholastic performance would yield a student population in which Jews were disproportionately represented. Because of this so-called invasion, the less quantifiable concept of a high school graduate's "character" became a factor in admission. This new system of admissions, inaugurated by Ivy League schools and adopted rapidly elsewhere, categorically rejected the premise that academic achievements alone merited admission. A "modernized" college entrance system featured face-to-face interviews with applicants, application forms with questions about family background, and an increased value placed on extracurricular activities—all measures designed to limit the Jewish student population.[26]

Jewish students' attendance at elite schools was a "problem" not only for administrators who controlled admissions. Their unprecedented access to colleges also fostered anxiety within Jewish communities. Rabbis and Jewish educators feared that college students might ignore or forget all that was particular to Jewish religion and culture as they integrated into their new environments. As Jewish college attendance soared, Jewish authorities established committees within existing organizations to combat the perceived assimilative power of higher educational institutions. In 1906, the same year as the founding of the Harvard Menorah Society, the Union of American Hebrew Congregations (UAHC) formed a Department of Synagog [*sic*] and School Extension, which hoped to win "the allegiance of Jewish college men and women for the cause of Judaism." Also in 1906, the Central Conference of American Rabbis (CCAR), the governing body of Reform rabbis in America, established the Committee on Religious Work in Universities.[27] The "duty" of the CCAR committee was "to secure [Jewish college students'] loyalty, while they are in a Christian environment, and their co-operation after they return to their homes." CCAR annual reports of this era reveal that some Reform rabbis were particularly concerned about compulsory chapel attendance. Yet many rabbis did not want to appear to insult other religious traditions by publicly declaring that Jews should not attend chapel. The CCAR committee therefore determined to have rabbis visit college campuses regularly and to welcome students in local synagogues. Jewish students' loyalty to Judaism was best secured, these rabbis argued, through the "elevating influence of worship."[28]

Yet the relationships between the UAHC and CCAR committees and college students on the ground never proceeded smoothly. Painted only perhaps a bit too broadly, students resented advice from outside authorities, and rabbis resented students who were unwilling to heed their directives. Although the rabbis who served on UAHC and CCAR committees eventually became exasperated by Jewish students' failure to participate in religious observances, most were mistaken in lamenting that Jewish college students had lost all interest in their Jewish identity. Religious activities did not hold the attention of the majority of Jewish college students during this period, but by 1908 students had founded at least five Jewish organizations (excluding fraternities) on campuses in the eastern and midwestern United States.[29] Just as Harvard students formed the Menorah Society in 1906, Jewish students at the University of Chicago organized a Maimonides Club, with the similar objective of promoting Jewish culture and humanities.[30] Jewish students at the University of Minnesota, the University of Illinois, and Yale University also established clubs by 1906.[31] Although the purpose of these clubs was to foster Jewish identity and group cohesion on campuses, none of the organizations defined its central function as religious.[32] Jewish students sought instead to articulate Jewish identity in a way that did not necessarily insist on religious observance at its core.

The Harvard Menorah Society

The sixteen Jewish students who first gathered at Harvard in October 1906 knew their general mission. They shared a pervasive feeling that they should encourage fellow Jewish students to take pride in being Jewish. They insisted that Jewish interests be broadly defined, rather than restrictive. Many of the original members of the group were staunch Zionists and belonged to the Harvard Zionist Club, formed one year before the Menorah Society, in 1905. Some early Harvard Menorah Society meetings even closed with students singing "Hatikvah" (The Hope), the Zionist hymn that eventually became the State of Israel's national anthem.[33] Members of the Harvard Menorah Society, which effectively replaced the Zionist Club, argued that a Jewish campus organization should be entirely non-partisan and based on a broader conception of Jewish identity than Zionism alone.[34] Moreover, advocating Zionism as a sole purpose risked fanning the flames of antisemitism—charges of "dual loyalty" during this era frequently rested on claims that Jews could not be both Zionists and loyal Americans.

The society's founding members also did not advocate forming a club for religious purposes. The majority of those who had any interest in religion believed that the synagogue, rather than campus, was the proper place for worship. There was more to this decision than a separation of religious and secular spheres. Most Harvard Menorah Society members had a sense that their acceptance by non-Jewish classmates at Harvard was somewhat tenuous and contingent. Establishing a religious organization, rather than a cultural society, might have threatened their quest for belonging. Forming a club where members behaved like other Harvard students mattered. So, instead of emphasizing religion, they likened themselves to other organizations on campus that promoted particular cultures.[35]

Although the Harvard Menorah Society founders supported Zionism and did not have antipathy toward religion, they remained in search of a broader, more enticing mode of pursuing Jewish interests. Not surprisingly, given their location at the most storied university in America, these young men turned to study. At the organization's second meeting, members announced that their object would be "to foster the study of Jewish History and Culture" through rigorous discussions on Jewish topics, lectures, dramatic presentations, service to the Jewish community, and support of similar organizations at other universities.[36] The service element soon dropped out of the program, signaling a more inwardly focused examination of Jewish history, politics, and culture, but the remaining purposes would endure throughout the organization's history.

By November 20, 1906—the third meeting of Harvard's newly formed Jewish organization—membership had increased from sixteen to twenty-eight members. The growing organization needed a name. After rejecting "Harvard Maccabees" and "Harvard Hebraic Club," two options remained: "Agudah Leivrith" (Hebrew Society) and "Menorah Society."[37] The students' ultimate selection of Menorah Society indicated both the club members' self-understanding and the way in which they hoped to be perceived by non-Jewish observers. The group's founding members viewed the menorah, or candelabrum, as a primary symbol of Jewish enlightenment. Members interpreted the menorah as encapsulating the "invincible spirit through defeat, of unquenched hope, of renaissance, and of freshly radiant service to mankind."[38] The choice of "renaissance" in this description was not made lightly. It signaled the students' greatest ambition, even from their modest beginning, to promote a cultural renaissance of Jewish humanities in the United States.

The menorah itself, moreover, symbolized not only Jewish enlightenment in ancient times, but also echoed the modern Western Enlightenment tradition. The European Enlightenment of the eighteenth century, as historian Michael A. Meyer argues, "brought self-consciousness and, especially for intellectuals, the need to achieve self-definition."[39] With newfound access to American institutions, these Jewish students needed to reconsider their self-definition as Jews in a liberal society. The menorah proved the most apt symbol for refiguring Jewish identity in the face of modernity's challenges. It ultimately announced that being Jewish was to be celebrated, not hidden.

Just as significantly, the Menorah Society, unlike Agudah Leivrith, would not have to be translated to educated non-Jews or to Jews who lacked knowledge of Hebrew. "The Menorah," society members would later explain, "is at once a Hebrew word and one euphonious in English."[40] Furthermore, the Hebrew word had been adopted for English-language usage for nearly a generation.[41] The choice of a name that would not sound too strange to outsiders, or be too difficult to pronounce, should not be underestimated, especially for a group eager to prove the compatibility of Jewish identity and American citizenship. A Hebrew word that already was accepted in the American lexicon embraced the possibility of synthesis between Jewish identity and American identity.[42]

The Harvard Menorah Society looked to at least two models on campus: the Deutscher Verein and the Cercle Francais, student clubs that promoted, respectively, the study of German and French language and culture. The Deutscher Verein was established in 1884 and the Cercle Francais in 1886, each staging plays and hosting lectures in German or French.[43] The Harvard Menorah Society's earliest activities closely resembled these language and cultural clubs; the founders claimed at the outset that, considering the campus presence of the Deutscher Verein and Cercle Francais as well as the Circolo Italiano and the Sociedad Española, the absence of a student organization devoted to Jewish culture needed to be remedied.[44] The existence of a Semitic department and the Semitic Museum at Harvard already signaled the worthiness of studying Jewish history and culture, Menorah Society founders argued, but in their view these offerings in Semitics were geared too specifically for the academic specialist.[45] The Harvard Menorah Society, in contrast, would promote Jewish humanities more broadly than an academic program in Semitics could.

During its first few years, the Harvard Menorah Society's membership grew impressively. A 1909 report indicates that the society had nearly 90 members, though average attendance at meetings and public programs tended to hover around half that number.[46] The membership included Jewish men with both eastern European and German backgrounds, but those with eastern European heritage dominated.[47] Those who joined the club insisted that its primary purpose was not social, but intellectual. The same 1909 report explains: "In nowise a social club nor religious fraternity, the Menorah is a scientific society; though inspired, to be sure, by a great loyalty to the tradition and civilization which it aims to study."[48] From its earliest days, the founders had great ambition to become an intercollegiate society that would spread to campuses across the country.

Administration of the Harvard Menorah Society during these first years fell largely to Henry Hurwitz. Hurwitz, Harvard class of 1908, emigrated with his family from Lithuania to the Boston area in the early 1890s. The Hurwitz family retained its Orthodox religious practices after emigrating. Much later in life, Hurwitz remembered that he prayed "to beat the band from rising up in the morning to lying down at night" before matriculating to Harvard in 1904.[49] Hurwitz never turned away from religion entirely, but he profoundly believed in complementing religious ritual with study of Jewish humanities and culture. Reporting for his fiftieth college reunion in 1958, Hurwitz still described himself as "in the process of transfiguring (at least for myself) the inherited Judaism into humanism."[50] This was his life's mission, and the Menorah Society always remained his vehicle for accomplishing the mission.

Hurwitz sometimes singlehandedly ensured the survival of the Menorah Association for more than fifty years. He was the first and only chancellor of the Intercollegiate Menorah Association, founded in 1913, as well as the editor-in-chief of the *Menorah Journal,* the organization's magazine, from its founding in 1915 until his death in 1961—soon after which the journal died as well.[51] Hurwitz's papers contain a multitude of examples of the personal and financial sacrifices he, as well as his wife and two sons, frequently made to keep the organization and the magazine in business. He took great

UNIVERSITY DEBATING TEAM AGAINST PRINCETON

I. Dimond, '09   I. L. Sharfman 1L   R. W. Kelso, '04   H. Hurwitz, '08

Henry Hurwitz is pictured in this Harvard
University Class Album of 1908.
Harvard University Archives, HUD 308.04.5, p. 69.

pride (perhaps second only to the pride he took in his sons' accomplishments) in his stubborn insistence to maintain the intellectual and financial independence of the Menorah Association.

As a Harvard undergraduate, Hurwitz, like so many of his peers, was profoundly influenced by William James, George Santayana, and other faculty whose teaching instilled a love for the humanities. These professors helped Menorah Society members realize that they could promote particular Jewish interests without threatening their civic identity as Americans. These Jewish students, in turn, thus would not abandon Jewish identity; instead, they would seek ways to nurture Jewish identity by promoting the humanities.

Although Hurwitz and his peers were willing to wear their Jewish identity openly at a time of significant discrimination at Harvard and in America, they were not fully comfortable with their own class status or roots. Almost all the members of the Harvard Menorah Society during these early years were children of eastern European Jews, but they aspired to perpetuate intellectual traditions that originated among Jews in Germany during the nineteenth century.[52] The Menorah Association's academic philosophy relied heavily on its adaptation of *Wissenschaft des Judentums* to an American setting. For these young Jewish men, study of the Jewish humanities in a German tradition provided a measure of status, separating them from the masses of eastern European immigrants who teemed into the nation at the time.

One of the clearest ways in which their class aspiration manifested itself was through language. Although most members of the Menorah Society read and spoke Yiddish, the group consistently rejected Yiddish in all its activities. A member of the Russian Duma who spoke to the Harvard Menorah Society on January 12, 1907, asked whether he should deliver his lecture in Yiddish or in German. Members insisted on German.[53] Eight years later, the Harvard Menorah Society president would ask a visiting speaker to change the title of his lecture from "Yiddish Drama" to "Jewish Drama."[54] Rejecting Yiddish culture and language became a key theme at various points throughout the organization's history. These early examples signaled the students' desire to align themselves with a German Jewish heritage that they conceived as more refined than eastern European or Russian heritage. In seeking legitimacy on Harvard's campus, and in modern American society at large, these class aspirations remained central.

The Harvard Menorah Society members rejected not only the language of their parents but also the religious observance of their youth. Although the society sponsored Passover seders and Hanukkah festivals during its first two years of existence, they dropped religious activities from their programs by 1908, when members began to insist more vehemently that the Harvard Menorah Society was not a religious organization.[55] The early Harvard Menorah Society was not anti-religious, as some critics at the time claimed. Members instead believed that religious interests constituted only one facet of Jewish identity. Promoting a broader Jewish identity arose in part from a desire for acceptance by non-Jewish peers. By deemphasizing religion in favor of humanistic pursuits, members hoped to show that the Menorah Society's mission and Harvard's mission were compatible. As a 1914 self-published history of the organization made clear: "The purposes of a Menorah Society reflect in a particular direction the general purposes of a university. The first of these is an intellectual purpose. The university is designed primarily for study. So a Menorah Society is designed primarily for study."[56]

Minimizing the importance of religion not only represented posturing for gentiles, though. Society members also claimed that religion alone was not enough to captivate Jewish students or to hold their interest for the long term. Instead, as the organization's leadership explained, Jewish students should be lured through "history, science, religion, art, literature, and politics of the Jewish people."[57] This broad understanding of Jewish identity remained central to the Menorah Association's program as it spread to various universities throughout the 1910s and 1920s.

Downplaying religion fostered conflicts, however, with national religious organizations. The UAHC, already disappointed by its Department of Synagog and School Extension's inability to persuade very many Jewish students to sponsor religious activities on campuses, instituted an effort to cooperate with the Harvard Menorah Society that quickly turned sour. Rabbi George Zepin, the director of the UAHC's Department of Synagog and School Extension, attended one of the first meetings of the Harvard Menorah Society in the autumn of 1906. Zepin hoped to convince the students to focus on religious rather than cultural activities. Despite the students' refusal to follow his advice, Rabbi Zepin and the Harvard Menorah Society agreed that the UAHC would pay the expenses of UAHC-affiliated rabbis who traveled to speak to the society.[58]

The list of UAHC-approved rabbis quickly proved too exclusive. In the autumn of 1908, Zepin refused to pay the expenses for Rabbi Stephen S. Wise of the Free Synagogue in New York City to visit Cambridge because Wise's congregation did not belong to the UAHC. An outraged Rabbi Wise informed the Harvard Menorah Society president: "I cannot myself see how your Society can with self respect acquiesce to the arrangement advised. It is prescriptive, intolerant and therefore unJewish."[59] Wise eventually addressed the Harvard Menorah Society at the group's own expense. Communication between the Harvard Menorah Society and the UAHC continued after this conflict, but the Menorah Society's refusal to foster an exclusively religious spirit drove a long-lasting wedge between these bodies. Zepin continually expressed frustration at his own inability to "awaken in these men a love for Judaism and a sense of their obligations to the Jewish cause."[60] After successfully funding lectures at Harvard by some leading Jewish intellectuals and rabbis for a few years, Zepin became exasperated by his effort to spur Jewish students' religious interests.[61] Relations between the two organizations ceased in 1912, when Zepin equated the Menorah Society with fraternity elitism by calling Harvard's Menorah Society a "semi-secret" society.[62]

In fact, the Harvard Menorah Society explicitly criticized fraternal secrecy as deplorable. Menorah Society founders insisted that their organization must become "part and parcel of the life of its college or university.

It has to be openly approved as a campus organization by the authorities, and it should make itself known to the whole student body."[63] The group did not even require that its members be Jewish to join, though the evidence suggests that non-Jewish students never joined.

The group's transparency was generally acceptable to campus authorities. Although he proved to be much less sympathetic to Jewish students than Charles Eliot, A. Lawrence Lowell, who succeeded Eliot as Harvard's president in 1909, did not publicly criticize the Menorah Society during its early years. He did hope that "the Society would not work towards the segregation of its members from the other fellows in the university."[64] Despite this warning, Harvard officials' relative acceptance of a Jewish cultural organization was remarkable. (As we see in the next chapter, however, Lowell became outspoken about Jewish students' overrepresentation at Harvard by the early 1920s.)

Some fellow Harvard men were not as quick to welcome Jewish students to campus. In 1907, one recent Harvard graduate who signed his anonymous hate mail "J. Ewbaiter" informed members of the Harvard Menorah Society, "We white men have the same regard for the Jew as we have for the nigger." Claiming that all members of the "Hebrew race" lacked the decency required for Harvard, this writer challenged Jews' masculinity (as well as their status as whites), arguing that young Jewish men failed to join the militia or the National Guard in sufficient numbers to prove their loyalty to America.[65] Such vitriolic hate, representative of contemporary antisemitic beliefs about Jews' physical and biological weakness, does not seem to have been common amongst non-Jewish students. Or, at least those who held such beliefs did not bother to complain to the school's administration or threaten Jewish students so directly. Instead, most non-Jewish classmates ignored the Menorah Society, declining to mix with the increasing Jewish population on campus rather than openly threatening Jews.

Whatever their non-Jewish classmates' perceptions, the Menorah Society intended to allow students to combat any feelings of inferiority that might have resulted not only from blatant antisemitism like that of "J. Ewbaiter" but also from the more common silent derision of gentile students. Promoting Jewish culture as a means to foster pride should not be underestimated as a motivating force behind the Menorah Society's history. As one founding document of the Harvard Menorah Society explained, "To some Jews, a Jewish university organization may appear as an anomaly, but to those who are not ashamed of the fact they are Jews and who have principles and are willing to live up to them, the founding of a Jewish society at an American university will appear as nothing strange."[66] Menorah Society founders hoped that their study as well as their fellowship would combat the "indifference" and "shameful ignorance of things Jewish" by men on campus who "desire to forget or to hide their Jewish origin."[67] The Menorah Society conceived of this "Jewish origin" in the broadest terms, combining a variety of aspects of Jewish identity into its guiding philosophy, known as "Hebraism."

Hebraism and Horace Kallen

Menorah Society members used the term Hebraism to articulate a conception of Jewish identity based primarily on inquiry into the humanities, including history, language, literature, and the visual arts. For these students, curiosity about Jewish culture mattered more than religious ritual. Harvard Menorah Society members came to believe that scholarly study of Jewish topics would provide a solid foundation for modern Jewish identity. In its earliest prospectus, the Harvard Menorah Society coined the "Menorah idea," which "conceives the Hebraic spirit not as a matter of history only, but, quite as much, as a vital force of the present." "The first requirement" of the Menorah idea was "an intelligent appreciation of Hebraism, its nature and its achievements."[68]

Embracing Hebraism soon led Menorah Association members to advocate the study of Jewish history and culture alongside other traditions and cultures on campuses. As chapter 4 details, the Menorah Association's intellectual agenda for Jewish studies programs on American campuses relied heavily on historical consciousness as integral to Jewish identity. Members of the Menorah Association frequently acknowledged their debt in this regard to nineteenth-century Jewish intellectuals in Germany. Indeed, the Menorah Association founders would seek to position themselves as the intellectual descendants of Leopold Zunz and his six colleagues who in 1819 founded the *Verein für Cultur und Wissenschaft der Juden*. Historian Ismar Schorsch describes this society of young men as "fiercely intellectual" and "alienated from traditional Judaism," yet determined to invent a new mode of Jewish expression for emancipated Jews.[69]

Menorah Society members drew their understanding of Hebraism not solely from Jewish reference points like the *Verein für Cultur und Wissenschaft der Juden* but also from their Harvard teachers—notably philosopher William James and literature scholar Barrett Wendell. James and Wendell were especially influential for Horace Kallen, the individual most responsible for crafting the Menorah Association's particular understanding of Hebraism. From James, Kallen developed ideas about Hebraism's relationship to Pragmatism. From Wendell he came to the opinion that American culture, unlike European culture, was based not on enduring social institutions, but on ideals such as liberty, union, and democracy.

The dynamic interaction among Hebraism, Pragmatism, and foundational American ideals ultimately helped Kallen to find his way to articulate the theory known as "cultural pluralism," which advocated the harmonic co-existence of many ethnic groups in the United States. During the years immediately following the completion of his doctorate in 1908, Kallen began to write for various outlets of the American Jewish press on Hebraism and Zionism.[70] His essays reveal a dynamic interrelationship between the ideas he drew from his most influential professors and his experiences as a founding member of the Harvard Menorah Society. In these writings, we also see the earliest seeds of cultural pluralism.

In many respects Kallen's biography typifies those of the majority of founding Menorah Society members. Although he rejected his parents' religious orthodoxy, he did not think that doing so necessitated that he abandon being Jewish. Instead, Kallen believed, modern American circumstances necessitated a new basis for Jewish identity. Born in Bernstadt, Silesia, in 1882, Kallen immigrated to Boston with his father, an Orthodox rabbi, in 1887.[71] To his father's great disappointment, Horace did not follow him into the rabbinate. The younger Kallen disdained Orthodox Judaism as a young man and continued throughout much of his adult life to have animus for his father's strict adherence to tradition and ritual. After a truant officer threatened Kallen's father (who was educating his son at home), Kallen entered the secular public schools. There, according to historian John Higham, he developed "an uncritical enthusiasm for America."[72]

Kallen began his studies at Harvard College at the age of eighteen and there earned his bachelor's degree in 1903 and doctorate in philosophy in 1908.[73] He held teaching posts at Princeton (1903–1905) and at the University of Wisconsin–Madison (1911–1918). Kallen later claimed that, had Princeton known he was Jewish, he likely would not have been hired. At Wisconsin he was dismissed for advocating pacifism during World War I, after which he helped to found the New School for Social Research in 1919, where he taught until 1973, a year before his death.[74]

Just after his father's death in 1917, Horace Kallen described him as "among the last of the old school of Jews who would make absolutely no concession to their environment, but made their environment wherever they went."[75] Kallen's judgment not only signaled alienation from his father's traditional world, but also his opinion that individuals and groups must make certain accommodations to their host societies. Kallen rejected his father's Orthodoxy, but also claimed that modern Reform Judaism, which had won the allegiance of many American-born descendants of German Jews as early as the mid-nineteenth century, also failed to fully address the needs of young Jews who craved intellectual stimulation.[76] Yet Horace Kallen never turned away from Jewish identity or culture.

Kallen preferred literature and philosophy to religion. He matriculated to Harvard with his feelings toward Judaism "not only negative but hostile," according to historian Milton R. Konvitz.[77] Even with such disdain for traditional religious expression, however, Kallen still found assimilation more abhorrent. Assimilation could have come in a variety of ways, the most extreme being conversion, with a lesser extreme being a denial of Jewish identity or an attempt to pass as non-Jewish. Nearly half a century later, as he reflected on his years at Harvard, Kallen would claim that he could have passed as gentile relatively easily, but he chose not to; instead he sought new modes of defining Jewish culture that would allow it to thrive in America.[78]

Clearly influenced by the secularizing trends at Harvard under President Eliot, Kallen believed that religious practice too often became anti-intellectual and antithetical to modern notions of scientific inquiry. Kallen perceived Orthodox Judaism as dogmatic and incapable of questioning established assumptions and practices. Jewish rituals, Kallen later argued, "tend too easily to become mechanized and rigid and to become emptied of meaning."[79] Uncritical adherence to such rituals clearly contradicted the spirit of scientific inquiry that Kallen learned as a Harvard student.

Hebraism became so useful for Kallen and his cohort at Harvard because it provided them with a way to express themselves as Jewish without limiting that self-conception to what they viewed as their ancestors' antimodern worldview. The notion that Hebraism represented the modern infused all aspects of the Menorah Association's early history. Indeed, Hebraism defined what group members often called "the Menorah idea."

Kallen did not invent the term Hebraism but revised its meaning to address his concerns at the time. He likely became familiar with Hebraism from his reading of Matthew Arnold, perhaps the leading American literary critic of his day. In an 1869 essay, Arnold described Hebraism and Hellenism as two "forces" that each aimed for humans' perfection. These complementary forces sought to reach their goals in different ways. Hebraism was characterized by "conduct and obedience." Hellenism was characterized by the ability to "see things as they really are." Hebraism focused on duty; Hellenism emphasized knowledge and beauty. Hebraism endorsed action; Hellenism favored contemplation. Although Hebraism and Hellenism pursued different means, the final goal of each was human salvation. Arnold's essay argued for a greater balance between Hebraism and Hellenism in order to achieve this lofty goal.[80]

In Kallen's writings on Hebraism, he completely refigured one important aspect of Arnold's philosophy. Kallen understood a primary component of Hellenism to be its *resistance to change*, where Hebraism *allowed for change* as the essential condition of life. In a rapidly modernizing America, which Kallen called a "moving act," Hebraism proved more useful than Hellenism, which Kallen interpreted as emphasizing stasis and destiny.[81] According to literary scholar Susanne Klingenstein, Kallen associated Hebraism with American "equality, democracy, and freedom," where Hellenism "came to signify Europe's graven structures."[82] Relying on this notion of Hebraism's flexibility, Kallen would map his understanding of Hebraism onto the core American values taught to him by Barrett Wendell, who always emphasized the contrast between an American society based on ideals and a European society based on enduring social institutions more resistant to change. "To believe in life in the face of death," Kallen wrote in 1909, "to believe in goodness in the face of evil, to hope for better times to come, to work at bringing them about—that is Hebraism."[83] Honing in on this lack of fixity in modern life, Kallen later wrote, "Hebraism assigns to Becoming a oneness which is the same as the boundless succession of events, the evil as well as the good, the false and wrong as well as the true and right, the unbeautiful as well as the beautiful. Becoming is unceasing creativity."[84] Here, Kallen's Hebraism obviously drew upon his dissertation director's philosophy of Pragmatism. As Kallen wrote in 1909, only one year after completing his dissertation under James, any idea had "genuine survival value, if it endures, by working, in the flux."[85]

Kallen's linking of Hebraism to Pragmatism allowed him to employ Hebraism in the service of cultural diversity. Around the time that he began to use Hebraism, Kallen also started to portray America not as a fixed entity to which outsiders must adapt, but instead as a work in progress. As with any other idea, the American idea would remain current only if it could adapt to changing circumstances. James's worldview depended on change and progress. In fact, he so "hated the idea of undifferentiated oneness," in the words of cultural critic Louis Menand, that James "thought the universe should be renamed the 'pluriverse.'"[86] Kallen drew on James's logic by arguing for an America always in formation—an understanding that necessitated allowing for the cultural contributions of newly arrived immigrant groups.[87] By this logic, no peoples could be excluded from the nation on the grounds that they were "un-American." For, if one agreed that

America was always in the making, new cultural contributions should be welcomed provided that they did not contradict cornerstone ideals such as liberty and democracy. As we see in chapter 3, Kallen used this logic to propose that developing particular Jewish cultural interests meshed seamlessly with American ideals.

Despite his insistence on portraying all aspects of American culture as malleable, Kallen's notion of Hebraism ultimately proved quite inward looking, more focused on redefining Jewish identity, than outward looking, in the spirit of group cooperation. Indeed, for Kallen, linking Hebraism with change meant primarily that *Jewish* identity could adapt to the needs of the era. Because Hebraism provided such a capacious definition of Jewish identity, Kallen advocated that it replace religion as the cornerstone of Jewish self-understanding. As Kallen explained, "The term Hebraism covers the total biography of the Jewish soul, while the term Judaism stands only for a portion of it."[88] Hebraism was larger than religion. As Kallen wrote to Judge Julian Mack in 1915, "Religion is less than life, and as life becomes more and more secularized, the religion of the Jews becomes less and less the life of the Jews. I use the word Hebraism consequently to designate the whole of that life, of which Judaism is a part—in the case of Orthodoxy a major part."[89]

Kallen explained in a speech to those gathered at the Second Annual Menorah Society Dinner in December 1913, "Jews change their religion; I am myself no adherent of religion, but I should resent harshly a statement that I am therefore no Jew." Kallen declared that change could happen for Jews in two ways: either Jews would assimilate or they would find ways to perpetuate their particular culture in a manner that did not conflict with their modern setting. Of course, he urged the latter: "The Menorah [Association] very properly aims not only to study Hebraic ideals; it aims to *advance* Hebraic culture and ideals."[90] The organization not only was good for perpetuating Jewish culture, Kallen further argued, it was good for the American nation. Here is where the turn toward a pluralist logic began. As Kallen noted in 1913: "That [Jews] are distinct and will remain so, and that it is better for civilization that they do remain so, seems to me clear enough. This is particularly true for America."[91] In order to maintain their distinctiveness, Kallen contended, Jews and other cultural groups should proudly advance their own particular culture. To conceive of the nation as anything but a combination of many cultures during the early twentieth century was abhorrent to Kallen and his followers in the Menorah Society.

Kallen was apparently so convinced that promoting Hebraic culture "proved" Jews' loyalty to the United States that he even used Hebraism to support American Jews' advocacy for a Jewish homeland at a time when Zionists in America often were forced to fend off charges of dual loyalty. In his 1913 speech to the Menorah Society, Kallen contended that Zionism logically emerged from Hebraism. He also argued that Hebraism already had found it truest expression in Palestine. Kallen declared, "There [in Palestine], at present, and only there, the Hebraic spirit gets unmixed and adequate expression."[92] Kallen echoed the central figure in the move for cultural Zionism, Ahad Ha'am, by arguing that Zion provided a spiritual center from which Jewish culture would emanate.[93] Ahad Ha'am (Hebrew for "one of the people") was the pen name of Asher Hirsch Ginsberg, a Russian Jew who argued against the feasibility of settling large numbers of Jews in Palestine, but who did hope that the Zionist movement would foster cultural expression and promote the use of the modern Hebrew language.[94] Challenging the stereotype of Jewish males' physical weakness, Kallen closed the speech by imploring Menorah Association members to become "*active* soldiers on the field of battle" for Hebraism, Zionism, and Jewish culture.[95]

Kallen's early writings on Hebraism became guides for the nascent Menorah Association. As early as 1909, as Kallen first published on Hebraism, the Menorah Society defined its aim as instilling "a love for Hebraism in all its members." Demonstrating his hope that study of Jewish humanities would become the antidote to assimilation, Menorah Society founder Henry Hurwitz explained in 1909 that although "a great many Jews threw their whole Jewishness overboard into the roaring flood of liberty" after emancipation, a "modern and truly enlightened Hebraism" would come to define Jewish identity and strengthen American citizenship among Jewish youth.[96]

Although they were not yet using the term "cultural pluralism," Kallen and his peers in the Harvard Menorah Society already were seeking to broaden conceptions of American identity and to make room for specific forms of Jewish expression. The essence of the Menorah idea was to refashion Jewish identity in the image of the scholarly life they had come to admire. By the mid-1910s, the Intercollegiate Menorah Association had spread to campuses across the nation. As we see in the next chapter, the Menorah idea would catch on with students at these campuses, although not without conflicts and controversies along the way.

2

The Intercollegiate Menorah Association and the "Jewish Invasion" of American Colleges

By 1913, the Intercollegiate Menorah Association (IMA) could boast of significant accomplishments. In just over seven years, it grew from an idea espoused by sixteen students at Harvard to become the most influential Jewish organization on American campuses. During this time, the organization's leaders convinced competing Jewish student organizations to disband or be absorbed by the Menorah Association.[1] At campuses across the country, local Menorah Society chapters sponsored study circles in literature, history, and Hebrew language. They staged plays and maintained an actively circulating library of books of Jewish interest for their members. By the mid-1910s, the IMA's goal of promoting Jewish culture among college students seemed to be reaching fruition. As the University of Minnesota Menorah Society reported in 1915: "Most of the students who were indifferent before are now exhibiting a lively interest in things Jewish."[2] The Menorah idea resonated widely among Jewish college students.

The battle to combat assimilation by promoting Jewish culture, however, was hardly won. Jewish authorities across the United States remained unconvinced. As the Menorah Association began to thrive as a national intercollegiate organization, even those sympathetic with its efforts worried that college attendance would come at the cost of assimilation. Consider a claim Jewish Theological Seminary president Solomon Schechter made to an IMA gathering in December 1913. For many Jewish students, Schechter warned, "a college education meant the studied indifference to Judaism and Jewishness."[3] At the same event, I. Leo Sharfman, a Menorah Society founder at Harvard who became a professor of economics at the University of Michigan, topped Schechter by asserting that Jewish college students were "openly ashamed of Jewishness."[4] Some sympathetic non-Jewish observers agreed. Writing in *Harper's Weekly* in 1916, Norman Hapgood reported that differences between Jews and other students on campuses were not particularly pronounced. Surely some social obstacles existed, but, for the most part, Hapgood wrote, Jewish students "blend into the mass."[5]

Concerns about Jewish college students' ability to "blend into the mass" during the 1910s generally coalesced around two themes. First, critics portrayed the college campus as an open environment in which a variety of competing interests lured Jewish students away from activities that focused on Jewish culture. Second, they understood that Jewish students had become remarkably adaptable within college environments, often choosing to turn away from pursuits that had anything to do with being Jewish. Attending college, in other words, provided students with both the enticement and the possibility to cast off Jewish identity.

The Menorah Association was designed to address this new reality by encouraging students to take active interest in being Jewish, even as they embraced opportunities that previous generations of Jews in America never imagined. Winning Jewish students' loyalty became the organization's primary challenge. As it promoted Jewish culture on campuses, the Menorah Association encouraged Jewish students to conceive of their identity as plural, both Jewish and American. Long before Horace Kallen first used the term cultural pluralism, those who were most influential within the Menorah movement embraced pluralism as a lived experience. Concerns about assimilation would be answered by reframing students' self-understanding. They would not have to be "Jews" or "Americans" exclusively. They could be both, simultaneously and without contradiction.

By the late 1910s, the IMA became the largest Jewish student organization in the nation.[6] Advancing Jewish culture through study emerged as a clear mission. As the IMA won the affiliation of many Jewish students on campuses, though, the American college student population already was changing in ways that threatened the organization's long term viability. Even as the IMA became increasingly influential, it did not adapt to students' modern needs. Moreover, the association failed to make space for students' desire to foster Jewish cultural expression outside the realm of academic study. These shortcomings led to the IMA's decline by the 1930s.

The heyday of the Intercollegiate Menorah Association depended, of course, on the rapid increase in Jewish students' college attendance during the early twentieth century. This increase became an issue of significant distress at a handful of elite schools during the early 1920s, when some administrators sought ways to limit Jewish enrollment. Spurred primarily by a controversy about quotas at Harvard in 1922, many elite universities eventually did restrict Jewish student enrollment without ever declaring quotas an official institutional admission policy.[7] This brief storm over admissions quotas in the 1920s directly challenged the Menorah Association's pluralist ideal, as supporters of quotas usually portrayed cultural difference as negative. The debate over quotas, which occurred just as Jewish leaders worried that college attendance would ease the process of assimilation, demonstrated that Jewish students were caught in between, targeted by some for being unable to assimilate and by others as too willing to assimilate. One might suspect that these views of Jewish students would have been in conflict with each other, but they often were not. Concerns that students would cast off all distinctiveness readily coexisted with claims that college environments could do little to assimilate large numbers of students considered variant from the norm.

"If You Make Yourself a Sheep the Wolves Will Eat You"

Just two years after its founding in 1906, the Harvard Menorah Society membership grew to more than one hundred, and Menorah Society chapters began to spread to other campuses.[8] In some cases, the organization traveled with Harvard alumni. Louis L. Silverman, a Harvard graduate who joined the faculty at the University of Missouri in 1907, established the second Menorah chapter there.[9] Silverman eventually encouraged Jewish students at nearby Washington University in St. Louis to form a Menorah Society. On the East Coast, Harvard Menorah Society members invited Jewish students from local colleges to their meetings and encouraged them to form their own campus chapters. On December 20, 1907, the Harvard Menorah Society hosted Jewish students from Brown, Dartmouth, MIT, Tufts, Boston University, and Radcliffe College. Harvard president Charles Eliot spoke to those who gathered about the importance of perpetuating Jewish culture.[10] Each of these visitors, except for the Dartmouth representative, eventually founded a Menorah Society chapter on his own campus. Menorah Societies formed at Pittsburgh, the University of Illinois, and the University of Texas by 1908.[11]

The students involved in the early spread of the Menorah Society viewed their membership as an expression of pride in Jewish culture. One student who hoped to organize a Menorah Society at Clark College in Worcester, Massachusetts, especially took to heart the mission to promote Jewish students' dignity, informing the Harvard Menorah Society president, "The Jew has a feeling, which seems to be innate, that he is a foreigner and an alien, he is meek, humble and submissive at the very time when he ought to assert his rights." Jewish students at Clark banded together under Menorah Society auspices, this student wrote, to combat such feelings of inferiority. His language demonstrates the support that membership in the Menorah Society afforded some Jewish students: "If you make yourself a sheep the wolves will eat you. An association in the nature of the Menorah Society will greatly assist in eliminating this feeling."[12]

The formation of Menorah Societies at campuses around the nation provided fellowship between Jewish students and also allowed some Jewish students to create a stronger bond with their own universities. As the secretary of the Harvard Menorah Society explained, the existence of a Menorah Society at Yale forced Jewish Harvard men to become more "keen and alert; for now, to the long list of rivalries with Yale in many fields, is added the rivalry in the field of Menorah work."[13] Although some non-Jewish students might have blanched at the suggestion that a Jewish student organization could be a custodian of the venerable Harvard tradition, Jewish students in the Harvard Menorah Society perceived their organization as having a meaningful link with Harvard traditions. Participation in the Menorah Society buttressed their feelings of belonging to Harvard.

In January 1913, the existing Menorah Society chapters banded together to form the Intercollegiate Menorah Association. Nearly thirty societies had joined the rolls soon after the incorporation of the IMA. The IMA was intended both to regulate campus chapters' activities and to encourage organizational growth. By 1914, students as far west as the University of Colorado and the University of Denver founded campus chapters.[14] By the mid-1910s, the IMA enjoyed a more receptive audience than any contemporary effort to organize Jewish college students.

The Manhattan-based IMA became the central administrative body for a network of local Menorah chapters. Campus chapters did not have to pay dues to the IMA, and, as long as students agreed to act in the spirit of the Menorah Association and report regularly to the national organization, a Menorah Society charter would be granted. With this system of national affiliation in place, by the time that the IMA gathered for its second annual convention at Columbia University in December 1913, thirty-one Menorah Societies existed at colleges throughout the nation. The number of Menorah chapters had more than doubled since 1912, and did so again by 1919, when the IMA boasted nearly eighty campus chapters.[15]

A variety of staff members, including editors of the *Menorah Journal*, joined Chancellor Henry Hurwitz in the New York office. No individual would ever remain in any IMA position long enough to wield influence as Hurwitz did. Many alumni who had been active in the Menorah Society during their college days served on the Menorah Board of Governors. Rabbis and professors lent their support to the IMA in many ways, including traveling to campuses to address meetings of local Menorah chapters. The IMA defined itself as a nonpartisan organization, seeking to promote Jewish culture, but eschewing political or religious advocacy of any kind.

Hurwitz depicted the rapid growth of the movement as entirely natural: "The Menorah movement has advanced because it has not been pushed." Rather, Hurwitz claimed, the organization spread as a "notable testament to the fact that the Menorah movement is not only a spontaneous but a deeply genuine expression of the spirit of the American university both in its principles and in its ideals."[16] Although Hurwitz overstated his case, the idea that the Menorah movement was the most proper approach for reaching Jewish students dominated the organization's rhetoric. As Irving Lehman, a justice of the New York State Supreme Court and one of the Menorah Association's most prominent early supporters, wrote for the organization's promotional purposes: "We have a great and difficult task to perform if we are to succeed in bringing back to the Jewish youth a pride in their Jewish heritage and a knowledge of their Jewish past but I know that such work is worthy of all possible effort."[17] The sentiment that the IMA had embarked on a challenging struggle to counter disinterest on the part of Jewish youth dominated the organization's rhetoric and philosophy.

The IMA leadership was keenly aware that promoting Jewish cultural literacy on campus had to be presented as non-threatening to Jews' status as American citizens. Beyond sensitivity to charges of dual loyalty, though, IMA leaders made a much bolder claim that depended on the logic of pluralism. Menorah Association authorities claimed that students' pursuit of Jewish cultural literacy would strengthen their loyalty to America, rather than threaten it. Arguing for the symbiotic development of Jewish culture and American civic identity dominated the organization's rhetoric during the mid-1910s, and especially during World War I.

This line of thought, called the "cult of synthesis" by historian Jonathan D. Sarna, depended on "the belief that Judaism and Americanism reinforce one another, the two traditions converging in a common path."[18] The cult of synthesis, which rested in this case on the premise that the American nation was strengthened by the presence of a plurality of cultural groups, allowed the Menorah Association's leaders to argue that its organization's activities simultaneously promoted Jewish cultural identity and American civic loyalty. At the IMA annual meeting in December 1913, Sharfman explained that the organization "aims to produce better Americans and to enrich the content of Americanism, as well as to safeguard the future of the Jews and to contribute to the perpetuation of Judaism."[19] In a 1914 volume chronicling the history of the movement, Hurwitz and Sharfman articulated the society's purpose through the language of pluralism. They wrote: "The civilization of America is a composite of the cultures and the ideals of the various peoples that constitute the American nation. To the common treasury of American culture and ideals each constituent element must bring the full measure of its resources."[20] By this logic, failure to bring the full measure of Jewish cultural resources to Jewish students in America would deprive the nation of reaching its full potential.

Conflict on Campuses

The most active Menorah chapter outside Harvard was at the College of the City of New York (CCNY). (In 1929, The College of the City of New York changed the name of the educational institution to The City College of New York.)[21] Organized in 1910, CCNY's Menorah Society quickly overshadowed the only other Jewish organization on campus, the Zionist Circle, which ceased to exist after the large majority of its members joined the new group.[22] CCNY had no shortage of Jewish students from which to draw members; in fact, by 1915, the Menorah Society there estimated that nearly half the school's more than eight hundred Jewish students belonged. A large majority of the students lived in New York City, and many chose CCNY because they could attend without paying tuition.[23] During the 1910s, the Jewish student population at CCNY continued to increase rapidly, both by number and by percentage of the total student body. By 1921, approximately 40 percent of CCNY's ten thousand students were Jewish. By the late 1930s, that number rose to 80 percent.[24]

The CCNY Menorah Society sponsored meetings and special weekly forums, where leading Jewish figures addressed students. These forums drew locally from some of the best-known American Jews of the day, including Rabbis Mordecai M. Kaplan and Stephen S. Wise, and Columbia University Semitics professor Richard Gottheil.[25] Attendance at the forum meetings often topped 100 students, with Wise's 1916 lecture reportedly drawing 450.[26]

In addition to forum meetings, no fewer than fifteen separate, well-attended Menorah study circles met every other week during the academic year. Each member of the CCNY Menorah Society was required to join a study circle, but, as one member reported, "The attendance at the study circles is an obligation which has come to be felt as a privilege." The study circles focused on a wide range of topics, including discussions of *Menorah Journal* articles and studies in Judaism, Zionism, elementary Hebrew, Hebrew grammar, Hebrew conversation, and the Talmud. Students in the study circles who wanted to learn more could draw on the CCNY's growing library endowed by the IMA. The CCNY Menorah library contained 350 volumes by 1916.[27] The best work that emanated from these CCNY circles could even lead to lucrative rewards. At various points in its history, both Abram I. Elkus—ambassador to Turkey in 1916–17 and after 1919 a judge in the New York Court of Appeals—and Bernard Baruch—a CCNY graduate, Wall Street speculator, and advisor to President Wilson—contributed $100 annually for a CCNY Menorah essay prize.[28]

In addition to these activities, CCNY's Menorah Society welcomed rabbis and educators from the surrounding area to teach courses on Jewish history, Bible study, Jewish philosophy and literature, and elementary Hebrew. In January 1915, CCNY's Menorah chapter reported to the IMA that Jewish students had been "inspired" by the courses with a "lively interest in things Jewish and a serious desire for collegiate Hebrew instruction."[29] Later that year, in a Menorah-sponsored address to more than four hundred students at CCNY, Rabbi Judah L. Magnes suggested that CCNY should establish a permanent faculty chair in Jewish studies. Only a few days later, CCNY students had collected one thousand signatures on a petition to create such a chair.[30] This petition failed to convince the Board of Trustees, however, and CCNY would not institute a Jewish studies program until the late 1940s.

The IMA actively supported most of the CCNY Menorah Society's efforts. In matters related to Zionism, however, the national organization clashed so strongly with the CCNY Menorah Society that the IMA would eventually threaten to revoke the chapter's charter. Hurwitz always hoped students at CCNY would temper their passionate support of Zionism, but his requests failed to alter their behavior. CCNY students in turn criticized what they felt was the IMA's timid stand on Zionism.

Enthusiasm for the Zionist movement increased at many U.S. colleges and universities following the November 2, 1917, issuance of the Balfour Declaration, in which the British government expressed support for establishing a Jewish homeland in Palestine. Even after the Balfour Declaration, the IMA adhered to its nonpartisan, nonpolitical mission, despite the fact that most of the organization's leadership personally supported the movement for a Jewish homeland. In December 1917 the IMA passed a resolution supporting the Balfour Declaration, but many students argued that its language was not vigorous enough. The resolution said that the Balfour Declaration would create "a great opportunity for the further progress of

Jewish culture and ideals."[31] Even those Jewish students who did not consider themselves passionate Zionists recognized that this resolution was spiritless.

At many universities, Jewish students who were involved in the Menorah Association also joined Zionist organizations, but at CCNY the Menorah chapter actually merged with the Zionist organization on campus, renaming itself the "Menorah–Zionist Society" and proposing a new constitution. CCNY students insisted that the academic study of Zionism was no longer sufficient to satisfy their desires. In 1920, the CCNY Menorah Society informed Hurwitz, "Zionism has assumed a position in Jewish life where it must receive the active attention of every conscious Jew, for it has abandoned the field of theoretical speculation and has entered the sphere of immediate realities."[32] Hurwitz responded angrily, telling CCNY students that they had become too "opinionated, aggressive, and therefore impatient with counsel to disinterested study."[33] The IMA refused to sacrifice its own principles to the CCNY chapter, but, on the advice of CCNY philosophy professor Morris R. Cohen, Hurwitz backed off his aggressive effort to revoke CCNY's charter.[34]

The conflict with CCNY exposed the IMA's most crippling weakness; too often, the IMA stubbornly adhered to rigid organizational policies established upon its founding, rather than taking into account students' desires. By the 1920s, Jewish students' experiences had changed significantly enough that policies established at Harvard in 1906, or even upon the IMA's incorporation in 1913, seemed antiquated.

The conflict over political activity in support of Zionism proved to be one of many instances in which the IMA would stifle students' initiative. The national organization also entered into conflicts with various campus chapters based on matters of religion, politics, and new social mores. In each of these cases, the IMA remained motivated by its stubborn obsession with intellectualism at a time when students were seeking broader expressions of Jewish identity.

A dispute with the University of Cincinnati Menorah Society revealed the IMA's inability to accommodate differences of opinion over the role of religion in the association. The Cincinnati chapter thrived in the first few years after its founding in 1914, largely because it enjoyed strong student leadership. For example, Jacob Rader Marcus, who later became a leading scholar of American Jewish history and founder of the American Jewish Archives, served as the president of Cincinnati's Menorah Society in 1916–1917.[35] Many Jewish students who simultaneously attended the University of Cincinnati and Hebrew Union College (HUC), a seminary for training

Reform rabbis, joined the local Menorah chapter. The IMA's focus on study of Jewish history and culture rather than on Jewish religion, however, did not satisfy many of these rabbinical students.

HUC President Kaufman Kohler warned the IMA that it ran the "risk of making your endeavor an inevitable and certain failure" by declaring that the movement was "anti-religious."[36] Kohler's assertion was not technically correct. The IMA was not anti-religious. His perception was quite widely shared, however, and the organization always had trouble escaping this stigma.

The American Jewish Committee's Louis Marshall declined an invitation to address the Harvard Menorah Society in 1924, for example, telling them that his "point of view regarding the significance of Judaism as a religion is inconsistent with the views of a large proportion of the members of the Menorah Society."[37] HUC leadership, including Kohler, also labeled the Menorah Society a "veiled Zionistic society" that promoted separatism on the part of some Jewish students. Where its reticence to express its Zionism had hurt the IMA at CCNY, in Cincinnati, the organization's tacit support of Zionism prompted resistance. Kohler's antipathy toward Zionism led to his failure to sympathize with the Menorah movement. And Kohler was not alone. The Reform movement's official opposition to Zionism during this period most likely made some HUC students think twice before joining the Menorah Association.[38]

HUC students remained active in the University of Cincinnati's Menorah Society throughout the 1910s and 1920s, but their domination of the society's activities always kept it at odds with the IMA. These students tended to become involved in a wide variety of Jewish organizations. Many were members of the Menorah Society in name, but slighted the organization when it came to devoting their time and energy. As Sidney Regner, the University of Cincinnati's Menorah Society president, reported in 1924: "Due to the many other Jewish activities in this city we are having a hard time in keeping up interest in the Menorah."[39] Despite its early momentum, Cincinnati's Menorah Society, situated in the historic home of American Reform Judaism, never overcame its perception as an anti-religious, veiled Zionist club.

Even as the Menorah Association's positions on Zionism and religion complicated its relationships with local chapters during the 1910s, World War I provided an opportunity for the Menorah members to express their American patriotism under the auspices of a Jewish organization, and thus to emphasize the pluralist ideal at the heart of the movement.[40] The chance for the Menorah Association to tout Jewish students' military service, however, was undermined by the shift of students' attention away from campus activities during World War I. The IMA tried to make its movement useful to the war effort by encouraging students to collect money for war relief, but even this activity seemed to contradict the intellectual purpose at the heart of the Menorah idea. The Cornell Menorah Society, for instance, which had maintained some of the most active study circles until this time, disbanded all study circles by 1916 except for one "because the two or three men that led the circles have this year been engaged in collecting relief for the Jewish war sufferers."[41]

As attention to the war diverted students from Menorah Association activities, those Jewish students who enlisted were temporarily or even permanently lost to the Menorah movement. Wartime concerns led to the publication of a number of articles in the *Menorah Journal* regarding both Jews' loyalty to America and Jewish suffering around the world.[42] The IMA made efforts to remain in contact with students stationed abroad by sending them these publications, but it did little more than this, except for trying to maintain records of which Menorah Association students had enlisted in the United States forces.[43]

Even before World War I, local campus chapters had suffered from the perceived incompatibility of the Menorah Association's intellectual agenda with the increasingly social nature of college life. Although students expressed their desire to complement the Menorah Association's intellectually focused activities with social activities, the IMA officially rejected such suggestions. In preparation for the 1913 national meeting of the IMA at the University of Chicago, one of the organizers had suggested holding a dance at the conclusion of the proceedings. Harvard Menorah Society president Aaron Horvitz replied that a dance would be "entirely out of scope" with the purpose of the conference.[44]

Of course, there was a social aspect to the Menorah Association—students became friendly with each other and considered themselves to be members of an identifiable campus group—but these byproducts were never part of the organization's stated mission. Social functions such as dances or picnics were officially discouraged by the IMA, despite many students' desire for such activities. This failure of the IMA to respond to members' needs left students with a few options: assent to the IMA's directives, defy the IMA and sponsor social events, or quit the Menorah Society altogether.

The conflict over social functions between the IMA and local campus chapters existed even at Harvard, which always set the standard for other Menorah Societies around the country. Despite Harvard's reputation for intellectual rigor, alumni recalled that students' commitment to academics varied greatly. Some students could pass through Harvard with a minimal amount of intellectual investment. As Harold Stearns, Harvard class of 1913, later explained: "If you didn't want to become an educated man, it was nobody's business but your own."[45] Thus, even at Harvard, the Menorah Society's insistence on intellectual rigor may have dissuaded some students. In his 1917 report, Harvard Menorah Society treasurer Charles A. Rome informed the IMA that making the organization "as intellectual as possible . . . has failed to hold the interest of the members and has, I think, failed to accomplish its purpose to a large degree." Rome then bluntly stated: "There can be no question that there is something about this society that doesn't appeal . . . there's *something* missing . . . the society [is] *too* intellectual." Finally, Rome predicted a dire future for the Harvard Menorah Society: "All work and no play will ruin any man; all intellectual and no social side will end this society."[46]

The Menorah Society began to suffer a severe stigma because of this exclusively intellectual focus. In 1921, one member of the Harvard Menorah Society acknowledged that Jewish students who had not been accepted to Jewish fraternities joined the society only as a "last resort."[47] Three years later, the chairman of the Harvard Menorah Society membership committee reported great difficulty in enticing students to join. The situation could be assuaged, he urged, if the society ceased to remain so "narrowly confined." "We suggest more discussions, debates, perhaps a play, entertainment or dance, surely a social activity of some kind."[48] The IMA's leadership categorically rejected such suggestions. Many Jewish students who would have liked to have seen the organization's intellectual focus balanced with some of the fun that they felt belonged in college extracurricular life presumably stayed away from the Menorah Association.

Finally, the transitory nature of college life stymied the Menorah Association over time. The IMA insisted on student leadership at local chapters, both because of the belief that Menorah activities should be initiated from the ranks of students themselves and because of insufficient funding to employ regional secretaries or campus-based advisors. In many instances, inconsistent leadership compounded the challenges that Menorah societies faced on campuses. Some strong student leaders did emerge, but maintaining the continuity of the organization after these students graduated was difficult. The Portland Menorah Society, for example, was led in the early 1920s by Reed College undergraduate Jacob J. Weinstein, who would become one of the country's leading Reform rabbis during the middle of the twentieth century.[49] Weinstein directed an active campus society that even convinced W. E. B. Du Bois to visit campus and address Jewish students

Delegates of Menorah Societies Conference at
Brown University, November 1927.
*Courtesy of the Jacob Rader Marcus Center
of the American Jewish Archives.*

on racial problems in the United States.[50] No one of Weinstein's caliber followed after he graduated from Reed in 1923, and, without him, the Portland Menorah Society faltered.

The situation was similar at Harvard. Harry Starr, president of the Harvard Menorah Society in 1921–22, was described as an "excellent President but a poor executive, in that he does not train anyone of his members to take on the detail work or to relieve him." The IMA's corresponding secretary thus admitted, "I greatly fear that the Society will fall to pieces when [Starr's] influence is withdrawn."[51] This prediction about the lack of continuity ultimately harming the Menorah Association came to pass at Harvard and many other universities.

Competing Interests on Campuses

The Menorah Association, of course, was not the only campus-based organization that sought Jewish students' affiliation. From its earliest days after incorporation, the IMA faced competition from organizations with alternative strategies. One such group, the Intercollegiate Zionist Association of America (IZAA), splintered from the Menorah Association due in part to the Menorah Association's insistence on remaining nonpartisan in matters related to Zionism.[52] Even some of the Menorah Association's most prominent leaders, including Horace Kallen, became active in the IZAA, which, between 1918 and 1920, was funded by the Zionist Organization of America (ZOA).[53]

Like Kallen, some students who were active in the Menorah Association also affiliated with the IZAA. Aaron Schaffer, who earned a doctorate at Johns Hopkins University in 1917 and remained at the school as a faculty member, served as the president of both the Menorah Society chapter and the IZAA chapter in 1917. Although he assured Henry Hurwitz in 1917 that there would be no conflict between the two organizations at Johns Hopkins, Schaffer became upset when the IMA failed to issue a strong statement endorsing the Balfour Declaration. By early 1919, Schaffer told Hurwitz "to refrain from any effort to resuscitate the now absolutely defunct Johns Hopkins Menorah Society." Schaffer tempered the blow somewhat by blaming the failure of the Hopkins Menorah Society on the limitations placed on students' time: "Most of the boys have only a very few open hours at their disposal and these they are putting to Zionist work."[54]

Other critics were not as gentle with the IMA's Chancellor. After visiting Menorah chapters at the University of Pennsylvania, George Washington University, and Johns Hopkins, Rabbi Joel Blau informed Hurwitz that the students who actively supported Zionism had come to regard the Menorah Association as "superfluous."[55] Blau rightly observed that students were more likely to be mobilized by Zionist activity with an urgent political purpose, rather than by the Menorah Association's agenda to study the historical context of Zionism.

Enthusiasm surrounding the Zionist movement during this period trumped the Menorah Association on a number of campuses. By 1918, the IZAA's leadership disdainfully labeled the IMA "cautious about offending anyone" and "as interesting as a mid-Victorian debating society."[56] Nonetheless, Hurwitz and the IMA stood their ground, insisting on nonpartisanship and remaining a formidable competitor for student interest with the IZAA. After initial conflicts in 1917, in fact, the two groups began to cooperate in some venues, although they never did so at the national level. At Columbia University, for instance, local Menorah Society members voiced their support for Zionism and, in return, the Columbia Zionist Society committed itself to promoting the study of "all phases of the Jewish past and present in order to adequately equip the Jewish student for efficient service to his people."[57]

By the early 1920s, the IZAA was only one of the Menorah Association's concerns. The IMA faced more daunting competition from Jewish fraternities, which appealed less to students' academic or political natures than to their social desires. Jewish fraternities actually had preceded the Harvard Menorah Society by a decade.[58] The first Jewish fraternity in the United States, ZBT, was founded at the Jewish Theological Seminary in New York City in 1898. Under the guidance of Richard Gottheil, ZBT originally formed as a club for the study of Jewish history and culture. The acronym stood for *Zion Bemishpat Tipadeh,* Hebrew for "Zion shall be redeemed with judgment" (Isaiah 1:27). In 1906, the fraternity adopted the Greek name Zeta Beta Tau.[59] Other Jewish fraternities soon followed ZBT, and Jewish women also organized their own social societies on campuses.[60]

Jewish fraternities arose in large part as a response to the exclusion of Jewish students from existing fraternities. At many colleges, "old stock" American students who were unhappy with the overrepresentation of Jewish students on campus excluded Jews as well as blacks and other minority students from fraternities, athletic teams, and social and academic organizations.[61] On many campuses, only non-Jewish students who were unable to "make" fraternities would socialize with Jewish students. In response, students formed their own societies. Jewish students' primary opportunities for social life generally came through these separate Jewish organizations.[62]

The Intercollegiate Menorah Association officially remained opposed to fraternities throughout its history and claimed that fraternities of any kind represented the worst form of discrimination and exclusion. Even as outside observers sometimes mistakenly regarded the IMA itself as a fraternity, the Menorah Association's leadership worked hard to distinguish its intellectual goals from the social purposes at the heart of the fraternity movement. Consequently, the relationship between students who belonged to the Menorah Association and Jewish fraternity members was sometimes uncooperative. In 1915, Gottheil told IMA leaders that students in Cornell University's ZBT chapter kept aloof from Cornell Menorah Society activities. A frustrated Gottheil admitted that he failed to convince undergraduates of "the necessity of their co-operating in all Jewish movements at Cornell."[63]

The IMA's opposition did not stem the tide of fraternities' popularity. Indeed, the national fraternity movement boomed by the early 1920s. As historian Paula Fass found, 1,560 national fraternity and sorority chapters existed in 1912; by 1930 the number of chapters grew to 3,900.[64] The Jewish fraternity movement followed suit: at Harvard in 1922, for example, "forty of the forty-six Jews belonging to social clubs were members of Jewish fraternities."[65] The secretary of the University of Atlanta Menorah Society informed the IMA in 1920 that a group of Jewish students had left the campus Menorah Society to form a fraternity. Describing these students as afflicted with "fraternitis," the student explained, "The fact is that the boys really do not care enough about Jewish subjects to neglect a social good-time even for one afternoon."[66] Two years later, students reported to the IMA that conditions were similar for Jewish students at the University of Illinois, Ohio State University, and many other colleges.[67]

This changing nature of college life led some in the Menorah Association to call for a wholesale revision of the organization's approach to Jewish students. Julietta Kahn, a corresponding secretary of the IMA who had visited many campus chapters during the early 1920s, presented the case for change in a memo delivered to Hurwitz in March 1922. Kahn recognized that the college experience in 1906, at the founding of the Harvard Menorah Society, bore little resemblance to college life in 1922. In its earliest years, the Menorah Society was the only option for Jewish students who "wished to preserve their identity." By 1922, Kahn noted, competition from other Jewish campus organizations had increased markedly. Kahn bluntly added, "Aside from the multiple interests of the Jewish students on the campus, the plain fact remains that the intellectual level of students in 1922 is considerably under that of 1906, or even 1913." Most college students "think that jazz music and dance are the center of universe," Kahn reported. She closed by warning, "Something must be done, and done quickly."

Kahn predicted that appeals to make the Menorah Association a social organization would fail, and she recognized that fraternities had no incentive or interest in cooperating with the Menorah Association. "There must be a house-cleaning, from top to bottom, if the original Menorah idea is to be saved," Kahn wrote. "Organizations, to live as something more than relics, must change with changing conditions."[68] Just as Hurwitz and the IMA began to consider how to respond to Kahn's warnings, however, Jewish students' presence on campuses became further complicated by a crisis that centered on their overrepresentation at some of the nation's most elite colleges.

The "Jewish Invasion"

The rapid social and demographic changes occurring on college campuses came to a head in 1922, when the question of limiting Jewish students burst into the national headlines.[69] As in so many education-related issues, Harvard became the center of the storm. The Jewish student population at Harvard had increased from 6 percent of the student body in 1908 to more than 20 percent by 1922. Harvard was not alone. At Yale, the Jewish student population rose from 2 percent in 1901 to over 13 percent in the class of 1925. Princeton enrolled six Jewish undergraduates in the class of 1900; the class of 1926 had twenty-five Jewish students, making up nearly 4 percent of the student body. In 1922, Jewish students made up 27 percent of the Wharton Business School at the University of Pennsylvania.[70]

Debates about implementing restrictive admissions quotas for Jewish applicants to these schools garnered national attention. Admissions quotas, reflective of the rising tide of nativism in the United States during the 1920s, spoke not only to Jews' ability to matriculate to college, but also to their ability to be hired in desirable professions after graduation.[71] As Rabbi Louis Newman asserted, "The effort to bar [the Jew] from liberal and professional colleges is in reality designed to banish him from the field of competition with Gentile professional men. If the Jew loses his fight to gain admission to the college campus, he is defeated in a far more significant battle, namely the right to entrance into the higher spheres of professions and commerce."[72] Quotas influenced Jewish students most immediately, but some observers like Rabbi Newman also recognized that the debates over restrictive quotas, like the contemporaneous debates about implementing immigration quotas in the United States, had implications for Jews beyond campus life and even called into question the nature of American democracy itself.[73]

As soon as the story about limiting Jewish students broke, Harvard's Board of Governors initially tried to deflect attention from charges of anti-semitism. The board avoided ideological declarations and reported that it would act in response to what it perceived as a too-rapid increase in *total* student population, rather than a too-rapid increase in *Jewish* student population.[74] On May 31, 1922, the board issued a statement: "We have not at present sufficient class rooms or dormitories to take care of any further large increase [in the student population]." Even though the statement focused on practicalities rather than on ideology, the board tried to portray the problem as a complex web of issues. "This problem is really a group of problems, all difficult, some exceedingly difficult, and most of them needing for their settlement more facts than we now have." At the end of the statement, the Board of Governors signaled the most outstanding of Harvard's "group of problems": "It is natural that with a widespread discussion of this sort going on there should be talked about the proportion of Jews at the college."[75]

Despite its best efforts, the Board of Governors could not keep the issue of Jewish student enrollment in the background for long. Just two days after the release of the statement on admissions, a front-page headline in the *New York Times* declared: "Discrimination Against Jews Suspected In New Harvard Policy on Admission."[76] Harvard's infamous "Jewish problem," which would spread to other elite eastern universities, had begun.

Harvard's debate about quotas surely stemmed from a rapidly increasing Jewish student population, but it also was precipitated by a change in administration. A. Lawrence Lowell, Charles Eliot's successor as president in 1909, was deeply suspicious of Jewish students' ability to become true Harvard men. Eliot and Lowell differed in educational philosophy and did not like each other personally. One Harvard faculty member, David Gordon Lyon Jr., reported that Eliot believed Lowell hated Jews.[77] Lowell held what historian Richard Norton Smith called a "lifelong bias against hyphenated citizenship."[78] Indeed, Lowell was skeptical of any claim to pluralism. As president of Harvard, he wrote, "I long ago came to the conclusion that no democracy could be successful unless it was tolerably homogenous."[79]

So it should come as no surprise that, by the 1920s, Lowell did not support the presence of the Menorah Society at Harvard. Over the course of more than a decade, Lowell always rejected invitations to speak to the group, despite its persistent efforts to solicit a visit from him.[80] In 1915, Horace Kallen urged the president of the Harvard Menorah Society to ask Lowell to participate in the group's tenth anniversary celebration; Lowell declined.[81] In December 1917, Lowell again declined an invitation to speak to the Harvard Menorah Society. The language he chose for his rejection in this case was particularly telling. Instead of citing a schedule conflict for his inability to attend, as he usually did, Lowell expressed his displeasure with the Menorah Society's guiding principle of pluralism: "It seems to me that in America it is very unfortunate to keep up distinctions of race, that the hope of our future lies in a homogenous population, and that therefore societies like the Menorah which tend to segregate a race are undesirable."[82]

Lowell's antipathy toward Jewish students did not stop at the Menorah Society, either. During his tenure as president, he entered into many testy exchanges with students and rabbis regarding scheduling conflicts between Jewish holy days and Harvard's autumn entrance examinations. Lowell always refused to excuse Jewish students from exams on Jewish holy days, arguing that special allowances could not be made. To justify his position,

A. Lawrence Lowell, 1923.
Harvard University Archives, HUP Lowell, A. Lawrence (22).

Lowell frequently noted that students who fell ill also were not exempt from entrance examinations.[83] Jewish students, of course, bristled at the equation of being Jewish with being sick.

By 1922, Lowell had privately identified the increasing Jewish presence in the student body as a problem and also had issued the public statement from Harvard's Board of Governors about restricting total enrollment. Lowell claimed that it was not the individual Jew who was a problem for Harvard; instead, he contended that a critical mass of Jews would become inassimilable. "To a limited number of Jews," Lowell informed a prominent alum, "we can do a vast deal of good in making them American; but if the numbers increase largely, they cling together and are affected comparatively little."[84] The stereotypical portrayal of Jews as clannish rings loud here, as does a lack of faith in students' ability to socialize or learn with peers of different cultural or religious backgrounds.

After the quota issue made its way onto the front pages of newspapers, Lowell modified his rhetoric to emphasize that quotas actually were designed to help, not hurt, Jewish students. Harvard was not an antisemitic institution, Lowell insisted, but because the nation itself was witnessing growing antisemitic fervor, quotas needed to be implemented to protect Jewish students' best interests. In public, Lowell suggested that having too many Jews at Harvard had negative consequences for Jews, who would form an "unleavened lump" and would miss out on the ability to socialize with non-Jewish Americans.[85] In private, however, Lowell worried about Harvard's future if too many Jewish students matriculated. He told one colleague: "The summer hotel that is ruined by admitting Jews meets its fate, not because Jews are of bad character, but because they drive away the Gentiles, and then, after the Gentiles have left, they [the Jews] leave also."[86]

Surely, Lowell's motivations here were paternalistic at best and antisemitic at worst. Most importantly, for our purposes, Lowell believed that being American and promoting Jewish culture were contradictory. Moreover, Lowell claimed that Harvard had a duty to assimilate Jewish students. As he wrote just days after the quota issue became news: "The United States will not be in a comfortable position unless it succeeds in Americanizing the Jews."[87]

To deflect the heightened tensions surrounding the issue, Harvard's Board of Overseers referred the issue of Jewish students' admission to a newly created special faculty committee, which would wait for more than one year to deliver its findings. Lowell clashed with Judge Julian W. Mack, a Jewish member of Harvard's Board of Overseers, about which Jewish professors should serve on the faculty committee. Mack advocated the outspoken law professor Felix Frankfurter, but Lowell would not grant Frankfurter a position on the committee. Ultimately, professors Harry A. Wolfson (Jewish literature and philosophy), Milton J. Rosenau (medicine), and Paul J. Sachs (assistant director of the Fogg Art Museum and associate professor of fine arts) served on the committee.[88]

As Harvard's faculty committee met periodically throughout 1922 to discuss quotas, national journals of opinion took notice. "May Jews Go to College?" asked the title of an editorial in the *Nation* on June 14, 1922. After praising Harvard for being the "frankest" college to openly address a problem plaguing many colleges and universities, the author noted that a "larger proportion of Jews go to college than of any other race in America," and wondered about the "tendency in American universities to establish an academic Pale." Whether this comment was intended to blame Jews for failing to mix with non-Jewish college students or to criticize universities for segregating Jews is not clear. The unnamed author accepted as given that Jews formed such a large percentage of student bodies at many colleges that they no longer mixed with non-Jews. Thus his begrudging conclusions, common to many editorials written in the summer of 1922 in similar publications, were somewhat surprising. Even as the author stereotyped most Jewish college students as coming from "poor immigrant homes" and remaining "only half-assimilated," he also admitted: "America is changing; it is no longer a nation of Anglo-Saxon stock; it is a nation molded by that stock but perpetually being transformed by the later comers."[89] After denouncing quotas based on this ideal vision of America, the editorial closed by criticizing schools in Poland, Rumania, and Hungary that refused to admit Jews and urged American schools not to follow such "backward" practices.

That autumn of 1922, the *Nation* reported on an exam given in a Harvard Social Ethics class that asked students: "For the good of *all* persons concerned, is a college ever ethically justified in limiting to a certain percentage the number of any particular race who are admitted to the freshman class each year?"[90] Of the eighty-three students who took the exam, forty-one supported quotas, thirty-four opposed, and eight did not answer either way. Those who voted in favor of quotas justified their position by making statements about power rather than about ethics. Many students argued, for example, that Harvard was a private college and therefore could admit whomever it pleased. Others assumed that Harvard's alumni would not want to give money to a school with an overrepresentation of Jews. Some respondents were more adamantly against Jews' presence, claiming that Jews failed to integrate into the student body and "destroy the unity of the college." Other supporters of quotas wrote that all Jewish students were "grinds" (the contemporary epithet for students too concerned with scholarship) who ruined the curve on every exam.

By the time the *Nation* published these opinions, Harvard's Jewish students, led by Menorah Society president Harry Starr, already had been working for six months to mount a response to those who advocated quotas. Beginning in April 1922, Starr, who graduated from Harvard in spring 1921 and entered Harvard Law School that autumn, joined three other Jewish Harvard students who met with a small group of non-Jewish students and one unnamed faculty member to candidly consider the relationship between Jewish and non-Jewish students at Harvard.[91] Even though Starr reported that "social barriers" at Harvard had become "more tight" and "more discouraging than ever," he had a good experience with this small group of students.[92] Starr recounted that, after "self-consciousness wore away" among the students, the Jewish student leaders emphasized their main concern: "We wanted to clarify our basic principle: that no self-respecting Jew could allow any talk which would cast a shadow over the Jew as an American with the right to domicile not only on the soil but in the institutions arising from that soil."[93] The issue again was cast as one of quotas versus pluralism, with advocates of pluralism arguing for synthesis between Jewish identity and American identity.

Starr's defense of Jewish students rested not only on the belief that Jews' devotion to Harvard and to America should not be doubted, but also on a central tenet at the heart of the Menorah idea—that America is a nation always in the process of forming and that the contributions of various cultural groups strengthen the nation. Starr explained: "We were all Americans. Perhaps some of us had a lucky hundred years' start on the others in getting here. But that gave no cause for any hokum about the 'pure' American stock. We were all the American race in the forming: whatever traditions any of us possess we must be willing to exchange." Starr articulated his challenge to quotas based on the foundations of pluralism: "Either we are just as good Americans, or not. If we were, it would be absurd to draw lines between Americans."[94]

Although his argument rested entirely on the pluralist logic espoused by Menorah Association leaders, Starr exposed his naiveté in thinking that the pleadings of a student committee could convince Harvard's administration to reverse course. Ultimately, Starr and his Jewish peers on this committee submitted a letter stating their case to Harvard Dean Chester Greenough.

Starr also penned his own letter to the student paper, the *Harvard Crimson,* but little seems to have come of these efforts to affect the debate amongst Harvard's faculty and administration.[95]

Despite Starr's efforts, the IMA's leadership failed to mount a unified response to the situation at Harvard. Harvard faculty member Harry A. Wolfson, a lifelong supporter of the Menorah Society, became incensed by the suggestion that Jewish students should forego Jewish affiliations to be accepted in American colleges: quota supporters, he wrote, assume "that Jewish students coming to the University bring with them ideals and loyalties different from those of other students . . . that assimilation is not complete until no two Jews are ever seen to walk together in the College Yard."[96] Hurwitz was more tempered than Wolfson in his response, writing in an unsent letter to the *Jewish Tribune* that Harvard had entered into an "honest, straightforward endeavor" to address a "real problem." Although he did not deny that Jews had the same right as all other Americans to attend colleges based on merit, Hurwitz did admit that "Jewish students do form, on the whole, distinctly recognizable groups at every institution where they are to be found in appreciable numbers."[97]

It was indeed masses of Jews, not individual Jews, which led to the controversy at Harvard, but Hurwitz saw little to criticize in such grouping of students as long as they were not exclusive in their membership. Hurwitz thus overturned the stereotype of Jewish students' clannishness, arguing that Jews' "corporate" responsibility should be interpreted as a "challenge and an opportunity." The challenge was to overcome "small-minded discrimination." The opportunity, in strict accordance with the Menorah idea, was to study Jewish culture within a democratic, pluralist setting. Rather than profess "blind loyalties" to the group, Hurwitz told Jewish students that nurturing their Jewish identity necessitated "understanding," "free intellectual discovery," and "the *pursuit of studentship.*"[98] In a letter possibly intended to calm Wolfson, Hurwitz expressed trust in his alma mater: "It needs to be borne in mind, meanwhile, that no limitations of students on the basis of race or religion have been put into force by the Harvard authorities, and it may be confidently anticipated that they never will be."[99]

Hurwitz's faith in Harvard proved to be unfounded. Harvard President Lowell admitted to colleagues that his original plan to publicly acknowledge that the university was considering quotas was "crude" and "probably unwise."[100] The special faculty committee appointed by Lowell in 1922 eventually denounced quotas. Nevertheless, Harvard indirectly limited Jewish students' enrollment by establishing new application procedures, including mandatory interviews for applicants. Newly designed application forms required prospective students to declare their place of birth and religious affiliation and to state their father's name (including any change "made since birth in your own name or that of your father"), birthplace, and occupation.[101] Scrutinizing the answers to these questions did not necessarily ensure that Harvard would be able to determine which students were Jewish, but the information collected surely helped immensely in achieving that goal. Harvard, like a handful of neighboring colleges, also implemented geographical distribution requirements designed to accept fewer students from the northeastern United States, where most Jewish applicants lived.

Harvard again proved to be the trendsetter in higher education, as other elite institutions—including Yale, Princeton, Columbia, and Dartmouth—altered admissions policies to decrease Jewish students' enrollment during the 1920s and 1930s. These new policies led to a rapid drop in the percentage of Jewish students at elite colleges. The Jewish student population at Columbia fell from 40 percent to 22 percent during a two-year period between 1921 and 1922. Columbia's eight-page expanded application form—designed to learn as much as possible about each applicant's background and adopted by many other universities during the 1930s—further ensured that schools would stave off the "Jewish invasion" without having to officially adopt quotas. Some elite universities that did not employ such "selective" admissions standards during this era saw their Jewish student population soar. For example, the University of Chicago's Jewish student population more than doubled during the 1920s.[102]

The great irony in these new application procedures was that, even as colleges claimed that Jews would sully the character of their institutions, these colleges went to great lengths just to determine who had Jewish heritage. Indeed, many Jewish students acculturated so well by the 1920s that schools had a difficult time determining who was Jewish without being told by the applicant. Some Jewish students could, if they chose, pass as non-Jewish relatively easily. As educator Ralph Philip Boas noted in an October 1922 *Atlantic Monthly* article, quotas focused on Jews because "the problem of what to do with other groups—negroes, Armenians, Italians—is as nothing when compared with the problem of the Jews. . . . At one remove from the immigrant quarter, other groups do not go to college." Boas continued: "Then, too, other groups have not the Jew's adaptability. The Ethiopian cannot change his skin; but Jewish boys and girls differ from their Gentile companions often only in a racial tie so faint that insistence upon it is but a galling reminder of a difference that seems almost academic."[103]

Even schools' efforts to determine the percentage of Jewish students enrolled bore this point out. To determine its Jewish population, Harvard's

Law School relied on two staff members' "personal recollections," and the Medical School reported its number of Jewish students based on the unscientific method of looking at a photograph as well as hypothesizing if a student's name "sounded" Jewish.[104]

Horace Kallen summed up the issue best, undermining Lowell and others who claimed to be looking out for Jewish students' best interests. Kallen wrote in a 1923 *Nation* magazine article that Lowell relied on quotas to mask his own fears about the changing nature of the American nation: "It is not the failure of Jews to be assimilated into undergraduate society which troubles them [quota supporters]. . . . What really troubles them is the completeness with which the Jews want to be and have been assimilated."[105] Kallen correctly recognized that it was not the foreignness of Jewish students, but instead the *lack* of discernible difference between Jewish and non-Jewish students, that frightened those who advocated quotas. Because Lowell and those who supported him denied the possibility that a Jew could acculturate into an environment without completely casting off his Jewish identity, quotas became necessary, even if implemented in practice without being implemented in official policy.

Hillel Captures the Field

Even as elite universities set new admissions policies in place during the 1920s, Jewish students' affiliations on campus continued to shift, based in large part on their increasing options. The restrictions placed on admission of Jewish students in the United States lasted in some cases until after World War II, but these new policies ultimately proved to be less damaging to the Menorah Association than its own inability to respond to Jewish college students' changing interests and needs.[106] While some students chose not to self-identify as Jewish by joining campus organizations, those who did increasingly turned to bodies other than the Menorah Association, notably the B'nai B'rith Hillel Foundation.[107] In contrast to the almost exclusively academic focus of the Menorah Association, Hillel Foundations welcomed expressions of Jewish identity in multiple forms, whether religious (no matter the denomination), cultural, educational, or social.

A newly ordained rabbi, Benjamin M. Frankel, founded the first Hillel at the University of Illinois Urbana–Champaign in 1923. While a rabbinical student at Hebrew Union College in Cincinnati, Frankel traveled to a congregation near Urbana every other week to officiate at services and teach religious school. Frankel came to know some of the approximately four hundred Jewish students at the University of Illinois during his travels, and, in the words of one historian, considered these students "aimless, lacking leadership, without Jewish influence during their most formative years, hardly proud that they were Jews, and reluctant to declare themselves as such."[108] After being ordained in 1923, Frankel addressed this problem by founding Hillel. Frankel insisted that the primary purpose of the organization was religious, but he also encouraged non-religious activities. He intended Hillel to complement, not replace, other Jewish campus-based organizations; nevertheless, soon after the new organization was founded, the University of Illinois Menorah Society voted to disband, instead forming a Menorah Committee for academic interests under the auspices of Hillel.[109] This was a telling moment, as students expressed a broad vision of Jewish identity, with intellectual endeavors forming only one part.

It did not take long for conflict to ensue between the two organizations. On December 27, 1923, the *American Israelite* published a wire service story about the founding of Hillel. Although the content of the article was innocuous, the headline read: "To Supplant The Menorah."[110] A few Reform rabbis who supported Hillel wrote to Menorah Chancellor Hurwitz in an effort to clear up any misunderstanding following the publication of the notice and errant headline. They informed Hurwitz that Hillel had no intention of replacing the Menorah Association.[111] Nevertheless, after the appearance of a Hillel chapter on only one campus, Hurwitz confided to the prominent Cleveland rabbi Abba Hillel Silver, "It seems to me we're in for a lot of trouble, complications, and conflicts."[112]

Even in Hillel's earliest years, its leaders tended to dismiss the Menorah Association, regardless of the assurances they provided to Hurwitz. Adolf Kraus, the president of B'nai B'rith, insisted in 1925 that Hillel should assume primary responsibility for Jewish college students. Kraus declared: "The Jewish student is, as a rule, only passively Jewish. . . . It is part of our responsibility to help in their training if we Jews of America are to produce a generation of leaders."[113] Kraus acknowledged that the academic activity conducted by Menorah committees under the auspices of Hillel certainly had its place, but also claimed that this work, taken alone, would not prepare young men to become community leaders. Kraus praised Hillel for complementing study with religious activity and social welfare efforts, pursuits the IMA was unwilling to endorse.

Hillel quickly became a powerful influence in Jewish student life. It enjoyed many advantages over the Menorah Association on campuses, including funding from a national organization and support from many Reform rabbis. In response to Hillel's rapidly increasing popularity, Hurwitz in 1926 publicly suggested cooperation between the two organizations.[114]

Abram L. Sachar, a professor of history at the University of Illinois, responded by implying that the Menorah Association's influence on college campuses had waned too much for Hillel to gain anything from cooperation.[115] Sachar, who later would become the national director of Hillel and a prominent historian of modern Jewry, suggested that IMA's best work occurred in the realm of publication, specifically in the *Menorah Journal,* and that perhaps it should allow Hillel to "gradually step in" to replace Menorah Association campus chapters.[116] Hurwitz briefly considered Sachar's proposal before rejecting it.[117]

The Hillel Foundation was dealt a significant setback when its founder, Rabbi Frankel, just thirty years of age, died from heart disease on December 21, 1927.[118] Just two weeks after Frankel's death, Sachar informed Hurwitz that "the future is very hazy now."[119] Nevertheless, Hillel continued to expand its influence, while the IMA's struggles persisted. By 1927, Hillel had established itself at eight schools, with many requests for new chapters pending.[120]

Hillel's expansion during the 1920s further exposed the IMA's inability to meet college students' needs. This point was driven home acutely during a misunderstanding between Hurwitz and Rabbi Stephen S. Wise. Wise had actively supported the Menorah Association in its earlier years, but he had begun to sour on the movement by the late 1920s. The *Jewish Daily Bulletin* reported that, at a fundraising dinner for B'nai B'rith on March 20, 1928, Wise commented: "I say with full realization of my utterance, that the Hillel Foundations are doing the only effective Jewish work among our student youth."[121] When questioned by Hurwitz about this comment, Rabbi Wise insisted that he had been misquoted. Wise claimed that he also had spoken about campus work being conducted by the Menorah Association as well as by Avukah, a Zionist student group. Echoing the opinion of many of his colleagues, Wise added: "I have for some time believed that the one really significant aspect of the Menorah work in America today, is the publication of the Menorah magazine."[122]

Menorah Association leaders took great offense at the opinion of one of America's leading rabbis. When challenged further, Wise insisted that campus Menorah societies were not modern. He claimed that the Hillel Foundations conducted the type of work that "the Menorah would have undertaken if it had been organized twenty years later." Wise argued that the character of Jewish students had changed, but that the Menorah Association had not: "The Menorah began its work at a time when the cultural interest of the Jew was just a nice euphuistic name for the reluctance of the Jew to identify himself with the totality of Jewish life."[123] Wise contended that modern Jewish students were ready to embrace aspects of their Jewish identity in ways that the Menorah Association would not allow. There was no longer any cause for concern, Wise claimed, about expressing Jewish identity socially, politically, or religiously.

Sachar agreed with Wise. As he expressed the Hillel Foundation's reluctance to cooperate with the Menorah Association, Sachar's once-promising friendship with Hurwitz deteriorated. In 1930, Hurwitz informed Sachar that the Hillel Foundations were "merely Jewish Y.M.C.A.'s" and were "repugnant" to all Jews with real intellectual interests.[124] Sachar responded that the Menorah Association "has absolutely nothing to offer in the way of partnership" with Hillel, because "most students are not interested in purely intellectual pursuits."[125] Sachar's point was undeniable; college student life had changed dramatically by the 1920s, and Jewish students were no different from non-Jews in embracing this change.[126]

The IMA's insistence on intellectualism as the constitutive element of Jewish identity ultimately undermined its other stated goal of building community on campus by discouraging local variation or evolution of organizational traditions. Rather than allowing its traditions to evolve based on student initiative, the IMA leadership had tried to strictly prescribe the boundaries of acceptable activity, leading to conflict, or even to ill will, with students. Thus, the Menorah Association stifled itself in large part because of a contradiction inherent to its pluralist ethos: even as the Menorah Association promoted a culturally pluralist view of what it meant to be American, it endorsed a restrictive definition of proper expressions of Jewish identity on campuses.

Rather than acknowledging changes in students' mentality, Hurwitz in 1930 warned that the IMA would begin to compete more aggressively against the Hillel Foundations in fund-raising.[127] Even Hurwitz had to realize the emptiness of this threat. With the B'nai B'rith, Hillel had a large fund-raising organization in place. The IMA had no such support. By the early 1930s, with the onset of the Great Depression, the IMA encountered even greater difficulty raising money.[128] Hurwitz and the IMA's Board of Governors certainly had to realize their inability to compete effectively with Hillel. Hillel Foundations employed a permanent staff member, often a young rabbi, on each campus that had a chapter. The Menorah Association, in contrast, was unable to raise adequate funds to occasionally send scholars to speak to campus chapters.[129] From its peak at eighty campus chapters in 1919, the Menorah dwindled to fifty-one colleges by the spring of 1928. By the winter of 1932, many of its forty-four chapters existed in name but not in practice.[130]

In 1931, Adolph S. Oko, one of the *Menorah Journal* associate editors, described Hurwitz as "down and out and beaten" as a result of the group's struggle on campuses.[131] Oko suggested, as Rabbi Wise and many other colleagues had, that the Menorah Association should abandon its college work and focus solely on publishing the journal. These colleagues were correct in their praise of the *Menorah Journal*. The *Menorah Journal* had no peer in the United States as a location for Jewish cultural expression during the interwar era. Nevertheless, Hurwitz stubbornly pressed on with campus-based activities. Menorah Society chapters endured on some campuses until the late 1930s. By 1938, even Hurwitz struggled to muster a convincing response to Rabbi Louis I. Newman, who told him: "Everything I hear regarding activities of Jewish students in colleges and universities confirms my impression that the Menorah Societies exist only rarely, and exert a minimum of influence. The Hillel Foundation and the fraternities have captured the field."[132]

3

Cultural Pluralism
and Its Critics

The Menorah Association's plan for a student-centered cultural renaissance on campuses faltered due to its insistence on an academically rigorous ethos and activities. The rise of competing organizations that more readily appealed to Jewish students' desires also contributed to the IMA's decline. Yet the Menorah idea cannot be deemed a failure, for it enjoyed significant influence in both academia (well beyond the realm of a student club) and public culture. A significant number of those individuals who had been instrumental in the early success of the Menorah Association went on to teach in colleges and universities. Many of these professors developed programs for integrating the study of Jewish history and culture into secular curricula. Other influential members of the Menorah Association became writers for the nation's leading journals of opinion, including the organization's own magazine, the *Menorah Journal*. Even though Jewish college students gravitated away from the Menorah Association beginning in the 1920s, the Menorah idea continued to have influence, primarily through these Jewish studies programs and publications.

The Menorah Association's vision for an integrated program of Jewish studies on American campuses as well as its influence on Jewish historiography, politics, and literature all rested on the foundation of cultural pluralism. Therefore, we must here closely examine the origins of cultural pluralism and its relationship to the Menorah idea. Put simply, all the organization's academic and public initiatives depended squarely on the idea that came to be known as cultural pluralism. The individuals who shaped the Menorah idea—especially Horace Kallen—became some of the most important voices in public discussions of American pluralism. From the moment of its founding in 1915, the *Menorah Journal* emerged as the indispensable location for debating what pluralism would mean for American Jewish culture and people. Full comprehension of the Menorah Association's plan for a Jewish cultural renaissance requires a close examination of the pluralist idea. This examination ultimately reveals that the ideal of pluralism remained inexorably bound with the desire to promote Jewish culture specifically.

As noted, Horace Kallen did not publish the term "cultural pluralism" until 1924, but the idea had been evolving since his days as an undergraduate nearly a quarter of a century earlier. Hebraism and Pragmatism always remained central to Kallen's pluralist vision as it developed. Yet Kallen's portrayal of the nation as a federation of cultural groups raised as many questions as it answered. In order to promote pluralism, Kallen first had to address the idea of chosenness at the heart of Jewish ideology and religious experience. For how could a pluralist nation favor one group as chosen?

Even as he sought to clear this hurdle, Kallen had to contend with responses from Jewish and gentile colleagues alike. Some critics questioned how Kallen's theory would be translated to practice. Others raised significant questions about the relationship between culture and race. The group of intellectuals who most cared about pluralism entered into a sustained debate about whether Jewish cultural identity was inherited or learned. Of course, these thinkers would not solve these questions to any point of mutual agreement. Yet the debates themselves help us better understand the tensions surrounding Jewish identity in the United States during the interwar period. More, they show that the pluralist ideal—today so ingrained in our national narrative—has a history beyond the realm of abstract ideas and, indeed, a history wedded to the quite specific concern of promoting Jewish culture among youth.[1]

Pragmatism and Pluralism

As detailed in chapter 1, Kallen relied heavily on Pragmatism in his early writings because of its emphasis on flux. The influence of Kallen's advisor, William James, was decisive in this case. In 1908, Kallen completed his dissertation, "Notes on the Nature of Truth," under James.[2] The two philosophers remained in contact after Kallen left Harvard. While Kallen was on a fellowship to Oxford in 1908, he heard James deliver the Hibbert Lectures, which provided the material for James's book *A Pluralistic Universe*. Before James died in 1910, he asked Kallen to gather and prepare the writings that were published in 1911 as *Some Problems in Philosophy*.[3] Kallen also wrote the introductory essay to the Modern Library's edition, *The Philosophy of William James,* in 1925.[4]

As a loyal student of James, Kallen knew that Pragmatism valued the consequences of ideas. In 1907, James wrote: "It is astonishing to see how many philosophical disputes collapse into insignificance the moment you subject them to this simple test of tracing a concrete consequence."[5] For James, ideas retained their use only if they worked in a changing world— "worked" meant that an idea had some practical value that made a discernible difference in how individuals perceived the world. According to James, the very nature of truth itself could change based on given sets of circumstances. James conceived of Pragmatism as a challenge to staid dogmas, explaining in a 1907 lecture, "Pragmatism unstiffens all our theories, limbers them up and sets each one at work." Later in the same lecture, James claimed, "To a certain degree, therefore, everything here is plastic." He urged his listeners to be skeptical of "truths grown petrified by antiquity" and explained: "*The true is the name of whatever proves itself to be good in the way of belief, and good, too, for definite, assignable reasons.*"[6]

Kallen sought to apply James's ideas to the challenge of cultural heterogeneity in the United States. Indeed, as he worked his way toward naming cultural pluralism, Kallen might have been influenced by one of James's contentions about student diversity at Harvard. In a 1903 lecture to Harvard graduates who were concerned about the changing character of the school (Kallen graduated in 1903), James said that Harvard had to be tolerant of "exceptionality and eccentricity" and devoted "to the principles of individual vocation and choice." In a comment that foreshadowed the foundational ideas of cultural pluralism, James concluded: "The day when Harvard shall stamp a single hard and fast type of character upon her children, will be that of her downfall."[7] This statement was consistent with his promoting tolerance of difference as early as an 1899 lecture, "On a Certain Blindness in Human Beings." There, James urged his listeners to "tolerate, respect, and indulge those whom we see as harmlessly interested and happy in their own ways, however unintelligible these may be to us."[8] Letting others alone to develop their own interests became a defining characteristic of Kallen's pluralism, and one that would be criticized vehemently by those who sought ways to foster cooperation among cultural groups.

Harvard literature professor Barrett Wendell also profoundly influenced Kallen. Wendell was a much-beloved figure to generations of students who attended Harvard between the 1880s and the 1910s. Academic colleagues knew him for his publications on Cotton Mather and Shakespeare and textbooks on American and European literature. Chapter 1 discussed how Kallen integrated Wendell's ideas about Europe's institutionalized cultural norms and America's cultural adaptability. Wendell also convinced Kallen that the Old Testament and Hebraic traditions had profound influences on American Puritanism. With this new information in tow, Kallen was able to relocate his Jewish roots in two centuries of American history.

Accepting Wendell's lessons about the Hebraic influences on the American Puritans allowed Kallen to claim that Jewish culture and values preceded Jewish peoples' physical presence in America. By this logic, Jewish peoples' embrace of American culture could be portrayed as a *return* to Hebraic traditions—traditions that, not incidentally, lay at the foundation of the American experiment. The somewhat circular (and arguably dubious) lesson was transformative for Kallen.[9] As he expounded upon the virtues of pluralism during the 1910s and 1920s, Kallen regularly expressed his debt to Wendell. He even dedicated his 1924 collection of essays *Culture and Democracy in the United States* to Wendell, who had died three years earlier.[10]

Kallen's short semifictional essay, "A Convert in Zion," published in 1916, perhaps best expressed his reverence for Wendell. In the story, a Jewish student enters college with great shame about his own heritage. Over time, a professor of American literature "undid" this student's shame. "His 'Americanism' had, he discovered, unconsidered roots and origins," Kallen wrote. After learning what Americanism owed to the "Hebraic tradition," this young student conceived of his own identity anew, and he came to value Jewish culture. For anyone who knew anything about Kallen's undergraduate experience, the autobiographical quality of this tribute to Wendell was obvious, though Kallen mentioned neither himself nor Wendell specifically.[11]

Jewish intellectuals also influenced Kallen's move toward Jewish culture.[12] Solomon Schechter, the president of the Jewish Theological Seminary, heard Kallen deliver a speech on Zionism in 1906, and the two men remained friends after that first meeting. Years later, Kallen included Schechter as the only Jewish individual in a list of six thinkers who had shaped his intellectual development. The other five were Santayana, James, Wendell, psychologist Edwin Holt, and Canning Schiller, Kallen's tutor at Oxford.[13] Schechter helped Kallen to formulate ideas about how to promote Jewish culture within a "voluntaristic" American society. In the words of historian William Toll, Kallen learned from Schechter that "while Jews were a descent group, the experience of living as a Jew required creative responses to changing environments."[14] Kallen's Jewish self-understanding, always reliant on his theory of pluralism, grew directly out of this important lesson from Schechter, and contrasted radically with what he saw as the static, ritualized Judaism of his father's generation. By integrating Schechter's influences with those of James and Wendell, Kallen found ways to redefine—rather than to abandon—Jewish identity.

Pluralism and the Chosen People

Even as Kallen's ideas about pluralism began to take shape, a vexing problem specific to the Jewish tradition itself came to the surface. Ethnic pluralism butted up directly against the idea that the Jewish people were chosen by God. How could one group claim to be chosen within a model of the nation that emphasized equality among cultural groups? Yet how could Jews abandon all vestiges of the idea of a special relationship with God and still consider themselves Jews? Kallen had to confront these difficult questions, and, indeed, many of his earliest publications and speeches addressed the tensions between pluralism and chosenness. Marshaling a case against chosenness became a crucial step in the development of Kallen's pluralist thought.

Although the idea of Jews as the chosen people was one of the central organizing principles of traditional Judaism, touting a special relationship during the modern period between Jews and God could not be reconciled easily either with universalist Enlightenment sentiments in Europe or with the spirit of religious toleration being promoted in the United States.[15] One common approach for reconciling this tension emphasizes Jews' "mission" to the nations rather than their "election" by God. The concept of Jews' election depends on the claim of a special bond between God and the Jewish people stemming from the Mosaic covenant at Mount Sinai. Mission, on the other hand, is a more vaguely defined sense that the world needs improvement or repair (*tikkun olam,* in Hebrew), and that Jews are obliged to initiate this repair. The prominent German rabbi Leo Baeck captured the idea of mission in his 1905 *The Essence of Judaism:* "This mission goes beyond Israel itself; it is an election for the sake of others. All Israel is the messenger of the Lord, the 'servant of God,' who is to guard religion for all lands and from whom the light shall radiate to all nations."[16] During the nineteenth and early twentieth centuries, the Reform movement in particular championed the mission idea as central to Jewish self-understanding.[17]

Although he was not affiliated with the Reform movement, the prominent rabbi Mordecai M. Kaplan is often credited with recasting chosenness for the twentieth century. Kaplan, a professor of homiletics at the Jewish Theological Seminary in New York City, encouraged Jews to interpret

Judaism not solely as a religion, but also as a particular cultural, artistic, ethical, and organizational way of life. Beginning in 1915 and continuing through the late 1920s, Kaplan published seven articles in the *Menorah Journal* that examined chosenness and suggested that Judaism needed to be reconstructed.[18] Although he was not seeking to form a new denomination, Kaplan is now credited as the founder of Reconstructionist Judaism. In his 1934 opus *Judaism as a Civilization,* Kaplan encouraged Jews to disavow chosenness because he believed that the idea was so misunderstood and antithetical to modern ways of thinking that it was better discarded rather than reformulated.[19]

Kaplan's criticism of chosenness has garnered much more scholarly attention than Kallen's.[20] Yet the two men developed their ideologies about chosenness simultaneously and read each other's works on the subject in the *Menorah Journal.* During an era of dramatic debate about the proper expression of Jewish identity, both Kaplan and Kallen struggled to find ways to adjust Judaism to modern conditions in order to ensure the continuity of Jewish identity across generations. Each claimed that chosenness, which was frequently cited by religious authorities as the safeguard that would ensure Jewish continuity, actually had the opposite result. Both men ultimately argued that chosenness, whether expressed as election or mission, potentially had counterproductive effects on Jewish individuals and communities. Moreover, both relied on pluralist ideas to express their displeasure with the idea that one cultural group could conceive of itself as superior to others. As Kaplan wrote in 1934, "Judaism is but one of a number of unique national civilizations guiding humanity toward its spiritual destiny."[21]

Despite their shared concerns, Kaplan and Kallen did not always agree. Although both argued that chosenness could not be reconciled with the modern Jewish condition, Kaplan's emphasis on God required a different vision from that of Kallen, who focused more on cultural expression. Kallen would replace chosenness with Hebraism; Kaplan would replace chosenness with "vocation." As historian Arnold Eisen explains, "'Vocation' connoted the call of individual and group to a particular task, issued by a divinity certainly no less vague than the God imagined in much of non-Orthodox theology."[22] The task, according to Kaplan, was to find meaning in life, which came from joining God to work for unity rather than chaos.

Five years before the *Menorah Journal* first published Rabbi Kaplan, Kallen scrutinized the idea of a Jewish mission to humankind in a June 1910 *American Hebrew* article entitled "Judaism, Hebraism, and Zionism."[23] Like all good Pragmatists, Kallen assessed the idea's consequences. Doing so led

Kallen into an attack on Jewish mission that was alternately insightful and snide. Kallen began the essay by discrediting mission as an improper justification for perpetuating Jewish culture and Judaism. He declared that those Jews who steadfastly clung to the mission idea were actually those most wayward and lost. "People are bothered about their work or their destiny," Kallen wrote, "only when they are out of work and do not know what to do with their lives." Chosenness (Kallen more often used "mission" here) thus signaled a fundamental insecurity about destiny.[24]

Even more insidiously, such insecurity actually had the potential to support the hateful claims of antisemites. Endorsing a Jewish mission, Kallen claimed, "presupposes the anti-Semitic challenge of Jewry's right to that life." Jews, as a national group, "need no excuse for their existence," Kallen wrote.[25] Their existence itself, for the sake of perpetuating Jewish culture, should be their only purpose.

Some key ingredients of cultural pluralism emerge here: Kallen imagined Jews as a coherent enthocultural group and argued that their destiny need not be justified to those who are not members of the group. A group should not develop its culture for the sake of others, in other words, but instead should concern itself primarily with its own members. Kallen seemed to be suggesting that relations among various groups in society remain secondary to vibrant group culture itself.

Kallen was not utterly naïve, though. He realized that ethnic groups must and do interact with each other. Anyone who knew only the basics of Jewish history had to have real concerns about Jewish peoples' integration in society, or what Kallen here called the "Jewish problem." Kallen drew out the relationship between chosenness and integration: "'Mission' and 'problem' are correlated terms in the history of Jewry. Human groups that are, as groups, normally and vigorously functioning in civilization do not offer problems and do not proclaim missions."[26] Again, mission signals weakness and an unnecessary rationalization for group existence. One does not hear about "the Russian problem," or "the Japanese problem," or "the English problem," so, Kallen asked, why had the Jewish problem become so pervasive and troubling? The answer, Kallen asserted, was the very idea of mission itself. That is to say, mission is not the proper *solution* to the Jewish problem; rather, it is the very *catalyst* to the problem. Its presence necessarily makes the problem unsolvable. The idea of a mission—in effect a continually repeated and unnecessary justification for Jews' existence—ensures that the Jewish problem will endure. The logical implication of mission is that Jews will unendingly restate the existence of a Jewish problem without working toward a solution.

Kallen did move past his vigorous critique of mission in this 1910 *American Hebrew* article to offer his own corrective. He saw two possibilities: first, the disappearance of the Jews, either by "violent and speedy destruction or by slower absorption into the neighboring peoples, by assimilation"; or second, gathering a "remnant" of the Jewish people to "reconstitute the Jewish polity in Palestine or elsewhere." For Kallen, there was only one real option: "I am a Zionist. I look toward the concentration and renationalization of the Jews."[27] Kallen did not articulate the belief, as he would a few years later, that a Jewish person could be a patriotic American and a Zionist without risking dual loyalty. This absence may be attributed to underdeveloped thought or to the publication of this article in a journal of which the large majority, if not the near entirety, of readers were Jews. Nevertheless, Kallen eventually would categorize Zionism as a cultural loyalty and assert that an individual could have multiple cultural loyalties that did not contradict a singular political loyalty.

Yet Kallen spent less time in 1910 on Zionism than he did criticizing mission. After announcing his support for Zionism, he returned to philosophical abstraction, discussing the moral goodness of individuals and then mapping those understandings of individuals onto cultural groups. Turning to a musical example, as he frequently did in later writings on cultural pluralism, Kallen noted that a talented fiddler does not speak of his "mission" to play the fiddle. Instead, when the fiddler fiddles he enters into "the perfect exercise of his natural function." He fiddles by "instinct," and fiddling brings him "happiness," but not because he has a "moral responsibility" to others to do so.[28] Instead, one who develops his own talents does so to make the most of his individuality. If this benefits humankind, as fiddling sometimes does, so be it, but this is not the essence of the fiddler's vocation. To be sure, not all "natural" talents should be developed for their own sake—Kallen provided the counterexample of a skilled thief—but the point stood that one would not rightly ask if the fiddler has a "mission" to fiddle.

Kallen continued with an analogy: as the fiddler produces music, groups produce their own cultures. Groups are somewhat different than individuals, Kallen admitted, because group cultures often come into conflict with each other, and social harmony is often more difficult to achieve among groups than among individuals. Kallen nevertheless dismissed these potential conflicts without providing satisfactory resolution, and instead advocated that groups act just as the fiddler does, by promoting their own cultures. He warned, however, that cultures still would be judged according to their contributions to society. Returning to musically inspired language, Kallen envisioned each cultural group contributing its own "tone" or "individual note" to civilization. The collection of these notes ultimately "enriches and changes the harmony" of civilization as a whole. As long as each individual note is not too dissonant, it will contribute to the harmony of society.

Kallen next applied the test to modern Jews, asking if their culture met the condition of harmony rather than dissonance. Jews, like any other cultural group, would be "entitled to life" if their Jewish "difference is elementally and by its very nature contributory to the values of culture and civilization."[29] History informed Kallen's answer; he argued that the history of the Jews represented not just the history of a religious group, but also the history of a people's culture. He claimed that those who championed Jewish mission—especially those who advocated the primacy of religious identity—missed this fundamental point. To reduce the Jewish people and its history to a religious essence with a mission to the nations was "dangerous to Jewish survival," because it prioritized religion over a cultural wholeness.[30] Kallen explained that religious expression depended on the existence of the Jewish people. The obverse, however, was not true—the Jewish people did not depend on religious expression for its existence.[31]

Three years later, in a speech delivered to the Second Annual Menorah Society Dinner in December 1913, Kallen echoed many of the ideas that informed his *American Hebrew* article. Here, he moved closer to defining Jews as a cultural group and, at the same time, articulated a clearer vision of his understanding of American identity.[32] He opened his speech with what had become a favorite theme: modern Jews had a problem. How would Jews ensure the distinctiveness of the Jewish people in a society that offered them the freedom to integrate, or at least to mute their difference? And why should Jews promote their particular culture, rather than blend into the mass? The traditional answer provided by Reform rabbis and some Jewish intellectuals, and now familiar to readers of Kallen, was that Jews "have a 'mission' to teach mankind morality and 'pure monotheism.'" Kallen's venom for the concept had not abated at all over three years; he described the idea of mission as "attractive to our vanity" and "colossal egotism."[33] Kallen continued to insist that such vigorous touting of mission actually signaled a lack of direction rather than a common purpose.

In the time that had elapsed between his *American Hebrew* article and his 1913 speech, Kallen developed three additional criticisms of mission. First, the logical implications of mission bothered Kallen, because the existence of a mission depended upon that mission never being achieved fully. As Kallen argued, if Jews must "be everlastingly teachers of 'pure monotheism' and high morality, then the rest of mankind must just as everlastingly cling to impure monotheism, or to polytheism, and low morality." There was no clear endgame to the Jewish mission. The expression of a Jewish mission therefore validated an ever-present view of non-Jews as somehow inferior. Kallen wondered how Jews, in good conscience, could accept such a mission that "requires the rest of mankind to be ignoble and wicked."[34]

Second, Kallen introduced a distinction based on class between Jews from central Europe and Jews from eastern Europe to support his doubts about mission. He wondered how Jewish "compatriots in Russia, the push-cart peddlers on Canal Street, the whole great, dumb, impoverished and suffering mass of our people, who have to fight with their heart's blood to keep body and soul together," would promulgate a mission. How could Jews who fought against pervasive economic hardship and antisemitism, including "the struggle for bread," "pogroms," and "ritual murder accusations," be expected to fulfill such a mission?[35] By highlighting the fact that protracted poverty and antisemitism forced many Jews to focus only on the bare necessities of existence, Kallen intended to raise doubts about whether most Jews truly could concern themselves with the ambitious spiritual elevation of humankind.

This speech notwithstanding, Kallen usually tended to avoid writing about discrimination or class difference during this era. Indeed, he downplayed divisions among Jews, and instead emphasized the shared culture that had the potential to unify them. Perhaps somewhat paradoxically, Kallen de-emphasized intra-group conflict even as he based a central component of his own Jewish self-understanding on the claim that Jews who touted mission were entirely misguided. The issue also may be one of audience: Kallen's most vehement criticisms of Jewish mission appeared in journals (e.g., *Menorah Journal, American Hebrew*) or at events (Menorah Society Annual Dinners) primarily directed to Jewish audiences. His essays that appeared in the *Nation,* to name one of many other venues, were never so harshly critical of other Jews. In forums with more diverse audiences, he tended instead to imagine Jews as a coherent cultural group.

Third, and vital to the development of pluralism, Kallen claimed in his 1913 speech that arguments for a Jewish mission were undemocratic, for they valued Jewish contributions to society above those of all other peoples. Kallen described the idea of a Jewish mission as "unfit for citizens of a democratic country, of which the cardinal principal is that of the essential equality of all men, according to their own natures."[36] To claim a Jewish mission was so offensive because it implied that other groups' cultures had lesser value than Jewish culture. Mission simply could not be reconciled with advocating cultural difference because of the claim of superiority inherent in the concept.

Kallen nevertheless understood that the idea of mission was crucial to Jews' self-understanding. He anticipated the criticism that Jewish identity without religious content would be too weak to ensure continuity across generations, and he answered the charge by insisting that Jewish culture could serve modern Jews more effectively. American Jews could discard the belief in mission, or even their religious identity altogether, and still remain Jews. What made Jews distinct was not religious identity (represented by mission) but culture. Then, however, in a curious and inconsistent turn of logic, Kallen suggested that remaining a distinct cultural group was effectively *guaranteed* by ancestry. He explained that a Jew who "is a member of a Jewish race and insists that he is a member of a religious sect, called Jews, will find it very much harder to change his grandfather than to change his religion."[37] This sense of distinct peoplehood, guaranteed by "inborn nature," would ensure Jewish continuity, Kallen argued.

Kallen's pluralist vision here relied on imagining the nation as a conglomerate of co-existing groups. He said little about cooperation and rejected the premise that cultures somehow would meld together to form a new, homogenized American culture. He described the nation as akin to a "meeting of a great many different nationalities at some international conference."[38] Kallen invoked the example of Switzerland, where cultural groups cooperated politically and free expression of distinctiveness was highly valued. The duty of each ethnic group within a nation was therefore to ensure political harmony but at the same time to resist cultural or biological uniformity.

Jews had a unique challenge in this regard. Even though Jews the world over had developed a strong cultural tradition, they did not have a "national center to look to, in Europe, where the spirit of their races lives freely, and flourishes, and expresses itself in the arts and literature and social forms of the French, the German, the Scandinavians."[39] This brief but significant mention of Europe betrays the fact that Kallen's version of pluralism included what we today call "white ethnics" only.[40] As Kallen would indicate more clearly two years later, pluralism emerged with distinct racial boundaries; European immigrant groups would contribute to America's cultural formation. Kallen sometimes made promises to address the particular cultural challenges of non-European groups in later writings, but these promises went unfulfilled until the 1950s.[41] Consequently, many late-twentieth-century critics have vilified Kallen for the limitations of his pluralist vision.[42] For our purposes, it is important to note these troubling limitations. Yet the limitations themselves reinforce the point that Kallen formulated cultural pluralism in large part to address concerns specific to American Jews.

A second factor that spoke directly to Jews' particular condition was Kallen's claim that Jews needed to put themselves on equal footing with other cultural groups by working for a Jewish homeland. Kallen consistently argued that Hebraism would have its most vital expression in a Jewish homeland, and he closed his 1913 address to the IMA by urging the young men in the audience to remain in exile ("*Galuth*") but to support Zionism.[43] Kallen's faith in pluralism was so well developed by 1913 that he could confidently declare that being Zionists would make Jews better Americans. He suggested that support for Zionism actually would strengthen Jews' American identity and the nation itself, as it was cultural diversity that ensured a nation's health.

The Melting Pot and Beyond

Kallen's emerging pluralist philosophy competed against other theories during the first decades of the twentieth century. No ideology for addressing cultural difference was more dominant than the melting pot. As noted earlier, Israel Zangwill's popular 1908 play *The Melting Pot* powerfully injected the language of "melting" back into American popular discourse.[44] Jean de Crèvecoeur had used the term "melted" to describe the process of adjustment to America as early as 1782 in his *Letters from an American Farmer*, but it remained almost entirely absent from America's discourse about acculturation in the nineteenth century.[45] The twentieth-century emergence of the melting pot metaphor was so troubling to Kallen precisely because he interpreted "melting" as wholesale assimilation, despite evidence that Zangwill did not intend it to be read that way.[46]

Zangwill was born in 1864 in London's East End to parents who had emigrated in the 1840s from czarist Russia. Moses Zangwill, Israel's father, struggled his entire life to make ends meet financially. Despite economic struggles, Moses emphasized the importance of religion in the Zangwill's home and community. Daily visits to the synagogue with his father imbued Israel Zangwill with a love of Jewish liturgy. As he came of age, however, Israel Zangwill did not remain observant.

Ellen Hannah, Israel's mother, was rescued from a Polish pogrom in the 1850s and brought to London with a group of Jewish children. Though barely literate, she has been described by one Zangwill biographer as "feisty and vocal" with a determination strong enough to keep "the family afloat."

Ellen found ways for Israel to stay in school rather than be sent to work. Indeed, Israel attended the Jews' Free School in London, which combined a religious and secular curriculum, including a strong emphasis on English language and culture. Reflecting on these roots from adulthood, Israel Zangwill described himself as a "Cockney Jew."[47]

Zangwill's play *The Melting Pot* particularly worried Jewish audiences because it featured an intermarriage between two immigrants from Russia— a Jewish man and a Christian woman. This was no ordinary intermarriage, either. During the course of the drama, the Jewish man at the center of the play learned that his parents were murdered in a pogrom in Russia orchestrated by his future bride's father. The two wed anyway, confirming that America erases all differences, ancestry, and personal history for immigrants. A front-page review of the play in the *American Israelite* best summed up American Jews' anxiety: "Ethnologically the Jew is doomed to extinction in America and this perhaps is the real message that lies at the heart of Israel Zangwill's great play."[48] In short, respondents to both the play and the ideas it spawned feared that, with the combination of coercive Americanization efforts and the freedom to intermarry, Jews eventually would "disappear."[49] This was just one of many competing responses to the melting pot idea in 1908, but, for the majority of Jews, it carried the day.

The multiple interpretations and misinterpretations of the melting pot over the past century are a barrier to understanding its importance in the discourse of American cultural difference. As early as 1908, the "melting pot" became a shorthand description both for complete assimilation and for the blending of various cultures to produce "the new American." A better description of complete assimilation—where members of a cultural group would lose any vestige of their own culture as they became American— actually is "Anglo-conformity." The differences between the melting pot and Anglo-conformity are often confused, but they are real. Anglo-conformity rests on the notion that the United States is "Anglo" at its core, in its culture and its history, and therefore should not absorb any trace of foreign cultural influences. The more common (though not universal) usage of the melting pot imagines a nation that finds ways to blend the cultural influences of its many ethnic groups. Anglo-conformity thus portrays American culture and nationality as much more fixed than the melting pot does. But Anglo-conformity never gained as strong a cultural or linguistic foothold as the melting pot did. As a result, the melting pot has been used too frequently and inconsistently as a catch-all term to cover many competing proposals for immigrants' Americanization.[50]

In 1908, Jewish critics of the melting pot metaphor tended to focus not on such nuance but on the intermarriage of a Jewish man and a gentile woman at the center of Zangwill's play. Kallen, however, was upset less by the intermarriage in the play than by what he considered its deeply flawed method for addressing cultural diversity within the United States. (Kallen himself married a non-Jewish woman.) Kallen's response to both the melting pot and to Anglo-conformity was motivated instead by the great offense he took at what he perceived to be the fixed idea of American identity at the heart of both these philosophies. In promoting pluralism, Kallen chastised both melting pot ideologues and Anglo-conformists, decrying them (and conflating them, despite their differences) for promoting the loss rather than the retention of individual group cultures.

Kallen's theory of cultural difference gained its broadest public attention when the *Nation* magazine published his essay "Democracy versus the Melting Pot" in two parts in February 1915. Writing to an audience of both Jews and non-Jews, Kallen described America as a "federation or commonwealth of national cultures" and imagined a United States in which each ethnic group could develop its own culture and traditions while acquiring citizenship and rights.[51] At the core of this essay Kallen argued that cultural particularity need not disappear as immigrants and their children became Americans. He again compared the nation to an orchestra in which each ethnic group played its own instrument, and he declared that the different players in this national orchestra should focus on harmony rather than on unison. America's many ethnic groups should coexist in one political entity, but political coexistence did not require cultural conformity. Kallen pressed the point by claiming that cultural difference was not weakening the nation. In fact, just the opposite was the case. Writing in direct opposition to nativist academics—especially sociologist E. A. Ross, who was a colleague of Kallen's at the University of Wisconsin–Madison in 1915—Kallen insisted that ethnocultural difference supplied the United States with its national strength.[52]

"Democracy versus the Melting Pot," published about a decade into Kallen's consideration of both Jewish identity and American cultural particularity, also relied heavily on his training as a Pragmatist. Kallen spent much of the article endorsing the adaptability of ideas. This allowed him to portray American identity as a work in progress rather than as a fixed entity to which outsiders must conform. He demonstrated this point by turning to the nation's founding documents, especially the Declaration of Independence. Kallen explained that when the American colonists declared independence from England in 1776 the writers of the Declaration "were not confronted by the practical fact of ethnic dissimilarity among whites of the country. Their descendants are confronted by it."[53] According to Kallen, because the cultural composition of America had changed so significantly over nearly one hundred and fifty years, the meaning of the Declaration's germinal phrase, "all men are created equal," needed to be refigured. Kallen did this refiguring by explaining that equality did not require conformity. "Equal" need not mean "the same." One of the nation's primary assets, according to Kallen, was that the meaning of American identity could endure such reinterpretations.

Kallen consistently argued that progress was impossible without continual change; reaching definite conclusions closed off the possibility of progress.[54] In accordance with this belief, continual reinterpretation of the American idea was absolutely essential to the nation's future health. The American idea itself had to adapt to changing circumstances. In short, the American idea was always in formation. One who accepted this premise would have to allow the influences of newly arrived peoples and cultures provided that they did not contradict cornerstone ideals such as liberty and democracy. By this logic, no group could be excluded from the nation on the grounds that it was "un-American."

Kallen also contended that individual groups' expressions of their own culture could change. Jews were no exception to this rule. As Kallen argued in "Democracy versus the Melting Pot," Jews were suited particularly well to these changing times because they were the "most self-conscious" of any American cultural group. Jews' survival in exile across so many generations depended on this self-consciousness, which enhanced their ability to adapt to their particular circumstances. There were no limits to this flexibility. Kallen described Jews as "the most successful in eliminating the removable differences between themselves and their social environment. Even their religion is flexible."[55] Kallen here echoed his earlier writings on Hebraism. One of the contentions underlying the claim about adaptability was that Jewish identity need not rest on a religious foundation. Casting off particular religious practices or beliefs did not cause Kallen great anxiety because, as he had been explaining for at least a decade by this point, Jewish identity depended on the self-conscious promotion of Jewish culture rather than on an essentially religious self-understanding.

Despite his emphasis on the adaptability of Jewish identity, Kallen closed "Democracy versus the Melting Pot" with a troubling, inconsistent assertion. After explaining the potential for cultural coexistence in America, he implied a belief in the immutability of ancestry. As noted earlier, in a 1913 speech Kallen had said that Jewish identity was guaranteed by "inborn nature." He returned to the same idea in the 1915 *Nation* article: "Men may change their clothes, their politics, their wives, their religions, their philosophies, to a greater or lesser extent: they cannot change their grandfathers. Jews or Poles or Anglo-Saxons, in order to cease being Jews or Poles or Anglo-Saxons, would have to cease to be, while they could cease to be citizens or church members or carpenters or lawyers without ceasing to be."[56] Kallen stated the claim even more strongly in a 1918 book: "So an Irishman is always an Irishman, a Jew always a Jew. Irishman or Jew is born; citizen, lawyer, or church-member is made. Irishman and Jew are facts in nature."[57]

In other words, Jews and other ethnics maintained a biological connection to their ancestors that could not be severed and that implied some cultural transmission inevitably would occur. The assertion was particularly troubling because it suggested that, even as Kallen criticized American nativists, he shared their belief in what literary critic Werner Sollors has described as "the eternal power of descent, birth, *natio*, and race."[58] Indeed, Sollors—who has argued that American ethnicity should be understood as a combination of descent and consent—has chastised readers as naïve for believing that cultural pluralism should be a "redemptively transcendent category that removes its advocates from prejudice," but, for most readers, Kallen's assertion about descent-based Jewish identity nevertheless remains troubling.[59]

All the more disturbing is the fact that the claim seems to contradict Kallen's own biography and history. It was not his father or grandfather who informed Kallen's Jewish identity, but his adopted (and non-Jewish!) "ancestors" Barrett Wendell and William James who had a profound (although not exclusive) influence on his own self-understanding.[60] Kallen's life history at the very least should have demonstrated to him the invalidity of his claim regarding the immutability of ancestry and identity.

Asserting Jewishness as an essential, inherent characteristic was also a troubling turn for Kallen because he based his vehement anti–melting pot argument on a denial of any essential American identity. In addition to contradicting principles of change and flux fundamental to Pragmatist philosophy, insinuating a singularly descent-based Jewish identity should seemingly have erased all anxieties about Jewish continuity that lay under the surface of Kallen's pluralist vision. For, if being Jewish was inherited, how could one escape it? What reason would there be to express concern about the perpetuation of Jewish culture in the United States? Here, we witness Kallen's logic at its most inconsistent.

Even more frustrating is the fact that Kallen avoided responding directly to those who challenged pluralism's internal contradictions and lack of specificity. His failure to expound on the issue of consent and descent in shaping identity has confounded even the most insightful historians, such as Philip Gleason, who writes about the "extreme sketchiness" and "obscurity of language" running throughout Kallen's thought.[61] Though Kallen's silence remains unsatisfying, it has foreshadowed one of the most difficult challenges in understanding ethnicity that persists to the present day—the role of ancestry in shaping ethnic identity. Historian David A. Hollinger notes that Alex Haley, the author of *Roots,* could have chosen to trace his father's bloodline back to Ireland, rather than his mother's back to Gambia. (Similar claims were made about Barack Obama during the 2008 presidential election.) As Hollinger explains, this view, which he labels "postethnic," would allow Haley "to be both African American and Irish American without having to choose one to the exclusion of the other."[62] This is one of many instances in which Kallen and his critics help to set the terms of debate about diversity in America that would persist, unsolved, well beyond their time.

"Different Instruments Playing Simultaneously"

Kallen's ideas about culture, kinship, and descent became a flashpoint for debates during the 1910s, especially among writers who were concerned with the specific case of Jews. American Jewish educators, community leaders, rabbis, and other authorities responded vigorously to Kallen's writings, as did some leading non-Jewish intellectuals of the day, including John Dewey, then a professor of philosophy at Columbia University, and Randolph S. Bourne, a frequent contributor to the *New Republic,* the *Atlantic Monthly,* and *Seven Arts.* The editors of the *Menorah Journal* filled the magazine's pages with these considerations of American identity and Jewish identity. The magazine itself became the locus for some of the most important and enduring expressions of American pluralism. The writers discussed here generally agreed on the dual goals of embracing American citizenship and preserving Jewish culture, but they vigorously debated the best means to achieve these goals.

Although not all the *Menorah Journal* writers were Jewish, the most frequent contributors belonged to an active intellectual community centered in New York City.[63] Discussions of pluralism during this era were dominated by a cosmopolitan, New York–based, Jewish intelligentsia.[64] Almost all the Jewish writers in this discussion claimed to advance a broadly conceived theory that would apply readily to any European immigrant cultural group. Time and again, however, the Jewish authors who concerned themselves with pluralism turned almost exclusively to Jews as their primary (or sole) example. Many of the non-Jewish intellectuals in the heavily New York–centered intelligentsia also gave primacy to the Jewish case to illustrate their opinions on pluralism.

The first issue of the *Menorah Journal*, published in January 1915, featured both a message of welcome and an article by Louis D. Brandeis, who the next year would become the first Jewish justice on the U.S. Supreme Court. Brandeis, born in 1856 in Louisville, Kentucky, was the son of non-practicing Jewish parents who emigrated in the wake of repressions that followed the unsuccessful uprisings of 1848. Brandeis earned his law degree at Harvard at age twenty, receiving the highest marks ever awarded. Nevertheless, he needed a waiver from Harvard's requirement that graduates be twenty-one years of age, which President Eliot and the Harvard trustees granted on the morning Brandeis graduated. Brandeis soon opened a firm in Boston, but he rejected an offer to teach law at Harvard simultaneously because of his concern that practicing law and teaching would put too much strain on his health. He frequently defended laborers in his early career, perhaps most famously in the 1908 case *Muller v. Oregon*. President Woodrow Wilson's nomination of Brandeis to the Supreme Court in 1916 aroused some opposition; scholars have since debated whether those opposed were motivated by antisemitism or by the business community's fear of a trust-busting "people's attorney" sitting on the nation's highest court.[65]

Brandeis became aware of the Menorah Association through his acquaintance with Kallen, which dated back to 1903. Brandeis never exhibited much interest in Zionism or Jewish culture before the 1910s. His mediation of a New York City garment worker's strike in 1910 likely instilled in him a new sense of kinship with eastern European Jewish immigrants and left him deeply concerned with the welfare of world Jewry.[66] Yet it was Brandeis's contact with Kallen that proved even more formative.[67] Brandeis read and thought highly of Kallen's "Judaism, Hebraism, Zionism." Furthermore, as Brandeis found his public voice on Zionism during the mid-1910s, he borrowed heavily from Kallen's language.[68]

In his 1915 welcoming message to the *Menorah Journal*, Brandeis echoed Kallen by arguing that a Jewish cultural renaissance, "in which the [Menorah] Society is certain to be a significant factor, is of no less importance to America than to its Jews."[69] Jews already had made a particular contribution to American culture, Brandeis suggested, by advancing the principles

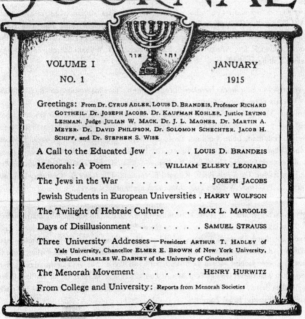

Cover of the first issue of the *Menorah Journal,* January 1915.
*Courtesy of the Jacob Rader Marcus Center of the
American Jewish Archives.*

of brotherhood and social justice shared by American and Jewish traditions. Only five years earlier, such a show of support from Brandeis would have been unimaginable. Brandeis's endorsement of the Menorah organization in 1915 represented a profound shift in his thinking; in fact, prior to 1910, Brandeis equated hyphenated Americanism with disloyalty.[70] Over a period of only ten years, however, Brandeis recast his understanding of Jews' place in American society and within the matrix of world politics, due in large part to the influence of Kallen's pluralist philosophy.[71]

Like Kallen, Brandeis separated cultural loyalty from political citizenship. Kallen's portrayal of America as a "federation of nationalities" echoes loudly in Brandeis's 1915 assertion that "a nation may be composed of many nationalities, as some of the most successful nations are."[72] Brandeis also understood the nation as a composite of many diverse groups acting together for the good of the polity rather than a homogeneous mass of people devoid of cultural particularity. Development of particular cultures still entailed responsibilities to the nation. Brandeis argued that, in exchange for the rights granted by citizenship, all Americans must dedicate themselves to patriotic causes. Then, through one significant leap in logic, Brandeis wed Jewish history to American patriotism: "The twentieth century ideals of America have been the ideals of the Jew for more than twenty centuries."[73] These ideals, according to Brandeis, included democracy, social justice, the duties of citizenship, high intellectual capability, submission to leadership, and a sense of community. By going beyond a claim for the compatibility of Jewish and American ideals to insist upon a Jewish basis for American ideals, Brandeis dissolved any possible tension between preserving Jewish culture and observing American political traditions.

Brandeis's writings on this subject, like Kallen's, stemmed from a profound anxiety about assimilation. "Assimilation is national suicide," Brandeis declared in his *Menorah Journal* contribution. "And assimilation can be prevented only by preserving national characteristics of life as other peoples, large and small, are preserving and developing their national life." Although he urged American Jews to become Zionists to avert assimilation, at no time did Brandeis call for American Jews to emigrate to Palestine. In fact, he counseled just the opposite, like Kallen and Ahad Ha'am before him. His support of cultural Zionism instead envisioned Palestine as "a center from which the Jewish spirit may radiate and give to the Jews scattered throughout the world that inspiration which springs from the memories of the great past and the hope of a great future." Support and fund-raising for the Zionist movement, not migration, would ensure the continuity of Jewish culture in America. In turn, the achievements of Jews in

Palestine would help to inspire Jews in the United States. Brandeis closed his 1915 article with a challenge to the young members of the Menorah Association: "We Jews of prosperous America above all need [a Jewish home in Palestine's] inspiration. And the Menorah men should be its builders."[74]

A year and a half later, Norman Hapgood—a prominent Progressive Era journalist, editor of *Harper's Weekly,* and a non-Jew—weighed in on the question of Jewish acculturation within the pages of the *Menorah Journal.* The magazine editors' decision to include Hapgood as well as subsequent articles by other non-Jewish intellectuals such as Dewey and Bourne served many functions. It may have brought a non-Jewish readership, albeit a small one, to the journal, and it may have helped to legitimize the journal to some skeptical non-Jewish intellectuals. More important, essays by non-Jewish authors protected the magazine from being viewed as provincial, either by Jews or by non-Jews. Giving space to non-Jewish authors in the debates about perpetuating Jewish culture in America strengthened the case that this particularly Jewish question also was a universal American question.

In "The Jews and American Democracy," published in the October 1916 issue, Hapgood echoed pluralists' claims that diversity strengthens democracy, explaining that true democracy should "encourage differences": "Our dream of the United States ought not to be a dream of monotony. We ought not to think of it as a place where all people are alike."[75] Hapgood cited Brandeis's confirmation to the Supreme Court as the highest evidence that pluralist principles governed the American nation, noting that President Wilson and the American people could appreciate Brandeis's legal "genius" and his fitness for the Supreme Court. His cultural background did not matter; what mattered were his qualifications.

At the end of a uniformly positive article about Jewish contributions to American society, however, Hapgood somewhat ominously declared, "Jewish affairs are in something of a crisis at the present moment."[76] This crisis centered on the pressures put upon Jews to cast off their particular culture. Almost one year earlier, Hapgood had sounded an even more dire note about Jewish assimilation in a series of articles published in *Harper's Weekly.*[77] In the *Menorah Journal,* Hapgood explained that, although there were many competing opinions about the proper means of Jewish adjustment to American society, in the end Americans hopefully would come to realize that Jews "can be truest to the country of their residence only when they are truest to the ideals of their inheritance."[78] Here, Hapgood fully embraced the synthesis between American identity and Jewish culture at the heart of pluralism. Hapgood acknowledged that assimilative pressures in

America were great, but he claimed that particular Jewish cultural interests could develop without contradicting either patriotic or civic duties to the United States.

In their contributions to the *Menorah Journal*, Bourne and Dewey criticized Kallen's pluralist claims more directly than Hapgood would. Bourne did not enter college until the age of twenty-three, when he received a full scholarship from Columbia. There, he studied under John Dewey and devoured the writings of William James in philosophy classes. Bourne was always deeply guarded about his appearance. His features had been "badly mangled" by a forceps delivery at birth and he developed a hunchback after contracting tuberculosis at the age of four. "He was always self conscious about his condition," according to Louis Menand; "he thought his appearance made people underestimate his capacities, and he compensated for it with a brilliance that could be exceptionally caustic."[79] Yet when defending ideas he believed in, Bourne balanced his caustic nature with passionate, careful argumentation.[80]

Raised as a Presbyterian, Bourne became one of the 1910s most cogent defenders of the American Zionist movement. He best articulated the case for Zionism in his December 1916 *Menorah Journal* article, "The Jew and Trans-National America." The article, which he also had delivered as a speech to the Harvard Menorah Society on November 8, 1916, was a revised version of his July 1916 *Atlantic Monthly* essay, "Trans-National America."[81] The *Atlantic Monthly* article and *Menorah Journal* revision both echoed Kallen in their anti–melting pot rhetoric. Like Brandeis, Bourne also cogently separated nationality and citizenship in support of American Zionism: "Zionism does not propose to prevent Jews from living in full citizenship in other countries. The Zionist does not believe that there is a necessary conflict between a cultural allegiance to the Jewish centre and a political allegiance to a State."[82] According to Bourne, Jews in America already were "proving every day the possibility of this dual life."[83]

Despite these significant notes of support, Bourne's understanding of pluralism's goals differed significantly from Kallen's. Bourne expressed concern about cultural particularity leading to prejudice and chauvinism, rather than to what he called "co-operative Americanism."[84] Bourne's co-operative Americanism endorsed a group's cultural development not for its own sake but instead in the hope that ethnic groups would move beyond the inwardly focused particularities to eventual interaction with other groups. For Bourne, beyond cultural pluralism lay cosmopolitanism, defined by historian David A. Hollinger as "the desire to transcend the limitations of any and all particularisms in order to achieve a more complete human experience and a more complete understanding of that experience."[85] Bourne's cosmopolitanism ultimately had greater ambitions for cross-cultural cooperation than Kallen's pluralism.

John Dewey also criticized the excessive particularism he perceived in Kallen's thought, and he warned Kallen more directly than Bourne did about the possible dangers. Dewey was in his mid-fifties by the time he started corresponding with the much younger Kallen, and their backgrounds contrasted starkly. Dewey had descended from a long line of farmers in Vermont, though his father had chosen to run a grocery business rather than farming.[86] Dewey graduated from the University of Vermont and, after a short time as a school teacher, earned a doctorate at Johns Hopkins in 1884. The breadth of Dewey's writing over his ninety-three years—from psychology to ethics, education, logic, religion, politics, philosophy, and art—is staggering. So perhaps it is no surprise that he weighed in to clarify what he viewed as the vagaries of Kallen's pluralism.

In March 1915, shortly after Dewey read "Democracy versus the Melting Pot," he congratulated Kallen. "I quite agree with your orchestra idea," he wrote in a letter to Kallen. His praise came with a warning, though, that the orchestra metaphor only worked "upon [the] condition we really get a symphony and not a lot of different instruments playing simultaneously." Dewey advised Kallen that the nation would only benefit if each group developed its cultural heritage in order "to contribute to others," rather than to remain turned inward.[87] In a letter to Kallen written two weeks later, Dewey argued that Jews had a unique opportunity not only to develop their own heritage but also to learn about the cultures of other groups in America. "I only feel pretty strongly," Dewey informed Kallen, "that the more groups different in the past (different merely because of isolation) interact the greater is the probability that genuinely individual reactions will get called out and get a footing."[88] For Dewey, as for his student Bourne, a cultural group could not contribute to the improvement of American society by developing its own culture in isolation, which is where they thought Kallen's pluralism rested. Without interaction among cultural groups, America would not truly become a federation of nationalities but rather a nation of distinct, non-cooperating groups.[89] Excessive particularism without cooperation, Dewey argued, eventually would prove dangerous because it would not foster any understand among different peoples who had to coexist in the same polity.

In an October 1917 contribution to the *Menorah Journal*, Dewey echoed Kallen by denouncing the melting pot, separating nationality and citizenship, and endorsing Zionism. Noting that "the theory of the Melting Pot always gave me rather a pang," Dewey supported the Menorah Association's effort to nurture Jewish culture. He partially veiled his concern about cultural pluralism leading to excessive particularism in this article, but he did touch on the point by declaring that there must be interest taken between members of various cultural groups to further discourage "uniformity and unanimity." Dewey championed "give and take of culture" among the nation's many groups.[90] In his hope for cultural exchange, Dewey, much like Bourne, actually was looking a few steps beyond the immediate aspirations of Kallen and the Menorah Association in 1915, most of whose active members were more concerned with promoting Jewish culture to prevent already acculturated Jews from abandoning their Jewish identity.

Pluralism's Jewish Critics

Jewish respondents to Kallen focused less on cooperation among cultural groups than on perpetuating Jewish culture. Like Bourne and Dewey, many Jewish critics sympathized with Kallen's general tenor, but they criticized him for failing to articulate how to put his pluralist theory into practice. Moving from theory to practice became of dire importance in this case because these critics considered complete assimilation the peril of an undefined program for Jewish cultural development. Some Jewish authorities of the day—most importantly Julius Drachsler, Smith College professor of economics and sociology, and Isaac Baer Berkson, a student of Dewey's at Columbia University and Teachers College and supervisor of school and extension services at the Bureau of Jewish Education of New York—sought to temper Kallen's vagaries by more clearly defining programmatic, educational, and institutional steps for maintaining Jewish continuity.

Drachsler immigrated to the United States in 1903, as a teenager. He attended CCNY and later earned a doctorate in sociology at Columbia's School of Social Work in 1920. Active in Jewish social services throughout his life, Drachsler applied social scientific methods to studying Jews in the United States.[91] In two articles published in the *Menorah Journal* in 1920, Drachsler addressed acculturation.[92] He endorsed the public school system as the best means to instill respect among Jewish youth in their culture and heritage. Jewish youth would become interested in things Jewish, Drachsler claimed, if public schools celebrated cultural particularity rather than ignored it. He wrote that public schools should acknowledge "all the cultural contributions of the races and nations represented in the student body . . . and thus . . . build up the attitude of intelligent and sympathetic insight into the life of diverse peoples."[93] Drachsler's proposal celebrated each ethnic group's agency to teach its own culture to its youth and advocated respecting other cultural traditions within a democratic society.

In his 1920 book *Democracy and Assimilation* (from which his two *Menorah Journal* articles were excerpted), Drachsler warned readers about the consequences of failing to teach Jewish youth about their heritage. He argued that a "fatal disease" was "gnawing" at Jewish continuity in America. The "diluted second generation" already had entered into a "death-struggle between two worlds, two cultures, two civilizations" with their immigrant parents.[94] This "death-struggle" was perhaps best represented by intermarriage, an ever-increasing phenomenon that Drachsler attributed to "a lack of knowledge and appreciation of the cultural heritage of their group and . . . a lack of affiliation with specifically communal undertakings."[95] As historian Eric L. Goldstein argues, Drachsler viewed intermarriage "as the only meaningful form of assimilation."[96] He explained that the first generation of Jews in America intermarried at a rate of 0.64 percent; the second generation intermarried at a rate of 4.51 percent. Drachsler focused on the rate of increase: "In other words, in the second generation, Jews intermarry about seven times as frequently as the first."[97] If intermarriage continued to rise at such a pace, as Drachsler predicted that it would, the most important means of combating the disappearance of Jewish identity would be to "foster an intelligent cultural community consciousness."[98] Drachsler maintained that consciousness of Jewish identity would have to be encouraged at the highest cultural levels, and he endorsed the Menorah Association, which he claimed was in the most ideal position to take on the required educational work amongst intelligent Jewish youth through its college campus chapters.

Yet, in the conclusion to *Democracy and Assimilation*, Drachsler noted the steady progress of cultural amalgamation occurring in the United States. Such progress could not be stopped, Drachsler wrote, but he did claim that the "social and economic settings with which the fusion is taking place" could be improved.[99] In this instance, Drachsler portrayed cultural amalgamation as inevitable and even seemed to endorse it.

Like Drachsler, Berkson emphasized that in a democracy each ethnic group should be encouraged to develop its own culture. In a December 1920 contribution to the *Menorah Journal*, the Brooklyn-born Berkson, who had been the president of the CCNY Menorah Society as an undergraduate in 1911, introduced the "community theory of American life," which would allow all ethnic groups "to maintain their identity in the midst of American democratic life."[100] Berkson's community theory insisted "on the value of each ethnic group as a permanent asset in American life" and claimed that culture, rather than race, religion, or philanthropy, remained Jews' only hope for continuity in an open, democratic society. Berkson endorsed educational institutions as crucial to the fight against assimilation because "culture is not inherited but must be acquired."[101] Dewey's influence becomes quite apparent here, as Berkson described the school as the most potent agent for both societal change and cultural preservation.

Berkson's community theory echoed Kallen's pluralism in claiming that political and cultural allegiances could be separate but not contradictory. Berkson made this distinction based on his contention that political allegiance constituted a "duty" while ethnic allegiance constituted a "loyalty." By keeping duty and loyalty separate, Berkson rejected all claims that perpetuating Jewish culture, even Zionism, could be interpreted as contradictory to patriotic Americanism.[102]

Berkson also added a positive twist where Kallen had rested at defending Jews against criticism. Dual loyalties, or in Berkson's favored term "double allegiance," signaled a rich individual life of great dimensions. Acquiring a second language or studying a variety of cultures opened minds to new concepts and, in Berkson's words, "destroys provinciality."[103] As long as one's political allegiance remained singular, multiple cultural allegiances signaled "broad-mindedness" rather than national betrayal.

Berkson's most strident criticism of Kallen stemmed from the insinuation of a racial theory of Jewish descent. Recall that in his 1915 *Nation* article and elsewhere, Kallen claimed that although Jewish immigrants and their descendants may have been cut off "externally" from their pasts, the same did not apply "internally." Kallen's contention that men "cannot change their grandfathers" did not sit well with Berkson.[104] He seized on this illogical claim, denying that being born Jewish guaranteed that one would live as a Jew. Berkson of course was not alone here; leading contemporary anthropologists including Franz Boas already were questioning the connection between race and culture and soon came to question classifying Jews as a race.[105]

Berkson disagreed with Kallen's claim about descent-based Jewish identity because it argued that one's ancestry determined one's destiny. If it were true that Jewish identity came through bloodlines, educational programs to preserve Jewish culture would be absolutely unnecessary. Berkson directly refuted Kallen's claim: "A moment's reflection would show that 'we can change our grandfathers' and in two specific ways." First, one could assimilate by passively forgetting or actively neglecting the traditions and culture of one's grandfather. Berkson explained this possibility, "What we are depends not only upon our original nature, but also upon its interaction with the environment."[106] Second, Berkson pointed out that a Jewish person effectively did change one's grandfather by intermarrying. Kallen had not addressed the fact that the lineage of an intermarried couple would become a mixture of ethnic backgrounds. Based on this recognition that intermarriage effectively mixed descent, Berkson rephrased Kallen's dictum as a warning, emphasizing education rather than inheritance. "A man dare not fail to know who his grandfathers were," Berkson counseled.[107] This rephrasing again emphasized the importance of educating Jewish youth about their history and culture and revealed intellectuals' anxiety about the consequences of the attenuation of such knowledge.

Although Kallen did not explicitly acknowledge the influence of Berkson's criticisms, his position concerning the best means of preserving Jewish culture changed dramatically over the ensuing decade, as he moved toward naming cultural pluralism for the first time in 1924. In fact, Kallen adopted the logic of his critics. Kallen's seemingly inconsistent claims about inherited Jewishness in 1915 stemmed in part from a desire to articulate a surefire theory to stem a tide of assimilation and reject the claims of Anglo-conformists and melting pot advocates. By 1925, Kallen aligned himself with Dewey, Drachsler, and Berkson by proposing a more proactive agenda for preserving Jewish culture through institutionally based educational efforts.

By the mid-1920s, Kallen had set aside the notion of descent-based identity. Any reference to individuals not being able to change their grandfathers would be absent from his writing from that point forward. Instead, consent—in the form of educational programs designed to foster knowledge and pride in Jewish heritage—became primary to ensuring Jewish continuity across generations. In his 1925 *Menorah Journal* article provocatively titled, "Can Judaism Survive in the United States?" Kallen declared, "The future of Judaism depends on the educational institutions of Judaism. . . . They are the official conservators and keepers of Judaism."[108] Kallen included both religious institutions (from the Orthodox religious school to the Reform Sunday school) and communal organizations (from Jewish charities to community centers) under the rubric of educational institutions. He concluded by 1925 that the only way to ensure Jewish continuity was to call for a personal commitment to Jewish culture among acculturated descendants of immigrants. "To ensure the survival of Judaism in the United States," Kallen declared, "requires the transformation of this passive and occasional interest into an active and constant one."[109]

Nearly thirty years later, by the time he had become widely known for cultural pluralism, Kallen issued his clearest rejection of his earlier claim that identity would be guaranteed through ancestry. In his 1956 *Cultural Pluralism and the American Idea,* Kallen insisted that identity comes through "associations" that tend to be a matter of choice. He claimed that an individual could "reënforce 'accident of birth' by consent and loyalty or nullify it by withdrawal from all association with the members of the family and the refusal of family responsibility."[110] Surely, this contrasted starkly with his 1915 contention that one could not change one's grandfather. It also placed affiliation, personal choice, at the center of ethnic consciousness in a way that would not become fashionable among scholars for at least another twenty years.[111] But that is jumping ahead too quickly. In the more immediate term, as cultural pluralism evolved during the 1910s and 1920s, it would inform the Menorah Association's efforts to initiate programs of Jewish academic study on campus.

— 4 —

Jewish Studies in
an American Setting

During the college graduation season of 1919, an author who identified him-self as "S. Baruch" published an "undelivered commencement address" in the *Menorah Journal*. Baruch announced, "There was never a time in his-tory when it was more urgent and needful that the intellectual and spiritual energy of the Jewish people" be "set in motion and kept in full swing." Fol-lowing this grand declaration, Baruch sounded a dire warning: too many Jewish students were "breaking away" from Jewish culture. Baruch declared that Jewish culture could be saved from extinction only by cultivating "a scientific mind towards Jews and Judaism" through university-based learn-ing. Using pugilistic language, Baruch explained, "The fight for our political and social freedom must also be a fight to exchange intellectual and spiri-tual goods with it. To liberate our Judaism, Jewish study must first win for itself a background analogous to general study."[1]

This commencement address, penned by a Menorah Association in-sider, justified one of the organization's defining campus-based efforts. Be-ginning in the late 1910s, the IMA's leadership complemented its existing extracurricular efforts for students by seeking to integrate Jewish studies in American college curricula. The IMA provided syllabi and reading lists in modern Jewish history, purchased books for university "Menorah librar-ies," and lobbied administrators to create faculty positions in Jewish studies. During the 1920s, even as its influence with students waned, the IMA also began efforts to raise funds for endowed faculty chairs in Jewish studies.

The stakes of this effort were high, as indicated by S. Baruch's claim that Jews were fighting both for their freedom and against their extinction.

According to the IMA, nothing less than the future of the Jewish people hung in the balance of these Jewish studies initiatives. If the Menorah Association could not demonstrate the relevance of its academic programs, students would be deprived of any meaningful knowledge of Jewish history and culture. Furthermore, failing to secure a place for Jewish studies in college curricula would be a significant blow to the theory of cultural pluralism, which was designed precisely to facilitate the pursuit of distinct cultural interests within a democratic setting. Winning a place for Jewish studies, conversely, would mean a significant victory for pluralism. Those who led the effort to integrate Jewish studies into college curricula insisted that securing school administrators' endorsement would signal at least a tacit admission that Jewish culture had value equal to that of other cultures studied.

Few individuals showed more passion for the Menorah Association's initiatives in Jewish studies than Adolph S. Oko, the librarian at Hebrew Union College (HUC) in Cincinnati and an associate editor of the *Menorah Journal*. It was Oko who authored the 1919 commencement address using his preferred pseudonym of "S. Baruch." Oko, born in Russia in 1883, was educated in Germany before immigrating to the United States in 1902. He settled in New York and worked at the Astor Library until 1906, when he accepted the librarianship at HUC and moved west to Ohio. Oko expanded HUC's library collections significantly over the next quarter century, acquiring collections from across the United States, Europe, and China. After his wife died, Oko married the ex-wife of an individual closely tied to HUC, causing a scandal on campus that led to Oko's resignation. In 1933, he moved to England, where he remained for five years while completing a bibliography of Baruch Spinoza. He returned to New York in 1938, working for the American Jewish Committee (AJC) until his death in 1944, including a brief tenure as editor of the AJC's short-lived magazine, the *Contemporary Jewish Record*.[2]

Oko's undelivered commencement address was representative of his work for the *Menorah Journal* during the 1910s and 1920s.[3] Although American Jews were "materially more or less prosperous," Oko claimed that they were becoming "spiritually dull." He asked: "And if we do not cultivate Jewish learning, and if we do not foster Jewish ideals—what is the meaning of our distinctive existence?"[4] Oko and his colleagues at the IMA looked to secular campuses as the natural environments to encourage the study of Jewish culture, and they faulted Jewish academics on these campuses for failing to push hard enough to integrate Jewish humanities into the gen-

Adolph S. Oko.
*Courtesy of the Jacob Rader Marcus Center
of the American Jewish Archives.*

eral curricula. They ultimately hoped to enlist the many Menorah Association graduates who held academic positions around the nation to promote Jewish studies to their fellow faculty members and administrators.

The Menorah Association, of course, did not invent secular Jewish studies. Indeed, Jewish learning existed at some American campuses when Oko published his 1919 commencement address, but it tended to be located in Semitics programs, which focused primarily on philology rather than on Jewish history and culture. By the late 1910s, most Semitics programs that had thrived around the turn of the century no longer remained vibrant.[5] Oko and his colleagues at the Menorah Association sought to address the perceived failings of these programs by replacing Semitic philology with the study of Jewish history, literature, and modern Hebrew language. These efforts, some of the first of their kind in the United States, depended fully on the logic of cultural pluralism.

Germanic Models for Jewish Studies

Promoting the study of Jewish history and culture to answer the challenges of modernity was not a wholly original idea. As noted earlier, the Menorah Association found its model in the *Verein für Cultur und Wissenschaft der Juden,* the group of Jewish intellectuals who came together in Germany during the 1810s to advocate scientific study of Jewish history, culture, and religion.[6] These men self-consciously turned to *Wissenschaft des Judentums* at a moment of great fluidity in expressions of Jewish identity, precipitated in part by the fact that some European states had begun to offer political citizenship to Jews.

IMA chancellor Henry Hurwitz and others frequently cited these nineteenth-century thinkers as inspiration for solving the dilemma of becoming modern while remaining Jewish. In 1920, Hurwitz emphasized that modern Jews' "prime need" was "that more and more of our brilliant Jewish youth must be attracted to Jewish learning and thought—not orthodoxy or reform or any *tertium quid,* but *Juedische Wissenschaft* in the spirit of Leopold Zunz."[7] In December 1919, the IMA inaugurated its annual Leopold Zunz Memorial Lecture.[8] The IMA named the series for the man whom they considered their progenitor.[9] Leopold Zunz, a young Jewish intellectual who completed his graduate studies at the University of Halle, joined the circle of seven young men in Germany in 1819 who founded the *Verein für Cultur und Wissenschaft der Juden.*[10] By 1823, Zunz was the editor of the organization's journal *Zeitschrift fur die Wissenschaft des Judenthums*

(Journal for the Science of Judaism), which published Jewish scholarship in a new, scientific mode.

The regularity with which Menorah Association leaders described their Jewish studies program as "scientific" and their frequent acknowledgment of Zunz and his contemporaries signals that they understood their project as a continuation of that initiated by German Jews one hundred years before. Here, the Menorah Association's elite self-understanding comes into clearer focus. As Hurwitz wrote in 1916, "The future attitude of this country towards the Jews is going to be determined by the educated classes."[11] Menorah Association leaders sought to align themselves with German Jewish ancestors not only because they interpreted their challenges similarly but also because they internalized the opinion that Jews of German heritage in the United States were more refined and therefore more acceptable to their non-Jewish neighbors than the more recent arrivals from eastern Europe.[12]

The founders of the *Verein* believed that Jewish studies should not focus exclusively on religious interpretations of texts. Even their use of the term *Judentums* (Judaism) connoted the modern. Prior to the 1810s, Jews used the term "Torah" to refer not solely to the Pentateuch, but to many texts central to Jewish religious tradition. Advocating *Judentums* instead of Torah, German Jewish intellectuals signaled the modernizing of Jews' self-perception and self-presentation.[13] In one of his most influential works, *Etwas über die rabbinische Literatur* (On Rabbinic Literature, 1818), Zunz defined a dividing point between the old-style learning of the rabbinic, classical study of religious texts and "new Jewish learning," which was to take its place alongside general humanist study by including history, literature, and culture.[14]

The movement for new scholarly understandings of Jewish tradition had both an internal and an external audience. It was intended to unite the Jewish people, reading Jewish history and texts in ways that addressed the complexities of modern Jewish existence. It simultaneously sought to legitimize Jews in the eyes of non-Jews by proving Jewish culture worthy of rigorous study alongside other cultural and religious traditions.

The birth of *Wissenschaft des Judentums* in Germany thus represented one response to the challenge of modernity for Jewry. Before emancipation, few Jews in European lands would have considered it necessary to defend the study of Jewish history or texts to Jews or to gentiles.[15] After all, throughout Jewish history, the study of Torah has required no justification by Jews to outsiders.[16] The modern freedoms available to Jews, however, called into question both the limits of acculturation and the best means of adapting Jewish study to modern circumstances.

The IMA's leadership hoped that transferring the ideals of *Wissenschaft des Judentums* to American colleges would instill in Jewish students a love of Jewish culture. In enumerating the organization's goals for its 1918 annual conference, Hurwitz noted that 1919 marked the centenary of the *Verein für Cultur und Wissenschaft der Juden* and indicated that it was "most necessary" for the IMA to continue the *Verein's* "constructive work, with emphasis upon liberal and humane and comparative point of view."[17] In looking to the heritage of *Wissenschaft des Judentums,* the Menorah Association both claimed a modern tradition for its efforts and defined the parameters of its vision for Jewish studies in the United States.

In the third annual Zunz Memorial Lecture in 1921, George Foot Moore, professor of the history of religions at Harvard, described Jewish studies as an alternative to assimilation. Moore himself embodied the Menorah Association's ideal: as a Christian who taught Jewish history and world religions at Harvard, Moore legitimated Jewish studies within an elite American setting. Moore posited that Judaism, Christianity, and "Mohammedanism" (Islam) must be understood in relation to each other.[18] In his Zunz Lecture, Moore said that the Jewish people faced a conflict between progress and tradition, or, in Moore's words, "modernism and reaction." Moore embraced the Menorah idea, defending modernism without completely discarding tradition. "The great epochs in the history of Judaism," according to Moore, were those during which Jews had found ways to adapt their lives to the present and "to shape the future." He insisted that religion remain central to Jewish identity, but he also claimed that religion must be "living and progressive," rather than fixed and inflexible.[19] Here again, the rhetoric so important to the Menorah idea emphasized adaptation as central to the modern experience.

In focusing so intently on the hundred-year tradition of *Wissenschaft des Judentums* for inspiration, the Menorah Association failed to fully recognize the similar goals of their own contemporary, philosopher and theologian Martin Buber. In 1901, Buber called for a renaissance of Jewish culture, intended to reinvigorate Jewish life by promoting arts, culture, and scholarship.[20] Buber's program had four objectives: supporting the arts, establishing publishing houses, founding newspapers and journals, and modernizing scholarship. Buber contended that Jewish studies belonged not in seminaries or to philology programs, but instead to modern disciplines such as history, anthropology, and ethnology. Like the founders of *Wissenschaft des Judentums,* Buber intended to synthesize Judaism and modernity.

Following World War I, Buber also attempted to popularize *Wissenschaft des Judentums* by appealing to a broad population of intellectually engaged Jews. The new element that Buber sought to integrate into this cultural renaissance was Zionism. Echoing the philosophy of Ahad Ha'am, Buber maintained that a homeland could become a spiritual center for the Jewish people, even though he did not expect the majority of Jews in the West to immigrate to Palestine.[21] Despite sharing similar goals and philosophies, IMA authorities rarely turned to Buber in their efforts to define a program of integrated Jewish learning.

Jewish Learning in the United States

In 1916, the Menorah Association took a census of Jewish studies courses offered in American higher educational institutions. The goals of the project were both informational and promotional, and the unsurprising results allowed the Menorah Association to highlight its own work on campuses. The census found that, although undergraduates at many schools could enroll in courses that surveyed the literature or history of the biblical period, there were almost no opportunities to learn about the modern period of Jewish history, literature, or culture. The evidence suggested that the few courses covering the modern period represented "only vestiges of a dissolving tradition." Hebrew language was studied as a "curiosity of ancient times." Professors offered courses in the Bible only because they "still seem proper." Despite these findings, the anonymously authored report on the study cited efforts initiated by the Menorah Association to reassure readers not to abandon hope. The author explained: "Happily there has arisen in academic circles a new force through whose influence the collegiate interest in Jewish knowledge is steadily increasing." Due to this force, a "renewed interest" in Jewish studies appeared quite likely.[22]

Although this survey accurately represented the dearth of opportunities, it did overlook the fact that some significant efforts to advance Jewish learning already were well underway in the United States by 1916. The Jewish Publication Society (JPS) was founded in 1888 to publish books of Jewish interest in English.[23] Among its many achievements, JPS published Heinrich Graetz's multivolume *History of the Jews* in 1891 and issued a new English translation of the Bible in 1917. In 1891, Isidore Singer, an immigrant to the United States who earned his Ph.D. from the University of Vienna in 1884, proposed compiling an encyclopedia of Jews and Judaism intended for both Jewish and non-Jewish audiences. Singer would become the managing editor of the twelve-volume *Jewish Encyclopedia*, published between 1901 and 1906.[24] In 1892, the American Jewish Historical Society was founded, followed in 1893 by the Jewish Chautauqua Society, which sponsored home-based education, study circles, and summer institutes.[25]

Significant institutional initiatives in higher education also occurred in the United States around this time. The Jewish Theological Seminary, reorganized in 1887, lured leading European scholar Solomon Schechter to New York to serve as its president. Schechter successfully recruited a group of scholars to the seminary who were committed to Jewish studies.[26] In 1907, the first non-rabbinical Jewish postgraduate institution, Dropsie College for Hebrew and Cognate Learning, opened in Philadelphia. Fifteen years later, in New York City, Rabbi Stephen S. Wise founded the Jewish Institute of Religion (JIR), a school intended to prepare students either for the rabbinate or for Jewish communal service and research.[27] These initiatives, all occurring within about thirty-five years, signaled the beginning of a shift of Jewish scholarship's center from European to American shores that culminated during the 1930s, accelerated in large part by Jewish scholars' exodus from Europe following the rise of the Nazi Party.

Another significant effort in Jewish education occurred in 1908 with the founding of New York Kehillah (Hebrew for "community"), an organization that hoped to unite different classes of New York City's Jews and to provide an organizational center for the city's Jewish activities. The Kehillah and the Menorah Association shared a similar purpose in that Kehillah leaders also hoped to promote a Jewish cultural renaissance through educational initiatives.[28] The Bureau of Jewish Education, founded in 1910 as an arm of the Kehillah, was intended to transmit knowledge to youth. Under the direction of Samson Benderly, the Bureau of Jewish Education (which would outlast the Kehillah) reformed Jewish education in the United States, using modern teaching methods and employing American-born teachers.

Although educators did not often agree on the best means of teaching Jewish youth, they concurred on the importance of the task at hand. Without proper education, educators worried, pressures to conform to a predominantly Christian environment would lure Jewish youth away from living meaningful Jewish lives. As Horace J. Wolf, an advocate of religious school reform, explained in 1917, "To my mind this problem is more vital than any question which faces American Jewry today." Without proper education, Jewish children "will be well along the road to complete amalgamation. . . . The menace of complete assimilation seems remote to us; but it may not seem so far removed, nor so very unwelcome, to our great-grandchildren."[29] Just two months later, Alexander Dushkin, then completing his doctoral dissertation on Jewish education at Columbia University, confirmed the view of his contemporaries, calling educational efforts the Jewish people's "guarantee for the future."[30] These educators were not asking for a return to the traditions of their ancestors, but they insisted that knowledge of such traditions, and of Jewish history and literature, were vital to Jewish survival.

Most of these prominent Jewish educators focused on Jewish communal efforts to educate Jewish youth rather than on secular institutions of higher education. By the time Benderly, Dushkin, and others began to publish their opinions, a number of American colleges had opened their doors to Jewish faculty. Many of these faculty members, however, taught Semitics or Hebrew language rather than general humanities topics. In 1874, Cornell University appointed Felix Adler, the son of prominent New York City rabbi Samuel Adler, as professor of Hebrew and Oriental literature and history. Adler's contract was not renewed in 1877.[31] Under initiatives led by Charles W. Eliot, Daniel Coit Gilman, and William Rainey Harper, presidents at Harvard, Johns Hopkins, and the University of Chicago, respectively, three elite colleges initiated Semitics departments and included Judaic studies under their rubrics.[32] Semitics departments at Columbia and the University of Pennsylvania offered instruction in rabbinic and medieval Jewish texts.[33] Jewish professors also were hired to teach Jewish studies at the University of California, New York University, Temple, and Tulane during the late nineteenth and early twentieth century.[34]

Despite these advances, restrictions against hiring Jews, more often tacit than officially acknowledged, prevailed at the majority of American universities.[35] Jewish faculty were not always welcomed or retained in the same manner as their non-Jewish colleagues. Jewish students too were discouraged from entering many fields of graduate study, precisely because few schools would hire Jewish faculty. According to Julian W. Mack, Columbia University professor John Dewey advised Jewish students not to pursue doctoral degrees in philosophy during the 1910s. Mack wrote, "Dewey told me at that time [around 1916] that he advised his Jewish post-graduate students, especially the Russians, not to go in for an academic career in philosophy, that the road ahead was too hard. He told me that the academic career for Jews generally was not easy, but in philosophy, just because it was linked up more or less with religion, the path to advancement was almost insurmountable."[36] The situation in anthropology was similar; Franz Boas, also at Columbia, sought to portray himself as German rather than as Jewish because of prejudice against Jews in his field.[37] In history departments, as historian Peter Novick explains, "there seem to have been no professional historians of recent immigrant background, none of working-class origin, and hardly any who were not Protestant," before World War I.[38]

To illustrate the trend in sociology, consider Louis Wirth's experiences as a graduate student and later a professor of sociology at the University of Chicago. Wirth chose to write his dissertation, "The Ghetto: A Study in Isolation," on a subject related to Jews, despite widespread antisemitism in academic circles in the 1920s.[39] Indeed, even though his mentor Robert E. Park and the University of Chicago faculty considered his dissertation brilliant, Wirth was rejected for an appointment at Chicago upon his graduation. He waited another four years before being hired as a professor there. One cannot definitively prove that Wirth's Jewish heritage or his dissertation topic directly caused the delay, but the University of Chicago employed only one Jewish professor in 1927. Wirth's Jewish heritage likely influenced the sociology department's decision to put off hiring him.[40] Perhaps Wirth considered his difficulty in securing a faculty position at Chicago a bitter lesson—he never produced another scholarly work on any Jewish subject. Although he often spoke in public to Jewish organizations on topics relevant to Jewish life in America, Wirth limited his participation in Jewish activities to a world outside of the academy.[41]

Despite these prevailing trends in academia, a small group of professors remained committed to integrating Jewish faculty and Jewish studies courses into American colleges. As early as 1914, the Menorah Association's leadership noted that the "new type" of Jewish professors would not have to "hide or ignore or minimize their Jewishness," but instead should remain "attached to Jewish interests" and thereby influence their Jewish students also to remain so attached.[42] With the help of the Menorah Association, Jewish studies did develop in American colleges during the interwar period. Even though many of these efforts were short-lived, they laid the groundwork for successful Jewish studies initiatives in the second half of the twentieth century.

The Menorah Association's Jewish Studies Program

"Pure studentship," in the words of IMA Chancellor Hurwitz, was at the heart of the Menorah Association's Jewish studies program. This "studentship," designed to illuminate Jewish contributions to Western civilization, had to occur within the confines of secular colleges in order to demonstrate that, "more than perhaps that of any other historic people, not excepting the Greeks, the life of the Jews has permeated our general civilization."[43] The crux of the problem, according to Hurwitz and his cohort, was ignorance of these Jewish contributions. The most dangerous effects of this failure were readily observable on campuses. Too many professors taught that Jewish culture and civilization had ceased to develop. Menorah Association leaders claimed instead that Jewish culture had continued to evolve with great consequences for the course of modern civilization.

In 1914, IMA promotional literature explained, "The Jewish influence, for example, upon the Reformation and the Renaissance, upon the development of medical science, upon the growth of capitalism and of socialism alike, is now only beginning to be brought to attention."[44] Teaching students about these contributions by Jews to the societies in which they lived would be a means of combating prejudice, Hurwitz hoped. As he told Horace Kallen in 1916, "Academic anti-Semitism in the student body anywhere is based on the ignorance of what the Jew is and has stood for." The Menorah Association could affect significant change "in mitigating that anti-Semitism by spreading knowledge of the history and character of the actual Jew."[45] According to the Menorah idea, scientific study would replace prejudicially based fictions with accurate portrayals of Jewish history and culture.

The Menorah Association's Jewish studies program pointedly rejected religiously based education. Instead the IMA emphasized the humanities, broadly conceived. "Judaism will be frail indeed," one Menorah Association leader wrote, "if it depends wholly on such education as is available for our children in *chedorim* [Torah schools] and religious schools."[46] Religious education had its place in Jewish learning, but it should not replace teaching of Jewish history and culture. For this reason, most of the organization's leadership criticized the Jewish studies work occurring at seminaries. Here, the American Pragmatists' influence on the Menorah Association's leading thinkers again prevailed: scholarship based in the academy, they argued, allowed for questioning of truths and openness to new knowledge that seminary-based learning denied. Some of the organization's leaders exposed their snobbery in rejecting seminaries as well, disparaging what they perceived as rabbis' lack of critical intellect. As Oko wrote, "The expounding of Judaism is work more for the professor's chair, and less for the pulpit, where half-knowledge may pass for real knowledge."[47]

In order to accomplish its goals, the Menorah Association convened a committee of supportive faculty, called the Menorah Educational Conference (MEC), in December 1918. The object of the newly formed conference, according to its constitution, was "to foster and to guide Menorah education in American colleges and among university graduates and other men and women in the general community interested in Jewish culture and ideals."[48] Membership in the MEC was open to all college and university officers and instructors. The MEC coordinated scholarly work related to Jewish studies across the country, but it did not admit students or confer degrees. It instead administered, subsidized, and published work in Jewish studies with the ultimate goal of promoting student interest in Jewish culture.[49] Hurwitz became the chairman of the MEC and was assisted primarily by Oko and Nathan Isaacs, a professor at Harvard Law School.[50] The remaining members of the MEC Executive Committee included many of the most prominent Jewish educators in the United States: Alexander M. Dushkin of the Bureau of Jewish Education; Israel Friedlaender, Jewish Theological Seminary; Richard Gottheil, Columbia; I. L. Kandel, Columbia Teachers College; Simon Litman, University of Illinois; Max L. Margolis, Dropsie College; Max Radin, University of California, Berkeley; and Harry A. Wolfson, Harvard.[51]

Instructors from seventeen colleges and universities gathered in New York City for the first MEC meeting on December 28, 1918. Expressing both the angst and the hope central to their effort, Hurwitz told the conference, "No graver period than the present has ever challenged the coming of age of a Jewish educational organization." He referred to the Menorah Association's debt to *Wissenschaft des Judentums* as he urged the group to rekindle the "Jewish Renaissance, started a century ago."[52] The MEC determined to support activities in three areas: lectures, forums, and study circles. It would train future leaders by endowing teaching fellowships and running a summer school, and it also would advocate hiring professors to teach Jewish studies in American colleges.

The executive committee was careful to note the danger of focusing too intently on Jewish studies at the expense of what they called "general knowledge." Based on the opinion that seminary-based training of rabbis produced only "ordinary" Jewish men, Oko argued that the MEC could provide an alternative for young Jewish men who were disillusioned with religious institutions. Although some members of the MEC, particularly Israel Friedlaender, disagreed with Oko's disparaging view of modern rabbis, even Friedlaender admitted that the MEC should "have real sympathy with the Jewish man who is not religious on principle."[53] Hurwitz articulated the IMA's ideal for a culturally based Jewish identity in 1921, when he wrote that the MEC's ultimate triumph would come when "our magistral Jewish experience throughout the centuries and our enduring ideals may be studied as an integral part of the whole of Western civilization in its every manifestation, and not merely in the theological or religious aspect."[54]

This vision of an integrated Jewish studies curriculum guided the MEC as it sought to create educational programming that would appeal to undergraduates.

Prior to the founding of the MEC in 1918, the IMA's initiatives in the realm of Jewish studies had not been coordinated well. In an effort to standardize Jewish learning, the IMA cooperated with the Jewish Publication Society to distribute a set of monographs on Jewish history and literature to more than forty campuses during the mid-1910s.[55] The libraries included surveys of Jewish history, literature, theology, and essays on Zionism.[56] Before 1918, the IMA conducted both formal and informal surveys of Jewish studies courses and had offered students cash awards for Menorah prize essays.[57] It also called for the creation of syllabi on topics including "The Jew in the Modern World," "Introduction to Jewish History," and "Jewish Factors in Western Civilization" during the late 1910s.[58] By the mid-1920s, Columbia University had instituted a course based on the Menorah Association's "Jewish Factors in Western Civilization" syllabus.[59]

With the founding of the Menorah Educational Conference, the IMA began systematizing this loose confederation of efforts. Rather than relying on the generosity of scholars to travel at their convenience to address campus chapters, for example, the MEC standardized what had been a haphazardly formulated Menorah College of Lecturers, compensating lecturers enough to produce "consistently high, responsible work, involving adequate preparation, [and] full accountability to the organization."[60] A program that in 1914 seems to have been based solely on convenience for the lecturer was, by the late 1920s, organized and advertised to the public.[61] These lectures promoted knowledge of Jewish civilization and sought to increase students' morale. The MEC also hoped that some of the young men who witnessed this impressively managed effort would be enticed to become the organization's future leaders.

The MEC also organized forums, or discussions on the present topics of interest, such as Zionism or antisemitism. Hurwitz hoped that lively debate between forum leaders and students would put "'pep' into this sacred (and hitherto rather dull) domain" of Jewish studies.[62] The MEC realized that forums would fail without well-informed Jewish students, and for this reason they continued to sponsor study circles, a component of the Menorah Association program from its earliest days. Like forums, study circles were guided by a faculty leader, but took a longer focus, meeting many times over the course of a semester or academic year.[63] The MEC soon observed sustained student interest in study-circle topics such as Zionism and modern Jewish problems. At some universities, study circles in Jewish history, literature, and elementary Hebrew also drew a committed follow-ing. Over time, however, the MEC found it increasingly difficult to entice students to participate in study circles because many students considered such activities analogous to classroom work.

The MEC also aimed to solve the problem of inconsistent student leader-ship that hindered the Menorah Association's progress on many campuses by introducing a bureaucratic structure into what they previously hoped would be a democratic, self-perpetuating student movement. In propos-ing to endow Menorah Teaching Fellowships, which never came to pass, Hurwitz wrote with a tone more characteristic of Progressive Era efficiency than of his normally impassioned pleas for funding. Hurwitz hoped that ten teaching fellowships, each paying a stipend of $500 per year, would al-low Menorah fellows to do "sufficiently promising work, both in research and instruction."[64] Adequate funding and an efficient strategy for train-ing, he hoped, would produce the leaders required to sustain the growth of the Menorah movement. Although standardizing the Menorah Associa-tion's educational efforts did produce some immediate results, ultimately the movement still remained dependent on initiatives generated by the or-ganization's leaders in New York, rather than by students themselves.

In addition to teaching fellowships, the MEC proposed founding a sum-mer school that would bring together both Jewish and non-Jewish scholars, graduate and undergraduate students for a six-week period.[65] Hurwitz ide-alistically proposed that individuals interested in Jewish learning remove themselves from the routine of their daily lives, perhaps to "some agree-able country spot, where study, discussion, and recreational life in the open might be combined."[66] The MEC sponsored three sessions of the Menorah Summer School, in 1922, 1923, and 1930. In seeking to lure a potential do-nor, Hurwitz expressed the ideals central to the Menorah Association's edu-cational philosophy, again highlighting the influence of *Wissenschaft des Judentums*. The general subject of the 1922 summer session, Hurwitz wrote, would be "Jewish history and thought, and the position of the Jew in the modern world. In the purely scientific spirit, and from the point of view of the community as a whole." Emphasizing integration of Jewish studies, Hurwitz added that the scholars present would "endeavor to look upon the Jew dispassionately, neither ghettoishly or anti-Semitically."[67]

In his remarks at the opening session of the first Menorah Summer School on July 10, 1922, Hurwitz called for a "fresh understanding between Jew and Gentile." The lessons learned from integrating Jewish studies into college curricula, he claimed, could illuminate the "common human in-heritance" of all "civilized mankind." Studying particular aspects of one's own people necessarily would strengthen the great diversity in Western civilization. The endpoint of such study, however, should emphasize commonalities. As Hurwitz explained to those who gathered, "How prodigiously the scientific yet sympathetic study of Jewish life in its entirety, in all ages and all environments can illuminate the ways of mankind." Like the founders of the *Jüdische Wissenschaft,* whom Hurwitz referred to as the "Menorah of a century ago," the summer school faculty would teach students to search for truth rather than to defend staid beliefs. Noting his pride in the school, Hurwitz boldly predicted that the Menorah Association could achieve in the United States what Zunz's efforts had failed to accomplish in Germany "by establishing Jewish learning as an integral, permanent part of our University curricula."[68]

The second session of the Menorah Summer School, lasting for six weeks in 1923, brought students into contact with more than a dozen instructors.[69] Hurwitz could not achieve his vision of a school meeting in the countryside, so the courses were held in New York City at the building of the Society for the Advancement of Judaism.[70] Elliot Cohen—who would soon become the managing editor of the *Menorah Journal* and later, in 1945, the founding editor of *Commentary* magazine—attended the school as a student and lauded its accomplishments: "The students of the Menorah Summer School have returned to their universities and communities with a far clearer conception of their place as Jews in the modern world." Because the school did not treat "the life of the Jew as an isolated phenomenon but as an integral part of the life of humanity as whole," Cohen predicted, students who attended the Menorah Summer School would become leaders not only to fellow Jewish students, but to the entire student body. Cohen concluded that the Menorah Summer School perfectly synthesized Judaism and Americanism: in promoting a Jewish cultural renaissance as part of a pluralist American project, the school "rendered a patriotic service of inestimable value to the country as a whole no less than to the Jew himself."[71]

Due to budget shortfalls, the Menorah Summer School did not operate between 1923 and 1930. The school reopened in 1930 as a result of generous funding from Jewish philanthropists Julius Rosenwald, S. W. Straus, Edward Lasker, and Lucius N. Littauer.[72] Much of the faculty changed between 1923 and 1930, but, when the school reopened in 1930 at the Jewish Institute of Religion's facility on West 68th Street in Manhattan, the purpose remained the same: training future Jewish lay leaders through the study of Jewish culture. Hurwitz told the more than one hundred students in attendance in 1930 that the summer school instruction would avoid the "emotional propaganda" that characterized so much of Jewish teaching of

Henry Hurwitz.
*Courtesy of the Jacob Rader Marcus Center of
the American Jewish Archives.*

the moment. Instead, the school's teachers sought "to connect the modern Jew with his past, in terms of his present, living, day-to-day interests."[73]

Despite Hurwitz's enthusiasm, the MEC, and indeed the entire Inter-collegiate Menorah Association, faced considerable obstacles. The Menorah Summer School ran its final session in 1930. Economic challenges that plagued the Menorah Association with the onset of the Great Depression combined with a lack of student interest led to the school's demise. Looking back many years later on the history of the MEC, one member summed up the group's challenges: "We aimed too high, we overestimated the willingness and the ability of the rank and file of Jewish students to participate in a program which offered them nothing more than intellectual food; they had enough of it in their University courses."[74]

Jewish Studies and University Faculty

IMA leadership always acknowledged that students' varied interests as well as their transience might hinder the ability to achieve long-lasting Jewish studies initiatives. The IMA sought to address this problem by lobbying school administrations to create permanent faculty positions in Jewish studies. Leaders of this effort viewed faculty chairs as a logical step in a successful long-term organizational plan. In a December 1919 address, MEC chair Nathan Isaacs claimed that, before the Menorah Association came along, most Jewish college students had been disconnected from surrounding Jewish communities and even from fellow Jews on campus. Isaacs congratulated the Menorah Association for stepping into this void, creating connections among Jewish students, and encouraging them to take pride in their Jewish heritage. More could still be accomplished, however.

After lauding the Menorah Association's progress to date Isaacs declared, "We have succeeded in 'selling' our Menorah brands to the student body, and now we must 'deliver the goods!'"[75] By "the goods" Isaacs meant scholarship—to meet its goals, the Menorah Association had to provide encouragement and support that would enable scholars to produce material worthy of study. Although Isaacs's call did not signal the abandonment of student-led initiatives, it did mark an important shift in focus from the consumers to the producers of scholarship in Jewish studies.

The MEC's effort to secure faculty positions meant that it would have to convince college administrators to integrate Jewish studies into curriculums rather than to conceive of these activities as extracurricular. Soon after the founding of the MEC, IMA leaders called for an increase in Jewish studies courses and faculty chairs. In his 1919 undelivered commencement address, Oko acknowledged that the strong force of academic tradition worked against implementing Jewish studies programs where they previously had not existed. Yet he insisted that "tradition was also against the several subjects that have been taken up by universities during the last sixty or seventy years: demands were made for their recognition."[76] The time had come, Oko and his colleagues determined with this empowering call, for the IMA to make similar demands. No other organization was in a position to do so; the IMA had a presence on more campuses than any other Jewish student association well into the 1920s.

Harry Austryn Wolfson, a leading authority in Jewish education who had been an active member of the Menorah Association since his undergraduate days, supported Oko's call for greater recognition of Jewish studies.[77] Wolfson, a yeshiva scholar who immigrated from Russia to the United States at the age of sixteen in 1903, graduated from Harvard in 1912. Described as shy and lonely by those who knew him best, Wolfson spent a life passionately committed to scholarship, never marrying but finding a sense of family among a few close colleagues in academia and in the Menorah Association crowd.[78] Following graduation, he spent two years in Europe on Harvard's prestigious Sheldon Fellowship, studying Crescas, the fourteenth-century Spanish Jewish philosopher and critic of Aristotle and Maimonides. Upon his return to the United States in 1915, Harvard appointed Wolfson an instructor in Jewish philosophy and literature, under the condition that his salary be raised from outside sources.[79] Wolfson was the first Jewish person appointed to Harvard's faculty of arts.[80]

In 1921, the Menorah Journal published Wolfson's essay "The Needs of Jewish Scholarship in America." Wolfson explained that the Jewish scholarly community in the United States was different from that in Europe because it had "not reached the stage where it can produce native scholars of its own." He implored American Jewish leaders and institutions to endow fellowships for study that would lead to the publication of new scholarship. Wolfson hoped these fellowships would be instrumental in "bringing to light many treasures of Hebrew literature which are now rotting in the holds of the world's libraries."[81] The organization most equipped to awaken Jewish consciousness through scholarly initiatives, Wolfson claimed, was the Menorah Association. The IMA, however, would spend most of its energy in this realm trying to secure a position for Wolfson himself.

Because financial support for Wolfson's position at Harvard became more uncertain, he began in 1921 to split his time between Harvard and Rabbi Wise's Jewish Institute of Religion in New York City. In 1922, Wise offered

Wolfson a full-time position at JIR, with a guaranteed salary much higher than Harvard would pay. Offers for a more secure position also came from Hebrew Union College in Cincinnati and from the newly established Hebrew University in Jerusalem in 1924 and again in 1925. With characteristic snobbery, some of the Menorah Association's most prominent leaders encouraged Wolfson to remain at Harvard. For example, Oko told Wolfson to accept the JIR offer if he preferred to teach "Y.M.H.A. students" rather than Harvard students.[82] By 1925, Harvard notified Wolfson that his position would be terminated if he did not find permanent funding from outside the university to support it. Although he would later assume more credit than he perhaps deserved, Hurwitz helped to encourage Lucius Littauer, Harvard class of 1878, to endow a position in honor of his father, Nathan. Wolfson held the Nathan Littauer Professorship of Jewish History and Philosophy from 1925 until 1958 and remained at Harvard as a professor emeritus until his death in 1974.[83]

Wolfson's decision to stay at Harvard during the 1920s must be explained by his unbending loyalty to the institution where, as one scholar has noted, he "entered in 1908, died as Professor Emeritus sixty-six years later, and never left in between, save his research period in Europe (on a Harvard scholarship) and a few months in the Army."[84] The encouragement from leaders of the IMA, to which Wolfson also remained devoted, also influenced his decision. The guiding principle of the Menorah idea, in fact, played an important role in Wolfson's decision to remain at Harvard. Wolfson prioritized integrating Jewish studies and disparaged efforts to segregate Jewish learning in seminaries such as Hebrew Union College or the Jewish Institute of Religion. Attaining a chair in Jewish studies at Harvard in 1925—which occurred on the heels of the debates over admissions quotas for Jewish students—validated both the presence of Jews at America's most elite institution and the Menorah Association's philosophy of synthesis between Americanism and Judaism. Wolfson's position at Harvard implied an acceptance of the contribution of Jewish culture to the humanities. Recognition of a Jewish scholar by Harvard's administration, even if not wholeheartedly enthusiastic, might have done little to counter the pervasive antisemitism in academia during the 1920s, but its significance should not be minimized.

Following Wolfson's appointment, other efforts to institutionalize Jewish studies in colleges both in the United States and abroad continued, with initiatives extending far beyond the Menorah Association's efforts.[85] In Columbia University's history department, Salo W. Baron was named the first chair of "Jewish history, literature, and institutions" in 1929.[86] New

York University began offering instruction in modern Hebrew in 1933; individual Hebrew classes blossomed into a Jewish studies department, and the NYU program became a model for programs instituted at Brooklyn College (1938), Hunter College (1940), CCNY (1948), and Temple University (1948).[87] In Weimar Germany, Martin Buber held a lectureship in religion and Jewish ethics at the University of Frankfurt am Main.[88] Further east, influential Jewish scholarly institutions opened their doors: in 1925, YIVO (Yiddish Scientific Institute) was founded in Vilna as a center for Yiddish-speaking scholars to study the history and folklore of eastern European Jewry.[89] That same year, in April, Hebrew University opened in Jerusalem.[90]

The Menorah Association actively supported Hebrew University as a symbol of dynamic Jewish culture in Palestine and as a home for Jewish scholars who were excluded from European institutions because of anti-semitism. Shortly after Hebrew University's cornerstone-laying ceremony in July 1918, the *Menorah Journal* began publishing articles about the institution. In December 1918, Ben Zion Mossinsohn, an educator and Zionist who had been barred from Russian universities, echoed a sentiment that recurred in many of these *Menorah Journal* articles: "A Hebrew University in Palestine is the first step towards the creation of a Hebrew national culture."[91] In later issues, noted cultural critic Lewis Mumford wrote about the architectural plan of the university, and frequent contributor Jessie E. Sampter compared Hebrew University to a new temple arising to redeem the Jewish people.[92] After the school opened, journalist William Schack reported that Hebrew University would forge the way to a renaissance of Jewish culture, promoting Hebrew language and literature, and perhaps even fostering greater understanding between Arabs and Jews in Palestine.[93]

The IMA officially supported Hebrew University, basing its endorsement on Ahad Ha'am's cultural Zionism, which viewed Palestine as a center from which Jewish culture would radiate to the rest of the world. As a center of Jewish culture, Jerusalem needed a singular institution devoted to Jewish scholarship. Moreover, Palestine needed a Jewish university as a refuge for Jewish students and professors who had been excluded from European universities.

The Menorah Association rejected the idea of establishing a Jewish university in the United States, however, even as a couple of proposals to do just that were raised during this period. In a 1917 speech to the Clark University Menorah Society, Clark president G. Stanley Hall, noted educator and an authority in psychology, suggested creating a Jewish university in the United States as a means to preserve Jewish culture. Hall did not argue that all Jewish students should attend the Jewish university, but instead that, even as Jewish students enrolled at various secular universities, the opportunity to choose a Jewish university should exist. Hall described his proposed institution as a "monument of the Jewish race, of its past and future, a repository of its learning, and a conservator of its loftiest spirit."[94] In their correspondence, Hall told Hurwitz that, without strong Jewish institutions to promote and teach Jewish humanities, the pressures to conform to Protestant environments could prove too enticing for Jewish youth to resist.[95]

At first glance Hall's support of scholarly programs in Jewish studies might have seemed to mesh with the Menorah Association's philosophy. Yet because a Jewish university would segregate a large portion of Jewish students, Hall's proposal actually directly contradicted the Menorah idea. Nathan Isaacs viewed Hall's suggestion as too limited. Expressing the IMA's party line, Isaacs agreed that a Jewish university in America may indeed be a "great thing," but he insisted that it should be founded only after established institutions accepted Jewish studies within their curriculums.[96] The Menorah Association did not act in any way to support Hall's proposal, and no other Jewish organization had enough influence in 1917 to pursue it in any meaningful way.

Five years later, on October 27, 1922, the *Jewish Tribune* printed an editorial by Rabbi Louis I. Newman, a former supporter of the IMA who had become disillusioned with the organization. In the editorial, Newman wrote that a Jewish university should be founded in the United States because it would foster "self-help" and "self-emancipation" as an answer to antisemitism. Newman envisioned an institution that would become a home for a Jewish cultural renaissance which would spread across the United States. Reactions to Newman's editorial came from so many sources that the Bloch Publishing Company issued a book in 1923 containing a further elaboration by Newman on the need for a Jewish university in America with a host of responses from all sides.[97]

Most of the active members of the Menorah Association strongly opposed Newman's suggestion. Hurwitz stated the case against segregating Jewish studies in America. "It is grossly inadequate," Hurwitz wrote, "and also dangerous, to limit such studies to the Jewish theological seminaries, or to any special segregated 'Jewish University.' Jewish experience and expression through the ages are part and parcel of the heritage of mankind, and must be critically appreciated in relation to all other elements in Western Civilization."[98] No organized movement to establish a Jewish university immediately followed Newman's editorial, and Brandeis University, a non-sectarian but Jewish-sponsored institution, would not come into being for more than twenty years, in 1948.[99]

In proposing a Jewish university in the United States, Newman was reacting to what he interpreted as the Menorah Association's lack of influence with college administrators. This reaction arguably was justified. Ultimately, the Menorah Association made little headway in convincing colleges to establish Jewish studies programs or endow faculty chairs during the 1920s. Too many factors stymied the IMA's goals. Many university administrators, perhaps motivated by antisemitism, did not support the idea of establishing chairs in Jewish studies. The funding for such positions at Harvard and Columbia originated not from university coffers but wealthy benefactors. The Menorah Association never established the necessary fund-raising structure for such an effort.

Hurwitz's inability to raise enough money to endow a chair in honor of retiring Harvard Professor David Gordon Lyon in 1922 demonstrated the difficulty of securing Jewish studies positions without backing from wealthy benefactors. Upon hearing of Hurwitz's campaign to honor Lyon, Wolfson bluntly counseled Hurwitz: "You know as well as I that the Intercollegiate [Menorah Association] cannot do anything but lend its moral support. As for the Harvard Menorah, it will take from 100 to 150 years to raise the funds [necessary to endow a chair]."[100] Just as distressingly, as Hurwitz and his supporters were forced to admit during the mid-1920s, few qualified Jewish scholars existed to fill such positions. As Elliot Cohen conceded in a 1926 internal memorandum, he could not think of any Jewish scholar in America "worthy to occupy a chair" even if the IMA raised the money.[101]

A Coda: Jewish Studies in the Postwar Era

By the 1930s, most Jewish students who cared to affiliate with a Jewish organization gravitated toward fraternities or Hillel. Some of the IMA's most active supporters, including Horace Kallen, nonetheless remained committed to the Menorah idea even after the association lost its influence on campuses. Kallen consistently argued against removing Jewish studies from the general humanities curriculum, telling an audience in 1951: "The whole education of the Western world isolates [Jews] from the liberal idea altogether and the consequence is that our children learn by default that somehow the Jewish content is not important for the life of a Jewish man or woman who is being educated in the subject matter of the liberal spirit." He told his listeners that he always directed his own academic efforts toward treating "the whole of the Jewish cultural component as part and parcel of the liberal tradition."[102] He called on other scholars to do the same. Supporters of the Menorah Association's academic initiatives, however, would have to wait nearly two more decades to see Kallen's call realized.

Indeed, the seeds planted by the IMA's interwar initiatives began to bear fruit nearly fifty years after the peak of the association's influence. Where only a small handful of schools offered modern Jewish studies courses in the 1910s, by the late 1960s one in three liberal arts colleges offered at least one course in some aspect of Jewish religion, history, language, or culture.[103] Exactly fifty years after the Menorah Association's 1916 survey of Jewish studies programs, a 1966 survey on the same topic reported being "repeatedly impressed" by the "bewildering diversity of [Jewish studies] programs in the United States." Jewish studies courses included offerings in near eastern languages and civilizations, history, and religious studies departments at more than sixty-five American universities by 1966, with more than sixty full-time faculty teaching Jewish studies across the country.[104] Scholars in the field founded the Association for Jewish Studies, a professional academic organization, in 1969. By 1972, the Hillel Foundation counted Jewish studies courses at more than three hundred colleges and universities in America, with undergraduate majors in Jewish studies at forty institutions and graduate programs at twenty-seven.[105]

Jewish studies courses and programs increased rapidly in response to ethnic consciousness movements beginning in the 1960s and 1970s. This precipitous rise also can be attributed to the growth of academic literatures outside the mainstream, the founding of the State of Israel in 1948, and the continually expanding offerings in Holocaust studies.[106]

By 1992, Jewish studies courses were offered at 410 institutions of higher learning, with 104 endowed professorships at non-Jewish colleges and universities in the United States and Canada.[107] The field also spread internationally. At the close of the twentieth century, nearly 300 European institutions in twenty-two countries included Jewish studies courses.[108]

These contemporary Jewish studies initiatives stemmed from some of the same concerns that drove the Menorah Association to promote learning in the Jewish humanities during the 1910s and 1920s. Professor of education and Hebrew literature William Cutter wrote during the mid-1990s that modern Jewish studies represents "a marker of self confidence" as well as signals "that Jewish academics may not yet be certain about the endurance" of modern Jewish identity.[109] As was the case with the Menorah Association, Jewish studies today may still be intended not only to demonstrate

Jews' belonging in the United States, or any other host country, but also to address a pervasive anxiety about the continuity of Jewish identity. The "renewed interest" in Jewish studies that the Menorah Association called for in its 1916 survey has had to be refigured in each successive generation, but the reliance on group survival through education, transmitting Jewish culture across generations, has remained relatively constant.

A Pluralist History and Culture

Even as they sought to integrate Jewish studies into college curricula, the leaders of the Menorah Association grew frustrated by the lack of scholarly publications available to support their effort. The problem was especially acute in the field of history. In a 1927 book review titled "Wanted: A New Kind of Jewish History," Herbert Solow, an assistant editor at the *Menorah Journal*, declared students' ignorance of Jewish history an irrefutable truth. Rather than blaming students for this shortcoming, Solow faulted historians. He insisted that readers needed more modern histories, by which he meant works that focused on Jews' social and economic contributions to the societies in which they lived, rather than histories of religion or political segregation.[1] New historical writing needed to look outward, emphasizing the ways that Jewish culture had thrived—sometimes against great odds—rather than looking inward to examine religious matters or responses to discrimination.

Solow's trenchant criticism came in the midst of a remarkable dozen-year run of articles in the *Menorah Journal* in which contributors articulated the need for a new, comprehensive Jewish history that would replace nineteenth-century historical syntheses and integrate Jews firmly into modern Western civilization. During this period, approximately from 1918 to 1930, many of the authors who called for a new Jewish history also criticized what they saw as American Jewry's barren cultural landscape.

Solow's voice was one of the most harsh. He was part of a "circle of precocious Jewish students" at Columbia during the 1920s—including Lionel Trilling, Meyer Schapiro, Clifton Fadiman, and others—who were drawn to the *Menorah Journal* by its young managing editor, Elliot Cohen.[2] Solow, born in 1903 and raised in Manhattan, had little interest in Judaism or Jewish culture as an undergraduate, but he grew deeply intrigued by Cohen and the Menorah crowd's effort to make Jewish culture relevant to modern America life. Solow remained closely associated with the *Menorah Journal*, first as an associate editor and later as a contributing editor, until 1931, when a series of anti-Zionist articles he wrote precipitated a split with Hurwitz.[3] Solow went on to work closely with John Dewey in his defense of Leon Trotsky in the Moscow Trials during the 1930s. By the 1940s, Solow had repudiated Trotskyists. After working for a couple of years at *Time* magazine, Solow became an editor at *Fortune* in 1945.[4]

Solow and others at the *Menorah Journal* set their sights especially on the Reform movement and on excessive materialism, both of which they portrayed as undermining the pluralist ideal. This cohort hoped that their reflections on Jewish history and culture would provide a foundation to steel Jewish youth against assimilation. Hurwitz articulated this grand hope in 1930 when he confided to a colleague, "Out of this newer scholarship may come that living interest in Judaism which we all desire."[5]

Most of the writers at the center of this discussion about Jewish historiography—especially historians Salo Baron and Cecil Roth, philosophers Horace Kallen and Harry A. Wolfson, and journalists Elliot Cohen and Marvin Lowenthal—argued that the future of Jewish culture in America depended on producing material that readers would regard as relevant. Without engaging products to interest Jewish youth in their history and culture, assimilation would continue apace. In advocating new sources in Jewish humanities, these writers were motivated primarily by the two complementary strains of pluralist ideology—encouraging Jews to cherish Jewish culture and persuading the majority to recognize Jewish contributions to the broader civilization.

Asserting the particular contributions of one's own group to the nation already was commonplace for many American ethnic groups by the mid-nineteenth century, but this trend represented a significant departure from previous Jewish histories.[6] The goals of those who wrote Jewish history during the 1910s and 1920s—preserving Jewish distinctiveness and ensuring that Jewish culture would be passed from generation to generation—may have been shared, but the tones in which these historians advanced these goals usually occupied different registers. Some writers claimed that Jewish history should be read alongside Greek and Roman histories as one of the pillars of modern civilization; others, more temperedly, called for recognizing Jewish influences on the history of Christianity. Within the American context, some historians argued that the nation's foundational ideals had been borrowed from Jewish historical tradition. Other writers claimed that America was a pluralist nation at its founding and always made room for Jewish cultural particularity. Although the treatments of Jewish history in the *Menorah Journal* did not inaugurate this conversation about the proper means of history writing, they did advance the discussion significantly. The journal itself became an important locus of debate about history writing during the interwar period.

Even the strident criticisms of modern American Jewry that characterized this era of the *Menorah Journal* were motivated by a constructive agenda. Although these writers often reveled in their own cleverness, they also wrote from a position of perceived responsibility. Wolfson, Lowenthal, Cohen, and their colleagues understood that they were living at a moment during which the cultural center of world Jewry was shifting from Russia and Europe to North America. (Although Lowenthal especially was troubled by European antisemitism during the 1920s, none could have known at the time that the annihilation of Europe's Jews during World War II would shift Jews' cultural center so dramatically.) They placed a burden upon themselves to produce material that mattered to Jews and that proved American Jews could handle the responsibility of creating meaningful Jewish culture. The *Menorah Journal*'s editors and frequent contributors sought through the magazine to redefine the Jewish humanities for a modern age. In doing so, they became some of the leading arbiters of interwar American Jewish culture.

German Precursors and American Ideals

As in its effort to integrate Jewish studies at American colleges, the Menorah Association's leaders looked to the hundred-year tradition of *Wissenschaft des Judentums* to inspire a new Jewish history. They turned to this tradition because they interpreted it as modern, free from religious doctrine, and integrated into the fabric of world history. As they positioned themselves as the inheritors of this intellectual movement, they again lionized Leopold Zunz, who posited in his influential 1845 *Contributions to History and Literature* that Jews' cultural contributions could be evidenced not only in the Bible, but also in their literature, poetry, and other writings.[7]

Even more influential than Zunz in this case, though, was Heinrich Graetz's enduring survey *History of the Jews*. Graetz, a professor of history at the University of Breslau, wrote the eleven-volume history between 1856 and 1873, setting a standard that writers who followed could not ignore.

Graetz hoped that *History of the Jews* would restore Jewish consciousness to a rapidly assimilating German Jewish population.[8] He always sought to produce works of scholarship that operated by the same standards as the most modern methods of historical inquiry and thus to create a space for Jewish historical works alongside those of their non-Jewish contemporaries. Graetz explained Jewish history not by analyzing religious texts, but instead by examining the social and cultural history of Jewish people.[9] His *History of the Jews* evoked criticism from nearly all directions, including vigorous opposition from Orthodox circles, but it served to popularize Jewish history to some extent and to validate *Wissenschaft des Judentums* to a larger audience than it previously had enjoyed.

By the 1920s, Graetz's mid-nineteenth century work still had no peer. In the words of historian David N. Myers, Graetz remains "one of the three grand narrators of Jewish history in the modern age."[10] One of the other two grand narrators, Simon Dubnow, would begin to publish his monumental *History of the Jewish People* in 1925. Dubnow's work included the history of Jewish life in Russia and Poland, which Graetz largely ignored. Salo Baron, the third grand narrator that Myers identifies, developed some of his foundational arguments in the *Menorah Journal* as part of the organization's intellectual project in the 1920s. Baron's twenty-seven volume *A Social and Religious History of the Jews* would be published between 1952 and 1983. During the post–World War I era, however, Graetz's *History of the Jews* was the dominant survey of Jewish history. It became a cornerstone of the libraries that the Menorah Association sent to college chapters.[11] Yet availability was not the sole factor in making it the preeminent publication on Jewish history. The work was especially appropriate to the Menorah idea in that it firmly positioned Jews as cultural contributors to the societies in which they lived.

The Menorah Association's founders did not need to look very far for an inspiration to claim Jewish contributions to civilization. David Gordon Lyon, a professor of Semitics at Harvard and a mentor to some of the founders of the Harvard Menorah Society, had delivered a lecture before the World's Parliament of Religions at Chicago's 1893 World's Columbian Exposition that enumerated civilization's debts to Jews. The speech celebrated the ways that Jews had made lasting contributions to humanity despite the fact that "the Jew has been for many cruel centuries a wanderer on the face of the earth." Lyon said that Jews gave Western civilization both the Bible and the concept of monotheism. He emphasized that Jesus was a Jew by birth and urged his audience to consider Jews and Christians as siblings under the same fatherly God.[12]

Many other writers in the *Menorah Journal* noted the close relationship between Judaism and Christianity. Most of the authors who did so rejected the concept of supersession, contending that Jewish ideals continued to exist resiliently even after the rise of Christianity. Unitarian minister R. Travers Herford, for example, contended in 1919 that, even after Judaism gave birth to Christianity, it persisted alongside Christianity as one of the great world religions. Herford praised the tenacity of Judaism, arguing that "Judaism is a living religion, now at the end of nearly nineteen centuries from the time at which it is said to have received its death blow." He also claimed that it would be incorrect to interpret the continuous existence of Judaism as oppositional to Christianity. Judaism instead provided a necessary foil to Christianity, and helped Christians to hone and defend their own beliefs. Herford closed by asserting, "The human race in general and Christianity in particular would have been much the poorer if there had not been that presence and influence [of Judaism throughout history]."[13] Herford's contribution to the *Menorah Journal* embodied the ideal of encouraging discourse between Jews and non-Jews, complementing the Menorah Association's emphasis on preserving Jewish culture for the good of Jews and non-Jews alike.

Writers close to the IMA echoed Lyon and Herford by highlighting Jewish contributions to Western civilization and to Christianity. Nevertheless, the tenor underlying these claims shifted subtly during the 1920s, as some essayists began to urge Jews more directly to preserve their own culture rather than to focus on commonalities between religions. In articles published after 1920, many *Menorah Journal* contributors emphasized Jewish contributions to civilization more heavily. This strategy ultimately was based on the journal's perceived readership. In focusing on religious commonality between Jews and Christians, Lyon and Herford had intended to reach out to Christians. The histories produced in the 1920s tended to focus first on Jewish audiences, highlighting particularities of Jewish culture rather than shared religious values. These essays were intended to instill pride among Jewish readers and to combat assimilation among Jewish youth.

Felix Perles, scholar and rabbi of the Jewish community in Koenigsberg, demonstrated this shift in emphasis in a 1922 article, "Culture and History: A Summary of Jewish Experience."[14] Perles criticized works of Jewish history that divided social history from religious history. To solve what he saw as this artificial and misrepresentative separation, Perles wrote that historians instead should emphasize "the history of culture." Culture, Perles argued in accordance with Kallen and contemporary American Pragmatists, was not a fixed thing, nor a "ready possession, but an everlasting pursuit, for the individual as well as for the nation and the whole of humanity." Perles urged his readers to interpret "culture" as greater than the specific fruits of scientific inquiry, philosophy, or poetry.[15] Instead, culture should be understood as the continual process of creating and questioning knowledge, rather than solely assessing the product of knowledge itself. Based on this definition of culture, Perles issued a challenge to modern Jewry: "Culture must always be created anew."[16]

Perles acknowledged that his call to continually reinvent Jewish culture would be achieved more easily in some settings than in others. Prejudices in many European nations likely would limit Jews' cultural production to some extent. Perles therefore looked to the United States and predicted that its Jewish communities would have "the determining influence upon the whole of Jewry, and especially upon its future cultural development."[17] Perles contended that only in the United States did Jews enjoy the freedoms to make this unfettered, continual re-creation of Jewish culture possible. He hoped that American readers would interpret his article as a call to action. The opportunity was great, as was the challenge, especially in an American political climate increasingly hostile to cultural particularity in the mid-1910s.[18]

Many contributors to the *Menorah Journal* focused on Jewish history in the United States prior to the wave of eastern European immigration. These writers chronicled multiple examples of Jewish influences on early American society in order to underscore both that Jewish culture long had thrived in America and to remind skeptical readers of the guarantees of liberty and religious tolerance at the heart of the nation's political rhetoric.[19] For example, the frequent *Menorah Journal* contributor Marvin Lowenthal published "Minutes in Colonial Jewry" in April 1916. Lowenthal noted the continuous presence of Jewish congregations in New York City since the early eighteenth century and described early American history as coexisting with the "continuous narrative of early American Jewry."[20]

A more audacious variation on the same theme came from New York rabbi Moses Hyamson. "Like Abraham Lincoln, [Hillel] was a woodchopper," Hymanson wrote, in a less-than-artful attempt to equate the most beloved U.S. president with the first-century hero of classical Judaism and thus to demonstrate the complementarity of American and Jewish cultures.[21] An unsigned snippet that ran in the *Menorah Journal* two years later asserted the centrality of the Old Testament in the formation of the United States: "Lincoln fed on it. Woodrow Wilson was born and bred in it."[22] An undated address delivered to the Harvard Menorah Society by Dr. Lyman Abbot credited Hebrew tradition for inventing popular government, freedom of speech, criminal codes, and public education.[23] These notable examples, however clumsy, represented a common effort to inject Jewish ideals into the narrative of U.S. history.

Some writers also noted the ways that prominent non-Jewish Americans embraced Hebrew language and literature. In a 1916 article, rabbi and educator George Alexander Kohut mentioned that prominent Puritans such as John Cotton, Richard Mather, Increase Mather, and Cotton Mather read Hebrew. "The Hebrew spirit permeated their consciousness," Kohut wrote, "colored their view of life and influenced their deliberations."[24] Kohut also celebrated the appointment of Judah Monis to Harvard's faculty in 1722—although he downplayed the fact that Harvard required that Monis be baptized before accepting the appointment. (Kohut did gently chastise Harvard for not graduating any Jews between 1637 and 1800.) In an article published the following year, Kohut lauded Ezra Stiles, president of Yale from 1778 to 1795, for his ability to read the Old Testament in its original Hebrew, for teaching Semitics at the university, and for maintaining a close friendship with Rabbi Raphael Hayyim Isaac Carregal.[25] In 1920, former U.S. Secretary of Commerce and Labor Oscar S. Straus (the nation's first Jewish cabinet member) declared that Pilgrims "drew their inspiration chiefly from the Hebrew literature."[26] Even as their declarations of Jewish influence bordered on the apocryphal, none of these writers were naïve enough to claim that Jews should be given full credit for the evolution of American democracy. Instead, these essays implicitly asserted that Jews were one group of many that had influenced the history of the American nation. As long as American history was interpreted in this manner, pluralism could be portrayed as a long cherished ideal in the United States, rather than as a new solution to a perplexing problem of how to deal with an influx of Jewish and other immigrants.

An Integrated Jewish Historiography

Advancing a pluralist agenda through history writing could not be accomplished, of course, through facile comparisons of American presidents to Jewish heroes or by celebrating Puritans who knew how to read Hebrew. What was needed were new syntheses of Jewish history that attracted a broad readership of Jews and non-Jews. Specifically, many Jewish intellectuals agreed that it was time to replace Graetz's *History of the Jews* with new works that would combat Jews' "indifference" to their own history. The two individuals with the ability to write such histories were British historian

Cecil Roth and American historian Salo W. Baron. In articles published in the *Menorah Journal* between 1928 and 1929, Roth and Baron each articulated a vision intended to guide their colleagues.

Roth earned his doctorate at Oxford University and wrote a dissertation on sixteenth-century Florence. He came to Jewish history not from the world of religious education, therefore, but from an interest in early modern Europe. He likely turned to Jewish history in the late 1920s because of his inability to find work in his chosen field.[27] Roth lamented the state of the field of Jewish history for its failure to reach broad publics. In private correspondence with Hurwitz, Roth wrote, "I do not belong to the dryasdust [sic] school of history, and I think that all historical work worthy of the name must be accessible to the public."[28] Roth taught at the JIR in New York in 1925 and 1926. He rejected an offer of a full-time appointment there in 1927 after a falling out with JIR founder Rabbi Stephen S. Wise. Roth would not hold another academic appointment until 1939, when he became a Reader in Jewish history at Oxford University. He taught at Oxford for twenty-five years, producing more than 600 works, praised by historians for their accessibility to a broad audience of readers.[29]

In his May 1928 *Menorah Journal* essay, "Jewish History for Our Own Needs," Roth lamented the anemic state of Jewish history writing and argued that "only from an appreciation of his past" could a Jew "be imbued with self-respect and hope for his future." The histories his contemporaries produced were "moribund" and "still-born," Roth wrote.[30] He declared that the time had come for a Jewish history written in English to update Graetz's more than fifty-year-old survey. Roth explained that Graetz's work had been figured too strongly as a response to pressures from the Christian world. He also contended that Graetz focused too exclusively on the Jews of Germany and, with few exceptions, most historians who came after Graetz followed his lead in this regard.[31] "For the last half century," Roth wrote, "bands of earnest students have engaged in inquiries into the bypaths of German-Jewish history."[32] A new history also had to remove German Jews as the central protagonists in order to give more emphasis to American Jewry and to Zionism. "Ordinary" readers, according the Roth, needed to see some of themselves and their own local experiences in the histories they read. Jews in the United States, the majority of whom had ancestry in Russia and Poland, would not even be able to recognize their parents' or grandparents' histories in Graetz and other extant works.

Roth also criticized what he considered the poor writing style common to Jewish history along with its excessively narrow focus. Although other academic historians criticized him for being a popularizer, Roth thought histories should be readable and entertaining for an educated populace. He saved his harshest rebuke in "Jewish History for Our Own Needs" for histories produced by rabbis and theologians: "Jewish history is written and taught today by persons whose education may qualify them to deal with Rabbinical texts, but who have not mastered even the elements of the historian's craft."[33] Both Roth and the *Menorah Journal* editors criticized seminary faculty's teaching of Jewish history. The motivation here might have been personally driven, but only to a point. Roth may have believed he failed to secure a position at JIR because he had not trained at a seminary.[34] He wrote to Henry Hurwitz in 1928: "I couldn't help resenting the imputation that, for a person to teach Jewish history, the only sine qua non is apprenticeship over the folios of the Talmud!"[35]

Nevertheless, Roth's call to remove Jewish history from seminary confines was likely motivated by more than any lingering vendetta. Roth believed that seminarians' histories suffered from their lack of training. "Without special study," Roth claimed, theologians "know nothing of the background of the events about which they presume to write." Theologians search for explanations, whereas historians enter into an ongoing debate, Roth asserted. Theologians' histories emphasized religious ideology and texts rather than social history, or what Roth called "things human." Therefore, Roth urged, "Jewish history must be democratized. Let us leave the rabbis and *parnassim* [administrators] to their disputes, and try to trace the story of Everyjew [*sic*] through the ages."[36] For Roth, the "only hope" lay in training the younger generation to produce Jewish history that would both instill pride in being Jewish and make a significant intellectual contribution to "universal history." He warned of the dire consequences of not producing a new Jewish history: "The eager young Jew with an enthusiasm for things Jewish, but not for a rabbinical career, stands today in a positively dangerous position."[37]

Roth's criticism of the rabbinate echoed the sentiments of *Menorah Journal* editors, especially Hurwitz, Solow, and Elliot Cohen. Hurwitz liked the article so much that he sent a reprint to every member of the Menorah Association Board of Governors, with a note explaining that Roth's piece "indicated clearly the kind of historical research and writing that are essential today for the modern Jew."[38] Solow commended Roth's "Jewish History for Our Own Needs," but urged Roth to state even more boldly the importance of Jewish history for a people without a nation. Solow had written to Roth: "I think it would be well to point out that History is more important to the Jew than to anyone else, because in it he can sink his roots, while others have a bit of solid ground they may call their own, and use for the same purpose."[39] History needed to stand in for the absence of home-land, monuments, and national memory common to other national groups. Solow wrote in an unpublished memo that the historical work that did exist tended to be "wholly apologetic," in a desperate attempt to "'justify' to the American the presence of the Jew in America." This "parochial" approach actually undermined the pluralist project, Solow believed, because it ne-glected the reciprocal influence of Jewish culture and national culture. In this regard, Jews should not be treated as unique, apart from other "such groups as the Italians, Germans and Irish" who were "undergoing similar experiences."[40]

Roth's second important treatment of historiography in the *Menorah Journal* addressed periodization. In April 1929, he lamented that Jewish historians operated in a vacuum, rather than abided by generally accepted standards of periodization of European history when writing Jewish his-tory. In an effort to bring Jewish history into accord with general history, Roth endorsed the dominant paradigm of ancient, medieval, and modern European history, claiming that these divisions also were significant to the telling of Jewish history. As Roth wrote, "The history of the Jewish people marches with that of Europe as a whole, epoch for epoch."[41] Although Roth acknowledged that Jews were originally an Asiatic people, he proposed that they be considered according to the European model, based on the fact that two-thirds of world Jewry resided in Europe by the 1920s. More-over, Roth claimed, half of Jewish history—the past 1,500 years—was pre-dominantly European.[42] Roth here hoped to integrate the telling of Jew-ish history with European history. His implicit contention was that Jewish historians needed to be trained in general world history in order to fully consider the context in which Jews lived. A theologian educated in a semi-nary, Roth implied, lacked the necessary training, and histories produced by theologians lacked the necessary context.

Salo Baron's essays on Jewish historiography in the *Menorah Journal* did not criticize methodology to the same extent that Roth's did, but they an-swered Roth's call for a richly textured social history.[43] Baron, born in Gali-cia in 1895, moved to Vienna during the 1910s. Between 1917 and 1923, he earned doctorates in philosophy, political science, and law at the Univer-sity of Vienna, finding time during that six-year period to be ordained at the Jewish Theological Seminary of Vienna as well. In the mid-1920s, Rabbi Wise invited Baron to JIR in New York, where he remained from 1925 to 1929.[44] Baron would go on to have a distinguished career at Columbia Uni-versity, holding the first Miller Chair in Jewish History beginning in 1930. Baron maintained strong ties to the IMA throughout this period, reviewing submissions to the *Menorah Journal* for the editors and publicly supporting the Columbia University Menorah Society.

Baron's first contribution to the journal was his most important. "Ghetto and Emancipation: Shall We Revise the Traditional View?" appeared in the June 1928 issue, immediately following Roth's "Jewish History for Our Own Needs." Baron's consideration of European Jewish history in this essay challenged commonly held perceptions about the effects of segregated living. Baron here famously coined the term "lachrymose conception" of Jewish history, and he rejected the linear narrative that told Jewish history as a story of progress from the suffering of the Middle Ages to the freedoms of the modern period.[45]

Baron opened "Ghetto and Emancipation" by explaining that Jews' emancipation in Europe had influenced the writing of modern Jewish history more than any other fact. Graetz, Dubnow, and others had treated emancipation as "the dawn of a new day after a nightmare of the deepest horror."[46] A more textured consideration of Jewish life both before and after emancipation revealed deep flaws in this treatment, according to Baron. Although Jews surely did not enjoy equal rights prior to emancipation, Baron challenged standard interpretations in two ways: first, he questioned the claim that Jews suffered more discrimination than other minorities. Second, he posited that Jewish historians erroneously treated the concept of equal rights as a timeless truth, rather than as an idea born primarily out of the French Revolution. Jews lacked political rights before being emancipated, but many peoples, save for nobles and clergy, did as well. In ghettos, Jews married each other freely, established their own courts, and judged their community members according to their own laws. Jews could not own land or join guilds, but Baron pointed out that these options were barred to many others as well. "In origin," Baron wrote, "the Ghetto was an institution that the Jews had found it in their interest to create themselves." Baron also maintained that Jews' autonomy in the ghetto had financial advantages as well as benefits to safety, especially for Jews who were not required to serve in the military. He expressed sympathy with some writers who had sounded "a note of romantic longing towards the Jewish ghetto." He insisted, moreover, that emancipation did not initiate a "Golden Age," even though it reduced some historic obstacles that Jews faced.[47]

In Baron's next contribution, "Nationalism and Intolerance," he extended his previous claims about misinterpretation of Jewish history by reminding readers that the modern tension between "assimilation" and "national persistence" had a precedent. "We fail to recognize," Baron wrote, "that what we experience now is merely a new form of an ancient clash, merely a single phase in a long evolving process."[48] Baron took a long view of Jewish history, beginning in Babylon and continuing to the present day, and he argued that the chief predictor for the treatment of Jews was the host society's state structure. He noted that, in many European lands after 1700, Jews became national citizens while retaining their own culture. The Jewish condition in the United States, however, was always slightly different because the presence of so many other minorities—especially those who were not white—served to make Jews appear more assimilable in comparison. The appearance of assimilability at times led to the fact of assimilation, allowing some Jews to cast off all vestiges of Jewish identity more easily than Jews in European lands. Baron concluded by wondering about the "ultimate solution" to this problem, and by expressing his hope that rising acceptance of minority rights and cultural differences in America would allow Jews to retain their distinctive culture. Baron hypothesized that he was living through a period of "profound transformation in the very essence of the relation between State and nationality."[49] As a rule, Jews were likely to thrive in places where there was an intended separation between citizenship and cultural affiliation, as in the United States. This separation would mitigate against any accusations of dual loyalty at the same time that it put the burden of maintaining Jewish culture squarely on Jews themselves.

In two *Menorah Journal* articles published the following spring, historian Hans Kohn advanced Baron's argument, exploring ideas about nationalism as a response to emancipation.[50] Kohn, not yet thirty years old when these articles were published, would go on to have a distinguished career as a scholar of nationalism, teaching at the New School for Social Research, Smith College, and CCNY, in addition to holding visiting appointments at many other universities.[51] In his April 1930 *Menorah Journal* article, "The Jew Enters Western Culture," Kohn disparaged the Reform movement in both Germany and the United States for too readily casting aside Jewish traditions, effectively severing Jews from their collective past and leaving them rootless. His private opinion on the matter was particularly scathing, as revealed in a 1931 letter to Hurwitz. Kohn wrote: "There may even come a day when America's Reform Rabbis . . . will not be shy to speak on God and Judaism . . . instead on [sic] new plays on Broadway, on books of the day (and not longer than a day) or on business. Then—perhaps even in American Jewry—the true position of a Rabbi will not be measured by the salary he gets or the niceties of his golf or bridge, but by the sanctity of his life and power of his message of God."[52]

In his published work, especially an essay titled "The Teaching of Moses Hess," Kohn declared that Judaism had reached its "lowest ebb" in Germany during the 1870s and 1880s because of the extent to which Jews at that time collectively strived to emulate their Christian neighbors. Into this story of decline entered Kohn's hero, Moses Hess, an early Zionist thinker. Hess taught that Jewish people must preserve their nationality—even in exile— in preparation for the establishment of a Jewish state.[53] According to Kohn, Hess demonstrated the reality that Zionism was set "within the framework of humanity as a whole." Jews needed to be educated about Zionism, Hess taught, while emphasizing that a Jewish nation was not an end in itself but instead a means to "the social education of the entire human race."[54] Having their own nation-state would increase Jews' self-awareness in the Diaspora, and would allow them to simultaneously embrace traditions and modernity. Kohn's treatment of Hess made the case for the Menorah Association's cause—a movement that supported a cultural renaissance and a national homeland, even one that did not require Jews to move to Palestine, would reconnect Jews with their history, increase self-awareness among youth, and ultimately unify world Jewry. As Kohn indicated, Jews' "escape" from their past must be corrected by a "return" through a national homeland.[55]

Cecil Roth encapsulated the IMA's stance on Jewish history in a lecture to inaugurate the 1930 session of the Menorah Summer School. Roth told students to learn their past in order to guide their future. He explained that the modern attenuation of Jewish culture had not occurred because of rampant antisemitism, but rather was due to the indifference of Jews themselves.[56] He would build on this point two years later, arguing that portraying Jews solely as a persecuted minority removed Jews' agency from their own history and grossly misrepresented the past.[57] The decay of Jewish culture would be solved through what Roth termed the "eternity and indestructibility" of the Jewish people. As Roth told his audience, "The Jewish people has withstood the action of thirty centuries and it is not to be imagined that it will suddenly collapse at the thirty-first."[58]

"Pomegranates"

Declaring the need for a new historiography constituted one branch of the Menorah Association's vision for a Jewish cultural renaissance. The *Menorah Journal*'s editors also turned their attention to the contemporary scene, commenting critically upon Jewish life in the United States. This commentary, which often focused on what the authors perceived as the failure of American Jews to engage intellectually with Jewish culture, was deemed especially important by the magazine's editors because, as they recognized, "the center of gravity and influence in world Jewry" was shifting.[59] Forty years of immigration to the United States had precipitated profound changes in the balance of the world's Jewish population, and the editors insisted that American Jews therefore had to assume new responsibilities. These responsibilities were not solely financial or philanthropic, but also cultural and political.

During the 1920s, a new group of editors joined the *Menorah Journal*'s staff, and the most frequently explored topics shifted to a more critical assessment of modern Jewish life. Both Adolph S. Oko and Harry A. Wolfson became associate editors in 1921. Marvin Lowenthal, who previously worked for Zionist organizations in America, also signed on as an associate editor. Two editors who sparked particular controversy were Elliot Cohen, managing editor from 1925 to 1931, and Solow, assistant editor from 1928 to 1929 and contributing editor from 1929 to 1931. Although Hurwitz remained the editor in title, Cohen in particular became more involved in the day-to-day operations of the magazine than any staff member ever had or would. During Cohen's seven-year tenure as managing editor, the journal transformed itself from a chronicler of Jewish life on campuses and promoter of cultural pluralism into a forum for lively debate about the state of world Jewry, religion and secularism, and Zionism.

The incendiary articles published regularly in the *Menorah Journal* during the 1920s had a precedent. In 1918, Wolfson penned two columns under the pseudonym "El. Lycidas," the Greek translation of his Hebrew name, Zvi Wolfson.[60] These columns, titled "Pomegranates," consisted of brief reflections on the modern Jewish condition. Wolfson explained the title with the epigraph he chose from the *Jewish Encyclopedia:* "Pomegranates are eaten raw, their acid juice being most refreshing."[61] By describing his columns as "raw," Wolfson signaled his intention to reveal the unprocessed and unbiased condition of American Jewry without manipulation from his own pen. Of course, Wolfson's observations were anything but innocently presented, and the "acid juice" he promised exposed his desire to provoke his readers.

What one biographer describes as Wolfson's "Puck-like quality of mind" emerged in these short commentaries as they did not in his academic writing.[62] He used the columns to defend the IMA against critics and to condemn American Jews for blindly following every passing cultural preoccupation of the day, but he saved his harshest criticisms in "Pomegranates" for those he described as "The Yiddish People," or more often the "Yidds." "The Yidds" were a people clearly distinguishable from "the Jews," Wolfson explained. The distinction was more than between those who spoke Yiddish and those who spoke English, although that did separate the two

Harry A. Wolfson.
*Courtesy of the Jacob Rader Marcus Center of
the American Jewish Archives.*

peoples. More important, Yidds and Jews were divided by class, culture, and politics. Wolfson was particularly offended by the Yidds' socialist politics. Yidds were tribal people, driven by individualism and vengefulness, while Jews were nationalist, motivated by altruistic ideals, such as the establishment of a Jewish state for the good of world Jewry.[63]

Yidds' "morality," according to Wolfson's observations of "their newspapers, their stage, their talks and discussions in workshops and clubs," was "essentially the product of twentieth-century slums and Bohemias." The Yidds' "spirit is fed on ignorance, on risqué literature, and on tainted dilutions of the anti-social heresies of the time." Jews, in contrast, created and embraced Hebrew literature and Jewish traditions.[64]

Wolfson's harsh rebuke of "Yidds" peaked in his last "Pomegranates" installment, "Palestine and the Undesirables." Wolfson argued that the division between Jews and Yidds must not cripple the Zionist movement. He evoked Abraham Lincoln by counseling against building a nation of both Jews and Yidds with a "household divided against itself." He concluded, "We shall be recreant to our national duty if we do not adopt at once drastic measures to exclude the Yiddish undesirables from Palestine."[65]

The editors' perceived superiority over America's "new immigrant" Jews was never more starkly stated in their magazine.[66] Perhaps Wolfson wrote with such vitriol because he, like many of those most active in the Menorah Association's founding, traced his own ancestry to eastern European Jews and wanted to distance himself from this past in order to portray himself as an inheritor of German Jewish traditions and customs. The irony here is especially striking: as Jewish philosopher and historian Gershom Scholem commented in 1979, Wolfson "remained essentially a Yeshiva Bocher," even after spending almost his entire life at Harvard.[67] Moreover, according to another scholar, when Wolfson was a Harvard undergraduate, Kallen "corrected Wolfson's English grammar, and removed the Yiddishisms from his essays."[68] Kallen himself responded well to "Pomegranates" but warned Wolfson in a February 1918 letter: "The manner is too irritating for those who do not agree with you and what is needed is persuasion."[69]

Wolfson eventually heeded Kallen's suggestion when writing "Escaping Judaism," an essay that Wolfson published under his own name in the June 1921 *Menorah Journal*. Here, Wolfson struggled in a more tempered way with the conflict between assimilating and maintaining Jewish identity. He criticized those Jews who felt they needed to escape Judaism in order to live a meaningful intellectual life. Still, the "Yiddish masses" remained his primary target. Wolfson wrote that "Yiddishized masses are gradually becoming a new, distinct people" from the Jews.[70] He urged his readers instead to focus on the types of cultural and aesthetic satisfaction being offered by the Menorah Association rather than by the Yiddish masses. He also sought to offer something constructive to his readers by taking a long view of Jewish history. Modern Jews surely faced a new test, but, throughout their Diaspora history, Jews always met the challenges associated with living as a minority within any society. The modern American experience would be no different if Jews made some sacrifices, including choosing loyalty to Judaism and Jewish culture over the temptations and trappings of the moment.

To demonstrate the point, Wolfson focused on the world he knew best—Harvard. Each autumn, Jewish students at Harvard complained to an unsympathetic president, A. Lawrence Lowell, about entrance exams that coincided with the holiest days of the Jewish calendar. Wolfson expressed no sympathy for these students, arguing that they had no right to complain about qualifying exams on Yom Kippur, when, on most other occasions, they "defile" themselves with non-kosher food and fail to observe the Sabbath. These students, according to Wolfson, needed to skip the qualifying exams in favor of attending synagogue, stop complaining about the conflict, and realize that being Jewish in a meaningful way demanded the willingness to make such a sacrifice. These young men could live in the Harvard (or, by extension, the elite American) world, Wolfson claimed, without casting off their past entirely in order to do so. Jews need not ignore modernity, but embracing modernity should not entail ignoring Jewish commandments and culture. Wolfson hoped "Jews" would learn this lesson, but doubted that those he labeled "the Yiddish people" ever would.[71]

"The Adversary's Notebook"

Like Wolfson's, Marvin Lowenthal's outlook was shaped in part by time spent with Kallen. Raised in a Reform Jewish household in Bradford, Pennsylvania, Lowenthal entered the University of Wisconsin–Madison in 1912 at the age of twenty-one. There he met Kallen, an instructor in philosophy and psychology, who was in the midst of publishing on Zionism, Hebraism, and pluralism. At the request of Louis Brandeis and Jacob de Haas, the former secretary to Theodor Herzl and one of Brandeis's most trusted advisors, Lowenthal moved to San Francisco in 1916 to become head of the Zionist Bureau of the Pacific Coast. In 1919, Kallen urged Lowenthal to return, telling his former student that his talents "do not lie in the direction of money raising," and that he had "a moral obligation" to develop his "literary powers, both because they are your own and for the good of the cause."[72] Lowenthal eventually did move east to write for the *Dial,* the *New Republic,* the *Nation,* and the *Menorah Journal.* He would become best known for translating the seventeenth-century *Glückel of Hameln* (1932), compiling the *Life and Letters of Henrietta Szold* (1942), and editing and translating the *Diaries of Theodor Herzl* (1956).[73]

Lowenthal became one of the most prolific *Menorah Journal* writers during the 1920s, contributing more than a dozen articles as well as thirty-one installments of the mischievous "Adversary's Notebook" column, which ran from June 1921 until February 1927. These first-person columns—the same series that called for a replacement to Graetz's history in 1921—included "man on the street" observations about political, social, and cultural matters relevant to Jewish life. Lowenthal wrote the series under the pseudonym "H. Ben-Shahar," by which he meant to evoke Lucifer.[74]

In the first six installments of "The Adversary's Notebook," which focused on the Jewish condition in the United States, Lowenthal sought to foster pride in Jewish culture. He playfully yet stridently praised Jews' cultural creativity and poked fun at Jews who viewed every social and historical problem solely through a Jewish lens. The first few items in the April 1922 "Adversary's Notebook," for example, considered the dilemma that Jews faced in acquiring wine for religious ceremonies under Prohibition, which began in 1920. Lowenthal comically reported on a Jewish wine company owner who fretted over how to determine if his clients with non-Jewish names were Jews who had tried to blend in to the American scene or gentiles trying to circumvent Prohibition.[75] In the fashion typical to these columns, Lowenthal explored the serious side of an otherwise humorous anecdote by musing on the malleability of Jewish identity and emphasizing that American Jews were involved in a "struggle to adjust our national habits of thought and action to an alien world, and yet preserve them."[76] In so doing, he successfully mocked Jews' anxieties in a way that exposed the simultaneous seriousness and absurdity of their concerns.

When "the Adversary" turned to the Jewish condition across the Atlantic, he could not remain lighthearted. Lowenthal moved to Europe in February 1922, traveling extensively for the next decade in his capacity as the European editor of the *Menorah Journal.* The prevailing sentiment of his European "Adversary's Notebook" columns can be described as wonderment at the ghostlike quality of a once vibrant Jewish culture mixed with anger about antisemitism. Lowenthal wrote of the shadows of Jewish life in Western European centers, countering antisemitism with biting sar-

Marvin Lowenthal, 1930.
*Courtesy of the Jacob Rader Marcus Center of
the American Jewish Archives.*

casm. Commenting on his Atlantic passage, for example, Lowenthal wrote, "If a ship carries five hundred passengers, with one Jew, it carries a Jewish problem."[77]

As Lowenthal moved east through Europe, he witnessed a degree of antisemitism he had never previously observed, and his tone changed dramatically. Visiting Berlin in 1922 obviously had a deep impact. Lowenthal must have sensed that the typical sarcasm of "The Adversary's Notebook" was not appropriate for the political realities he encountered there. While he continued to deliver the "Adversary's" series, Lowenthal also wrote a four-part article for the *Menorah Journal* entitled "The Jew in the European Scene."[78] He warned that weakening economic conditions had led to an increase in antisemitism, the likes of which would shock his readers. In Germany, Lowenthal heard from many "regular citizens" that the Jews had failed to do their part for the German side during World War I. In response to this "stab in the back" propaganda that effectively blamed Jews for Germany's ills, Lowenthal wryly noted, "Everything but the weather was blamed on the Jews."[79]

The few notes of sarcasm that lingered in his writing disappeared as he moved east to Bavaria, where he witnessed the new National Socialist (Nazi) Party and the fervor of its young leader, Adolf Hitler. Throughout Berlin and Bavaria, Lowenthal reported, it had become increasingly easy to purchase hate literature in stores. Violence against Jews, in the form of desecration of Jewish cemeteries, was also rising. In an eerily prophetic (and surely unintended) conclusion to his coverage of Germany, Lowenthal warned that if the government shifted any further to the right, "the Jews are in the fire."[80]

In his last two installments of "The Jew in the European Scene," Lowenthal informed his readers that antisemitism in Berlin was matched in Lithuania, Poland, Yugoslavia, Rumania, and Latvia. In Vienna, efforts were underway to bar Jews from universities, which in turn would preclude their entrance into professions in Austrian society. Lowenthal treated this same subject in a *Nation* article of November 14, 1923, turning a common antisemitic trope on its head by arguing that the "universities are poisoning the wells" of Europe, fostering hatred just as fervently as nationalist leaders.[81] He also commented that the two hours he spent in Poland was two hours too long for any Jew.

The series ended on a pessimistic note: increasing nationalist sentiment singled out Jews for all Europe's miseries. Lowenthal detected a "concerted effort to drive [Jews] into a new ghetto" in the countries he visited. He presented Zionism as an imperfect solution to these problems, and he argued that European Jews who continued to advocate acculturating into their host societies were sorely misguided. He called on American Jews to vigorously protest the treatment of their European brethren. Giving money and promoting Jewish culture may not be enough. What European Jews desperately needed, Lowenthal concluded, were "munitions for a siege."[82] Readers likely could not miss the subtext of Lowenthal's series—that the current and future center where Jews could live freely and develop their own culture was the United States.

Although antisemitism in the United States paled in comparison with that in Europe, the heyday of the *Menorah Journal* coincided with a rise in antisemitism unlike any other era of the century. Discrimination against Jews went far beyond elite universities seeking to keep Jewish students from enrolling. Beginning in the late 1910s, proponents of the "Red Scare" portrayed Jews and Bolsheviks as synonymous. The Ku Klux Klan experienced a resurgence in the 1920s. Henry Ford's *Dearborn Independent* aided the reissue of *The Protocols of the Elders of Zion,* a forged document "proving" Jews' intentions to dominate the world, as well as its own series of articles entitled *The International Jew: The World's Foremost Problem.*[83]

For all its coverage of challenges to Jews abroad, only a few articles in the *Menorah Journal* focused on antisemitism on the American scene. When the editors did take note of antisemitism at home, they tended to mock it. A single article warning of Henry Ford's activities in 1920 called his antisemitic rants "amusing" and claimed that only a "really good fool" would believe his lies about Jews.[84] An occasional piece on the psychological "malady" of antisemitism would appear, but the journal rarely commented directly on increasing nativism and antisemitism in the United States during the 1920s. The editors did not have anything to say, for example, about Father Charles Coughlin, Michigan's increasingly popular, antisemitic radio priest.[85]

This absence is notable for what it reveals about pluralism. The Menorah Association, from its earliest days, relied on a logic of cultural pluralism that portrayed being American and being Jewish as complementary. The editors surely could have reported on antisemitism as an anti-American phenomenon, but they chose instead more often to criticize American Jews for their faults than to defend them against accusers. Their choice to either ignore or poke fun at antisemitism on their home soil signaled a hope that, as pluralism emerged as the modern response to cultural difference in the United States, antisemitism and other forms of discrimination would be regarded as out of step with modernity.

Elliot Cohen's "Notes for a Modern History of the Jews"

Beginning in the mid-1920s, the *Menorah Journal* editors' criticism of American Jewish culture became more strident, in large part because of Cohen's influence as managing editor. Cohen's upbringing did not resemble that of his colleagues. He was neither raised nor educated on the East Coast of the United States.[86] Born in Iowa in 1899 and raised in Mobile, Alabama, Cohen—described as a "prodigy from birth"—matriculated to Yale at age fifteen.[87] He later downplayed speculation that his childhood experiences separated him from his peers. As Cohen told a journalist in 1949, he was like many of his contemporaries in that "there was only one thing important in my family. Books."[88] Cohen's childhood was more complicated than he let on in that interview. His father, an immigrant to the United States, opened a dry goods store in Mobile. The elder Cohen studied Jewish texts at home, but also conducted business on the Sabbath. Other tensions between maintaining religious observance and accommodating American practices pervaded Cohen's childhood home to the extent that he emerged, in the words of historian Lauren B. Strauss, "deeply scornful of both Reform and Orthodox Judaism, charging the first with displaying overweening zeal in imitating the trappings of American life and the second with spiritual stagnation."[89] This dissatisfaction with Judaism would inform many of Cohen's works for the *Menorah Journal*.

Cohen served as the president of the Yale Menorah Society during his senior year, 1917–1918. While an undergraduate, he wrote "The Promise of the American Synagogue," which won the award for the best essay by a member of a collegiate Menorah society. The essay spelled out Cohen's hopes for both Reform and Orthodox Judaism. He surmised that Judaism must "appeal strongly to the modern man" or be doomed. Orthodox Judaism faced the greatest challenge in this regard because its practices had become "foreign to modern American conditions." Reform Judaism confronted a different but "equally gloomy" future because social functions and charitable services had begun to dominate the denomination's activities.[90] Cohen wrote that religion, in order to become more modern, had to become more "democratic," by which he meant that Judaism had to appeal to a larger portion of American Jews.

Judaism could meet this challenge, Cohen claimed, if synagogues and rabbis made significant adjustments to organizational life and provided real leadership. Cohen described the ideal synagogue as "the community center of all Jewish activities."[91] Here, he borrowed from Rabbi Mordecai M. Kaplan, best known for his 1934 book *Judaism as a Civilization*. In a June 1916

Menorah Journal article, Kaplan wrote that the synagogue must become "a social centre where the Jews of the neighborhood may find every possible opportunity to give expression to their social and play instincts."[92] Echoing Kaplan, Cohen emphasized that rabbis would have to redefine their role as leaders of American Jews. He implied that the successful rabbi to the modern Jew would have to be a sage, a saint, and a proficient executive all rolled into one. By the time Cohen became managing editor of the journal, however, this youthful idealism that characterized his prizewinning essay would disappear. He instead reveled in cleverly articulated excoriations of the Reform movement.

After graduating from Yale at age eighteen, Cohen continued there as a graduate student in the English department for five years. The near impossibility of a Jew gaining an appointment to a university English department in the 1920s probably contributed to Cohen's failure to pursue his dissertation as avidly as he otherwise might have. Cohen also suffered from perpetual writer's block, although it is not clear whether this dated all the way back to his time in graduate school.[93] He left Yale in 1923 and found his niche in New York, working at the *Menorah Journal* from 1924 until 1931. In 1945, he became the founding editor of *Commentary* magazine, a post he held until he committed suicide in 1959.

Following Cohen's death, Lionel Trilling remembered him as a man obsessed with the "subtle interrelations that exist between seemingly disparate parts of culture."[94] Cohen's successor at *Commentary,* Norman Podhoretz, agreed. Recalling the first time he met Cohen at the *Commentary* editorial offices, Podhoretz wrote, "In the first hour I spent with [Cohen] he jumped from literary criticism to politics, from politics to Jewish scholarship, from Jewish scholarship to the movies, from the movies to sports, and indeed spent a good deal of time trying to find out how much I knew about baseball."[95]

These qualities that Trilling and Podhoretz described were most evident in Cohen's *Menorah Journal* series, "Notes for a Modern History of the Jews." Between 1924 and 1927, Cohen conducted a study of Jewish life in America by bringing together already published items from the Jewish press, announcements from Jewish organizations, and bits and pieces from rabbis' sermons. Cohen never interjected his own voice into this series. Instead, he highlighted contradiction and ambiguity in his source material by carefully and often ironically juxtaposing quotations to construct a fragmented narrative that mocked the prevailing concerns of American Jewish authorities. These painstakingly crafted columns sought to deflate American Jewish leaders' grandiose claims about American Jews' excep-

Elliot Cohen.
Courtesy of the American Jewish Committee, New York.

tionalism, combat stereotypes about Jews, and question community leaders' priorities.

Cohen's columns deserve attention not only because of his pointed criticism of American Jewry, but also because of the form that he adopted to
articulate his opinions. Similar to other literary works produced during
the 1920s and 1930s, "Notes for a Modern History of the Jews" also resemble quintessentially modern forms of cultural production emerging in
the visual arts during the 1920s, especially photomontage.[96] Guided by his
incisive wit, Cohen's juxtaposition of artifact quotations used authors' own
words to carry out a rebellious style of criticism. Cohen's columns are akin
to photomontage in the way that they take decontextualized scraps from
already published mass media to compile a new whole. Like photomontages, Cohen's columns startle the viewer/reader by presenting words in new
and unexpected formats.[97] His achievements in compiling these columns—
undermining simplistic stereotypes about Jews, criticizing American rabbis, and questioning the priorities of American Jewry as a whole—all contributed to a larger desire to realign the center of American Jewish life and
culture. By positioning himself as the compiler of truth—after all, he was
merely quoting others' words—Cohen sought to expose what he and his
colleagues perceived as the false rhetoric endemic to so much of American Jewish life.[98]

Cohen was not the only cultural critic to use this format at this time. He
idolized perhaps the greatest American satirist of the 1920s, *American Mercury* editor H. L. Mencken. In the first issue of the *American Mercury,* published just one month before Cohen's first "Notes" installment, Mencken
authored his first "Americana" column, which extracted items from local
presses in various states and coupled these items with Mencken's charac-
teristically biting commentary.[99] The technique caught on elsewhere: three
years after Cohen's final "Notes" column appeared, novelist John Dos Passos used a similar style in his *U.S.A.* trilogy in sections entitled "Newsreels," which combined popular song lyrics, full paragraphs from newspaper stories, and headlines of the day.[100] While Cohen's "Notes" columns
surely took inspiration from Mencken and may have foreshadowed Dos
Passos's "Newsreels," there is no evidence to suggest that Cohen knew of
Walter Benjamin's contemporary *Arcades Project,* a well-documented effort
to critically examine modern life through a montage of previously published quotations.[101]

Cohen opened his first "Notes for a Modern History of the Jews" column
in the February 1924 *Menorah Journal* with the following stream of extracts:

"The Jews exist to safeguard monotheism for the world."—*Rabbi Nathan Krass*. . . . Joseph Diamond and 'Whitey' Diamond have confessed to planning and helping execute the robbery and murder of two bank messengers in Borough Park, Brooklyn. . . . Ellis S. Joseph, the world's foremost collector of rare animals, has arrived in New York with an assortment of 58 Australian camels, 97 kangaroos, 3 lions, 12 Tasmanian devils, 12 wombats, a leopard, a tiger, and many snakes. . . . Miss Sophia Waldman of the George Washington University Girls Rifle Teams scored 100 in a match with the University of Maryland . . . Of two thousand actors engaged on the legitimate stage last year two hundred were Jews. . . . The whist team of the Cosmos Club, claimants of the championship of Roxbury and Dorchester (Mass.), challenge any team. Harry Miller and H. Flashner are the captain and manager. Any club desiring games please address the Cosmos Club, care of Jewish Welfare Center, Intervale St., Roxbury. . . . Nathan Rothschild, head of the London branch of the famous banking family, died recently leaving a collection of 70,000 fleas to the British museum.[102]

After contrasting Rabbi Krass's lofty understanding of Jews' purpose in life with Jewish criminals, animal collectors, rifle champions, performers, card players, and flea collectors, Cohen continued on for another two pages, juxtaposing quotations on weighty matters of science with a pastiche of quotes about Jewish strongmen, incidents of antisemitism, and the "Santa Claus craving" common amongst Jewish children.

Cohen hoped that "Notes for a Modern History of the Jews" would undermine stereotypes that contributed to antisemitism, an urgent task in an era of resurgent immigration restriction, anti-radicalism, and Anglo-Saxonism. Henry Ford, the Ku Klux Klan, and American Jewish Committee founder Louis Marshall made appearances in Cohen's first "Notes" installment of February 1924:

"We Jews are happy in America and contented with conditions. We don't care for Ford and the Ku Kluxes. We don't notice them."—*Louis Marshall*. . . . "Louis Marshall devoted a large part of his annual report as President of the American Jewish Committee to a spirited attack on the Ku Klux Klan."—*The American Israelite*[103]

Although the reader's first reaction to such an obvious contradiction might have been a confused shake of the head, Cohen's fear about American antisemitism underlies this couplet of quotations. As he exposed the contradictions in the rhetoric of one of American Jewry's most prominent leaders, Cohen also suggested that deflecting attention from the Klan could not mask real anxieties.

Cohen specifically combated age-old stereotypes about Jews. For example, he followed a quote from a non-Jewish business owner who had "never found [Jews] remarkable for cleanliness" with the following: "The president of the Pennsylvania State Association of Master Plumbers recently said that Jewish young men are the most scrupulously clean in the United States, judging from the amount of shower baths and fixtures sold to Jewish institutions."[104] In this juxtaposition, the absurdity of the "evidence" for Jews' superior cleanliness is exceeded only by that used to support the claim that Jews are dirtier than others. Only if one can believe the premise that sales of plumbing fixtures to Jews "proves" their cleanliness can one accept the claim about Jews being dirtier than other people.

An avid sports fan, Cohen saved his most vigorous attacks on anti-semitism for the stereotype of Jewish men as weak and frail. Sociologist E. A. Ross (the target of Kallen's criticism in the 1915 *Nation* magazine article "Democracy Versus the Melting Pot") had written in 1913 that "Hebrews are the polar opposite of our pioneer breed," and described Jews as "undersized," "weak-muscled," and "exceedingly sensitive to pain."[105] In response, Cohen littered his columns with instances of Jewish physical triumphs in track and field, football, wrestling, and boxing.[106] Most common were straightforward reports of male athletic prowess. In the February 1925 column, for example, Cohen included three consecutive items that introduced his readers to three Jewish boxing champions.[107] Cohen's focus on Jewish physical triumphs accomplished even more than negating a stereotype in the realm of athletics. For, as scholar Sander Gilman has persuasively argued, the stereotype of Jewish weakness often stands in for beliefs about "Jews' inability to serve as a citizen."[108] By emphasizing Jewish athleticism, Cohen tacitly asserted that Jewish men were as strong as all other American laborers, and, should the call come, would serve in the military just as well as any other American citizen.

Cohen did not neglect women's victories, either. He closed a 1926 installment of the "Notes" column with Sonia Witkoff, an eighteen-year-old Russian who "can meet and beat any man in a Greco-Roman wrestling match and is also a serious opponent for any athlete in the world in the weight lifting and long distance running event." He simultaneously emphasized and undermined Witkoff in the next and final item of this installment, which read, "'Grand and glorious are the achievements of the Jewess beautiful wherever she abides.'—*American Hebrew*."[109]

Even as he effectively dismantled antisemitic stereotypes, Cohen saved his harshest criticism for American Jews themselves. Country clubs, fund-raising drives, and Christmas celebrations were among Cohen's favorite targets to demonstrate what he interpreted as the excessive materialism and waywardness endemic to American Jewry.[110] The examples are numerous; consider the following as representative. In a 1924 "Notes for a Modern History of the Jews" column, Cohen allowed the following item to stand on its own without comment from surrounding snippets: "'With four country clubs to its credit, Philadelphia Jewry is certainly entitled to rank as a leading Jewish center.'—*Jewish Exponent*."[111] Materialism and status had begun to stand in for meaningful intellectual culture in American Jewish life.

Many of Cohen's readers, especially the rabbis, were not amused. Rabbi Horace J. Wolf of Rochester, New York, condemned the "bad taste shown by the publication of such cheap material by a Journal which simultaneously solicited the support of the American rabbinate."[112] Rabbi Wolf promptly cancelled his subscription. Many other rabbis also pulled their own and their congregational support for the *Menorah Journal,* citing Cohen's column among their many reasons for growing disillusionment. Even Nathan Isaacs, a professor of law at Harvard and one of the most dedicated supporters of the IMA, lambasted Cohen: "You know as well as I do how much more you have loved acerbity than accuracy."[113] Cohen ignored Isaacs's warning, and the rift between Cohen and American rabbis continued to grow.

"Why Do the Heathen Rage?"

The scorn for Reform rabbis and the distress over American Jews' lack of interest in Jewish culture was not confined to Cohen's columns. Writing in his own words in 1925, Cohen labeled the modern Jewish era "The Age of Brass." As he explained, "By an Age of Brass we mean simply an age that substitutes rhetoric for knowledge, bold assertions for learning, vainglorious pretensions for soundly-based convictions, bluster for strength, and braggadocio for an inwardly felt security."[114] Cohen claimed that assimilated Jews who had little knowledge of Jewish religion or culture favored achievement over learning.

Cohen did not hold back in "The Age of Brass." He attacked Jewish leadership in business, social services, and religion as vacuous, narcissistic, and shallow. Cohen claimed that he did not want to blame "the present low state of the Jewish life in America" on the rabbis, but, in almost the same breath, he indicted American rabbis for "a too meek acquiescence in the degradation of the rabbinical function to that of a spokesman—i.e., mouthpiece—of the ignorance, ambitions, and fears of the influential Jewish laity."[115] Cohen did not give up on religion entirely; instead he yearned for sincere leadership by the rabbinate. This leadership, Cohen hoped, would emerge as a product of a vibrant intellectual and cultural renaissance spearheaded by the Menorah Association.

Like many other writers who published in the *Menorah Journal* during its heyday, Cohen longed for the development of a more meaningful American Jewish culture. He put his faith in the Menorah Association's call for a cultural renaissance, but he offered little practical direction to his readers. At this stage in his career, Cohen more easily mocked Jews rather than explained how to achieve a rebirth of Jewish culture. The montage form of critique that Cohen employed in "Notes for a Modern History of the Jews" and the accusatory tone of "The Age of Brass" were perfect for exploring the absurdities of Jews, but they offered no plan for addressing the hard choices between assimilation and revitalization.

"The Age of Brass" ran in the *Menorah Journal* during the same twelve-month period as two other highly critical and controversial articles. In April and December 1925, Kallen published a two-part article with the provocative title, "Can Judaism Survive in the United States?" In February 1926, Hurwitz also assessed the state of American Jewry in "Watchmen, What of the Day?" Together, Cohen, Kallen, and Hurwitz would exacerbate emerging conflicts between the *Menorah Journal* and leading Reform rabbis, especially Cleveland's prominent rabbi, Abba Hillel Silver.

Kallen's article opened with a story about his chance meeting on a train with a former student who had become a successful businessperson. The young man was blond and blue eyed. Kallen wrote, "Whether this young man was a Jew not even the most sensitive and expert taste in Nordics could determine." Nevertheless, "There seemed to be a suggestion of Jew in the feel of him—something in his expression."[116] Kallen's deepest anxieties about American Jews were encapsulated in this physical description alone. The relative ease of passing as gentile inhered in the man's physical attributes, yet a feeling of connectedness to other Jews lingered.

Beyond describing him physically, Kallen portrayed the young man as representative of the American Jewish condition more generally. The young man was a member of a synagogue, but he did not attend very often. He did not care for the rabbi but he sent his children to religious school out of obligation. Most of his friends were Jewish. Relationships he had with Christians were strictly formal but without conflict. Kallen's assessment of the situation verged on the hopeless: "He was stranded, alone, between the Jews he could not warm to and the Christians who would not warm to him." The metaphors became increasingly melodramatic. This young man was "entangled in the network of the crossing strands of American life like a honey bee in a spider's web."[117] After parting with this man, Kallen wondered to himself (and to his reader, of course), "Can Judaism Survive in the United States?"

Kallen then moved beyond the specific case of his former student to offer some solutions to ensure Jewish survival. Modern America did not contain any institutional anchor for Jewish group life, Kallen argued. Synagogues did not provide Jews with the spiritual sustenance or communal ties for which many longed. "Judaism," Kallen declared, "tends to be no more than a survival worn down to dietary intolerances, an occasional *kaddish* for the dead, and perhaps a ticket admitting to synagog or hall on Rosh Hashana and Yom Kippur." Young Jewish adults did not care about the Hebrew language or the "transmission of Judaism to their children" as their ancestors had. "Concerning Judaism, the young listen and look and turn away."[118] The only hope for Jewish survival in the United States, Kallen wrote, rested with Jewish educational institutions, which had to teach children about the pleasures of Jewish life, making Jewish identity an active commitment rather than a passive burden. Because Jewish youth had so many options in the marketplace of potential affiliations, Jewish institutions had to entice young men and women to join. One monumental problem to be overcome on Kallen's path was the many conflicts within and between Jewish organizations and denominations. American Jews, Kallen argued, were "too bitter against each other to combine even against non-Jewish competitors."[119]

Kallen blamed rabbis for both the failures of educational institutions and the internal divisiveness of organizational life. He cited three seminaries— Jewish Theological Seminary, HUC, and JIR—as out of touch with the needs and realities of modern Jews. These seminaries educated rabbis in a deeply flawed way; they produced graduates who learned about "historical Judaism" as a "dead antiquity." Rabbis actually were being trained in a manner that ensured they remained out of touch with the needs of modern Jews. The Reform synagogue, according to Kallen, also failed to provide Jews with either the spiritual sustenance or communal ties for which many longed.[120] Finally, the Reform movement's official rejection of Zionism further fueled Kallen's criticism of the denomination as out of sync with the needs of world Jewry.[121]

Kallen returned to Hebraism, the broadly conceived sense of Jewish identity, to argue that rabbis neglected the "total fullness of the life of the Jewish people." Although he expressed little hope in seminaries, Kallen insisted that they must change their curricula to ensure survival: "For it is Judaism that must return to the Jew, not the Jew to Judaism."[122] If seminaries could not modernize, rabbis could not lead effectively, and the future of the Jewish people would remain in peril. Kallen closed with a pessimistic barb: "I confess, sadly, that I have no great confidence that anybody who has the means and the power will also have the imagination and the courage to try to do it."[123]

In February 1926, two months after publishing Kallen's bleak assessment, *Menorah Journal* editor Henry Hurwitz proposed a more optimistic solution to modern Jewish problems in an article titled "Watchmen, What of the Day?" Hurwitz's title echoed at least two sources. First, the question "Watchman, What of the Night?" appears in Isaiah 21:11. Second, in Carnegie Hall on October 14, 1923, Israel Zangwill had delivered an address to the American Jewish Congress titled, "Watchman, What of the Night?" In the speech, Zangwill stridently criticized the AJC and American Jews for their failure to commit resources beyond philanthropy to the Zionist movement.[124]

Hurwitz began by reviewing the litany of charges made by Cohen and Kallen: American Jewish life had become all "brass" but remained hollow on the inside. Jews' financial priorities did not adequately address the most pressing issues for world Jewry. American Jews lacked leadership.[125]

Hurwitz agreed that philanthropic and institutional aspects of American Jewish life were not enough to ensure continuity, but he would not endorse Kallen's doomsday prophecy. Predictably, he cited the Menorah Association's program as vital to the renaissance of American Jewry. "A people lives indeed through its creative individuals," Hurwitz wrote, "its thinkers, scholars, writers, artists." If these individuals were nurtured instead of neglected, the future of Jewish culture would be assured. Hurwitz then reiterated the initiatives that already would have been familiar to a regular reader of the *Menorah Journal*—schools and foundations for Jewish historical study, general scholarship, art, publishing, and all forms of culture. This "passion for creative Judaism" would solve the problems cataloged by Cohen and Kallen.[126]

One of the first responses to Hurwitz's call came from Rabbi Mordecai M. Kaplan, who praised Hurwitz for writing a statement about Jews' "cultural needs that has body to it." He criticized the total vision, however, as a "tire" without a "hub." The hub of a Jewish cultural renaissance, Kaplan insisted, must be religious institutions. Yet Kaplan was not uncritical of seminaries. "If the Jewish seminaries and colleges would do their work not with an eye to numbers and prestige, but with a regard to high cultural standards and the future of Judaism," Kaplan wrote privately to Hurwitz, "Jewish culture, such as you so eloquently plead for, would experience a rena-scence."[127] Hurwitz disagreed. He wrote to Kaplan a few weeks later, telling the rabbi that he "cannot see how the theological seminaries can meet the situation."[128] A new type of humanistic school, not only for future clergy but also for lay people, was in order. Hurwitz remained stubbornly com-mitted to this point, despite the likelihood of alienating those rabbis who otherwise might have been sympathetic to his call.

Responses from other rabbis and from seminary administrators were not as generous as Kaplan's. Julian Morgenstern, the president of HUC in Cincinnati, took the opportunity to criticize Hurwitz's article as well as the *Menorah Journal* more generally. He told Hurwitz that he found the maga-zine's criticism of seminaries "superficially constructive, but at heart ma-licious or perhaps even venomous." He went on to deride Hurwitz's plan (and therefore the raison d'être of the Menorah Association), calling it "un-founded, fruitless and ill-advised."[129] Morgenstern's harshness signaled the *Menorah Journal's* declining reputation among Reform Jewish leaders and rabbis, many of whom agreed that the magazine criticized the seminaries with too much cleverness and not enough tact.

The deterioration of a once-promising alliance between the Menorah Association and Reform rabbis would become complete during the sum-mer of 1926, when Rabbi Abba Hillel Silver submitted his article in response to Cohen, Kallen, and Hurwitz. For years, Hurwitz pleaded with Silver to write an article for the *Menorah Journal* and to urge his congregants to sub-scribe.[130] Correspondence between the two men was cordial, though Silver never demonstrated much enthusiasm for Hurwitz's requests. The articles by Cohen, Kallen, and Hurwitz finally elicited more than just a polite re-sponse from the Cleveland rabbi. Because he lacked trust in the magazine's editorial staff, Silver made two requests upon submitting the article in April 1926. He asked the editors to publish the long piece in full in a single is-sue without changes and without comment or response within the same issue.[131] Hurwitz acquiesced to these requests.

Silver, who was born in the Lithuanian village of Neustadt-Schirwindt, landed at Ellis Island with his mother and siblings in 1902 when he was nine years old. At the age of eleven, Silver and his older brother founded the Dr. Herzl Zion Club, the first Hebrew-speaking Zionist club in America. The club, which was open to boys eleven to sixteen years old for a five-cent membership fee, sponsored programs on Zionism, Jewish history, and Jew-ish literature. In 1911, Silver surprised his young colleagues by enrolling at Cincinnati's Hebrew Union College, the Reform seminary known for an anti-Zionist stance. Silver graduated from both HUC and the University of

Cincinnati in 1915. In 1917, after serving a congregation in Wheeling, West Virginia, for two years, Silver assumed the pulpit at one of the leading Reform congregations in the United States, Cleveland's Tifereth Israel (known there as "The Temple"). He was twenty-four years old at the time. Silver remained a leading advocate of Hebrew culture and Zionism until his death in 1963.[132]

Silver could not abide the attacks on the Reform movement that had become so pervasive in the *Menorah Journal* during the mid-1920s. His essay's title, "Why Do the Heathen Rage?"—taken from the second chapter of the Book of Psalms—clearly indicated his opinion of Cohen, Kallen, and Hurwitz. Despite its savage criticism of the three men most responsible for defining the Menorah idea, Silver's article continued to move forward through the publication process. Hurwitz sent page proofs to Silver in May 1926, with a message that the article would run in a summer issue.[133] A few days later, however, managing editor Elliot Cohen attempted to stop publication of the article. In a long memorandum to his fellow editors, he argued that the style and temper of Silver's article were beneath the standards of the magazine. He also claimed that Silver misrepresented and distorted the arguments made by himself, Kallen, and Hurwitz. The damage to the journal would be great were the article to run, Cohen claimed.[134]

Hurwitz immediately relayed the contents of Cohen's memo to three of his most trusted advisors, associate editors Oko and Wolfson, as well as Nathan Isaacs, the Harvard Law School professor who was so critical of Cohen's "Notes" columns. Oko wired Hurwitz, telling him to keep his promise to publish Silver's article. Wolfson informed Hurwitz that refusal to publish the article would "do Menorah more harm" than any statement Silver made in the article itself. Isaacs agreed and took the opportunity to criticize Cohen again for attacking others so stridently in his own pieces but being unwilling to be the object of an attack. He informed Hurwitz that the *Menorah Journal* must publish the article.[135] Despite the counsel they received, Hurwitz and Cohen ultimately broke their promise to Rabbi Silver and informed him that they would not publish his article.

Silver resigned from the board of the IMA on July 13, 1926, one week before the first installment of "Why Do the Heathen Rage?" ran in a competing publication, the *Jewish Tribune*.[136] The article was released as a pamphlet by the *Jewish Tribune* later that year. In the essay, Silver angrily attacked Cohen's "Age of Brass," claiming that, "for sheer 'brass' in this sad Age of Brass one need not look elsewhere."[137] He contended that because Cohen, Kallen, and Hurwitz seldom entered a synagogue, they were not qualified to comment on what occurred there. Had they any knowledge of

Judaism or contact with Jewish religious leaders, Silver claimed, these three critics would realize that religion must remain the central component of Jewish life. The Jewish cultural renaissance advocated by the IMA would enrich Jewish life, Silver admitted, but without religion there would be no Jewish life to enrich. "When the American Jew abandons his faith he will swiftly and surely assimilate," Silver wrote. Moreover, "no quantum of Jewish music and Jewish art or books on Jewish literature and philosophy will be potent enough to save him. The anti-religious Jew will be the first to go, as he always has been."[138] In a final salvo, Silver announced that to expect American Jews to unite around the Menorah Association's cause was not only "frightfully naïve" but sheer "folly."[139]

Predictably, Cohen reacted angrily, firing off a thirty-one page internal memo intended to refute what he claimed were Silver's misstatements and misinterpretations.[140] Hurwitz was more tempered. He wrote to the *Jewish Tribune* in an attempt to control the damage done to the *Menorah Journal's* reputation. He ignored his original promise to Silver that the article would be published "as is" and claimed that "any magazine aiming at a high literary standing, must be subject to editorial scrutiny and correction as to style, logic, and statement of facts." Hurwitz then easily slipped into a belligerent tone, criticizing the *Jewish Tribune* for its contention that the *Menorah Journal* had "attacked 'American Judaism' and the 'faith and works of the Jews of America.'" Hurwitz claimed instead that the *Menorah Journal* offered "honest analysis of Jewish conditions and activities in America, and proposals for the elevation and greater effectiveness of Judaism."[141]

The harm done to the *Menorah Journal's* reputation was profound. An editorial in one Jewish newspaper reported that "the rabbis of this country [have] been hauled over the coals" by Cohen, Kallen, and Hurwitz, and criticized as insincere the journal's claim to "fair play" as an open forum for critical thought on Jewish life. The editorial granted *Menorah Journal* writers the right to be "radicals," but argued that they remained "very intolerant of the views of others."[142] Reform rabbis generally agreed: many wrote to the *Menorah Journal's* editors to cancel their subscriptions and express their dismay. HUC ceased running advertisements in the *Menorah Journal*. HUC President Morgenstern informed Hurwitz, "I have completely lost confidence in the [Menorah] Society and have even begun to believe that it is hostile to a religious interpretation of Judaism."[143] Solomon Freehof, a Chicago rabbi, spoke for many Reform leaders when he wrote, "I think that the Journal is fair to every section of Jewish life except ours."[144]

For years to come, the *Menorah Journal* carried the reputation as an antireligious magazine, open only to publishing opinions that complemented its own. A line was drawn distinctly between rabbis and the Menorah Association, now labeled as anti-religious "radical intellectuals." The rift would not be easy to solve. Even those still sympathetic to the Menorah Association, such as Rabbi David de Sola Pool, called the magazine an "antagonizing influence in Jewish life." As de Sola Pool informed Hurwitz just one year after the controversy over Silver's article, "I do not like a steady sauce of flippancy and smart aleckism liberally spattered over my Judaism."[145]

— 6 —

Pluralism in Fiction

During the 1920s, the *Menorah Journal* introduced readers to a cohort of young writers, many of whom would go on to have distinguished careers as authors, critics, and academics. In contrast to the acerbic essays by Cohen, Kallen, Hurwitz, and others, much of the fiction in the *Menorah Journal* commented entertainingly on the dilemmas of American Jewish life. Still, its primary purpose was intended to be instructive. The journal's editors hoped that readers would easily recognize the assets and the foibles of fictional characters, and would take counsel from them on proper means of expressing Jewish identity. The short stories and fictional essays published in the journal usually hewed closely to the pluralist logic that defined the Menorah idea, even as they revealed a troubling contradiction inherent to the Menorah Association's pluralist project. Although these fiction writers portrayed the United States as a nation that welcomed the cultural distinctiveness of multiple ethnic groups, their conception of how to constitute Jewish identity was often restrictive.[1] This tension between broadly imagining the nation as pluralist yet narrowly conceiving of Jewish culture defined the fiction published in the *Menorah Journal* during the magazine's heyday.

Stories published between the mid-1910s and the early 1920s tended to focus on immigrants' struggles to Americanize, but this gave way over time to works that voiced concern about the attenuation of Jewish identity in America. In stories that ran between 1924 and 1930, protagonists found themselves searching for an acceptable means of expressing Jewish identity in an American context. The subject of these later 1920s works was often a child of Jewish immigrants who rediscovered or learned to appreciate his (they were almost always men) own Jewish difference as he matured. As in the contemporary nonfiction published in the journal, this later 1920s fiction continually found the solution to the dilemmas of identity in pluralism.

The thematic shift that characterized the fiction in the *Menorah Journal* over this fifteen-year period mirrored a significant evolution occurring in American Jewish life between the 1910s and 1920s. Children of immigrants tended to interpret the relationship between being Jewish and being American differently from how their parents had. We should not assume, however, that the relationship between these identities became less complicated; for the young writers examined here, the opposite was often the case. They sought to articulate, through character types, how Jews could reinvent Jewish culture for an American setting. Many of them were motivated by the same dilemmas that led Kallen to formulate pluralism. That is, they sought to be two things at once without contradiction. Most writers discussed in this chapter vigorously protested the "Jewish writer" label precisely because it represented a fundamental rejection of the ethos of pluralism. These authors rejected any essential Jewish identity and any fundamental distinction between Jewish culture and American culture, thus rendering the label of "Jewish writer" meaningless in their minds, even while they demonstrated a commitment to perpetuating Jewish identity and culture.[2]

This significant shift in fictional themes between the 1910s and the 1920s transpired not only because of the passage of a decade during which a second generation of American Jews matured, but also because of the retooling of the magazine's editorial staff. Elliot Cohen, only in his twenties when he assumed the role of managing editor at the *Menorah Journal* in 1925, became the mentor to a talented young cohort of writers during the mid-to-late 1920s, undoubtedly the magazine's most dynamic period.[3] The writers he recruited to the journal included Kenneth Fearing, Albert Halper, Meyer Levin, Henry Rosenthal, Lionel Trilling, Anzia Yezierska, and many others.[4] Many members of this cohort met weekly for dinner, and a few even banded together to found a social association with the tongue-in-cheek mission of celebrating "the pleasanter Jewish festivals."[5] One chronicler has called these young men and women a "traveling Jewish Algonquin circle of wits."[6] The existence of this circle of writers is significant both for its contribution to the evolution of pluralist thought and for its function as a training ground for many young intellectuals who would go on to shape the fields of Jewish-themed fiction and cultural criticism through the middle of the twentieth century.

The Immigrants and the Acculturated

The stories about pluralism and Americanization that this talented group produced had precedent. Perhaps the two best-known tales of Jewish Americanization written during the first quarter of the twentieth century were Mary Antin's 1912 autobiography *The Promised Land* and Abraham Cahan's 1917 novel *The Rise of David Levinsky*.[7] Antin's tale is one of rebirth, as she announced in her first paragraph: "I am absolutely other than the person whose story I have to tell."[8] Her passage from the Old World to the New meant casting off Jewish identity and looking back on her past as if it belonged to another person. Cahan's protagonist Levinsky experienced a less linear adjustment to the New World, but Cahan's novel still portrayed American and Jewish identities in conflict.[9] Neither Antin nor Levinsky, both immigrants to the United States, found ways to readily express Jewish identity fully in harmony with American identity.

Much of the earliest fiction published in the *Menorah Journal*, like the works by Antin and Cahan, also focused on immigrants' experiences, but this early fiction differed in significant ways, especially from Antin's work. The enticements of Americanization certainly loomed powerfully in stories that appeared in the *Menorah Journal* during the late 1910s and early 1920s, yet the protagonists ultimately felt a deep loss as a result of assimilation. The experience of becoming American was less one of "rebirth" than one filled with pangs of guilt and sometimes regret.

Writers including Anzia Yezierska and Meyer Levin struggled in their fiction with the conflicts between maintaining Jewish traditions and becoming modern Americans. Class conflict is central to Yezierska's "The Lord Giveth," published in the *Menorah Journal* in February 1923. Yezierska herself had arrived in the United States as a young girl, settling with her family on the Lower East Side around 1890. After a childhood of poverty, Yezierska taught herself English, attended school at night, and earned a scholarship to Columbia University, where she graduated in 1904. She would go on to write novels and stories that focused in particular on women's Americanization, including the 1925 novel *Bread Givers*.[10]

The difference in expected gender roles between the Old World and the New pervades Yezierska's "The Lord Giveth." Two recent immigrants to the United States, Reb Ravinsky and his wife, are at the center of this tale. Reb Ravinksy was a revered scholar in the Old World, where his community had provided for his family, allowing him to pursue study rather than work for wages. In the New World, where a man is expected to support his family in addition to being pious, Ravinksy is unable to find ways to earn money.

He has neither the skills nor the desire to do so, and he spends his days immersed in prayer and study. The landlord demands rent from the Ravinsky family, which they cannot pay. The wife laments, "Home, in Russia, they kissed the ground on which he walked, and in America, they throw him in the street." She can only put food on the table by taking handouts from neighbors who are only slightly better off than herself but who also live in poverty. Neither she nor her husband see any way out of their economic predicament. Foreshadowing the title of Yezierska's 1950 fictionalized autobiography, *Red Ribbon on a White Horse*, Reb Ravinsky declares: "Poverty is an ornament on a Jew like a red ribbon on a white horse."[11]

The defining action in "The Lord Giveth" occurs after Mrs. Ravinsky has collected a bounty of food from charitable neighbors. Usually, she would have denied herself most of this food, eating only the scraps that her husband and child had left. On this particular day, however, Mrs. Ravinsky treats herself to a solitary "gluttonous indulgence." Eating well reminds her of the Sabbath dinners in the Old World, "when she was the honored wife of Reb Ravinsky." In the midst of this feast, however, the "charity lady"— a social worker sent by a charitable agency to ensure that the Ravinskys in fact require assistance—arrives. A panicked Mrs. Ravinsky hides the food in the oven and in a bureau before the charity lady enters. Mrs. Ravinsky then lies to the social worker, telling her that the family has no food.

A short time later the charity worker returns to the Ravinsky home with a delivery boy who bears groceries for the family. With the groceries comes a lecture about the differences between the Old World and America. "The first principle of religion is for a man to provide for his family," the charity worker insists, denying Reb Ravinksy's belief in the primacy of study and reinforcing the different gendered expectations between the Old World and the New. She also condescendingly informs Mrs. Ravinsky, "Soap and water are cheap." Before leaving, the charity worker surveys the apartment, insisting that it could be kept cleaner. As she does so, she discovers the hidden food. She assumes that the Ravinskys have been duping the charitable organization all along, and she orders the delivery boy to return the groceries to the store. The charity worker scorns Mrs. Ravinsky, especially for teaching her child to lie. The story concludes as Mrs. Ravinsky wails for the lost food and Reb Ravinksy assures her by saying, "The Lord giveth; the Lord taketh away. Blessed be the name of the Lord."[12] Yezierska's reader learns that Old World traditions and New World economies do not harmonize. Religious fulfillment and material hunger are in conflict in the lives of the new arrivals, and systems designed to help new immigrants often fail them.

Meyer Levin introduced generational conflict into this tension between new immigrants and acculturated Jews in his April 1924 *Menorah Journal* story, "A Seder." Though just a senior at the University of Chicago in 1924, Levin already was working as a part-time reporter at the *Chicago Daily News* and had published a short story about Chicago Jews in the previous *Menorah Journal* issue.[13] Levin later became well known both for *Compulsion*, his account of the trial of Nathan Leopold and Richard Loeb—two wealthy Jewish students from the Hyde Park neighborhood of Chicago who were convicted of murder in 1924—and for *The Old Bunch*, a 1937 novel about children of immigrant Jews on Chicago's West Side. Less than ten years after the end of World War II, Levin would introduce American readers to what would become the most widely read source on the Holocaust, *Anne Frank: The Diary of a Young Girl*, in his front-page *New York Times Book Review* of June 15, 1952.[14]

In "A Seder," one of Levin's earliest published works, the Americanized Berger family desperately tries to orchestrate a Passover meal even though they have long given up all other religious observances. The father, an immigrant storeowner, frequently works late and misses family meals altogether; he even arrives late on the Passover evening during which the story takes place. Despite his late arrival, Mr. Berger hopes to conduct a traditional seder but is discouraged by his children's lack of interest as well as his own feeling of disconnection from his ancestors, especially his deceased parents. This immigrant Jewish father is caught in between, alienated from both the Old World Judaism of his parents and the hyper-Americanism of his children. The family goes through the motions of the traditional meal but does so without any real feeling. The youngest daughter, disobeying her parents' wishes, does not even attend. She opts instead to go to the movies, one of the most potent symbols of American modernity.

According to Passover tradition, Jews leave a cup of wine on the table for the prophet Elijah and open a door to invite him into their homes. At the conclusion of Levin's story, instead of filling the cup for the prophet Elijah with wine, as is customary, a distraught Mr. Berger puts water in Elijah's cup and declares, "Let him change it into wine."[15] His act, more than a reference to Jesus's miracle, is a clear rejection of Elijah, the prophet whom Jews expect to announce the coming of the messianic era. Mr. Berger's refusal to carry out this symbolic invitation of Elijah signals his admission of the defeat of Jewish religion and culture in his home.

The Berger home is meant to represent the United States in microcosm. According to Levin's story, Judaism cannot survive with any meaning in a country where economic obligations and popular entertainments have trumped religion and familial ties. A marginally interested first generation (Mr. Berger) half-heartedly tries to observe Jewish traditions, but does so with a mixture of sadness and contempt. His children, representing the second generation of Jews in America, for the most part ignore the traditions altogether.

The loss of Jewish tradition and culture becomes especially apparent during this Passover holiday on which Jews celebrate their freedom from slavery. Levin leaves his reader wondering if embracing American freedoms, especially the pursuit of individual wealth and mass entertainment, have permanently damaged Judaism and Jewish culture. As in Yezierska's story, the protagonists find themselves unable to balance being Jewish and being American. These characters struggle through the cultural, economic, and religious challenges of Americanization but fail to find solutions. Yezierska and Levin both ended their tales pessimistically, leaving readers to wonder whether Jewish culture will disappear completely over the course of another generation or two.

Fitting in as Americans

The editorial staff that joined the *Menorah Journal* in the mid-1920s initiated a shift in the journal's fiction. Where stories of the late 1910s and early 1920s examined class and generational conflicts between immigrant Jews and acculturated Jews, stories published after 1924 more baldly criticized what was perceived as the absence of meaning in modern Jewish life. This literature suggested that the intellectual vacuity endemic to the modern Jewish condition would have to be corrected. Rather than providing a pathway for such correction, however, most writers focused on what they saw as the fallacies of assimilation. Readers of fiction in the *Menorah Journal* during the second half of the 1920s would meet many characters who believed that they had been accepted by mainstream America and who thought little about perpetuating Jewish culture. Many stories depicted young Jewish men who could not figure out how to integrate Jewish cultural interests into a modern American life as they came of age.

Beginning in 1924, a feature entitled "Commentaries" began to appear in the *Menorah Journal*. The journal's editors described the recurring "Commentaries" as "brief, informal and personal" contributions of "stray insights and chance inspirations" about modern Jewish life. Cohen, Hurwitz, and their co-editors compared this column to *Atlantic Monthly*'s "Contributors' Club" and *Harper*'s "The Lion's Mouth."[16] Cohen in particular envisioned these columns as literary portrayals of "the Jewish reaction to the American environment" that would be both humorous and insightful.[17] Within "Commentaries," readers would meet various types of Jews, including those too eager to promote Jewish exceptionalism, those disdainful of eastern European Jewish immigrants, those with no knowledge of Jewish religion or culture, and those too willing to assimilate. Through these stock character types, writers parodied what they perceived as an absence of meaning in American Jewish life.

The first few "Commentaries" lamented American Jews' tenuous connection to Jewish tradition and mocked their filiopietistic tendencies. In a 1924 column representative of the genre entitled "Necrologues and Noodles," Maximillian Hurwitz (no relation to Henry Hurwitz)—an editor at both the *Jewish Tribune* and at *The Day*, a Zionist Yiddish daily—presented a narrator whose most passionate expression of Jewish identity was consuming noodle soup every Sabbath dinner. The noodle soup–loving narrator took great pleasure in making fun of the American Jewish weekly newspapers' "specialty of emphasizing the Americanism and the American background of the Jew." The narrator decried Jews' tendency to claim full responsibility for the nation's founding. He demonstrated the extent of this absurdity through imitation, speaking of a Jew who "conclusively proved that the first white man to sneeze on American soil had a cousin who knew a man whose grandmother had been a *Shabbos goy* in the Old World." This fact, he jokingly continued, could be used to prove "that the Jews are no newcomers in America."[18] Although the narrator claimed "no kinship to the first white man who sneezed or yawned in America," he insisted that his recent arrival on American shores made him no less an American than a Jew (or any other immigrant) who had been in the United States for generations. The moral of this soup eater's rant was that those Jews who measured American identity according to personal or family longevity in the nation were mistaken. Instead, a dedication to the principles of American democracy ensured belonging, no matter how long ago one's ancestors arrived.

A number of other "Commentaries" published in 1925 and 1926 made light of what the authors saw as Jews' propensity to excessively celebrate their own people. In one installment of April 1925, the first-person narrator described his friend Franklyn, who continually claimed to be "a fourth—or is it fifth?—generation Jew" living in the United States.[19] Franklyn repeatedly reminded the narrator that their great-uncles had served together in the American Civil War. This assertion emphasized Jews' presence in the United States before the heavy influx of eastern European immigrants between the 1880s and the 1920s. It also overstated Jews' roles as agents in the war that saved the Union and countered the antisemitic stereotype of Jewish men as too weak to serve in the armed forces.

One year later, in an April–May 1926 "Commentaries," advertising executive and author Alexander Javitz parodied the skills necessary to become a publicity writer for Jewish organizations in the United States. The steps to achieving success in this field were simple, Javitz explained. First, a publicity writer for Jewish organizations had to "memorize one or two admonitions from the Talmud" to use in press releases. Here, ready quotations could substitute for real knowledge. Second, "learn the phonetically correct English spelling of *rachmonas* [compassion]." Javitz concluded his sarcastic counsel by telling publicity writers to teach your "heart, mind, fountain pen and typewriter keys that all the virtues of charity, pity and altruism are the sole property of the Jewish people." Javitz advised that article headlines such as "Jews Lead Nation!" and "Prominent Authority Says Jewish Institution Best" could suffice on multiple occasions and should be kept readily on hand.[20]

Press releases should avoid any mention of unmarried Jewish mothers, mostly for fear of negative response from gentiles. No press release should address the sweatshop conditions in which so many immigrant Jews labored. Above all, the Jewish publicity writer in America "must be Jewish (yet not un-American), American (yet not un-Jewish) [and] throw in a paragraph about Palestine (but be neither Zionist nor anti-Zionist)."[21] In other words, celebrate Jewish contributions to the United States and never take any stance too strongly for fear of offending any potential constituency or of providing fodder for antisemites. Javitz's mockery of the task at hand spoke directly to the challenge of pluralism—there had to be real substance to the argument that Jewish identity and American identity could exist in full concert with each other. Empty rhetoric would undermine pluralism's goals.

In a subsequent contribution to "Commentaries," Javitz identified a target for his biting satire. His biographical sketch portrayed the "genteel Jewish lady" who was always seeking to raise one million dollars for some charitable cause.[22] The lady demonstrated her skills best at banquets, mingling with the rich and presenting checks to foundations on behalf of the ladies' auxiliary. Javitz's story demonstrated the tendency of Jewish men to project negative accusations about materialism onto Jewish women.[23]

Javitz suggested a psychological motivation to the genteel Jewish lady. After being raised in poverty in New York City's Bowery, she overcame early disadvantages and became a leader of the cultured set. She memorized the necessary cultural references that facilitated her aspiration to the upper classes. But, because her persona was based on such a shallow understanding of Jewish culture and traditions, Javitz dismissed her activities as fleeting, without real significance.[24] The technique employed here was not exclusive to Javitz. Many contributors to "Commentaries" advocated the committed embrace of Jewish culture by negatively portraying those like the public relations man and the genteel Jewish lady who were uninterested in Jewish life beyond celebration and fundraising.

These barbed character sketches extended as well to assimilated Jews. In two separate "Commentaries" contributions, Albert Halper wrote of young American Jews who were ignorant of Jewish tradition. Halper, born in 1904 on Chicago's West Side, was a child of Jewish immigrants from Lithuania. He moved to New York City in 1928, though much of his early work is set in Chicago and rooted in his Chicago experience. Shortly after arriving in New York, Halper met Cohen, who published a few of Halper's stories in the *Menorah Journal*.[25] Cohen not only encouraged Halper, he brought him into a cohort of young writers—including Kenneth Fearing, Charles Reznikoff, Clifton Fadiman, Louis Berg, and Anita Brenner—who became friends and faithful critics of each others' work.[26]

Halper's April 1929 "Brothers Over a Grave" follows three brothers as they visit their mother's burial plot. They read the customary mourner's Kaddish prayer only by relying on English transliterations of the original Aramaic (the vernacular of Jews in the first century). One of the sons explains: "We had been raised in Christian neighborhoods, had received little Jewish education, and could not read Hebrew or Yiddish." The unfamiliar words of the prayer became "material objects stumbling over teeth" and came out in "broken bits."[27]

In another of Halper's "Commentaries," published one year later, five grown sons accompany their father to synagogue to say Kaddish for their mother. The sons are wholly ignorant of Jewish religious ceremony; they cannot follow the order of the service, and they only know to turn the page in their prayer books when they hear the rustling of pages by the "graybeards" at the front of the synagogue. Their greatest desire is "to get ahead in the world." Their economic aspirations leave them without Jewish content in their lives, unable to honor their mother according to Jewish tradition.[28]

In the story's climax, the competition between tradition and material gain rises to the surface. As the family leaves the synagogue, the rabbi responds derisively to the father's meager charitable contribution of two dollars; one of his sons steps into the conflict and hands the rabbi a ten dollar bill. The younger generation has greatly surpassed its elders' ability to earn and to provide charity, but this accomplishment has come at a great cost— the attenuation of knowledge. Jewish tradition has succumbed to the entrapments of class aspiration in America.

Even worse than forgetting one's Jewish past, as many of these grown children had, was actively choosing to cast off that past. In a 1925 "Commentaries" contribution titled "Assimilation," New York novelist Melvin P. Levy chronicled the daily life of Harry, a young Jewish salesman. This short story opens with Harry at his bathroom mirror, shaving before going out to work. Each day that he shaves, Harry remembers his father "bearded and bent over books with fine yellow pages." Harry "considered himself an American," meaning that he does not share his father's passion for study of Jewish texts. So Harry goes off to work, even on the particular Saturday/ Sabbath morning during which the story is set. Harry attends synagogue only on Yom Kippur and "was pleased when he was told that he had few Jewish traits." Harry has assimilated so fully that he wonders whether Jews are to blame for antisemitism. When he overhears his gentile co-workers' conversations, Harry begins to feel "a sudden hatred of those Jews who insisted on keeping alive differences."[29]

After eating a non-kosher lunch with his co-workers, Harry takes a young woman to a dance, as he does every Saturday night. Perhaps, on Monday morning before work, as he shaves again, he would briefly think of his father. But at all other moments, "He is not foreign, he is assimilated. He is an American." At the conclusion of this character sketch, Levy takes an extra step back to comment on Harry's embrace of being American: "He has never had occasion to wonder what that means."[30] The reader is meant to pity Harry for his inability to go beyond surface-level introspection. Levy uses the unenlightened fictional salesman Harry as an anti-hero to reinforce that becoming an American need not mean rejecting or hiding one's Jewish identity.

Reuben Goldstein, another fictional character who appeared in "Commentaries," put up only a bit more resistance to assimilating than Harry. Reuben moves his family to the fictional Chicago suburb of Mapleton in Kenneth F. Fearing's "Mapleton Welcomes the Stranger." In this piece, Fearing, a frequent contributor to the *Menorah Journal*, *Poetry*, the *New Masses*, and the *Nation*, assessed the reactions from Mapleton's community, which had not previously had a Jewish family in its midst. After an initial panic during which the "neighbors braced themselves for an attack upon their decent, right-living, suburban social world," all soon returns to normal in the small hamlet, with Reuben and his family ignoring their neighbors and all the neighbors ignoring the Goldsteins. Time passes, and the Goldsteins find themselves invited to a dinner party. Though he does not play golf, some of the men at the party (including a city councilman) invite Reuben to join the restricted golf club. Reuben awkwardly reminds his companions that he is Jewish, and, after "painful silence" and "shocked realization," the matter is dropped. More important than the uncomfortable silence is the ease with which Reuben's once panicked neighbors forgot that he is Jewish.[31]

Reuben soon finds himself in a predicament that he cannot solve by keeping to himself, after his son steals a Rolls Royce belonging to Mapleton's vice president. The city councilman who had asked Reuben to join the golf club offers to fix the situation if he applies for membership in the club. Reuben joins and becomes an ideal member—he pays his dues on time and rarely uses any club services. He even is elected to the membership committee, after the club's members determined that "anyone who had the sense to stay away from the weekly poker and business sessions of the club must, perforce, be a man of balance and sense."[32]

At the end of Reuben's second year in Mapleton, he finds himself in a conversation with the leading members of the club, during which they yet again seem to have forgotten that he is Jewish. As the men complain about the population boom in their suburb, one remarks that at least "Mapleton hasn't filled up with a lot of Polacks and Jews and that sort of people." When they ask, "Isn't that right, Goldstein?" he hesitates and sighs before answering "Yes" and wonders to himself: "What's the use?" Just two short years living among gentiles and severing connections to the Jewish community have broken Reuben's resolve to stand up for his fellow Jews who are the targets of discrimination. The Jew, originally the "stranger" of the story's title, is welcomed as soon as he sheds any outward sign of his Jewish identity. Reuben's process of relinquishing Jewish identity in public occurs with alarming ease and speed.

This handful of "Commentaries," representative of the nearly one hundred such columns published between 1924 and 1931, reveals the editors' concerns about the future of Jews' distinctive culture and existence in America. Middle-class Jews' desire for acceptance had produced damaging results. What lay just beneath the surface of all these bleak character sketches, of course, was the opinion that assimilation was a dangerous path, maybe even a fallacy. Though these criticisms were delivered with a heavy dose of condescension, the Menorah Journal's editors hoped that readers would recognize bad practices and worst-case scenarios in these characters and then would choose to live in ways that expressed real commitment to Jewish culture and traditions.

Heroic Pluralism

Other fictional portrayals in the *Menorah Journal* explored the dilemma of acculturation more gingerly than the "Commentaries" columns. One particularly intriguing example was the character sketch of "Reuben Cohen" written as a six-part series by Irwin Edman, a professor of philosophy at Columbia University.[33] Before he wrote the Reuben Cohen series for the *Menorah Journal,* Edman had published a novel in 1926 entitled *Richard Kane Looks at Life,* which followed a "sensitive American youth" in search of "an order out of contemporary chaos and an inner peace for [his] own troubled spirit."[34] In successive chapters, Kane entered college, traveled to Europe, considered marriage, and contemplated education, art, politics, and God.

Hurwitz knew Edman well from having recruited him to serve on the journal's editorial board. Hurwitz read *Richard Kane Looks at Life* in manuscript and told Edman the book was a "masterpiece of characterization—picturing vividly a particular individual and at the same time a large class of which he is representative."[35] Even before *Richard Kane* reached publication, Hurwitz suggested to Edman that he create a "portrait of a Jewish student in the same vein" for the journal.[36] Edman took Hurwitz up on the offer, immediately beginning what would become the series on Reuben Cohen.

The first installment, "Reuben Cohen Goes to College," which ran in the April–May 1926 issue of the *Menorah Journal,* is told in the first person by one of Reuben's non-Jewish professors. Here, Edman blended fiction with his own experiences, likely basing Cohen on an aggregate of his students at Columbia. By the time he invented Reuben Cohen in 1926, the thirty-year-old Edman rarely had strayed far from Columbia. Edman grew up in the Manhattan neighborhood of Morningside Heights, where Columbia is located, and he attended Columbia as an undergraduate and graduate student. He earned his doctorate in 1920 and that same year accepted a teaching position in Columbia's philosophy department.[37] Edman became a full professor in 1935 and remained at Columbia until his death in 1954.[38]

In writing the Reuben Cohen series, Edman had an agenda beyond entertaining readers: he sought to invent for readers an ideal type who demonstrated through his lived experience—rather than through a more detached academic argument—the possibility of being both Jewish and American.

He used Reuben Cohen to endorse cultural pluralism, making the case that modern Jewish youth could fully enjoy the opportunities and benefits of American citizenship while developing a meaningful Jewish identity. Edman's portrayal of Reuben Cohen should be read as both a cautionary tale for Jewish youth in the 1920s and as a corrective, replacing the possibility of assimilation (meaning the complete abandonment of Jewish heritage, religion, and culture) with a call for cultural pluralism. Indeed, Edman broke the wall of fiction entirely at the end of the series by having the fictional Reuben read nonfictional essays on pluralism by Kallen.

The fictional Reuben Cohen was an American-born child of Jewish immigrants, but his professor remarked that very little distinguished Reuben from his Protestant classmates. Most of the so-called obvious physical markers of Jewish identity are not apparent. True, the professor confessed to a "certain suspicion" about Reuben's nose, but he noted that Reuben's voice does not obviously mark him as Jewish.[39] Unlike other Jewish students on campus, Reuben does not don any markers of Jewish affiliation, such as a Jewish fraternity pin. Except for his name, Reuben is not easily identifiable as Jewish because he does *not* overtly tout his Americanism. The assumption here is that those who are most eager to demonstrate that they belong are also the most self-conscious about not belonging.

Perhaps it is not easy for his professor to recognize Reuben as Jewish because Reuben himself had not been particularly aware of his Jewish identity up to this point in his life. He initially describes himself to his professor as "none at all [*sic*]" a Jew.[40] Reuben's father kept his store open on the Sabbath and his mother displayed a "positive gusto" for such non-kosher food as lobsters, oysters, and "crisp fried bacon" that she served in their home. His family kept candlesticks on the buffet, but they no longer lit them on Friday evenings. Neither of Reuben's parents concerned themselves with providing a religious education for Reuben, either inside or outside the home. As he advanced through the public schools, Reuben's teachers encouraged him to strive for a "cosmopolitan kinship with all the world." Reuben's "friends at college included an O'Neale, a Smith and a Taylor along with a Rosenberg, a Rotkowitz and a Strauss."[41]

Reuben seems uncomfortable with his peers at college who limit their social and extracurricular activities within exclusively Jewish circles. When he gazes at the other Jewish students on campus, Reuben has trouble seeing any reflection of himself. Unlike some of his Jewish classmates, he is unable to read Hebrew and he has outright "contempt" for Yiddish. Jewish political and cultural activities interest him little. He shows no particular sympathy for the Zionists on campus and his brief flirtation with a fictional Jewish student association, the Society for Promotion of Jewish Culture, goes quite badly. After attending a few meetings, Reuben quips that the group should change its name to the Society for the Promotion of Jewish Bitterness, because the participants spend most of their time talking about prejudice, social exclusion on campuses, and how best to defend Jews' rights.[42]

In this initial episode, Edman set up his readers to believe that little distinguished Reuben from his non-Jewish peers and that it would be difficult to imagine the circumstances by which Reuben would become engaged in any way with being Jewish. Still, though Reuben remains alienated from these classmates, he does not forsake his Jewish identity altogether. Reuben tells the professor that many of his Jewish peers had abandoned Judaism fully. Perhaps they are passing as gentiles or just ignoring their Jewish heritage without claiming to be gentiles. Reuben cannot follow this path. He feels that doing so would not be an acceptable option for him. "Try as he would to deny it and to live like an urbane cosmopolitan," the professor observes of Reuben, "he found by the time he was a senior a strange perturbing response to and kinship with what he could only describe as the Jewish temper." Reuben wonders about this kinship and lacks the words to describe it. The professor calls it an "imprint" of "minor habits and associations" that defined a "man's spirit."[43] Twenty years of upbringing in even the most minimally conscious Jewish environment mattered. What also mattered was Reuben's own agency, as he consciously chooses to find ways to become more comfortable as a Jewish student, despite the many pressures and opportunities to abandon such a pursuit.

This initial essay provided Edman with a way to highlight the dramatic alteration of Reuben's character. By his senior year, Reuben notices an "intimacy" with Jewish friends that he cannot achieve with gentile classmates. He takes note of the number of "little things that one could take for granted with one's Jewish friends," including gossiping about "distinguished or wealthy Jews," "odd turns of Jewish humor," and "belonging to the same tradition even if one did not know much or care much about it." Reuben reacts to these realizations by determining to learn more about Jewish history and culture. Furthermore, Reuben begins to "take a positive active joy in being a Jew." He reconsiders the way he thinks about Zionism, realizing that Zionists not only advocate a haven for victims of persecution but that they also seek to revive a tradition. This dramatic realization leads Reuben to ask the question at the heart of Edman's series: "Where . . . did his loyalty lie—to that Jewish tradition and milieu in which he was beginning to find his basic attachments, or to that miscellaneous America, in which he had thought to live without any obtruding awareness of being a Jew at all?"[44] Outside the campus environment, the question would become even more vexing.

In the series' second installment, "Reuben Cohen Enters American Life," Edman reintroduces Reuben as a college graduate in search of employment. He finds many want ads that read "Gentiles Only Need Apply" or "Christians Preferred." At one point, he comes close to being hired at an advertising company until the potential employer remembers to inquire about Reuben's last name, Cohen. He assumes that it would be easier to find work were his name not such an obvious marker of his Jewish heritage. Reuben's hunch is confirmed when—"following a train of reasoning responsible for the sudden acquisition of white Protestant names by dark young Hebrews"—he changes his name to "Raymond Cogan" and quickly lands a job, vaguely defined by Edman as related to sales.[45]

Despite his name change, Reuben retains a fundamentally Jewish nature to his character. Edman explains: "It will be less confusing to the reader, and spiritually more accurate, perhaps, if throughout the remainder of this memoir he continue to appear as Reuben Cohen. For those sensible to such matters, there may even be a symbolism in continuing to call him Reuben."[46] Reuben's name change, in other words, is solely for outward appearances and economic survival. Although for many other Jews changing one's name constituted an important step on a path to assimilation, Edman made sure that his readers did not interpret it this way by giving it precisely the opposite outcome. Trying on this new name spurs Reuben to more awareness and pride in his Jewish identity. Although some academics by this time had begun to call into question the notion of an essential self, Edman here suggests that Reuben Cohen somehow has a fundamentally Jewish essence at his core.[47]

Changing his name to Raymond Cogan allows Reuben a deeper access than he previously had to gentiles' perceptions of Jews. Edman highlighted the contradictions at the heart of antisemitic beliefs when he explained what Reuben learns from clients and colleagues who think he is gentile. Some clients complain that Jews are "hard," others that they are "soft." Some associates call Jews "intrusive"; others label them "clannish." Some colleagues classify Jews as "spend-thrifts"; others criticize them as "misers."[48] Even as Reuben learns firsthand of antisemitism's elasticity and internal contradictions, he remains silent. Speaking out likely would not be worth the trouble, he assumes.

At a dinner party, Reuben hears his companions complain that New York City is overrun with Jews. They also comment that the ongoing murder trial of Leopold and Loeb exemplifies Jewish degeneracy. Suddenly, being a "pretender" bothers Reuben intensely. Although he does not defend Jews or reveal his Jewish identity during this party, the following day he writes a letter to the hosts to inform them that he is Jewish. Each member of the host family sends a letter to Reuben in return to apologize for their offensive comments. They continually invite him back to their home, but he never accepts.[49]

The episode teaches Reuben more about himself than about his hosts. His shame at concealing his Jewish identity leads Reuben to accept greater responsibility for his fellow Jews. In fact, after his experience at the dinner party, "He was almost for resuming his old name," Edman wrote of Reuben, "but only fear of being ridiculed for variability prevented him."[50] Reuben's reaction to his fellow diners' antisemitic remarks reveals the complex array of choices that some Jewish youths faced during the 1920s. Though initially too intimidated to speak out against discrimination, Reuben ultimately could not live with the consequences of being a bystander. Even as he stands up for Jews, he chooses to do so in a less confrontational way than he might have. Moreover, he does not risk revealing his Jewish identity to a broader public by reverting to his given name. He still finds himself between two worlds—the Jewish and the American—seeking to integrate the two.

The discoveries that Reuben subsequently makes as he enters American life hew closely to the pluralist agenda. He learns that Zionism and Americanism are entirely consistent and, despite a lifelong preference for dating gentiles, he decides to marry a Jewish woman. His encounters with antisemitism leave Reuben unwounded but also with a newfound conviction that the best way to respond to discrimination is to take pride in being Jewish. For Reuben, "entering American life" means allowing Jewish identity to blossom.

In the third essay, "Reuben Cohen Claims His Inheritance," Edman explored Reuben's innermost thoughts about the compatibility of American identity and Jewish identity. This installment does not include any narrative action, only Reuben's musings about whether "Jewish" should be understood as a race, a religion, a culture, or some combination of the three. Reuben does not settle on an answer, but he does come to believe that there is an "essence" within him that he can only describe as "Jewish." "If the Jew would but be himself," Reuben declares to himself, "he would find out quickly enough that he was a Jew." Any attempt to cast off that Jewish essence would constitute false living. Denial of self—assimilation—became a failing to avoid. "The Jew's uncanny capacity for assimilation was his defect," Reuben thinks. "It was up to the Jew to discover and exploit his own peculiar cultural contribution to America." Finally, Reuben fully embraces

Jewish consciousness. "One could now sail proudly under one's own colors," Reuben thinks. Edman described the realization as a "homecoming."[51]

This installment is particularly revealing of definitive dilemmas for some Jewish students during the interwar period. Edman marked Reuben's maturity by showing a process in which his typically youthful indecision disappears. By exploring the relevance of expressing his Jewish identity, Reuben begins to understand who he wants to be as an adult. Reuben's experience of finding ways for his Jewish and American identities to coexist in harmony precedes the philosophy used to name it. Consider, for example, Edman's pronouncement that "the day it had come to him clearly that he must live freely and authentically not only as an American but as an American Jew, Reuben felt that he had psychically come of age."[52] Indeed, Reuben here "claimed his inheritance," which was not financial wealth but the cultural wealth of the Jewish experience.

Reuben even directly echoes Kallen's pluralism when he asks: "Would one not be a better American for being a more complete and conscious Jew?" Edman made certain that readers would not be confused by the meaning of "Jew" here by spelling out that Reuben is not in search of religion in any denominational sense. Nor would models of Jewish culture from previous generations suffice. Reuben represents a new generation of American Jews who refuse to separate Jewish culture from American identity, and who instead find expressions that would be what Edman called "certainly Jewish in their source and color and just as certainly American in their possible realization." "What [Reuben] needed," according to Edman, "was a fusion of his Jewish blood and heritage with his American habits and environment. There was none to tell him where to find or how to make that amalgam."[53]

None, that is, until Kallen and cultural pluralism came along. Edman dismantled his thin fictional scrim fully in this installment, writing that "the Jew's uncanny capacity for assimilation was his defect: he assimilated by denying himself. It was at this time that Reuben came across that mystically mathematical phrase of Horace Kallen's: cultural pluralism. It was up to the Jew to discover and exploit his own peculiar cultural contribution to America."[54] It is crucially important that Reuben embraces a pluralist identity before he knows that Horace Kallen had given cultural pluralism its particular name. As a Jewish student and young man seeking to integrate himself into American life, Reuben's situation is particularly well suited to developing a pluralistic understanding of American society. Pluralism allows both Reuben's desire for acceptance and his commitment to difference to coexist without contradiction. From here, the tone of Reuben's self-expression changes. He is no longer a searching youth, but a young adult confident in his opinions about the world around him.

In the last three installments of Edman's series, Reuben acts on this new conviction. He attends a service at a synagogue and laments the failure of leadership and inspiration he finds there.[55] He reflects on the modern state of sex and marriage before determining that, despite a history of preferring non-Jewish companions, he would be "disinheriting himself" and future generations of Jews if he married a non-Jewish woman.[56] Finally, he philosophizes about the "vicious circle" of antisemitism and the possible options for Jews determined to avoid discrimination. The first option, which Reuben already had rejected, is "complete assimilation," or ceasing to be a Jew. The "more patient, more honest," and ultimately "more successful" option is to "be a Jew simply and honestly, and be at last at peace with one's own soul." Reuben's journey as told by Edman ends here, with the protagonist realizing that antisemitism is a "brutal" fact of life for Jews even in the United States, but that discrimination must not be the primary concern of American Jews or marker of Jewish identity. Rather, the "true defeat" of antisemitism would "be to develop a Jewish culture or idealism or express one's Jewish psyche, if there were any, so clearly and indefeasibly that they would be not only recognized but respected."[57]

Readers' closing moments with Reuben Cohen reveal a mature young man, confident in his beliefs about how to live a meaningful Jewish life in an American context. Over the course of Edman's six-part series, Reuben has progressed from indecision about how he is viewed by outsiders to conviction that he must define his adulthood by embracing Jewish identity. He has figured out how to live as an American Jew, and he has moved from this lived reality to a confidence in the ideology of cultural pluralism. The key to this confidence rested in placing culture at the center of Jewish identity and in envisioning America not as a nation of antisemites but instead as a nation that allows young people to develop and sustain particular cultural interests.

Reuben does not bury his head in the sand. He knows that antisemitism is "a fact, a brutal one." Yet he closes by declaring that hatred of Jews is "not a spiritual issue for a youth who was trying to find his way back to his place in Judaism." Reuben's journey, indeed, has been finding that way back on a path paved by cultural pluralism. This path, significantly, is not imposed upon him by his elders. Living with plural identities—American and Jewish—is a discovery Reuben makes in response to the challenges of his everyday life. As he discovers that cultural pluralism provides an answer to the dilemmas of his everyday life, Reuben comes of age as a young adult. This discovery represents Reuben's full maturity and allows him to turn to the "more important matters" of Jewish learning and Jewish culture.[58]

Jewish Students and Faculty in Fiction

Like Edman, many contributors to the *Menorah Journal* located their works in the world they knew best—the academy—and included only a thin veneer of fiction to explore the challenges of Americanization. Cohen solicited many of these contributions from writers, and some students, who lived in New York City. Two young contributors who would make a particularly significant mark on the magazine during the late 1920s were friends as Columbia University undergraduates, Henry Rosenthal and Lionel Trilling.

Rosenthal simultaneously parodied and lamented the typical Jewish faculty member's desperate desire to be accepted by colleagues in his April 1925 essay, "Emancipated Jew: Faculty Model."[59] The professor who provided the inspiration for this satire was likely either Columbia classicist Moses Hadas or philosopher Irwin Edman, the author of the Reuben Cohen series.[60] "Emancipated Jew: Faculty Model" chronicled the career path of a type: a "brilliant young Jew" who graduated from college with scholarly distinction but without passing the swimming test. Rosenthal's reference played upon stereotypes about Jewish men's lack of athleticism and thus lack of masculinity. To prove that he fit in, the semi-fictional young Jewish faculty member would pepper all his lectures with references to Christ and repeatedly insist on preferring Greek to Yiddish and English to Hebrew. In "his double-edged anxiety to create a good impression," Rosenthal explained, the "emancipated" faculty member could demonstrate that he belonged only by denying his Jewish consciousness that always lay just under the surface.[61] Rosenthal portrayed his professor's attempts to fit in as foolish.

Six months later, Rosenthal turned his satirical skills on students, using his own experience as inspiration. His character sketch, "Theological Student: Advanced Model," followed a graduate who wanted "to show a dubious world that one may be both genius and theologian, both rabbi and maker of paradoxes, both pious and clever."[62] Rosenthal's commentary on American rabbis' lack of intellectual acumen echoed the claims that Cohen had made in his 1918 essay "The Promise of the American Synagogue" and which had become commonplace for much of the Menorah circle's commentary on contemporary Jewish life. Unlike many of his colleagues at the journal, Rosenthal was not willing to give up on rabbis but instead challenged them here to advance both Judaism and intellectually rigorous expressions of Jewish culture.

Rosenthal later took it upon himself to answer this challenge. He would be ordained at the Jewish Theological Seminary after graduating from Columbia, and then became the religious director of New York's 92nd Street Young Men's Hebrew Association (YMHA). In 1942, Rosenthal returned to Columbia to earn a doctorate in philosophy, a subject he taught at Hunter College from 1948 to 1977.[63] While Rosenthal attended JTS during the late 1920s, he separated himself from Cohen and the Menorah Journal contributors. Although Rosenthal never wrote as frequently as the editors would have liked him to, his greatest contribution to the magazine actually may have come when he introduced his closest friend, Lionel Trilling, to Cohen.[64]

Trilling went on to become one of the most influential literary critics of the twentieth century, but in 1925, when the Menorah Journal ran his first contribution, he had never published before.[65] Trilling's six-year association with the journal had a profound influence. As historian Thomas Bender notes: "At the Menorah Journal, where [Trilling] published his early fiction and wrote reviews of Jewish novels, he came to understand and use ethnicity and class as social categories."[66] Between 1925 and 1931 Trilling published two "Commentaries," three fictional (but obviously autobiographical) short stories, two works of literary criticism, two translations from French, and at least twenty book reviews in the Menorah Journal.[67] Trilling forever claimed Cohen as a mentor, though he also thought Cohen resented his (relative) acceptance in academic circles.[68] Despite some tensions between the two men, Trilling remembered Cohen as the "only great teacher I ever had," especially high praise considering the regard in which Trilling held Columbia professors such as Mark Van Doren and John Dewey.[69]

Trilling's dedication to the Menorah idea of affirming Jewish particularity through cultural production and intellectual inquiry was substantial, as was his loyalty to the organization itself. Trilling worked as an assistant editor for the Menorah Journal in 1929 and 1930 and taught a course on representations of Jews in fiction during the 1930 session of the Menorah Summer School.[70] With Cohen's encouragement, Trilling wrote about his own Jewish identity for the Menorah Journal. Although Trilling's contributions tended to be set on college campuses rather than in the old neighborhood or the newly integrated suburb, the themes of alienation from the majority and disdain for the trappings of middle-class existence so common to the journal's fictional works also are present. Protagonists' reflections on their

Jewish identity, however, sometimes result in more positive ends in Trilling's stories than in many of the contributions considered earlier in this chapter.

The typical Jewish faculty member in Trilling's fiction was eternally lonely, exiled from New York City, and starved for Jewish companions and Jewish culture. Institutionalized antisemitism in academia and Jews' self-conception as outsiders pervaded these stories. One typical example was the story "Impediments," which ran in the June 1925 *Menorah Journal* when Trilling was just twenty years old.[71] "Impediments" examined a tenuous friendship between two Jewish undergraduates at Columbia, the unnamed narrator (based on Trilling) and the pushy Hettner (based on Rosenthal), who was desperate to become the narrator's friend.[72] Hettner, whom Trilling described as a "scrubby little Jew," visits the narrator too often in his room late at night for "intelligent and serious conversation." Little actually transpires in this short story beyond two Jewish college students talking in a room; this is instead a story about manners and mannerisms.

As two young men discuss philosophers including Dewey, Santayana, and Spinoza, the narrator observes Hettner with disgust—the way that Hettner lights his cigarette and sips his tea annoys the narrator to no end. Even as Trilling's narrator despises Hettner, he recognizes himself in the man: "I like people's outsides, not their insides," the narrator confesses to himself, "and I was particularly reluctant to see [Hettner's] insides; they would be, probably, too much like mine." Trilling here reflected on Jewish acculturation. Hettner's obviously Jewish sensibilities and mannerisms make the narrator uneasy. He is not disconnected from his Jewish past, but he fears and seeks to reject the more outward expressions that he associates with his "scrubby little Jew" companion. As literary critic Mark Krupnick notes, Trilling's anger is actually directed at both characters—the too-Jewish Hettner and the "paralyzingly self-conscious and proper" narrator who "yearns to break free."[73] In the end, neither character is sympathetic, but it is the narrator who struggles more because he is not being true to his Jewish self.

Trilling left New York from 1926 to 1927 to teach English as a lecturer at the University of Wisconsin–Madison. Some of Trilling's fiction over the next few years focused on his short experience there.[74] Trilling's move to Madison increased his sensitivity to considering what his Jewish identity meant to himself and to others. Much of his writing for the *Menorah Journal* during this period defined the Jew from the perspective of non-Jews. Frequently, this outsider's gaze was discriminatory, leading Trilling to wonder in a 1928 book review, "Is a Jew a Jew without a pogrom in the middle distance?"[75]

In an essay entitled "A Light Unto the Nations," Trilling wrote about one of his non-Jewish female students from New Jersey who sought a particular kinship with him because they both hailed from the East. The student told Trilling that she came to the Midwest for college because she could not compete with all the "Hebrews" in the entrance exams for East Coast schools. Trilling did not admit to the student that he was Jewish, but when another student—an Italian woman—visited his office in despair because she believed that being Italian had precluded her acceptance in America, Trilling did reveal his Jewish identity. "Her jaw dropped," he wrote. The student considered the situation for a moment after the shock wore off: "If he was a Jew, she was thinking, it could not be so terrible for her to be Italian." For the remainder of the semester, the Italian student wrote stories for Trilling's class about her ancestry and heritage.[76]

Following his meeting with the Italian student, Trilling's Jewish identity became known to the East Coast student who had commented to him about "Hebrews." For the remainder of the semester, she avoided eye contact with him and never again visited him in his office. Her work improved dramatically over the course of the semester, leading him to speculate that "she wanted to prove to a Jew that she was a considerable person." Even though these two students reacted so differently to learning that Trilling was Jewish, in both cases their perception of him inexorably changed. Neither student's reaction was particularly heartening to Trilling, nor was the tale intended to reassure readers about the potential of non-Jews to accept Jews. Although Trilling's identity was not initially obvious or easily discernable to these students, once it became known he was indelibly marked.[77]

Relationships with gentile faculty members differed from those with students. Trilling suspected that most of his colleagues knew he was Jewish. He reflected on being a Jewish member of the faculty at Madison most poignantly in his August 1927 story "Funeral at the Club, with Lunch." The story's narrator, a Jewish professor at a "non-metropolitan" university, goes to the faculty club for lunch, forgetting that a funeral service for a beloved professor is being held there that afternoon. At moments like this when a large number of faculty gathered, the narrator regards himself as "a stranger in a strange land." Although fellow faculty members never directly comment upon his being Jewish, the narrator worries that the funeral service would somehow bind the gentile faculty together with a "homogeneity and a particular essence" that he could not share.[78]

The narrator decides to sit alone for lunch on this particular day, rather than to join the young members of his department as he often does. As he eats alone, the narrator reflects on his behavior and his perspective changes significantly. Rather than feeling forced to be an "outlander," the narrator begins to understand his solitude as a conscious choice. "He has been kicked out not by intolerance," the narrator thinks, "nor by hatred, nor by prejudice (though probably some day that would happen), but by his own perception of the insufficiency of what was within."[79] The narrator then leaves the club, deciding not to attend the funeral of the fellow faculty member he had never met.

The narrator in "Funeral at the Club, with Lunch" forces himself to contend with his self-imposed segregation. Mark Krupnick recognizes this trait in much of Trilling's early writing: "Wherever Trilling's young protagonists go, they always secretly want to be part of the group, and at the same time they fight that impulse. They must discipline themselves always to affirm their difference."[80] At the end of this story, the narrator asserts that on days as beautiful as this, one should "set out on journeys" embracing the "company one can be to one's self."[81] Trilling's young instructor resolves to more fully consider his own Jewish identity, even at the cost of alienation from the majority.

Achieving this heightened awareness of Jewish difference, as well as embracing the desire to fully explore what that difference might mean, spoke to some of the limits of the Menorah Association's pluralist ideology during the 1920s. Pluralism more often entailed self-scrutiny and acceptance of Jewish cultural difference rather than practical suggestions to promote intercultural cooperation. The tinge of disdain for the mediocrity of non-Jews present in Trilling's story also cannot be denied as characteristic of the Menorah Association's pluralist ideology.[82]

Trilling left Madison in 1927, and he reflected on this experience in his May 1929 *Menorah Journal* story "Notes on a Departure." Again, Madison, or even the Midwest, is never mentioned specifically, but the story follows a professor as he says farewell to his many acquaintances in "the town" and prepares to return to "the city." As in "Funeral at the Club, with Lunch," Trilling's narrator in "Notes on a Departure" embraces the solitude of being Jewish in order to remain "free." Because he "embodied the separateness of his race," the narrator ensures that he will remain apart.[83] The narrator's greatest anxiety would be to remain too long in "the town" because he fears that would lead to a prolonged period of exile from his own culture. In his short stint in "the town," he already has found it too easy to blend into the majority, and he wants to close this option. Living in "the city" will return the narrator to a milieu in which he will no longer have to consider his difference in isolation.

Upon returning to New York, Trilling found the community he desired. As a part-time assistant editor of *Menorah Journal* beginning in 1929, he helped strengthen the Menorah Association's literary publications. Trilling ceased his affiliation with the *Menorah Journal* following a 1931 editorial dispute between Hurwitz and Cohen that led to Cohen's departure.[84] After Trilling's break with the *Menorah Journal* in 1931, he began to insist that he was not a "Jewish writer." Trilling's publications would never again address his own Jewish identity in such detail as did his 1920s work for the *Menorah Journal.*[85]

In 1932, Trilling would become the first Jewish person appointed to the faculty of Columbia's English Department, but this appointment was not without controversy. Trilling was dismissed in 1936—the faculty told him that because he was "a Freudian, a Marxist, and a Jew," he might be "more comfortable" at another school. In fact, he was not a Freudian or a Marxist, leaving only one "objectionable" label. Trilling protested, not on the grounds of antisemitism, but instead by arguing that the department would not be able to find a teacher more qualified than he. The majority of the professors within the department seemingly agreed. Trilling was reappointed and received his doctorate at Columbia in 1938. He retired in 1974 as a university professor, the highest honor Columbia bestows upon its faculty.[86]

The Fallacies of Assimilation

Ludwig Lewisohn, a leading Jewish fiction writer of the 1920s and regular contributor to the *Menorah Journal,* had quite a different experience with Columbia's English Department. Lewisohn was born into an acculturated Jewish family in Berlin in 1883. The Lewisohns immigrated to Charleston, South Carolina, in 1890 and sent Ludwig to Methodist Sunday School.[87] Reflecting on his childhood, Lewisohn wrote: "It is clear then that, at the age of fifteen, I was an American, a Southerner, and a Christian."[88] He eventually attended the College of Charleston. There, he experienced antisemitism that led to an awakening of what had been an almost entirely dormant Jewish consciousness.

Lewisohn went on to earn a master's degree in Columbia's English Department in 1903, but he was denied admission to the doctoral program in 1905. One of Lewisohn's professors, George Rice Carpenter, informed him that he had been rejected because Columbia's faculty thought it unlikely that he would be hired to teach English at any university following his graduation. Carpenter wrote to Lewisohn, "I do not at all believe in the wisdom of your scheme. A recent experience has shown me how terribly hard it is for a man of Jewish birth to get a good position."[89] Indeed, English departments would be among the last to open their doors to Jewish faculty in American universities, but this reality did not lessen the sting of rejection for Lewisohn.[90]

Following his inauspicious parting with Columbia, Lewisohn worked as a freelance writer and critic in New York City before moving to Madison in 1910 to become an instructor of German at the University of Wisconsin. He secured this appointment at Madison only after Columbia Professor Alexander Hohlfeld made a personal appeal to the department to hire Lewisohn despite the fact that he was Jewish.[91] Lewisohn lasted just one year in Madison before moving to Columbus to teach German at Ohio State University, where he remained until 1919. These years in Madison and Columbus were miserable ones for Lewisohn. His first autobiography, *Up Stream*, commented on his students' lack of intellectual curiosity and the antisemitism that pervaded university life during the 1910s. Lewisohn's German heritage and pacifist stance during World War I further compounded his difficulties at both Wisconsin and Ohio State.[92]

Lewisohn left academia and was hired by Oswald Garrison Villard as drama editor at the *Nation* in 1919. Between 1924 and 1934, he wrote from Europe and traveled to Palestine frequently, championing Zionism as the solution to antisemitism in Europe. This was especially evident in his 1925 autobiographical work *Israel*.[93] Lewisohn also credited his experiences with the Ohio State University chapter of the Menorah Society for his emergent interest in Jewish culture and Zionism.[94] From 1929 to 1931, he served as a contributing editor for the *Menorah Journal,* but he broke away in 1931, citing the excessively clever commentaries by young editors, including Cohen.[95] At the outset of World War II, Lewisohn (who was by then editing a journal called *New Palestine*) repudiated his earlier pacifism and endorsed Zionism as the best means to save Jews in Europe. He joined the faculty of Brandeis University upon its founding in 1948 and taught there until his death in 1955.[96]

As soon as Lewisohn became involved with the Menorah Society chapter at Ohio State, Hurwitz began to seek contributions from him for the *Menorah Journal.* Lewisohn continually refused.[97] Although Lewisohn finally did contribute to the journal in 1924, his work had been considered in its pages two years earlier, when Jacob Zeitlin reviewed Lewisohn's autobiography.[98]

Zeitlin was a provocative choice to review Lewisohn's book, because Zeitlin had been accepted as a graduate student in English at Columbia shortly after Lewisohn was denied admission to the doctoral program there. Zeitlin, who also was Jewish, went on to receive his Ph.D. in English at Columbia in 1908. That same year, he was appointed to the English faculty at the University of Illinois.[99] In his review, Zeitlin proved entirely unsympathetic to Lewisohn's failure to secure a position teaching English and he charged Lewisohn with using an excessively "rancorous tone" when recounting his experiences at Columbia. Moreover, Zeitlin suggested that being Jewish may not have been the primary reason for Lewisohn's exclusion. "In addition to being nominally a Jew," Zeitlin wrote of Lewisohn, "he was also indubitably a German." Zeitlin did praise Lewisohn's artistry in *Up Stream,* but he also wrote that "his being a Jew seems only to be an accident in the story."[100]

Lewisohn never responded directly to Zeitlin's review. If he had, he likely would have called Zeitlin an assimilationist. The insult would have been especially damning because Lewisohn dismissed assimilation as impossible, as he explained in his October 1925 *Menorah Journal* article, "The Fallacies of Assimilation."[101] The fallacy of assimilation was the belief that because certain opportunities or institutions opened to Jews, the Jewish people would blend in to such an extent that their distinct culture would cease to exist. Lewisohn passionately argued that Jews' continuous survival without a land, an army, or power should provide evidence enough that Jews would manage to survive the modern era, too, even with all its trappings and enticements to cast off Jewish identity.

Considering the public attention that *Up Stream* and *Israel* received, it was a coup for the *Menorah Journal* to serialize *Mid-Channel,* Lewisohn's third autobiographical work, before Harper and Brothers published it in 1929.[102] *Mid-Channel* appeared in nine consecutive issues, from July 1928 to March 1929. The book is a polemic against assimilation, a plea for a Jewish cultural renaissance, and a passionate endorsement of Hebraism. In other words, it is an expression of the Menorah idea encapsulated in autobiography.

Artists and intellectuals who truly committed themselves to a Jewish cultural renaissance embraced the wisdom of their ancestors' traditions even as they found ways to adapt these traditions for a modern setting. The greatest example of one who had achieved such a challenge, according to Lewisohn, was Martin Buber. In advocating a Jewish cultural renaissance in Germany beginning at the turn of the twentieth century, Buber worked in a German idiom even as his writings were "almost wholly Jewish in content."[103] Here, Lewisohn contrasted between "assimilation" and "self-emancipation." Assimilation, as he often noted, constituted "spiritual self-delusion" and "fraud."[104] Self-emancipation meant that Jews insisted on rights as a cultural minority from their host nation as they simultaneously demanded that their fellow Jews perpetuate Jewish culture and traditions. Lewisohn did not contend that achieving such a balance between American citizenship and Jewish culture was easy. In an echo of W. E. B. Du Bois's notion of double consciousness, Lewisohn wrote, "I carry a double burden and am wounded by a two-edged spear."[105]

For Lewisohn, as for the Menorah Association's intellectual progenitor Horace Kallen, Hebraism remained the linchpin that would allow Jews to solve this double burden. Lewisohn described Hebraism as the long "stream of tradition" within which Jews lived.[106] The stream may change its course and likely would not run straight, but that variance only proved the adaptive capabilities of Jewish people and Jewish culture. Hebraism, the totality of Jewish existence, had "adapted itself to civilization after civilization, to age after age, and kept its bearers a cultural and ethnic identity through all the storms and cataclysms of time."[107] Hebraism even complemented modern nationalisms, Lewisohn contended, because of its democratic qualities. It rejected authoritarianism and abided change, Lewisohn argued in the final chapters of *Mid-Channel*.

Lewisohn closed by issuing a challenge not to Jews in America but to gentiles throughout the world. "The Jewish problem is the decisive problem of Western civilization," Lewisohn asserted, but he claimed that it was a problem primarily for gentiles to address. Christian history, although it had produced gifted thinkers and creative artists, was also a history of war, cruelty, and hatred. The persistent lie that Jews had crucified Jesus was damning, but even more destructive was the way that Christians had abandoned Jesus' teachings by foolishly promoting hatred of strangers and fighting a world war that threatened to destroy civilization. The "belligerent nationalisms" endemic to Hellenism had to be balanced by the tolerance for difference that defined Hebraism. Lewisohn argued in closing that "the future of civilization needs a new synthesis of Hellenism and Hebraism, of nature and of spirit, of knowledge and righteousness" in order to secure peace.[108] Maintaining Jewish culture and advancing Hebraism therefore remained essential to the future not solely of Jews but to all of humankind.

Epilogue
"The Promise of the Menorah Idea"

———

In the autumn of 1931, Elliot Cohen and Herbert Solow resigned from the *Menorah Journal* after a bitter dispute with Henry Hurwitz about the magazine's editorial policies and future plans. These young editors' acerbic criticism earned the magazine a negative reputation in mainstream Jewish circles. Many IMA board members expressed their displeasure with the magazine's controversial articles of the late 1920s and early 1930s by quitting the organization. Reform rabbis increasingly spoke out against the *Menorah Journal* in their congregations. Some of the magazine's most talented writers, including Lionel Trilling, stayed loyal to Cohen and never wrote for the *Menorah Journal* again.[1]

The departure of the *Menorah Journal's* young editors in 1931 combined with a number of other factors during the 1930s to displace the magazine from the influence it once enjoyed. The financial challenges of the Great Depression slowed the publication schedule. After putting out twelve issues in 1928 and nine in 1929, the journal printed a total of only fifteen issues between 1932 and 1939. Economic constraints contributed to this drought, as did the fact that Hurwitz was forced for a time to edit the entire magazine himself. Increased competition from periodicals such as the *Partisan Review,* founded in 1934, and later *Commentary,* founded by the American Jewish Committee in 1945 (with Elliot Cohen as its first editor), also hurt.[2] Finally, the rise of the Nazi Party in Germany redirected the energies of many Jewish intellectuals from an inwardly focused discourse about Jewish particularity and American pluralism to considerations of how to best address the crisis abroad.

The *Menorah Journal*, without much staff or funding, did what it could during these years. It brought works by European Jewish intellectuals, including Hannah Arendt among many others, to an English-speaking audience for the first time and made efforts to help European scholars and intellectuals immigrate to the United States.[3] Although it continued to serve as a training ground for many Jewish scholars and refugees hoping to gain entry into English language publications, the quality of the journal and the attention it received between 1924 and 1931 would never be matched again.

The *Menorah Journal* soldiered on through the 1940s and 1950s, publishing at least one and sometimes as many as four issues a year until 1960.[4] In 1961 Henry Hurwitz died at the age of seventy-five, failing to reach the goal he had expressed late in life to see the *Menorah Journal* to its fiftieth anniversary in 1965. A final issue, published in 1962 by Hurwitz's son David Lyon Hurwood (who had changed his surname) and associate editor Leo W. Schwarz, celebrated and reflected on the IMA's accomplishments.[5]

Although Horace Kallen's *Menorah Journal* articles had generated some of the most strident criticism from Jewish authorities during the 1920s, he remained one of the magazine's champions all the way through its last issue. Appropriately, Kallen wrote the lead essay of the final issue, "The Promise of the Menorah Idea."[6] Kallen, by 1962 an eighty-year-old professor of philosophy at the New School for Social Research in New York City, used the occasion of returning to the *Menorah Journal* to reflect on the origins of pluralism in a revealing, memoir-laden essay. More than half a century after he responded so vigorously to the melting pot metaphor, Kallen again ruminated on what it meant to be American, and more specifically on what it meant to be Jewish in America. The concerns that prompted Kallen to coin cultural pluralism during the interwar period continued to resonate well into the Cold War.

It had been fifty-nine years since Kallen received his BA at Harvard. He reflected in 1962 on the dilemma of being a Jewish undergraduate at the turn of the twentieth century. "I felt the predicament myself when I entered college," Kallen wrote, "and desired to escape the handicaps laid upon one by being known as a Jew."[7] Calling Jewishness a handicap was not a product of melodramatic hindsight. When Kallen entered Harvard in 1900, he found himself at an institution that historically had been unwelcoming to Jews, and he lived in a national climate of increasing suspicion about the southern and eastern Europeans who continued to land on American shores.

Recall that Kallen himself had experienced a dramatic shift in his own self-understanding while at Harvard. The refiguring of his own Jewish identity accompanied an even bolder and inextricably related attempt to re-

Horace M. Kallen, 1968.
*Courtesy of the Jacob Rader Marcus Center of
the American Jewish Archives.*

define what it meant to be an American. In order to encourage a vibrant Jewish culture in America, Kallen had to imagine a nation that would make space for Jewish culture to flourish. The Menorah Association provided Kallen and his cohort with a structure to develop such Jewish culture, and it became the anchor of the social and intellectual pursuits of many Jewish college students during the 1910s and 1920s. The origins of cultural pluralism in the twentieth century were tied to these Jewish intellectuals' concerns about perpetuating Jewish culture. Moreover, a full understanding of cultural pluralism's origins depends on acknowledging the social and cultural milieu from which it emerged.

At mid-century, Kallen occasionally tried to downplay the connection between cultural pluralism and Jewish experience. In a 1953 letter to historian Moses Rischin, for example, Kallen claimed that his ideas about pluralism had a "strictly American derivation." He listed his intellectual influences and included his Harvard professors William James and Barrett Wendell. He also added Thomas Jefferson and Walt Whitman for good measure.[8] On other occasions, however, Kallen admitted that his desire to promote a renaissance of Jewish humanities informed his pluralist ideals. "The Promise of the Menorah Idea" is a particularly instructive example of Kallen's pointing directly to the connection between Jewish experience and cultural pluralism.

In "The Promise of the Menorah Idea," Kallen explained that a combination of lessons in history and math shaped his thinking about identity during his youth. In his American history courses, Kallen read and reread the Declaration of Independence. Perhaps it was no surprise that he focused on the words that embody the promise of America: "All men are created equal." In his math classes, Kallen learned that "equal" and "the same" were synonymous. With these lessons in tow, Kallen recalled himself wondering how to locate and identify the "'American' one craves to be 'the same as'?"[9]

Of course, Kallen never found what he called "'the American' that the imagination fashioned." As a young man growing up in Boston, and even as a Harvard student in the first decade of the twentieth century, he encountered a religious and cultural diversity that was unaccounted for in his American history lessons. Only occasionally did he even find the "superior sort of American," which he was taught to believe was "British and blond by ancestry and Puritan, Congregationalist, Unitarian, or otherwise Protestant . . . by religion." Instead, the "Americans" Kallen encountered were "Irish or Italian or German or Polish or French or Greek or Negro Americans."[10] Not all Americans were Protestant, and not all were blond.

As a young man, Kallen initially blamed himself for his inability to locate the true American. What he came to learn as his thinking on cultural pluralism evolved was that the fault was not in his searching but in his imagining. Kallen explained that during his undergraduate years, "It did not occur to me that 'equal' need not be a synonym of 'same' and that the Founding Fathers could not have intended it as a synonym."[11] Kallen's particular experiences allowed him to redefine his fundamental assumptions about American identity.

As Kallen reshaped these ideas, his understanding of what it meant to be Jewish also changed. Kallen credited Wendell, who "opened my eyes to . . . what [Jewish difference] might continue to signify, not in the American scene alone, but wherever it was unsuppressed and free to grow." Kallen then moved beyond the particulars of the Jewish case to claim that Jews could be a model for other ethnic and cultural groups in America. "And if this was true of the Jewish difference," he wrote, "it was of course true as well of any and all ethno-cultural groupings, each with its own singularity of form and utterance."[12] Kallen, however, did little to explain how the Jewish case actually would provide a model for other ethnic and cultural groups. What has so often been described as a shortcoming of Kallen's pluralist vision mattered more to critics than to Kallen, in large part because Kallen remained preoccupied with promoting Jewish culture as he conceived of pluralism.

In a revealing moment, Kallen next allowed himself to ask a difficult question, one he likely was not equipped to ask as pluralism was taking shape during the early twentieth century. To lead up to this question, Kallen returned to the idea that being Jewish was a "handicap" to "escape" at Harvard in 1900. "From my own experience I knew that my Jewish difference, even if it was only a seeming difference, yet could and did cripple my strivings for a life and a living." Jewish students' options were limited by restriction from social clubs at school and by exclusion from professions, neighborhoods, and organizations following graduation. Kallen eperienced discrimination firsthand while teaching in the English Department at Princeton, where his contract was not renewed shortly after his colleagues learned that he was Jewish.[13] Kallen recalled in 1962 that it seemed "reasonable" as an undergraduate to "rid myself" of Jewish difference "if I were able." In order to support the assertion that he would have been able to cast off his Jewish identity, Kallen turned to African Americans, though only as a foil to Jews in this case.[14] "I *was* able since, unlike the Negro, I could look and act and talk like the model of my choice. . . . In a word," Kallen wrote, "I could 'pass.'" Finally, he asked: "What then was the point of not passing, of suffering the lameness that not-passing entailed?"[15]

Before we turn to Kallen's answer, we should consider the meaning of pluralism at the specific historical moment when he penned this final *Menorah Journal* essay. It had been more than half a century since Kallen began to think about cultural pluralism. The idea never gained as much traction in American cultural life as the melting pot did. By the 1950s, few scholars even wrote about pluralism at all. The notable exception was Will Herberg, whose 1955 book *Protestant-Catholic-Jew* imagined the nation primarily as religiously pluralist.[16] Even Herberg's notion of religious plurality quickly came to be described as a "triple melting pot." It would be a profound mistake, however, to use this absence of the term "cultural pluralism" from public discourse to dismiss cultural pluralism as unimportant, or without a legacy in the national narrative about diversity.

The history of the melting pot metaphor itself bears this point out. The melting pot meant something significantly different by mid-century than it had in 1908.[17] In fact, its meaning had changed almost entirely. By the 1960s, the connotation of the melting pot actually resembled something close to what cultural pluralism had meant during the 1920s. Like many commentators on the melting pot metaphor during the 1910s, Kallen took offense at what he understood as its implication that immigrants and their children must leave behind their particular cultures in order to become American. Few observers still interpreted the melting pot in this way after World War II. By 1963, just one year after Kallen's final *Menorah Journal* essay, sociologists Nathan Glazer and Daniel Patrick Moynihan confidently declared, "The point about the melting pot . . . is that it did not happen." They did not mean that ethnics did not find ways to become American. They meant that becoming American did not necessitate discarding cultural particularity: "The notion that the intense and unprecedented mixture of ethnic and religious groups in American life was soon to blend into a homogenous end product has outlived its usefulness, and also its credibility."[18]

Although the idea of a culturally homogenized mass of Americans was discredited, the "melting pot" did not fall out of use—it just changed its meaning. By the 1950s, its meaning had come nearer to the idea that American culture would be reformed by the contributions of many different ethnic groups. Thus, as historian Stephen J. Whitfield reminds us, in 1958 Senator John F. Kennedy declared that "'the melting pot' need not mean the end of particular ethnic identities or traditions." In 1974, U.S. Supreme Court Justice William O. Douglas argued that the melting pot was not "designed to homogenize people." The melting pot instead implied a celebration, or at the very least a recognition, of the nation's cultural diversity. Kallen's theory—pluralism—though represented by that which he had meant to argue against—the melting pot—actually had "achieved the status of conventional wisdom" by the 1960s, according to Whitfield.[19] Indeed, it is an important lesson not only on the legacy of pluralism but also on how the meanings of key words in American history have the potential to change so profoundly over a relatively short time.[20]

Kallen's contribution to the national discourse about ethnic difference was not widely recognized during the 1950s or 1960s in part because of this very slipperiness of terminology.[21] Cultural pluralism only began to gain some attention later in the twentieth century when multiculturalists discredited Kallen for the shortcomings of his theory. Though Kallen had tried during the 1950s and 1960s to move away from the biological determinism suggested by his 1915 claim that one could not change one's grandfather, multiculturalists tended to remember him for what they interpreted as a theory of identity that essentialized descent. In his 1962 reflection on his early writings Kallen admitted, "At the time I shared the widespread belief—which I no longer hold—that these differences were rooted in race rather than created as cultures."[22] Critics ignored this correction, which Kallen also explained in a 1956 publication on cultural pluralism.[23]

Kallen's early conception of pluralism was anathema to many late-century multiculturalists because it failed to include non-Europeans. Recall that Kallen's institutional affiliations and social paths had crossed with both W. E. B. Du Bois and Alain Locke, but that his pluralist vision excluded African Americans. Long after the dissolution of the Menorah Association, in 1957, Kallen praised Locke as a "notable spokesman" for cultural pluralism.[24] Nonetheless, Kallen's credit to Locke came too late for his critics and did little to address the absence of non-whites from cultural pluralists' portrayal of the nation's cultural landscape.

As was so strikingly apparent in his 1962 claim that, "unlike the Negro . . . I could pass," Kallen continued to view Jewish difference as fundamentally unlike black difference in the United States. Kallen might have more clearly stated by the 1960s that what separated Jews from blacks was not something essential, but instead rested on the fact that Jews enjoyed different options for self-definition through affiliation.[25] In his claim about having the option to pass as gentile, we hear early echoes of the recent scholarship on ethnic and racial difference that has focused on "whiteness." Historian Andrew Heinze identifies "whiteness" as "academic shorthand for 'becoming American' (or becoming mainstream) by emphasizing the fact that one is not black." In seeking to dismantle the efficacy of whiteness as it relates to Jews, Heinze correctly recognizes that Jews' "legal status as free white citizens under the Constitution was never seriously challenged." Jews have in fact "enjoyed many of the privileges America offered whites and denied blacks."[26] As I have shown here, one of the most striking of these privileges has been the opportunity to redefine the limits and boundaries of inclusion in the nation itself. Kallen, like other Jews of his era, faced discrimination that should not be minimized, but he did not have to prove he was white—he simply had to recognize it and then ask himself whether he should also pretend to be gentile.[27]

The point here is not to unilaterally defend Kallen against criticism, but rather to historicize the origins of pluralism even as we recognize its limits. Even those multiculturalists who bristled at Kallen's logical shortcomings—after all, he never answered who would conduct his metaphorical orchestra of American cultural groups—and noted his failure to include non-European had to contend with pluralism as they reimagined possibilities for addressing diversity in the United States. As historian David A. Hollinger asserts, cultural pluralism "is an important precursor to multiculturalism."[28]

Moreover, the differences between pluralism and multiculturalism are particularly instructive. Multiculturalism imagines much broader boundaries of belonging in the national fabric. Multiculturalists tend also to enlist the help of the state in promoting diversity, where pluralists of the early twentieth century fought against state-sponsored Americanization programs. More troublingly, some multiculturalists have made victimhood a virtue. "In multicultural politics," Michael Walzer writes, "it is an advantage to be injured."[29] Despite these important differences, as Hollinger recognizes, Kallen "defended the rights of immigrants to resist assimilation and to maintain cohesive communities devoted to the perpetuation of ancestral religious, linguistic, and social practices."[30] Most late-century multiculturalists could endorse this agenda, at least in part. To do so, they would have to recognize that Kallen's pluralist ambition was no small thing in its time, and that it entailed real risks in the cultural and political climate of interwar America.

So why was the risk of not passing worth taking? We can now return to Kallen's question about "suffering the lameness" of being Jewish and opting not to pass. In his answer, Kallen argued for a reframing of perspective based on the logic of pluralism—cultural difference did not constitute "lameness" but strength. Accepting the logic of pluralism rendered passing antidemocratic. For, if pluralists succeeded, trumpeting cultural difference would no longer be perceived as un-American but as the very essence of being American.

A renaissance of Jewish culture as Kallen and his fellow Menorah Association founders imagined it would have allowed Jews to escape from feelings of inferiority, but it would have demanded that they not escape from Jewishness. In a society that valued cultural difference, promoting Jewish culture would not marginalize Jews but would create opportunities for them to coexist easily within a diverse ethnic landscape. According to Kallen, the cultural viability of the nation itself depended on this diversity. As he reminded readers in 1962, the "Menorah Idea," which he defined as promoting a renaissance of Jewish culture and humanities, depended fully on the "American Idea," which meant imagining the democratic nation as a federation of nationalities with distinct cultures.

A Jewish cultural renaissance not only benefited Jews. Kallen claimed that fostering the Jewish humanities "had the power to liberate . . . the non-Jews from their prejudices about Jews, [and] the Jews from their prejudices about themselves."[31] Kallen's own transformation from hostility for Judaism to a love of Jewish culture constituted a prime example of this possibility.

Kallen therefore made a place for Jewish culture only by first asking his readers to reconsider the meaning of American culture. There was no absolute "American." Therefore there was no norm to which Jews must assimilate, except in the minds of the nativists, who were so sorely mistaken. A norm to which all others adapted would have necessitated fixity, exactly the opposite of what pluralists believed about the modern world. In an ever-changing nation, attributing a fixed meaning to American identity was nonsensical. Just as American culture had to evolve continually, Jewish culture needed to remain a living entity. According to Kallen, the "social process" of American Jewish communities and organizations would determine the future of Jewish culture. If Jewish culture hoped to retain its value, it could not remain static. That, Kallen ultimately reminded readers, was exactly what a "*living* Jewish culture requires."[32]

NOTES

Abbreviations

AJA American Jewish Archives
HHMA Henry Hurwitz/Menorah Association Collection
HUA Harvard University Archives
RPALL Records of President A. Lawrence Lowell
RMS Records of the Menorah Society

Introduction

1. "Culture and the Ku Klux Klan" appeared in Kallen's 1924 collection of essays *Culture and Democracy in the United States* (1924; reprint, New Brunswick, N.J.: Transaction Publishers, 1998). The page numbers cited here refer to the 1998 edition.

2. Ibid., 16.

3. Gary Gerstle, *American Crucible: Race and Nation in the Twentieth Century* (Princeton, N.J.: Princeton University Press, 2001); John Higham, *Strangers in the Land: Patterns of American Nativism, 1860–1925* (New Brunswick, N.J.: Rutgers University Press, 1955, 1994); Nancy MacLean, *Behind the Mask of Chivalry: The Making of the Second Ku Klux Klan* (New York: Oxford University Press, 1994).

4. Kallen, "Culture and the Ku Klux Klan," 35.

5. Ibid.

6. Kallen, *Culture and Democracy in the United States,* 108. Reprint of Kallen's 1915 essay, "Democracy versus the Melting Pot."

7. Kallen, "Democracy versus the Melting Pot," *Nation* 100 (February 18 and 25, 1915): 190–94, 217–20.

8. There is no comprehensive biography on Kallen, but a number of scholars have published on his ideas. In a recent essay, Noam Pianko seeks to recover the importance of Kallen's Judaism and Zionism to the development of cultural pluralism. See Pianko, "'The True Liberalism of Zionism': Horace Kallen, Jewish Nationalism, and the Lim-

its of American Pluralism," *American Jewish History* 94 (December 2008): 299–329. Pianko also makes this point about Kallen's thought in *Zionism and the Roads Not Taken: Rawidowicz, Kaplan, Kohn* (Bloomington: Indiana University Press, 2010): see especially 41–47. See also Susanne Klingenstein, *Jews in the American Academy 1900–1940: The Dynamics of Intellectual Assimilation* (New Haven, Conn.: Yale University Press, 1991); Milton R. Konvitz, "Horace Meyer Kallen (1882–1974)," *American Jewish Year Book* 75 (1974–1975): 55–80; Konvitz, *Nine American Jewish Thinkers* (New Brunswick, N.J.: Transaction Publishers, 2000), 7–22; Konvitz, ed., *The Legacy of Horace M. Kallen* (Cranbury, N.J.: Associated University Presses, 1987); Sarah Schmidt, *Horace M. Kallen: Prophet of American Zionism* (Brooklyn: Carlson Publishing, 1995); William Toll, "Horace M. Kallen: Pluralism and American Jewish Identity," *American Jewish History* 85 (March 1997): 57–74.

9. Some of Kallen's often-cited works include *The Book of Job as a Greek Tragedy* (New York: Moffat, Yard, 1918); *The League of Nations: Today and Tomorrow* (Boston: Marshall Jones, 1918); *The Structure of Lasting Peace* (Boston: Marshall Jones, 1918); *Frontiers of Hope* (New York: Liveright, 1929); *Indecency and the Seven Arts* (New York: Liveright, 1930); *Individualism: An American Way of Life* (New York: Liveright, 1933); *The Decline and Rise of the Consumer* (New York: D. Appleton-Century, 1936); *Art and Freedom* (New York: Duell, Sloan and Pearce, 1942); *The Education of Free Men* (New York: Farrar, Straus, 1950); and *Utopians at Bay* (New York: Theodor Herzl Foundation, 1958).

10. On the Menorah Association, see Robert Alter, "Epitaph for a Jewish Magazine: Notes on the 'Menorah Journal,'" *Commentary* 39 (May 1965): 51–55; Lewis Fried, "The *Menorah Journal:* Yavneh in America, 1945–50," *American Jewish Archives Journal* 50 (1998): 77–108; Fried, "Creating Hebraism, Confronting Hellenism: The *Menorah Journal* and the Struggle for the Jewish Imagination," *American Jewish Archives Journal* 53 (2001): 147–74; Daniel Greene, "The Crisis of Jewish Freedom: The Menorah Association and American Pluralism, 1906–1934" (Ph.D. diss., University of Chicago, 2004); Elinor Grumet, "The Menorah Idea and the Apprenticeship of Lionel Trilling" (Ph.D. diss., University of Iowa, 1979); Louis Harap, "The Menorah Journal—A Literary Precursor," *Midstream* 30 (October 1984): 51–55; Jenna Weissman Joselit, "Without Ghettoism: A History of the Intercollegiate Menorah Association, 1906–1930," *American Jewish Archives Journal* 30 (November 1978): 133–54; Seth Korelitz, "The Menorah Idea: From Religion to Culture, From Race to Ethnicity," *American Jewish History* 85 (March 1997): 75–100; Mark Krupnick, "The Menorah Journal Group and the Origins of Modern Jewish Radicalism," *Studies in American Jewish Literature* 5 (Winter 1979): 56–67; Andrea Pappas, "The Picture at the *Menorah Journal:* Making 'Jewish Art,'" *American Jewish History* 90 (September 2002): 205–38; Lauren B. Strauss, "Staying Afloat in the Melting Pot: Constructing an American Jewish Identity in the *Menorah Journal* of the 1920s," *American Jewish History* 84 (December 1996): 315–31; Alan M. Wald, "The Menorah Group Moves Left," *Jewish Social Studies* 38 (Summer/Fall 1976): 289–320.

11. Thomas Bender, *New York Intellect: A History of the Intellectual Life in New York City, From 1750 to the Beginnings of Our Own Time* (Baltimore: Johns Hopkins University Press, 1987).

12. Diana Selig, *Americans All: The Cultural Gifts Movement* (Cambridge, Mass.: Harvard University Press, 2008), 11.

13. As Susan A. Glenn explains, "Jewish self-hatred" did not enter the lexicon in the United States until the post–World War II period. On Jewish self-hatred, see Glenn, "The Vogue of Jewish Self-Hatred in Post–World War II America," *Jewish Social Studies* 12:3 (Spring/Summer 2006): 95–136; Sander L. Gilman, *Jewish Self-Hatred: Anti-Semitism and the Hidden Language of the Jews* (Baltimore: Johns Hopkins University Press, 1990); Todd Endelman, "Jewish Self-Hatred in Britain and Germany," in *Two Nations: British and German Jews in Comparative Perspective,* ed. Michael Brenner, Rainer Liedtke, and David Rechter (London: Leo Baeck Institute, 1999), 331–63.

14. Michael A. Meyer, *Response to Modernity: A History of the Reform Movement in Judaism* (New York and Oxford: Oxford University Press, 1988), 75–99; Ismar Schorsch, *From Text to Context: The Turn to History in Modern Judaism* (Hanover, N.H.: Brandeis University Press, 1994).

15. Shmuel Feiner, *The Jewish Enlightenment,* trans. Chaya Naor (Philadelphia: University of Pennsylvania Press, 2002), xi.

16. On the Haskalah, see also Shmuel Feiner and David Sorkin, eds., *New Perspectives on the Haskalah* (London: Littman Library of Jewish Civilization, 2001).

17. Pierre Birnbaum and Ira Katznelson explain that emancipation "is a shorthand for access by Jews to the profound shifts in ideas and conditions wrought by the Enlightenment and its liberal offspring: religious toleration, secularization, scientific thought, and the apotheosization of reason, individualism, the law of contract and choice." They go on to write that emancipation led to a "double transformation: in standing" as Jews became political actors, "and in the creation of new options, based on rights, for them." The process of emancipation was neither uniform across nations nor linear within nations. A critical event in the process in many European countries was marked by Jews' admission to citizenship. See Birnbaum and Katznelson, eds., *Paths of Emancipation: Jews, States, and Citizenship* (Princeton, N.J.: Princeton University Press, 1995), 4.

18. As Noam Pianko writes, "Until recently, few scholars have analyzed Kallen's own claims about the role that his personal sense of discrimination and proud associations with Judaism and Zionism played in staking out his vision of integration without assimilation." Pianko, *Zionism and the Roads Not Taken,* 42.

19. Du Bois asked this question in his 1897 essay, "The Conservation of Races." See Du Bois, *The Souls of Black Folk* (Oxford University Press, 2007), 184. See also David Levering Lewis, *W. E. B. Du Bois: Biography of a Race, 1868–1919* (New York: Henry Holt, 1993), 172.

20. For James's influence on Du Bois, see Andrew R. Heinze, "Schizophrenia Americana: Aliens, Alienists, and the 'Personality Shift' of Twentieth-Century Culture," *American Quarterly* 55:2 (2003): 242.

21. On Jews and whiteness, see Heinze, "Is It 'Cos I's Black? Jews and the Whiteness Problem" (Ann Arbor, Mich.: Regents of the University of Michigan, Jean & Samuel Frankel Center for Judaic Studies, 2007). Although Heinze's short essay is the most convincing treatment, two other monographs that focus on Jews and whiteness are Karen Brodkin, *How Jews Became White Folks and What That Says about Race in America* (New Brunswick, N.J.: Rutgers University Press, 1998); and Michael Rogin, *Blackface, White Noise: Jewish Immigrants in the Hollywood Melting Pot* (Berkeley: University of California Press, 1996). Some of the works most useful for understanding historians' debate on whiteness are Eric Arnessen, "Whiteness and the Historians'

Imagination," *International Labor and Working-Class History* 60 (Fall 2001): 3–32; James R. Barrett and David R. Roediger, "Inbetween Peoples: Race, Nationality and the 'New Immigrant' Working Class," *Journal of American Ethnic History* 16 (Spring 1997): 3–44; Matthew Frye Jacobson, *Whiteness of a Different Color: European Immigrants and the Alchemy of Race* (Cambridge, Mass.: Harvard University Press, 1998); David R. Roediger, *The Wages of Whiteness: Race and the Making of the American Working Class* (London: Verso, 2007); and David R. Roediger, *Working toward Whiteness: How America's Immigrants Became White: The Strange Journey From Ellis Island to the Suburbs* (New York: Basic Books, 2005).

22. See Kallen, "Alain Locke and Cultural Pluralism," *Journal of Philosophy* 54 (February 28, 1957): 119–27. This 1957 article is a reprint of a speech Kallen delivered at New York University to the Alain Locke Memorial Committee on October 29, 1955. Louis Menand has pointed out that Locke did not share the same memories about the first use of "cultural pluralism." See Louis Menand, *The Metaphysical Club: A Story of Ideas in America* (New York: Farrar, Straus and Giroux, 2001), 391.

23. On Kallen and Locke, see Stephen Whitfield, "Introduction to the Transaction Edition," *Culture and Democracy in the United States,* 30–31; and Menand, *Metaphysical Club,* 388–91.

24. David Weinfeld, "What Difference Does the Difference Make? Horace Kallen, Alain Locke and Cosmopolitan Cultural Pluralism," unpublished paper, 2009. I thank David Weinfeld for sharing this paper with me. See also Ross Posnock, *Color and Culture: Black Writers and the Making of the Modern Intellectual* (Cambridge, Mass.: Harvard University Press, 1998).

25. Higham, *Strangers in the Land,* 198–99; Higham, *Send These to Me: Immigrants in Urban America* (Baltimore: Johns Hopkins University Press, 1984).

26. See Meyer, *Response to Modernity.*

27. On chosenness, see Arnold M. Eisen, *The Chosen People in America: A Study in Jewish Religious Ideology* (Bloomington: Indiana University Press, 1983); Daniel Greene, "A Chosen People in a Pluralist Nation: Horace Kallen and the Jewish American Experience," *Religion and American Culture* 16:2 (2006): 161–93; David Novak, *The Election of Israel: The Idea of the Chosen People* (Cambridge: Cambridge University Press, 1995); essays by Novak and Menachem Kellner in *A People Apart: Chosenness and Ritual in Jewish Philosophical Thought,* ed. Daniel H. Frank (Albany: State University New York Press, 1993); and Michael Walzer, Menachem Lorberbaum, and Noam J. Zohar, eds., *The Jewish Political Tradition, Volume II: Membership* (New Haven, Conn.: Yale University Press, 2000).

28. Most scholars agree that less than 5 percent of Jewish immigrants returned to Europe (and some of those likely immigrated again later). By comparison, according to Roger Daniels, 20 percent of Lithuanians, 36 percent of Slovaks, 66 percent of Romanians, and 87 percent of Balkan nationalities returned to their homelands after emigrating to the United States. Daniels, *Coming to America: A History of Immigration and Ethnicity in American Life* (New York: HarperCollins, 1990), 225.

29. Thorstein Veblen, "The Intellectual Pre-Eminence of Jews in Modern Europe," *Political Science Quarterly* 34 (1919): 41.

30. Andrew Heinze, *Jews and the American Soul: Human Nature in the 20th Century* (Princeton, N.J.: Princeton University Press, 2004), 70. Italics added.

31. On synthesis as a key principle in American Jewish history and culture, see Jonathan D. Sarna, "The Cult of Synthesis in American Jewish Culture," *Jewish Social Studies* 5 (1998/99): 52–79.

32. David Biale, "The Melting Pot and Beyond: Jews and the Politics of American Identity," in *Insider/Outsider: American Jews and Multiculturalism,* ed. Biale, Michael Galchinsky, and Susannah Heschel (Berkeley: University of California Press, 1998), 18.

33. Heinze, *Jews and the American Soul;* David A. Hollinger, "Ethnic Diversity, Cosmopolitanism and the Emergence of the American Liberal Intelligentsia," *American Quarterly* 27 (May 1975): 133–51; and Hollinger, *Science, Jews, and Secular Culture: Studies in Mid-Twentieth Century American Intellectual History* (Princeton, N.J.: Princeton University Press, 1996).

34. On the "Jewish problem," see Eric L. Goldstein, *The Price of Whiteness: Jews, Race, and American Identity* (Princeton, N.J.: Princeton University Press, 2006), esp. 119–37.

35. The writers and thinkers at the center of this book fit within the loose cohort of Progressive Era intellectuals who sought to recast meanings of American citizenship amid what historian Jonathan M. Hansen calls a "crisis of affiliation in American society." See Hansen, *The Lost Promise of Patriotism: Debating American Identity, 1890–1920* (Chicago: University of Chicago Press, 2003), xviii. Hansen's language echoes that of David A. Hollinger, who persuasively argues that identities are acquired largely through affiliation. See Hollinger, *Post-Ethnic America: Beyond Multiculturalism* (New York: Basic Books, 1995). See also Lynn Dumenil, *The Modern Temper: American Culture and Society in the 1920s* (New York: Hill and Wang, 1995), 251.

36. Edna Nahshon, ed., *From the Ghetto to the Melting Pot: Israel Zangwill's Jewish Plays* (Detroit: Wayne State University Press, 2006).

37. On the cultural resonance of Zangwill's play, see Werner Sollors, *Beyond Ethnicity: Consent and Descent in American Culture* (New York: Oxford University Press, 1986), 66–75.

38. Even those who championed the melting pot did not always agree on what it meant. See Biale, "The Melting Pot and Beyond: Jews and the Politics of American Identity"; Phillip Gleason, "American Identity and Americanization," in *Harvard Encyclopedia of American Ethnic Groups,* ed. Stephan Thernstrom (Cambridge, Mass.: Harvard University Press, 1980); Philip Gleason, *Speaking of Diversity: Language and Ethnicity in Twentieth Century America* (Baltimore: Johns Hopkins University Press, 1992); Neil Larry Shumsky, "Zangwill's *The Melting Pot*: Ethnic Tensions on Stage," *American Quarterly* 27 (March 1975): 29–41.

39. Milton M. Gordon, *Assimilation in American Life: The Role of Race, Religion, and National Origin* (New York: Oxford University Press, 1964), 84–114.

40. See Higham, *Strangers in the Land.*

41. Kallen, "Nationality and the Hyphenated American," *Menorah Journal* 1:2 (April 1915): 82. On hyphenation, see Higham, *Strangers in the Land,* esp. 194–233.

42. Authoritative definitions of "assimilation" and "acculturation" are elusive. Moreover, to define these terms in an absolute way immediately imposes a false unity on what historically has been an always messy conversation. On the shifting meanings of assimilation over time, see Gordon, *Assimilation in American Life;* Gleason, *Speak-*

ing of Diversity; Russell A. Kazal, "Revisiting Assimilation: The Rise, Fall, and Reappraisal of a Concept in American Ethnic History," *American Historical Review* 100 (April 1995): 437–71.

1. The Harvard Menorah Society and the Menorah Idea

1. *Harvard Crimson* (October 25, 1906); *Harvard Crimson* (October 27, 1906).

2. "Harvard College—Harvard Menorah Society: Minutes of Meetings, Constitution, correspondence, and newspaper clippings of the Society. 1906–1915." AJA Microfilm # 538.

3. Samuel Eliot Morison, *Three Centuries of Harvard, 1636–1936* (Cambridge, Mass.: Harvard University Press, 1936), 436.

4. Ibid., 417.

5. Minutes of Harvard Menorah Society meeting. November 1, 1906. AJA Microfilm #538.

6. Minutes of Harvard Menorah Society meeting. October 25, 1906. AJA Microfilm #538.

7. Higham, *Strangers in the Land;* Mae M. Ngai, *Impossible Subjects: Illegal Aliens and the Making of Modern America* (Princeton, N.J.: Princeton University Press, 2004).

8. Arthur A. Goren, *The American Jews* (Cambridge, Mass.: Harvard University Press, 1982), 2. A view across a larger span of time illustrates the increase in Jewish population in the United States. About 3,000 Jews lived in the United States in 1818. By 1918, the Jewish population in the U.S. reached 3.3 million. See Julius Drachsler, "The Trend of Jewish Communal Life in the United States," *Jewish Social Service Quarterly* 1:3 (November 1924): 2.

9. See Alfred Jospe, "Jewish College Students in the United States," *American Jewish Year Book* 65 (1964): 131.

10. Sherry Gorelick, *City College and the Jewish Poor: Education in New York, 1880–1924* (New Brunswick, N.J.: Rutgers University Press, 1981), 59.

11. Deborah Dash Moore, *B'nai B'rith and the Challenge of Ethnic Leadership* (Albany, N.Y.: SUNY Press, 1981), 137; Stephen Steinberg, *The Academic Melting Pot: Catholics and Jews in American Higher Education* (New York: McGraw-Hill, 1974), 8; Paula Fass, *The Damned and the Beautiful: American Youth in the 1920s* (New York: Oxford University Press, 1977), 123. Harold S. Wechsler notes, "In 1910, about 8.8% of the 17-year-old population was graduated from high school. By the early 1920s this percentage had doubled, and by the early 1930s it had doubled again." See Wechsler, *The Qualified Student: A History of Selective College Admission in America* (New York: John Wiley and Sons, 1977), 238.

12. Yuri Sleskine, *The Jewish Century* (Princeton, N.J.: Princeton University Press, 2004), 223.

13. Quoted in Paul Mendes-Flohr, *German Jews: A Dual Identity* (New Haven, Conn.: Yale University Press, 1999), 33.

14. Steinberg, *Academic Melting Pot,* 1.

15. See Marcia Graham Synnott, *The Half-Opened Door: Discrimination in Admissions at Harvard, Yale, and Princeton, 1900–1970* (Westport, Conn.: Greenwood Press, 1979), 30.

16. Jerome Karabel, *The Chosen: The Hidden History of Admission and Inclusion at Harvard, Yale, and Princeton* (Boston: Houghton Mifflin, 2005), 37. See also Hugh Hawkins, *Between Harvard and America: The Educational Leadership of Charles W. Eliot* (New York: Oxford University Press, 1972).

17. Louis Menand has written that Eliot's appointment as Harvard's president in 1869 signaled that "science, not theology, was the educational core of the future." See Menand, *Metaphysical Club*, 230. See also Christine Stansell, *American Moderns: Bohemian New York and the Creation of a New Century* (New York: Henry Holt, 2000), 57.

18. See Julie Reuben, *The Making of the Modern University: Intellectual Transformation and the Marginalization of Morality* (Chicago: University of Chicago Press, 1996), 101.

19. Nina Rosovsky, *The Jewish Experience at Harvard and Radcliffe* (Cambridge, Mass.: Harvard University Press, 1986), 8.

20. Jospe, "Jewish College Students in the United States," 131.

21. Synnott, *The Half-Opened Door*, 16.

22. "May Jews Go to College?" *Nation* 114 (June 14, 1922): 708.

23. "The creation of the country's first Office of Admissions, established at Columbia in 1910, was a direct response to the 'Jewish problem.'" Karabel, *The Chosen*, 129. For a discussion of elite universities' responses to increased Jewish student enrollment in the 1920s, see chapter 2.

24. Harvard raised its tuition from $140 to $150 per year just before Eliot became president in 1869. For the rest of his forty-year administration, he refused to raise Harvard's tuition, arguing that a tuition increase would prevent students who had attended public high schools from attending. Hawkins, *Between Harvard and America*, 170–71. David O. Levine, *The American College and the Culture of Aspiration 1915–1940* (Ithaca, N.Y.: Cornell University Press, 1986), 17.

25. For more on this point, see chapter 2.

26. See Karabel, *The Chosen*, especially chapters 1–4.

27. See Gary T. Greenebaum, "The Jewish Experience in the American College and University" (master's thesis, Hebrew Union College-Jewish Institute of Religion, 1978), 53.

28. "Report of the Committee on Religious Work in Universities," *CCAR Yearbook* 16 (1906), 188. See *Jewish Students: A Survey Dealing with the Religious, Educational, Social and Fraternal Activities among Jewish Students at Universities and Colleges* (Cincinnati: Department of Synagog and School Extension, 1915), 4. During the same era, Rabbi Kaufman Kohler, a pillar of the Reform movement, also proposed that Reform rabbis travel to colleges to teach Christian students about Judaism and the Jewish people. See Lila Corwin Berman, *Speaking of Jews: Rabbis, Intellectuals, and the Creation of an American Public Identity* (Berkeley: University of California Press, 2009), 11–33.

29. "Report of the Committee on Religious Work in Universities," *CCAR Yearbook* 22 [1912], 67. Jewish fraternities during this period included Zeta Beta Tau (founded 1897), Sigma Alpha Mu (1909), and Alpha Epsilon Pi (1913). See Marianne R. Sanua, *"Here's to Our Fraternity": One Hundred Years of Zeta Beta Tau, 1898–1998* (Hanover, N.H.: Zeta Beta Tau Foundation, 1998).

30. The Maimonides Club, "devoted to the consideration of problems of Jewish

interest," was advised by the nationally prominent Rabbi Emil G. Hirsch of Chicago Sinai Congregation. See RMS. Aaron Horvitz Correspondence, 1910–1913. Letter, Ida Perlstein, secretary of University of Chicago Maimonides Club to Aaron Horvitz, February 9, 1908. HUD 3568.515. HUA.

31. "Report of the Committee on Religious Work in Universities," *CCAR Yearbook* 18 (1908), 78.

32. *The Menorah Movement: For the Study and Advancement of Jewish Culture and Ideals* (Ann Arbor, Mich.: Intercollegiate Menorah Association, 1914), 6–7.

33. Harvard Menorah Society minutes. AJA Microfilm # 538. Allan Davis, Harvard class of 1907, was the first president of both the Harvard Zionist Society and the Harvard Menorah Society. See *Harvard Class of 1907: Twenty-fifth Anniversary Report* (Norwood, Mass.: Plimpton Press, 1932), 132–34.

34. *The Menorah Movement, 1.*

35. See Joselit, "Without Ghettoism: A History of the Intercollegiate Menorah Association 1906–1930," 137.

36. Minutes of Harvard Menorah Society meeting. November 1, 1906. AJA Microfilm #538.

37. Minutes of Harvard Menorah Society meeting. November 20, 1906. AJA Microfilm # 538.

38. *The Menorah Movement, 6.*

39. Michael A. Meyer, *Jewish Identity in the Modern World* (Seattle: University of Washington Press, 1990), 17.

40. *The Menorah Movement, 6.*

41. Webster's dictionary dates the first English language usage of "menorah" to 1888.

42. On synthesis, see Sarna, "The Cult of Synthesis in American Jewish Culture."

43. "The Cercle Francais," *Harvard Illustrated Magazine* (May 1900): 200–203. HUD 3262.200.95. HUA; "Deutscher Verein," HUD 3324.500. HUA.

44. *The Menorah Movement, 2.* The Menorah Society's literature refers to the German and French clubs at Harvard much more often than the Italian or Spanish organizations.

45. In 1889, Jacob H. Schiff gave $10,000 to the Harvard Semitic Department to purchase objects useful for instruction. The Semitic Museum formally opened on February 5, 1903. See David Gordon Lyon, "The Semitics Museum," *Harvard Alumni Bulletin* (February 9, 1916): 357–59; *The Semitic Museum at Harvard University* (Cambridge, Mass.: Harvard University, 1903).

46. "Harvard Menorah Society Annual Report 1908–1909," May 13, 1909. Harvard University Archives. HUA 3568.771.5.

47. Ibid.

48. Ibid.

49. Henry Hurwitz, "A Mother Remembered," *American Jewish History* 12 (September 1980), 21. Hurwitz's son, David Lyon Hurwood, discovered and published this manuscript long after his father's death in 1961.

50. *Harvard Class of 1908: Fiftieth Anniversary Report* (Cambridge, Mass.: Harvard University Printing Office, 1958), 339–41.

51. Ira Eisenstein, "Henry Hurwitz: Editor, Gadfly, Dreamer," in *The "Other" New York Jewish Intellectuals,* ed. Carole S. Kessner (New York: New York University Press, 1994), 191–205.

52. In 1908–1909, sixty-six Jewish students at Harvard were of eastern European birth or descent; eight were of German descent. The Jewish population at Yale was similar. Until the twentieth century, the few Jewish students at Yale had been descendants of German Jews who had immigrated to the United States during the mid-nineteenth century. Things changed in the early 1900s, though. "If we count both sons of immigrants and the foreign-born, Russian Jews numbered 71 of the 95 Jewish academic students [at Yale] in 1908," historian Marcia Graham Synnott notes. Synnott, *Half-Opened Door,* 44. See also Eve Rachel Markewich, "The Menorah Society, or Being Jewish at Harvard, 1906–11" (B.A. thesis, Harvard-Radcliffe College, 1983), 5.

53. Harvard Menorah Society minutes. January 12, 1907. AJA Microfilm # 538.

54. RMS. Correspondence, 1906–22. Unsigned letter, Frederick Greenman (most likely) to Meyer London, November 23, 1915. HUD 3568.510. HUA.

55. RMS. Harvard Menorah Society minutes, October 30, 1907. HUD 3568.505. HUA; Markewich, "The Menorah Society, or Being Jewish at Harvard," 22.

56. *The Menorah Movement,* 10.

57. "Harvard Menorah Society, Prospectus 1907–1908," 2. AJA Microfilm # 538.

58. "Documents Exhibiting the Relations between the Harvard Menorah Society and the Union of American Hebrew Congregations," May 15, 1913. HHMA 19/10. AJA. This document is also in the Harvard University Archives. HUD 3568.913.5.

59. Wise to Aaron Horvitz, November 7, 1908. Quoted in "Documents Exhibiting the Relations between the Harvard Menorah Society and the Union of American Hebrew Congregations," May 15, 1913. HHMA 19/10. AJA.

60. George Zepin. Annual Report, Director of Synagog and School Extension. October 31, 1910. HHMA 60/7. AJA.

61. In 1911, for example, the UAHC sent the following rabbis and Jewish leaders to address Harvard students: Samuel Schulman, David Philipson, Kaufman Kohler, Emil G. Hirsch, Israel Friedlaender, and J. Leonard Levy. See HHMA 60/7. AJA.

62. *CCAR Yearbook* 22 (1912), 216.

63. *The Menorah Movement,* 10. In 1913, Horace Kallen did found a secret Zionist organization, called the "Parushim," a Hebrew word meaning both "Pharisees" and "separate." Some Menorah Society founders, including Hurwitz, did belong to Kallen's secret organization. The Parushim's accomplishments were few, however, and the organization ceased to exist by the end of the 1910s. See Sarah Schmidt, "The *Parushim:* A Secret Episode in American Zionist History," *American Jewish Historical Quarterly* 65 (December 1975): 121–39.

64. "Jewish Students Active at Harvard," *American Hebrew* (April 1, 1910): 584.

65. RMS. Correspondence, 1906–22. "J. Ewbaiter" to Harvard Menorah Society president, December 23, 1907. HUD 3568.510. HUA.

66. Undated document, no title. HHMA 19/12. AJA.

67. *The Menorah Movement,* 4.

68. "Harvard Menorah Society, Prospectus 1907–1908," 2. AJA Microfilm # 538.

69. On the *Verein für Cultur und Wissenschaft der Juden,* see Ismar Schorsch, *From Text to Context,* 205–32.

70. See especially Kallen, "Hebraism and Current Tendencies in Philosophy," written in 1909 and republished in Kallen, *Judaism at Bay: Essays Toward the Adjustment of Judaism to Modernity* (New York: Bloch Publishing, 1932), 7–15; and Kallen, "Judaism, Hebraism and Zionism," *American Hebrew* (June 24, 1910): 181–83.

71. At the time of Kallen's birth, Bernstadt belonged to the German empire. Today, the area is part of Poland.

72. Higham, *Send These to Me*, 206.

73. Konvitz, "Horace Meyer Kallen (1882–1974)," 65.

74. Kallen also taught for one semester as an instructor in logic at Clark University. On his claim regarding Princeton, see Kallen, "The Promise of the Menorah Idea," *Menorah Journal* 49 (Autumn–Winter 1962): 12; and Kallen's obituary in the *New York Times* (February 17, 1974): 66.

75. Kallen letter to I. B. Lipson, December 8, 1917. Kallen Papers, AJA.

76. On Reform Judaism, see Meyer, *Response to Modernity*.

77. Konvitz, "Horace Meyer Kallen (1882–1974)," 65.

78. Kallen, "The Promise of the Menorah Idea," 9–16.

79. Kallen, *Judaism at Bay*, 47.

80. Arnold, "Hebraism and Hellenism," in *Culture and Anarchy*, ed. Stefan Collini (Cambridge: Cambridge University Press, 1993), 127.

81. Kallen, "Hebraism and Current Tendencies in Philosophy," in *Judaism at Bay*, 14.

82. Klingenstein, *Jews in the American Academy 1900–1940*, 44.

83. Kallen, "Hebraism and Current Tendencies in Philosophy," in *Judaism at Bay*, 13.

84. Kallen, undated, handwritten document called "HEBRAISM and the Ethos of Modernity," in Kallen Papers 57/5. AJA.

85. Kallen, "Hebraism and Current Tendencies in Philosophy," in *Judaism at Bay*, 12.

86. Menand, *Metaphysical Club*, 88.

87. This concept is expressed in many of Kallen's writings, one of the most notable being "Democracy versus the Melting Pot," *Nation* 100 (February 18 and 25, 1915): 190–94, 217–20.

88. "The Third Annual Convention of the Menorah Societies," *Menorah Journal* 1:2 (April 1915): 130.

89. Kallen to Mack, January 19, 1915. Kallen Papers 20/10. AJA.

90. *The Menorah Movement*, 84. Italics in original.

91. Ibid., 84.

92. Ibid., 86.

93. Pianko, "'The True Liberalism of Zionism,'" 301, 311–12; Pianko, *Zionism and the Roads Not Taken*, 46.

94. See Paul Mendes-Flohr and Jehuda Reinharz, *The Jew in the Modern World: A Documentary History*, 2nd ed. (New York: Oxford University Press, 1995), 543. On Ahad Ha'am, see Steven J. Zipperstein, *Elusive Prophet: Ahad Ha'am and the Origins of Zionism* (London: Peter Halban, 1993).

95. *The Menorah Movement*, 86. Italics in original.

96. "The Harvard Menorah Society," *American Hebrew* (May 14, 1909): 44.

2. The Intercollegiate Menorah Association and the "Jewish Invasion" of American Colleges

1. At the University of Minnesota, for example, the University Jewish Literary Society agreed to affiliate with the Menorah Association in 1911, changing its name to

the University of Minnesota Menorah Society and limiting its nonacademic activities. *The Menorah Movement*, 105; William E. Austin, "The Story of the Menorah Movement" (unpublished paper, 1963), 9. See "Report of Minnesota Menorah Society. December 1921," HHMA 73/7. AJA.

2. "Record of the Menorah Society of University of Minnesota for 1922–23," HHMA 29/10. AJA. "Report of Activities of Menorah Society of University of Minnesota for 1915," December 20, 1915, HHMA 73/6. AJA.

3. Schechter's speech was reprinted in *The Menorah Movement*, 67.

4. Quoted in ibid., 51.

5. Hapgood, "Schools, Colleges and Jews," *Harper's Weekly* 62 (January 22, 1916): 79.

6. By 1918, Menorah societies also were established at two Canadian universities, the University of Manitoba and the University of Toronto. See "Menorah Statistics—1915–1916," HHMA 67/9; Report to the officers of the IMA, November 25, 1918. HHMA 67/1. AJA.

7. See Karabel, *The Chosen;* Synnott, *The Half-Opened Door.*

8. "The Jewish Student at Harvard," *American Hebrew* (January 1, 1909): 248.

9. *The Menorah Movement*, 109.

10. Newspaper clipping, no source provided. AJA Microfilm #538.

11. RMS. Correspondence. HUD 3568.510. HUA; RMS. Harvard Menorah Society President's Reports. Annual Report 1908–1909. HUD 3568.771.5. HUA.

12. RMS. Aaron Horvitz Correspondence. R. Kaufman to Aaron Horvitz, November 2, 1910. HUD 3568.515. HUA.

13. RMS. Harvard Menorah Society, Minutes. Report of the Secretary, 1913–14. HUD 3568.505. HUA.

14. *The Menorah Movement.*

15. "Statistical Report of Menorah Societies: December 1919," HHMA 68/3. AJA. See also document entitled, "Growth of movement" in HHMA 69/8. AJA.

16. Hurwitz, "The Growth of the Menorah Movement," *American Hebrew* (March 26, 1915): 566.

17. Lehman to IMA convention, December 21, 1914. HHMA 29/7. AJA.

18. Sarna, "The Cult of Synthesis in American Jewish Culture," 52.

19. *The Menorah Movement*, 55, 51.

20. Ibid., 13.

21. S. Willis Rudy, *The College of the City of New York: A History, 1847–1947* (New York: City College Press, 1949), 386–87.

22. *The Menorah Movement*, 110.

23. Gorelick, *City College and the Jewish Poor,* ix. City College remained tuition free until 1976.

24. *Menorah Journal* 1:1 (January 1915): 59. CCNY Menorah Society Report. HHMA 74/4. AJA; Rudy, *The College of the City of New York,* 294.

25. *The Menorah Movement*, 112.

26. *Menorah Journal* 3:1 (February 1917): 56.

27. *Menorah Journal* 2:5 (December 1916): 326.

28. See *American Hebrew* (July 7, 1916): 287; Hurwitz to Baruch, September 27, 1917; Baruch to Hurwitz, November 18, 1921; Hurwitz to Baruch, November 14, 1922. HHMA 2/21. AJA.

29. *Menorah Journal* 1:1 (January 1915): 59.

30. *Menorah Journal* 3:2 (April 1917): 117–18.

31. "Resolution Passed by the Intercollegiate Menorah Association, December 31, 1917," HHMA 23/3. AJA; see also Joselit, "Without Ghettoism: A History of the Intercollegiate Menorah Association 1906–1930," 145.

32. Menorah Society of CCNY to Henry Hurwitz, December 1, 1920. HHMA 7/14. AJA.

33. "The Menorah Interest," no date (likely August or September 1921). HHMA 39/4. AJA.

34. See Cohen to Hurwitz, September 14, 1921. HHMA 39/4. AJA.

35. See Hurwitz to Marcus, May 29, 1916. HHMA 70/18. AJA.

36. "Intercollegiate Menorah Association: Third Annual Convention. Public Meeting, December 23, 1914," HHMA 67/7. AJA.

37. See RMS. Correspondence, 1906–22. Letter, Marshall to Everett H. Stahl, President, Harvard Menorah Society, August 26, 1924. HUD 3568.510. HUA.

38. Reform Judaism's official position on Zionism would undergo a transformation between the 1880s and the 1930s. An 1885 declaration by the Central Conference of American Rabbis declared Jews "no longer a nation, but a religious community." In 1937 this anti-nationalist stance would be overturned by the Reform movement's Pittsburgh Platform, which declared, "In the rehabilitation of Palestine, the land hallowed by memories and hopes, we behold the promise of a renewed life for many of our brethren." This history is chronicled in Mark A. Raider, *The Emergence of American Zionism* (New York: New York University Press, 1998). On these platforms, see 12, 173.

39. Sidney L. Regner to Francis Grossel, March 2, 1924. HHMA 71/4. AJA.

40. On this point, see Joselit, "Without Ghettoism," 142. See also "Menorah Students and Jewish War Relief," *Menorah Journal* 2:4 (October 1916): 266–67.

41. Cornell University. 1913–1917. HHMA 71/10. AJA.

42. See, for example, Richard Gottheil, "The War from a Jewish Standpoint," *Menorah Journal* 1:3 (June 1915); "Jewish Ideals and the War," *Menorah Journal* 3:3 (June 1917); Hurwitz, "The War and the Menorah Quinquennial," *Menorah Journal* 3:4 (October 1917); Julian W. Mack, "Jewish Hopes at the Peace Table," *Menorah Journal* 5:1 (February 1919).

43. Minutes of the informal Menorah conference, April 9, 1917. HHMA 55/7.

44. RMS. Correspondence of Aaron Horvitz, 1910–13. Horvitz to Blumberg, December 9, 1912. HUD 3568.515. HUA.

45. See Stearns, *Confessions of a Harvard Man* (Santa Barbara, Calif.: Paget Press, 1984), 70.

46. RMS. Treasurer's files, including reports 1906–1927. Treasurer's Report of Charles A. Rome, May 7, 1917. HUD 3568.787. HUA. Emphasis in original.

47. RMS. Treasurer's files, including reports 1906–1927. Treasurer's Report of David Stoffer, May 10, 1921. HUD 3568.787. HUA.

48. RMS. Membership Committee. Report, May 23, 1924. HUD 3568.654. HUA.

49. Weinstein was ordained by HUC in 1929 and served as rabbi at Chicago's Kehilath Anshe Maariv (KAM) Temple from 1939 until 1974. Presidents Kennedy and Johnson appointed him to civil rights and labor negotiating committees, respectively.

Janice J. Feldstein, ed., *Rabbi Jacob Weinstein: Advocate of the People* (New York: Ktav Publishing House, 1980).

50. See information in "Portland Menorah Society, 1922–23," HHMA 75/9. AJA.

51. Julietta Kahn's memo, dated March 22, 1922. Harvard University. 1919–1921. HHMA 72/1. AJA.

52. Raider, *Emergence of American Zionism*, 22.

53. Kallen taught at the IZAA's Zionist Summer Course in 1915. See "Bulletin: Intercollegiate Zionist Organization of America" 8 (May 25, 1917), in Kallen's papers 39/11. AJA; Alfred Jospe, "Jewish College Students in the United States," 137–38.

54. See Schaffer to Hurwitz, October 17, 1917, and January 30, 1919. HHMA 52/7. AJA.

55. See Blau to Hurwitz, December 11, 1917. HHMA 6/1. AJA.

56. Jonas S. Friedenwald, "The Intercollegiate: A Retrospect," in *Kadimah*, ed. David S. Blondheim (New York: Federation of American Zionists, 1918), 196–97, as quoted in Raider, *Emergence of American Zionism*, 23.

57. See I. B. Hoffmann to IMA, March 31, 1919. HHMA 71/9. AJA.

58. European Jewish fraternities preceded Jewish fraternities in America. As Marion A. Kaplan writes: "In 1886, as a result of their exclusion from [non-Jewish] student life, Jewish men formed the first Jewish fraternity. The *Viadrina*, as it was called, was intended to cultivate a sense of Jewish identity and to practice self-defence. In 1896, Jewish men founded a national association of Jewish fraternities, the *Kartell-Convent*." Kaplan, "Tradition and Transition: The Acculturation, Assimilation and Integration of Jews in Imperial Germany. A Gender Analysis," *Leo Baeck Institute Yearbook* 27 (1982): 31.

59. On ZBT, see Sanua, "*Here's to Our Fraternity*"; Sanua, "Jewish College Fraternities in the United States, 1895–1968: An Overview," *Journal of American Ethnic History* 19 (Winter 2000): 3–42; Sanua, "The Non-Recognition of Jewish Fraternities: The Case of Columbia and Brown Universities," *American Jewish Archives* 45 (Fall/Winter 1993): 129–30; Lee J. Levinger, *The Jewish Student in America: A Study Made by the Research Bureau of the B'nai B'rith Hillel Foundations* (Cincinnati: B'nai B'rith, 1937), 2.

60. Among the early women's Jewish societies, Sanua includes: "Iota Alpha Pi, founded at the predecessor to Hunter College in 1904 by the younger sister of a ZBT member; Alpha Epsilon Phi, founded at Barnard in 1900; Phi Sigma Sigma, founded in 1913, also at Hunter College; and Sigma Delta Tau and Delta Phi Epsilon, both founded in 1917, at Cornell and New York University." See Sanua, "The Non-Recognition of Jewish College Fraternities," 131.

61. Synnott, *Half-Opened Door*, 23. African American students first formed a Greek system 1906. In 1930, existing African American fraternities came together under an organization called the National Pan-Hellenic Council. See Sanua, "Jewish College Fraternities in the United States," 34n17.

62. Synnott, *Half-Opened Door*, 24.

63. Gottheil to Sharfman, May, 15, 1915. HHMA 15/6. AJA.

64. See Fass, *The Damned and the Beautiful*, 141–67; and Levine, *American College and the Culture of Aspiration*, 120–21.

65. Synnott, *Half-Opened Door*, 101.

66. Ida Feldman to Charles Mantinband, March 15, 1920. HHMA 70/8. AJA.

67. See Isador Lubin to Hurwitz, March 22, 1922. HHMA 33/9. AJA.

68. See Kahn's memo to Hurwitz, titled, "An Analysis and a Recommendation." There is no date on this memo, but Hurwitz sent it to some of his colleagues for their opinion on March 22, 1922. The memo can be found in many different locations at the AJA, including HHMA 20/9; 67/2; 67/3; and in the Adolph S. Oko Papers 8/5.

69. Jewish student enrollment at Columbia University became an issue earlier than at other institutions. Columbia president Nicholas Murray Butler expressed concern about the large percentage of Jewish students in the college in 1915. Historian Harold S. Wechsler convincingly demonstrates Columbia's "not-so-graceful withdrawal" from liberal admission standards. See Wechsler, *Qualified Student,* especially chapter 7: "Repelling the Invasion: Columbia and the Jewish Student."

70. See Steinberg, *Academic Melting Pot,* 22; Synnott, *Half-Opened Door,* 19; Synnott, "Anti-Semitism and American Universities: Did Quotas Follow Jews?" in *Anti-Semitism in American History,* ed. David A. Gerber (Urbana: University of Illinois Press, 1986); and "May Jews Go to College?" *Nation* 114 (June 14, 1922): 708.

71. See Levine, *American College and the Culture of Aspiration,* 90–95.

72. Louis I. Newman, *A Jewish University in America?* (New York: Bloch, 1923), 11.

73. On the debates about immigration quotas, see Mae M. Ngai, "The Architecture of Race in American Immigration Law: A Reexamination of the Immigration Act of 1924," *Journal of American History* 86:1 (June 1999); Mae M. Ngai, "The Strange Career of the Illegal Alien: Immigration Restriction and Deportation Policy in the United States, 1921–1965," *Law and History Review* 21:1 (Spring 2003); Ngai, *Impossible Subjects.*

74. Many schools did limit total student enrollment during the 1920s. Harvard capped its freshman class at 1,000, Yale at 850, and Princeton at 600. See Synnott, *Half-Opened Door,* 14.

75. "Harvard Is Overcrowded," *New York Times* (June 1, 1922): 6.

76. *New York Times* (June 2, 1922): 1.

77. See Wechsler, *Qualified Student,* 161–62; Hawkins, *Between Harvard and America,* 282–84.

78. Richard Norton Smith, *The Harvard Century: The Making of a University to a Nation* (New York: Simon and Schuster, 1986), 74.

79. Quoted in Synnott, *Half-Opened Door,* 35.

80. Lowell's papers are littered with his rejections of invitations to address the Harvard Menorah Society. See, among others, Lowell to Henry Hurwitz, December 26, 1908; Lowell to Aaron Horwitz [*sic*], February 3, 1909; Lowell to Aaron Horvitz, February 12, 1912; Lowell to R. A. Newman, January 25, 1915. RMS. Correspondence. HUD 3568.510. HUA.

81. See RMS. Correspondence, 1906–1922. Kallen to Frederick Greenman, November 20, 1915. HUD 3568.510. HUA.

82. Harvard University. RPALL. Official correspondence. Lowell to Hurwitz, December 12, 1917. UAI5.160, fol. 1934. HUA.

83. Among the many examples, see Harvard University. RPALL. Official correspondence. Lowell to Rabbi H. G. Enelow, January 5, 1921. UAI5.160, fol. 716. HUA.

84. Harvard University. RPALL. Official correspondence. Lowell to Rufus S. Tucker, May 20, 1922, UAI5.160, fol. 1056, HUA.

85. See Synnott, "Anti-Semitism and American Universities"; and Lewis Gannett, "Is America Anti-Semitic?" *Nation* 116 (March 21, 1923): 232.

86. See Harvard University. RPALL. Official correspondence. Lowell to Professor William E. Hocking. UAI5.160, fol. 1056, HUA.

87. Harvard University. RPALL. Official correspondence. Lowell to John R. Lazenby, June 8, 1922. UAI5.160, fol. 1056. HUA.

88. See Harvard University. RPALL. Official correspondence. Mack to Lowell, June 9, 1922. UAI5.160, fol. 1056, HUA; Papers of David Gordon Lyon. Correspondence and Other Papers Relating to Admission of Jews to Harvard, ca. 1922. HUG 1541.7 HUA; Synnott, *Half-Opened Door,* 70.

89. "May Jews Go to College?" *Nation* 114 (June 14, 1922): 708.

90. "Harvard Student Opinion on the Jewish Question," *Nation* 115 (September 6, 1922): 225–27. Italics in original.

91. See Harvard University. Harry Starr. Miscellaneous letters 1917–22. Hurwitz to Wolfson, September 29, 1922. HUD 922.4. HUA. Professor Harry A. Wolfson unofficially advised these four Jewish students, but it is unlikely that he was the faculty member who sat in on these meetings.

92. RMS. President's reports. Harry Starr's Presidential Report, 1921–22. HUA 3568.771.5. HUA.

93. Starr, "The Affair at Harvard," *Menorah Journal* 8 (October 1922): 265.

94. Ibid., 268.

95. These letters were reprinted in ibid., 269–70, 274–75. Starr's long-term influence at Harvard is worth noting. He eventually became a member of the Harvard Overseers Committee to Visit the Departments of Semitic and Egyptian Civilizations and of Middle Eastern Civilizations. In 1976, the Littauer Foundation, of which Starr had long served as president, endowed the Harry Starr Professorship in Jewish Studies at Harvard. The Harvard University Center for Jewish Studies now offers a "Harry Starr Fellowship in Judaica" to university faculty. See William Bentinck-Smith and Elizabeth Stouffer, *Harvard University History of Named Chairs: Sketches of Donors and Donations* (Cambridge, Mass.: Secretary to the [Harvard] University, 1991), 506; see also *Harvard Class of 1921: Fiftieth Anniversary Report* (Cambridge, Mass.: Harvard University Printing Office, 1971), 479.

96. Harry Austryn Wolfson, "Remarks on proposed changes in admission policy in Harvard University," May or June 1922 (Estate of David Gordon Lyon Jr.), Harvard University Archives, as quoted in Synnott, *Half-Opened Door,* 67.

97. Hurwitz to Nehemiah Mossessohn, editor of *The Jewish Tribune,* June 5, 1922. HHMA 63/3. AJA.

98. Hurwitz, "Morale! To the Jewish Students in our Colleges and Universities," *Menorah Bulletin* 5 (October 1922): 1–2. Italics in original.

99. Unpublished "Editorial Note" attached to Hurwitz to Wolfson, October 19, 1922. HHMA 63/3. AJA.

100. See Harvard University. RPALL. Official correspondence. Lowell to Cyrus Brewer, December 1, 1925. UAI5.160, fol.184. HUA.

101. Harvard University. RPALL. Official correspondence. "Report of the Committee Appointed to 'Consider and Report to the Governing Boards Principles and Methods for More Effective Sifting of Candidates for Admission to the University,'" UAI 5.160. HUA. (The application form is in Lowell's correspondence, UAI5.160, fol. 8. HUA.) One significant consequence of this new system was that an increasing number of students failed to report their religious affiliation to Harvard College. Of the mem-

bers of the class of 1921, 20.6 percent of Harvard students asked about their religious affiliation answered "none" or left the question blank. By the class of 1929, 40 percent chose to answer "none" or leave the question blank. See Morton and Phyllis Keller, *Making Harvard Modern: The Rise of America's University* (New York: Oxford University Press, 2001), 48.

102. Wechsler, *Qualified Student,* 221.

103. Ralph Philip Boas, "Who Shall Go to College?" *Atlantic Monthly* 130 (October 1922): 445.

104. See Synnott, *Half-Opened Door,* 62.

105. Kallen, "The Roots of Anti-Semitism," *Nation* 116 (February 28, 1923): 242.

106. President Truman's Commission on Higher Education released a report in 1947 acknowledging the damaging effects of quotas in higher education against minorities, particularly Jews and blacks. See Mark Dollinger, *Quest for Inclusion: Jews and Liberalism in Modern America* (Princeton, N.J.: Princeton University Press, 2000), 206.

107. Beginning in 1925, the Hillel Foundation affiliated with B'nai B'rith, the world's oldest Jewish service organization.

108. Winton U. Solberg, "The Early Years of the Jewish Presence at the University of Illinois," *Religion and American Culture* 2 (1992): 227–28. On Hillel, see Moore, *B'nai B'rith and the Challenge of Ethnic Leadership,* 135–63; Susan Roth, "And the Youth Shall See Visions: The Jewish Experience in Champaign-Urbana and the Founding of Hillel" (master's thesis, Eastern Illinois University, 1995).

109. "The Hillel Foundation," *B'nai B'rith News* (March 1924): 204.

110. *American Israelite* (December 27, 1923), in HHMA 14/7. AJA.

111. See, for example, Rabbi Solomon Goldman to Hurwitz, January 15, 1924. HHMA 14/14. AJA; and Rabbi David Goldberg to Hurwitz, January 2, 1924. HHMA 14/7. AJA.

112. Hurwitz to Silver, January 4, 1924. HHMA 56/12. AJA.

113. "Excerpt of Report of the President to 1925 Convention of B'nai B'rith (12 Annual Convention): B'nai B'rith Hillel Foundations" in "B'nai B'rith Hillel—Small Collections" file. AJA.

114. See Hurwitz, "The Menorah Movement," *B'nai B'rith Magazine* 40 (April 1926): 230.

115. Howard M. Sachar, *A History of the Jews in America* (New York: Vintage, 1992), 418.

116. Sachar to Hurwitz, October 2, 1927. HHMA 51/2. AJA.

117. Just a few days after receiving Sachar's letter, Hurwitz wrote to a few close friends asking them what they thought of Sachar's proposal. See, for example, Hurwitz to Herbert B. Ehrmann, October 7, 1927. HHMA 10/2. AJA; and Hurwitz to J. J. Kaplan, October 12, 1927. HHMA 23/10. AJA.

118. See Solberg, "Early Years of the Jewish Presence at the University of Illinois," 244n64.

119. Sachar to Hurwitz, January 6, 1928. HHMA 51/2 AJA. After some seemingly difficult deliberation with the University of Illinois, Sachar became the director of Hillel in 1931. Among the letters between Sachar and Hurwitz on this matter, see Sachar to Hurwitz, June 7, 1929. HHMA 51/3. AJA. See also Moore, *B'nai B'rith and the Challenge of Ethnic Leadership,* 142.

120. See Roth, "And the Youth Shall See Visions," 59.

121. See Hurwitz to Wise, March 21, 1928. HHMA 62/11. AJA.

122. Wise to Hurwitz, March 21, 1928. HHMA 62/11. AJA.

123. Wise to Harry Starr, March 23, 1928. HHMA 62/11. AJA.

124. Hurwitz to Sachar, March 11, 1930. HHMA 51/3. AJA.

125. Sachar to Hurwitz, March 20, 1930. HHMA 51/3. AJA.

126. As historian David O. Levine writes, "Amidst the activities and fraternities, one type of student was bound to be unhappy—the serious student." Levine, *American College and the Culture of Aspiration*, 121.

127. See Hurwitz to Sachar, April 4, 1930. HHMA 51/3. AJA.

128. The *Menorah Journal* cost 35 cents per issue in 1915. It increased in cost only occasionally over the years. By April 1930, the IMA's deficit ran to nearly $60,000. The association's income dropped 80 percent between 1929 and 1933. See Hurwitz to Edward B. Benjamin, March 5, 1931. HHMA 3/10; Hurwitz to Frederick Greenman, April 8, 1930. HHMA 15/12; Hurwitz to Frederick Greenman, September 5, 1930. HHMA 16/2; Hurwitz to Kallen, March 2, 1933. HHMA 23/4. AJA.

129. See, for example, Hurwitz's report to the Menorah Board of Governors, April 25, 1928. HHMA 25/16. AJA.

130. Counting the exact number of active college Menorah chapters at any given moment is difficult, as archival sources on this matter are contradictory. Any numbers given throughout this book reflect the most plausible information that I have found. See Hurwitz's April 25, 1928, report; Hurwitz to Jacob J. Kaplan, December 16, 1932. HHMA 24/2. AJA; Austin, "The Story of the Menorah Movement," 23.

131. Oko to Elliot Cohen, June 23, 1931. Oko Papers 7/5. AJA.

132. See Newman to Hurwitz, July 7, 1938. HHMA 38/1. AJA.

3. Cultural Pluralism and Its Critics

1. The scholarship on the intellectual origins of pluralism and its relationship to white ethnicity during the interwar era is extensive. My indebtedness to the works in this field is evident throughout the footnotes of this book. Among the most informative works on the origins of pluralism, see Gary Gerstle, "The Protean Character of American Liberalism," *American Historical Review* 99 (October 1994): 1043–73; Gleason, *Speaking of Diversity*; Higham, *Send These to Me*; Hollinger, *Postethnic America*; Kazal, "Revisiting Assimilation."

2. See Werner Sollors, "A Critique of Pure Pluralism," in *Reconstructing American Literary History*, ed. Sacvan Bercovitch (Cambridge, Mass.: Harvard University Press, 1986), 267.

3. Menand, *Metaphysical Club*, 399.

4. Kallen, "Introduction," *The Philosophy of William James* (New York: Modern Library, 1925), 9. On James and ethnic identity, see Larry C. Miller, "William James and Twentieth-Century Ethnic Thought," *American Quarterly* 31:4 (Autumn 1979): 533–55.

5. James, "What Pragmatism Means," in James, *Essays in Pragmatism* (New York: Hafner, 1948), 144.

6. James, "What Pragmatism Means," 145, 149, 151, 155. Italics in original.

7. James, "The True Harvard," *Harvard Graduates' Magazine* 12 (1903): 7, 8.

8. James, "On a Certain Blindness in Human Beings," in *Pragmatism and Other Writings*, ed. Giles Gunn (New York: Penguin Books, 2000), 285.

9. Menand, *Metaphysical Club*, 389.

10. The dedication reads: "To the Memory of BARRETT WENDEL Poet, Teacher, Man of Letters, Deep-seeing Interpreter of America and the American Mind, In Whose Teaching I received My First Vision of Their Trends and Meanings I Reverently Dedicate This Book."

11. See Kallen, "A Convert in Zion," in *Judaism at Bay,* 64, 65.

12. As noted in chapter 1, Kallen drew from Ahad Ha'am's Zionist vision as he moved toward cultural pluralism. On Kallen's debt to Ha'am, see Pianko, "'The True Liberalism of Zionism,'" 301, 311–12.

13. Schmidt, *Horace M. Kallen,* 26, 165.

14. Toll, "Horace M. Kallen: Pluralism and American Jewish Identity," 67.

15. See Michael Walzer, Menachem Lorberbaum, and Noam J. Zohar, eds., *The Jewish Political Tradition, Volume II: Membership.* On American Jews and chosenness, see Eisen, *The Chosen People in America,* and Greene, "A Chosen People in a Pluralist Nation."

16. See Baeck, "Revelation and World Religion," in *The Essence of Judaism,* ed. Irving Howe (New York: Schocken, 1948), 67.

17. On missionary Judaism prior to World War II, see Berman, *Speaking of Jews,* especially chapter 1.

18. See Kaplan's "What Judaism Is Not," *Menorah Journal* 1:4 (October 1915); "How May Judaism Be Saved?" *Menorah Journal* 2:1 (February 1916); "The Future of Judaism," *Menorah Journal* 2:3 (June 1916); "Where Does Jewry Really Stand Today?" *Menorah Journal* 4:1 (February 1918); "A Program for the Reconstruction of Judaism," *Menorah Journal* 6:4 (August 1920); "Toward a Reconstruction of Judaism," *Menorah Journal* 13:2 (April 1927); "Judaism as a Civilization: Religion's Place in It," *Menorah Journal* 15:6 (December 1928). Pianko discusses Kaplan's 1915 and 1916 *Menorah Journal* essays in *Zionism and the Roads Not Taken,* 105–8.

19. Mordecai M. Kaplan, *Judaism as a Civilization: Toward a Reconstruction of American-Jewish Life* (Philadelphia: Jewish Publication Society, 1934, 1994). See also "Mordecai Kaplan's *Judaism as a Civilization:* The Legacy of an American Idea," ed. Arnold Eisen and Noam Pianko, special issue, *Jewish Social Studies* 12:2 (Winter 2006).

20. Eisen, *Chosen People in America,* 73–98.

21. Kaplan, *Judaism as a Civilization,* 180.

22. Eisen, *Chosen People in America,* 83.

23. Kallen, "Judaism, Hebraism, Zionism." This article was reprinted in Kallen, *Judaism at Bay.* All the page citations here refer to the reprinted version of the article.

24. Ibid., 30.

25. Ibid.

26. Ibid., 30–31, 31.

27. Ibid., 32.

28. Ibid., 35.

29. Ibid., 37.

30. Ibid., 41.

31. Kallen relied on Ahad Ha'am here. In an 1897 essay, Ha'am wrote: "In my view our religion is national—that is to say, it is a product of our national spirit—but the reverse is not true. If it is impossible to be a Jew in the religious sense without acknowledging our nationality, it is possible to be a Jew in the national sense without accepting many things in which religion requires belief." See Ha'am, "The Jewish State and

the Jewish Problem," in *The Zionist Idea: A Historical Analysis and Reader,* ed. Arthur Hertzberg (New York: Atheneum, 1959), 262.

32. The text of the untitled speech was reprinted in *The Menorah Movement,* 81–86. All quotations from this speech hereafter refer to this reprinting of the speech.

33. Ibid., 83.

34. Ibid.

35. Ibid.

36. Ibid.

37. Ibid., 84.

38. Ibid., 85.

39. Ibid.

40. "The incompleteness and the bias of Kallen's pluralism becomes obvious once we ask what role it assigned to the Negro. The answer is: none." Higham, *Send These to Me,* 210.

41. See, for example, Kallen's essay "Americanization," where he wrote: "I do not discuss the influence of the negro upon the esthetic material and cultural character of the South and the rest of the United States. This is at once too considerable and too recondite in its processes for casual mention. It requires a separate analysis." Kallen, *Culture and Democracy in the United States,* 218.

42. See Sollors, "A Critique of Pure Pluralism"; Walter Benn Michaels, *Our America: Nativism, Modernism, and Pluralism* (Durham, N.C.: Duke University Press, 1995), especially 64–72; Posnock, *Color and Culture,* 187–88.

43. *The Menorah Movement,* 86.

44. Israel Zangwill, *The Melting Pot* (New York: Macmillan, 1909).

45. See Gleason, *Speaking of Diversity,* 5–6, 34.

46. On the suggestion that Zangwill imagined an American melting pot in which Jewish identity would remain distinct, see Shumsky, "Zangwill's *The Melting Pot:* Ethnic Tensions on Stage," 29–41; Biale, "The Melting Pot and Beyond: Jews and the Politics of American Identity"; and Nahshon, *From the Ghetto to the Melting Pot.*

47. See "Introduction" to Nahshon, *From the Ghetto to the Melting Pot,* 5–10.

48. "'The Melting Pot': Will the Jew Become Merged in It and Disappear?" *American Israelite* 55 (March 4, 1909): 1.

49. On coercive Americanization efforts, see Gary Gerstle, "Liberty, Coercion, and the Making of Americans," *Journal of American History* 84:2 (September 1997): 524–58.

50. See Gordon, *Assimilation in American Life.*

51. Kallen, "Democracy versus the Melting Pot," in *Culture and Democracy in the United States,* 108.

52. See Edward Alsworth Ross, *The Old World in the New: The Significance of Past and Present Immigration to the American People* (New York: Century, 1913). Kallen opened "Democracy versus the Melting Pot" by refuting *The Old World in the New* and by chastising Ross as a "nervous professor." Kallen, "Democracy versus the Melting Pot," 61.

53. Kallen, "Democracy versus the Melting Pot," 107.

54. One of his clearest statements of this idea is in Kallen, "Introduction," *The Philosophy of William James,* 47.

55. Kallen, "Democracy versus the Melting Pot," 104.

56. Ibid., 114–15.

57. Kallen, *The Structure of Lasting Peace* (Boston: Marshall Jones Co., 1918), 31.

58. Sollors, "A Critique of Pure Pluralism," 260. Italics in the original.

59. Ibid., 260, 273. John Higham and Philip Gleason also have provided convincing criticism regarding the lack of specificity in Kallen's pluralism. See Higham, *Send These to Me*; Gleason, "American Identity and Americanization." Louis Menand has concluded that, for Kallen, "ethnicity is immutable," and therefore that Kallen shared "the scientific assumptions of the anti-immigrationists." See Menand, *Metaphysical Club*, 392.

60. Werner Sollors has written: "Instead of accepting the possibility of a text's many mothers, pluralists often settle for the construction of one immutable grandfather." See Sollors, "A Critique of Pure Pluralism," 275.

61. Gleason, "American Identity and Americanization," 43.

62. See Hollinger, *Postethnic America*, 21.

63. On the New York intelligentsia, see Thomas Bender, *Intellect and Public Life* (Baltimore: Johns Hopkins University Press, 1992); Bender, *New York Intellect;* Terry A. Cooney, *The Rise of the New York Intellectuals: Partisan Review and Its Circle* (Madison: University of Wisconsin Press, 1986); James B. Gilbert, *Writers and Partisans: A History of Literary Radicalism in America* (New York: Wiley, 1968); and Christopher Lasch, *New Radicalism in America: The Intellectual as a Social Type* (New York: Alfred A. Knopf, 1965).

64. Gleason, "American Identity and Americanization," 46–47.

65. Melvin I. Urofsky, *Louis D. Brandeis: A Life* (New York: Pantheon Books, 2009). See also Robert A. Burt, *Two Jewish Justices: Outcasts in the Promised Land* (Berkeley: University of California Press, 1988); Philippa Strum, ed., *Brandeis on Democracy* (Lawrence: University Press of Kansas, 1995).

66. Raider, *The Emergence of American Zionism,* 25.

67. Urofsky, *Louis D. Brandeis,* 405–13.

68. Schmidt, *Horace M. Kallen,* 63.

69. *Menorah Journal* 1:1 (January 1915): 4.

70. Schmidt, *Horace M. Kallen,* 57.

71. Urofksy, *Louis D. Brandeis,* 410–11.

72. Brandeis, *The Jewish Problem: How to Solve It* (New York: Zionist Essays Publication Committee, 1915), 6.

73. Brandeis, "A Call to the Educated Jew," *Menorah Journal* 1:1 (January 1915): 15.

74. Ibid., 18, 19. One can find the same sentiments in Brandeis, *The Jewish Problem;* and Brandeis, *Zionism and Patriotism* (New York: Foundation of American Zionists, 1915).

75. Hapgood, "The Jews and American Democracy," *Menorah Journal* 2:4 (October 1916): 202.

76. Ibid., 205.

77. Hapgood's articles were "Do Americans Dislike Jews?" *Harper's Weekly* 61 (November 13, 1915): 460–62; "Jews and Intermarriage," *Harper's Weekly* 61 (November 20, 1915): 488–89; and "The Future of the Jews in America," *Harper's Weekly* 61 (November 27, 1915): 511–12.

78. Hapgood, "The Jews and American Democracy," 205.

79. Menand, *Metaphysical Club,* 40.

80. Bourne's promising career was cut short at the age of thirty-two when he died during the influenza epidemic of 1918. On Bourne's relationship with Dewey, see Bender, *New York Intellect*, 246–47; Lasch, *The New Radicalism in America 1889–1963*, 181–224; Stansell, *American Moderns*, 328–33. Bourne's essays are collected in Bourne, *The Radical Will: Selected Writings 1911–1918*, ed. Olaf Hansen (New York: Urizen Books, 1977).

81. On Bourne's visit to the Harvard Menorah Society, see RMS. Correspondence. HUD 3568.510. HUA; also Bourne, "Trans-National America," *Atlantic Monthly* 118 (July 1916): 86–97. Bourne confessed to "stealing" the term "trans-national" from a "Jewish college mate." See Mitchell Cohen, "In Defense of Shaatnez: A Politics for Jews in a Multicultural America," in Biale et al., *Insider/Outsider: American Jews and Multiculturalism*. Louis Menand has recently suggested that Bourne stole the term "transnational" from Alexander Sachs, a graduate student of Dewey's at Columbia. See Menand, *Metaphysical Club*, 402.

82. Bourne, "The Jew and Trans-National America," *Menorah Journal* 2:5 (December 1916): 281.

83. Ibid., 283. The editors of the *Menorah Journal* encouraged Walter Lippmann to respond to Bourne in the magazine. Although he expressed much interest in Bourne's article, Lippmann never did write a response. See the correspondence between Lippmann and Hurwitz in Kallen Papers 18/21. AJA.

84. Bourne, "The Jew and Trans-National America," 282.

85. David A. Hollinger, *In The American Province: Studies in the History and Historiography of Ideas* (Bloomington: Indiana University Press, 1985), 59.

86. Robert B. Westbrook, *John Dewey and American Democracy* (Ithaca, N.Y.: Cornell University Press, 1991), 2.

87. Dewey to Kallen, March 31, 1915. Kallen Papers 7/13. AJA.

88. Dewey to Kallen, April 16, 1915. Kallen Papers 7/13. AJA.

89. On this point, see Westbrook, *John Dewey and American Democracy*, 212–14.

90. Dewey, "The Principle of Nationality," *Menorah Journal* 3:4 (October 1917): 207, 206.

91. Goldstein, *The Price of Whiteness*, 180–81.

92. See Drachsler's "The Blending of Immigrant Cultures," *Menorah Journal* 6:2 (April 1920); and "Americanization and Race Fusion," *Menorah Journal* 6:3 (June 1920).

93. Drachsler, "Blending of Immigrant Cultures," 87.

94. Drachsler, *Democracy and Assimilation: The Blending of Immigrant Heritages in America* (New York: Macmillan, 1920), 79.

95. Ibid., 119.

96. Goldstein, *The Price of Whiteness*, 180.

97. See Drachsler, *Democracy and Assimilation*, 133.

98. Drachsler, "Americanization and Race Fusion," 134.

99. Drachsler, *Democracy and Assimilation*, 236.

100. Berkson, "A Community Theory of American Life," *Menorah Journal* 6:6 (December 1920): 311. For information on Berkson and the CCNY Menorah Society, see RMS. Aaron Horvitz Correspondence, 1910–1913. HUD 3568.515. HUA.

101. Berkson, "A Community Theory of American Life," *Menorah Journal* 6:6 (December 1920): 311, 312.

102. See Berkson, *Theories of Americanization: A Critical Study with Special Refer-*

ence to the Jewish Group (New York: Teachers College, Columbia University, 1920), 11. The *Menorah Journal* reprinted two sections of *Theories of Americanization:* "A Community Theory of American Life," *Menorah Journal* 6:6 (December 1920); and "The Jewish Right to Live," *Menorah Journal* 7:1 (February 1921).

103. Berkson, "The Jewish Right to Live," 45.

104. Kallen, "Democracy versus the Melting Pot," *Nation* 100 (February 25, 1915): 220.

105. See Boas, "Are the Jews a Race?" *World Tomorrow* 6 (January 1923): 5–6. On Jews and the idea of racial identity, see Goldstein, *Price of Whiteness.* On Boas and the Jewish question, see Amos Morris-Reich, *The Quest for Jewish Assimilation in Modern Social Science* (New York: Routledge, 2008), esp. 34–50; Leonard B. Glick, "Types Distinct from Our Own: Franz Boas on Jewish Identity and Assimilation," *American Anthropologist* 84 (September 1982): 545–65; Geyla Frank, "Jews, Multiculturalism, and Boasian Anthropology," *American Anthropologist* 99 (1997): 731–45.

106. Berkson, *Theories of Americanization,* 88.

107. Berkson, "The Jewish Right to Live," 43.

108. Kallen, "Can Judaism Survive in the United States?" *Menorah Journal* 11:2 (April 1925): 112. "Can Judaism Survive in the United States?" originally appeared in two parts in the April 1925 (11:2) and December 1925 (11:6) issues of the *Menorah Journal.*

109. Kallen, "Can Judaism Survive in the United States?" *Menorah Journal* 11:6 (December 1925): 548. Kallen here also articulated a new criticism of the "mission" idea by criticizing the historical relationship between Christians and Jews. He argued that so much antisemitism throughout history was based on Christians' belief that Jews were a people *once* chosen by God, who later became a people *rejected* by God in favor of Christians. "There is no mode of anti-Semitism," Kallen declared, "which does not take its departure from this presumption," that Jews are "inherently inferior" to newly chosen Christians (Kallen, "Can Judaism Survive in the United States?" 183). The results of this relationship for the collective psyche of the Jewish people were tragic, according to Kallen. And, because Kallen believed that the idea of a Jewish mission to humankind had its roots as a response to feelings of inferiority to Christians, it would continually and insidiously reinforce that very same inferiority. As I show in chapter 5, Kallen's article helped to widen an already growing chasm between the *Menorah Journal* cohort and prominent Reform rabbis in the United States.

110. Kallen, *Cultural Pluralism and the American Idea: An Essay in Social Philosophy* (Philadelphia: University of Pennsylvania Press, 1956), 22.

111. One of the clearest articulations of the relationship between ethnicity and choice is Mary C. Waters, *Ethnic Options: Choosing Identities in America* (Berkeley: University of California Press, 1990).

4. Jewish Studies in an American Setting

1. S. Baruch, "'Whither?'" *Menorah Journal* 5:3 (June 1919): 121, 122, 130.

2. Biographical information compiled from the Adolph S. Oko Papers, AJA; "Dr. Adolph S. Oko, Spinoza Scholar," *New York Times* (October 4, 1944): 20.

3. See, for example, Oko, "The Prague Haggadah," *Menorah Journal* 11:2 (April 1925); S. Baruch, "The Quest of a Jewish Intellectual," *Menorah Journal* 12:5 (October–

November 1926); and an undated, unpublished text titled "The Ethic of the Modern Jew," in the Adolph S. Oko Papers 9/14. AJA.

4. Baruch, "'Whither?'" 127.

5. See Paul Ritterband and Harold S. Wechsler, *Jewish Learning in American Universities* (Bloomington: Indiana University Press, 1994), 36–44, 75. The one exception to this trend of decline was the Semitics program at the University of Chicago's Oriental Institute.

6. Meyer, *Response to Modernity,* 75–99; Schorsch, *From Text to Context,* 205–32, 345–59.

7. Hurwitz, "The Prime Need," *Jewish Forum* (February 1, 1920). HHMA 5/5. AJA. Emphases in original.

8. The 1919 Zunz lecture featured Hartley Burr Alexander on "The Hebrew Contribution to the Americanism of the Future." In 1920, Louis Ginzberg, a professor of Talmud at the Jewish Theological Seminary, spoke. The 1921 lecture was delivered by George Foot Moore, professor of the history of religions at Harvard, and, in 1922, Max Leopold Margolis, philologist at the Dropsie College for Hebrew and Cognate Learning in Philadelphia, delivered the final Zunz Memorial Lecture.

9. Oko (using the pseudonym "S. Baruch") wrote the three-part biographical article, "Leopold Zunz—Humanist," that ran in the February, June, and August 1923 issues of the *Menorah Journal.*

10. In addition to Zunz, the group included Eduard Gans, Moses Moser, Isaac Marcus Jost, Isaac Levin Auerbach, Joel List, and Joseph Hillmar. See Mendes-Flohr and Reinharz, *The Jew in the Modern World,* 218n1; 221n2.

11. Hurwitz to M. R. Travis, January 26, 1916. HHMA 5/7. AJA.

12. Schorsch describes the "impervious elitism" of the *Verein,* a quality shared by much of the IMA's leadership. Schorsch, *From Text to Context,* 206.

13. I am indebted to Paul Mendes-Flohr for clarifying this point in a conversation with me.

14. Schorsch, *From Text to Context,* 242–48; see also Nahum N. Glatzer, "The Beginnings of Modern Jewish Studies," in *Studies in Nineteenth-Century Jewish Intellectual History,* ed. Alexander Altmann (Cambridge, Mass.: Harvard University Press, 1964), 36.

15. For a fuller understanding of the processes of emancipation, see Birnbaum and Katznelson, *Paths of Emancipation.*

16. See Byron L. Sherwin, *Context and Content: Higher Jewish Education in the United States* (Chicago: Spertus College of Judaica Press, 1987), 71.

17. Hurwitz to Harry Wolfson, December 11, 1918. HHMA 62/21. AJA.

18. See Moore, *History of Religions* (New York: Charles Scribner's Sons, 1919). Ritterband and Wechsler, *Jewish Learning in American Universities,* 69.

19. Moore, "The Idea of Torah in Judaism," *Menorah Journal* 8:1 (February 1922), 13–14.

20. Michael Brenner, *The Renaissance of Jewish Culture in Weimar Germany* (New Haven, Conn.: Yale University Press, 1996). See also Inka Bertz, "Jewish Renaissance—Jewish Modernism," in *Berlin Metropolis: Jews and the New Culture 1890–1918,* ed. Emily D. Bilski (Berkeley: University of California Press, 1999), 175–76; and David A. Brenner, *Marketing Identities: The Invention of Jewish Ethnicity in Ost und West* (De-

troit: Wayne State University Press, 1998), 33. A similar phenomenon would occur in France, with a flowering of literary clubs, historical societies, and journals dedicated to Jewish history and culture. See Nadia Malinovich, "Le Reveil D'Israel: Jewish Identity and Culture in France 1900–1932" (Ph.D. diss., University of Michigan, 2000); and Paula Hyman, *From Dreyfus to Vichy: The Remaking of French Jewry, 1906–1939* (New York: Columbia University Press, 1979).

21. See Brenner, *Renaissance of Jewish Culture in Weimar Germany,* especially chapter 4: "Toward a Synthetic Scholarship: The Popularization of Wissenschaft des Judentums," 100–26.

22. Charles K. Feinberg, "Jewish Studies in American Universities," *Menorah Journal* 2:5 (December 1916): 319–21. This study counted classes in language, history, literature, religion, sociology, and archeology offered in 164 American universities. It grouped the courses into three historical periods: biblical, Second Temple period, and AD 70 to the present. Of the total courses counted, 486 were in the biblical period, 19 in the Second Temple period, and 11 in the AD 70 to early-twentieth-century period.

23. Jonathan D. Sarna, *JPS: The Americanization of Jewish Culture, 1888–1988* (Philadelphia: Jewish Publication Society, 1989).

24. Shuly Rubin Schwartz, *The Emergence of Jewish Scholarship in America: The Publication of the* Jewish Encyclopedia (Cincinnati: Hebrew Union College Press, 1991). Singer tried to find patrons for an encyclopedia project in Europe but could not.

25. Ibid., 13. On the Jewish Chautauqua Society, see Berman, *Speaking of Jews,* 24–32.

26. Ritterband and Wechsler, *Jewish Learning in American Universities,* 58.

27. Ismar Elbogen, "American Jewish Scholarship: A Survey," *American Jewish Year Book* 45 (1943–44): 47–65. The Jewish Institute of Religion merged with Hebrew Union College, the Reform seminary, in 1950.

28. On the Kehillah, see Arthur A. Goren, *New York Jews and the Quest for Community: The Kehillah Experiment, 1908–1922* (New York: Columbia University Press, 1970).

29. Horace J. Wolf, "A Remedy for the Sunday School," *Menorah Journal* 3:1 (February 1917): 36.

30. Alexander M. Dushkin, "The Profession of Jewish Education," *Menorah Journal* 3:2 (April 1917): 91. Dushkin's dissertation was published as *Jewish Education in New York City* (New York: Bureau of Jewish Education, 1918).

31. Ritterband and Wechsler, *Jewish Learning in American Universities,* 46. See also Benny Kraut, *From Reform Judaism to Ethical Culture: The Religious Education of Felix Adler* (Cincinnati: Hebrew Union College Press, 1979).

32. Ritterband and Wechsler, *Jewish Learning in American Universities,* 30.

33. Paul Ritterband and Harold S. Wechsler, "Judaica in American Colleges and Universities," *Encyclopedia Judaica Yearbook 1977/8* (Jerusalem: Keter Publishing House, 1979), 74.

34. "At least 16 Jewish scholars offered instruction in Jewish learning in U.S. universities during the late nineteenth and early twentieth centuries. These scholars included Max Margolis, James M. Philips, William Popper, and Jacob Voorsanger at the University of California; Emil G. Hirsch at the University of Chicago; Felix Adler (briefly) at Cornell; Richard Gottheil at Columbia; Cyrus Adler, Immanuel Moses Casanowicz, Caspar Levias, and William Rosenau at Johns Hopkins; Abram S. Isaacs at

New York University; Isaac Husik and Morris Jastrow at the University of Pennsylvania; Joseph Levy (briefly) at Temple; and Max Heller at Tulane." See Ritterband and Wechsler, *Jewish Learning in American Universities*, 237n5.

35. See Synnott, *Half-Opened Door.*

36. Mack to Roscoe Pound, September 23, 1926, from Roscoe Pound papers, Harvard Law School; copy in Kallen papers 20/10. AJA.

37. See Frank, "Jews, Multiculturalism, and Boasian Anthropology," 734.

38. See Peter Novick, *That Noble Dream: The "Objectivity Question" and the American Historical Profession* (New York: Cambridge University Press, 1988), 68–69.

39. Wirth's dissertation, "The Ghetto: A Study in Isolation," was accepted by the University of Chicago Sociology department in 1926, and published as *The Ghetto* (Chicago: University of Chicago Press, 1928).

40. Hasia R. Diner, "Introduction," in Wirth, *The Ghetto* (New Brunswick, N.J.: Transaction Publishers, 1998), xvi, xxiv–xxv.

41. It should be noted that Wirth did advise some dissertations and master's theses on Jewish topics at the University of Chicago. I am grateful to Professor Andrew Abbott and Linnea Martin of the University of Chicago sociology department for their assistance in determining Wirth's advisees.

42. *The Menorah Movement,* 53.

43. Hurwitz, "Menorah Fundamentals," undated (probably 1922). HHMA 56/25. AJA.

44. See *The Menorah Movement,* 3.

45. Hurwitz to Kallen, July 26, 1916. HHMA 14/1. AJA.

46. Undated, untitled speech (likely delivered by Hurwitz in 1923 or 1924) in HHMA 19/12. AJA.

47. Baruch, "'Whither?'" 133.

48. "Constitution of Menorah Educational Conference," no date. HHMA 69/8. AJA.

49. Nathan Isaacs to Hurwitz, July 9, 1917. HHMA 20/4. AJA.

50. Isaacs left his position as Acting Dean at the University of Cincinnati Law School for a one-year appointment at Harvard in the autumn of 1919. He taught at the University of Pittsburgh School of Law from 1920 until the spring of 1924, and returned to Harvard in the autumn of 1924. See HHMA 20/4. AJA.

51. Hurwitz to Oko, November 26, 1919. Oko Papers 7/13. AJA.

52. Hurwitz, "First Memorandum on Menorah Education," December 28, 1918. HHMA 19/11. AJA. Reprinted in *Menorah Journal* 5:1 (February 1919): 53–58.

53. See the "Minutes of the Executive Committee of the MEC, December 30, 1918," 13. HHMA 69/8. AJA.

54. Hurwitz memo, untitled, attached to Hurwitz to Louis D. Brandeis, February 16, 1921. HHMA 6/16. AJA.

55. See correspondence between Hurwitz and George Dobsevage, September 21, 1916; October 31, 1916; October 19, 1917. HHMA 22/9. AJA.

56. A list of Menorah library books, as of 1914, can be found in RMS. Harvard Menorah Society correspondence. HUD 3568.510. HUA.

57. Most often, the IMA was able to award $100 to the essay prizewinners. The funds for the awards usually came from businessmen sympathetic to the Menorah cause. Beginning in 1907, for example, Jacob H. Schiff endowed Harvard's Menorah essay prize. Upon Schiff's death, the Menorah Society at Harvard changed the name

of the prize to the Jacob H. Schiff Menorah Essay Prize. See RMS. Harvard Menorah Society Correspondence. President of Harvard Menorah Society to J. D. Green, Secretary to the President of Harvard. December 26, 1907; and statement issued by the Harvard Menorah Society. October 13, 1920. HUD 3568.510. HUA. For a sampling of suggested topics, see "Menorah Prize Essay Subjects," *Menorah Bulletin* (February 1919), 3.

58. "The Jew in the Modern World," was published in 1921. "Introduction to Jewish History" and "Jewish Factors in Western Civilization" both appeared in 1922. The IMA also published two shorter syllabi: "Jewish Reconstruction after the War," in 1917, and "Jewish Reconstruction," in 1919.

59. Hurwitz, "Watchman, What of the Day?" *Menorah Journal* 12:1 (February 1926): 20.

60. Hurwitz, "First Memorandum on Menorah Education," December 28, 1918. HHMA 19/11. AJA.

61. See Hurwitz to David de Sola Pool, February 5, 1914. HHMA 42/15. AJA. Lists of lecturers available ran in the *Menorah Journal* in 1927 and 1928 issues.

62. Hurwitz, "First Memorandum on Menorah Education," December 28, 1918. HHMA 19/11. AJA.

63. At Harvard, study circles organized by non-Jewish students also saw a revival in the late 1910s. In 1919, ten study groups were formed at Harvard, with a total student enrollment of 240 undergraduates discussing topics such as the League of Nations, Bolshevism, labor relations, international relations, and economics. Even though the groups met in Phillips Brooks House, where the Harvard Menorah Society often gathered, no mention of the Harvard Menorah Society study circles was made in the survey of discussion groups at Harvard published in 1919. See Thomas Nixon Carver, "Discussion Groups and Harvard," *Harvard Graduates' Magazine* 28 (December 1919): 263–65.

64. Hurwitz, "First Memorandum on Menorah Education," December 28, 1918. HHMA 19/11. AJA.

65. The summer school idea had been proposed by the MEC at least as early as 1920. See "Secretary's Report at Annual Meeting of Menorah Educational Conference. University of Chicago, December 29, 1920," HHMA 69/8. AJA.

66. Hurwitz, "First Memorandum on Menorah Education," December 28, 1918. HHMA 19/11. AJA.

67. Hurwitz to Barnard Baruch, March 27, 1922. HHMA 2/21. AJA. Baruch declined to offer funds to the Menorah's summer school effort. It is not clear who funded the school in 1922 and 1923. See Hurwitz to A. L. Sachar, January 8, 1930. HHMA 51/3. AJA.

68. See Hurwitz, "Towards a Revision," *Menorah Journal* 8:4 (August 1922): 254–58.

69. In addition to Hurwitz, Isaacs, and Oko, Julius Drachsler (CCNY, government and sociology), F. J. Foakes-Jackson (Union Theological Seminary, philosophy of religion), R. Travers Herford (Williams Library, London, librarian), Isaac Husik (Pennsylvania, philosophy), Horace M. Kallen (New School for Social Research, philosophy), I. M. Kandel (Columbia Teachers College, education), Jacob Z. Lauterbach (Hebrew Union College, Talmud), H. S. Linfield (Bureau of Jewish Social Research, director of information and statistics), Jacob Mann (Hebrew Union College, Jewish history and

literature), Max L. Margolis (Dropsie College, Bible), Marvin Lowenthal (*Menorah Journal,* associate editor), and Louis A. Mischkind (North Shore Congregation, Chicago, rabbi) taught at the Menorah Summer School in 1923.

70. The Society for the Advancement of Judaism was located at 41 West 86th Street in Manhattan.

71. Elliot Cohen, "The Menorah Summer School: A New Agency for Liberal Education," *Menorah Journal* 9:4 (October 1923): 342, 343. Cohen did not provide enrollment figures, but noted that students from seventeen different states attended the Menorah Summer School in 1923.

72. "Summer Courses on Jewish Life," *New York Times* (May 25, 1930): 33.

73. "Jewish Summer School," *New York Times* (June 22, 1930): N3; on the school attendance, see "Topics of Interest to the Church-Goer," *New York Times* (July 5, 1930): 19.

74. Simon Litman, "Hillel, Early Days" (1948), 4. B'nai B'rith Hillel Letters, Reports, and Various Other Items Reflecting the Early History of the Hillel Foundations, 1915–1945. AJA.

75. Isaacs, "A New Menorah Phase," *Menorah Journal* 6:1 (February 1920): 59.

76. Baruch, "'Whither?'" 129.

77. On Wolfson, see Leo W. Schwarz, *Wolfson of Harvard: Portrait of a Scholar* (Philadelphia: Jewish Publication Society, 1978); Lewis S. Feuer, "Recollections of Harry Austryn Wolfson," *American Jewish Archives* 28 (April 1976): 25–50; Hillel Goldberg, *Between Berlin and Slobodka: Jewish Transition Figures from Eastern Europe* (Hoboken, N.J.: Ktav Publishing House, 1989).

78. Isadore Twersky, "Harry Austryn Wolfson, in Appreciation," in Schwarz, *Wolfson of Harvard,* 13–27.

79. Julian Mack and Irving Lehman, both active donors to the Menorah Association, provided funds for Wolfson's salary during the late 1910s, as did Sol Rosenblum, Mortimer Schiff, and Felix Warburg (Ritterband and Wechsler, *Jewish Learning in American Universities,* 114). Wolfson earned $800 per year in 1915; his salary was later raised to $1,000 per year. Between 1918 and 1921, some evidence suggests, Frederick Greenman, IMA chairman and a Harvard Menorah Society alum, raised the $3,500 necessary to cover Wolfson's position for three years. See Harry Austryn Wolfson correspondence. Box 2. HUG (FP)-58.7. HUA.

80. Harvard's administration changed Wolfson's title to faculty instructor in 1918 and appointed him an assistant professor in 1921.

81. Wolfson, "The Needs of Jewish Scholarship in America," *Menorah Journal* 7:1 (February 1921): 28, 31.

82. See Wolfson correspondence. Oko to Wolfson, November 15, 1922. Box 8. HUG (FP)-58.7. HUA.

83. Bentinck-Smith and Stouffer, *Harvard University History of Named Chairs,* 322–23.

84. Goldberg, *Between Berlin and Slobodka,* 47. Scholars have been quite critical of Wolfson for his reluctance to press Harvard to welcome refugee scholars during the Nazi era. In addition to Goldberg, see Feuer, "Recollections of Harry Austryn Wolfson," 33, 42–43.

85. The *Menorah Journal* reported a notable achievement, celebrating the appoint-

ment of Dr. Abraham Shalom Yahuda as the first Jew since the expulsion in 1492 to obtain an academic or state appointment in Spain. Yahuda was named the Professor Ordinary of Rabbinical Language and Literature at the Central University of Madrid. See Max Nordau, "An Opportunity for American Students," *Menorah Journal* 2:1 (February 1916): 51–53.

86. The position was not funded by Columbia, but instead by Linda Miller, the widow of Nathan L. Miller, a New York businessman. On the search to fill this position, see Ritterband and Wechsler, *Jewish Learning in American Universities*, 150–71. On Baron, see Robert Liberles, *Salo Wittmayer Baron: Architect of Jewish History* (New York: New York University Press, 1995).

87. Ritterband and Wechsler, "Judaica in American Colleges and Universities," 76.

88. Brenner, *Renaissance of Jewish Culture in Weimar Germany*, 102.

89. YIVO, like the *Akademie für die Wissenschaft des Judentums* in Berlin, was not a seminary, but a research institution devoted to secular analysis of Jewish texts. YIVO founder Max Weinreich moved the central operation of YIVO from Vilna to New York City in 1940. See David N. Myers, *Re-Inventing the Jewish Past: European Jewish Intellectuals and the Zionist Return to History* (New York: Oxford University Press, 1995), 38.

90. Historian David N. Myers explains that, when Hebrew University formally opened in April 1925, it was not a "full-fledged teaching facility. Rather it consisted of three small research institutes: Chemistry, Microbiology, and Jewish Studies." Jewish studies offerings included courses in religion, Hebrew and other Semitic languages, literature, history, law, philosophy, and Palestine studies. See Myers, *Re-Inventing the Jewish Past*, 40.

91. Mossinsohn, "A Hebrew University in Jerusalem," *Menorah Journal* 4:6 (December 1918): 330.

92. Mumford, "The Vision of the Architect," *Menorah Journal* 8:1 (February 1922): 33–36; Sampter, "On the Mount of Olives," *Menorah Journal* 8:1 (February 1922): 36–40. See also Sol Rosenbloom, "The Chief Function of the Hebrew University," *Menorah Journal* 7:1 (February 1921): 36–40.

93. Schack, "Four Years of the Hebrew University," *Menorah Journal* 16:4 (April 1929): 325–34.

94. Hall, "A Suggestion for a Jewish University," *Menorah Journal* 3:2 (April 1917): 98–101; quotation from 101.

95. Hall to Hurwitz, March 22, 1917. HHMA 20/4. AJA.

96. Isaacs to Hurwitz, May 25, 1917. HHMA 20/4. AJA.

97. Louis I. Newman, *A Jewish University in America?* (New York: Bloch, 1923).

98. Hurwitz, "Objects," attached to Hurwitz to Leo F. Wormser, August 1, 1923. Oko papers 8/26.AJA.

99. Abram L. Sachar, who had served as the president of B'nai B'rith Hillel Foundations from 1933 to 1948, became the first president of Brandeis in 1948.

100. See Wolfson to Hurwitz, May 6, 1922. HHMA 63/2. AJA. Hurwitz instead honored his favorite professor by naming his second son David Lyon Hurwitz.

101. Cohen's memo is attached to Hurwitz to Isaacs, May 6, 1926. HHMA 21/3. AJA.

102. "Address by Prof. Horace M. Kallen and the meeting of Father and Son, held at The Jewish Club, June 6, 1951," Kallen Papers 62/1. AJA.

103. Ritterband and Wechsler, "Judaica in American Colleges and Universities," 73.

104. See Arnold J. Band, "Jewish Studies in American Liberal-Arts Colleges and Universities," *American Jewish Year Book* 67 (1966): 3–30. B'nai B'rith Hillel Foundations had endowed three of the ten Jewish studies chairs in the United States by 1966.

105. *Jewish Studies in American Colleges and Universities: A Catalogue* (Washington, D.C.: B'nai B'rith Hillel Foundations, 1972).

106. William Cutter, "Jewish Studies as Self-Definition: A Review Essay," *Jewish Social Studies* 3:1 (Fall 1996): 163. See Peter Novick, *The Holocaust in American Life* (New York: Houghton Mifflin, 1999), 188, 103.

107. Elizabeth Vernon, *Jewish Studies Courses at American Colleges and Universities* (Cambridge, Mass.: Association for Jewish Studies, 1992), 1.

108. See Ruth Ellen Gruber, *Virtually Jewish: Reinventing Jewish Culture in Europe* (Berkeley: University of California Press, 2002), 12.

109. William Cutter, "Jewish Studies as Self-Definition," 159.

5. A Pluralist History and Culture

1. Herbert Solow, "Wanted: A New Kind of Jewish History," *Menorah Journal* 13:3 (June 1927): 320–24. Solow was reviewing Ismar Elbogen, *History of the Jews* (Cincinnati: Union of American Hebrew Congregations, 1926). On Solow, see Alan M. Wald, "Herbert Solow: Portrait of a New York Intellectual," in *Prospects: An Annual of American Cultural Studies* 3, ed. Jack Salzman (New York: Burt Franklin, 1977); Alan M. Wald, *The New York Intellectuals: The Rise and Decline of the Anti-Stalinist Left from the 1930s to the 1980s* (Chapel Hill: University of North Carolina Press, 1987), especially chapters 1, 2, and 5.

2. Wald, "Herbert Solow," 421–23.

3. See Solow, "The Realities of Zionism," *Menorah Journal* 19:2 (November–December 1930); Solow, "Camouflaging Zionist Realities," *Menorah Journal* 19:3 (March 1931); "'The Realities of Zionism': A Discussion," *Menorah Journal* 19:4 (June 1931). Solow's resignation letter to the Board of Directors, dated October 12, 1931, is in HHMA 56/21. AJA. On this split, see Wald, "Herbert Solow," 428–31.

4. See Solow's obituary: "Herbert Solow, Fortune Editor," *New York Times* (November 27, 1964).

5. Hurwitz to George Alexander Kohut, October 6, 1930. HHMA 27/7. AJA.

6. Kathleen Neils Conzen argues that, for many American ethnic groups, history writing has served as a means to justify the group's belonging in America "by stressing the value of particular gifts it brought to its new homeland." See Conzen, "Phantom Landscapes of Colonization: Germans in the Making of a Pluralist America," in *The German-American Encounter: Conflict and Cooperation between Two Cultures, 1800–2000*, ed. Frank Trommler and Elliott Shore (New York: Berghahn Books, 2001), 7. Orm Øverland has also examined this phenomenon in *Immigrant Minds, American Identities: Making the United States Home, 1870–1930* (Urbana: University of Illinois Press, 2000).

7. Howard M. Sachar, *The Course of Modern Jewish History* (1958; reprint, New York: Dell, 1977), 151. See also Michael A. Meyer, *Origins of the Modern Jew: Jewish Identity and European Culture in Germany, 1749–1824* (Detroit: Wayne State Univer-

sity Press, 1967); Michael A. Meyer, *Judaism within Modernity: Essays on Jewish History and Religion* (Detroit: Wayne State University Press, 2001); Susannah Heschel, "Revolt of the Colonized: Abraham Geiger's Wissenschaft des Judentums as a Challenge to Christian Hegemony in the Academy," *New German Critique* 77 (1999): 61–85; Henry Wasserman, "The Wissenschaft des Judentums and Protestant Theology: A Review Essay," *Modern Judaism* 22 (2002): 83–98.

8. See Meyer, *Judaism within Modernity,* 60.

9. Shlomo Avineri, *The Making of Modern Zionism: The Intellectual Origins of the Jewish State* (New York: Basic Books, 1981), 25.

10. David N. Myers and David B. Ruderman, *The Jewish Past Revisited: Reflections on Modern Jewish Historians* (New Haven, Conn.: Yale University Press, 1998), 5.

11. See Hurwitz to Bernard J. Reis, February 1, 1916. HHMA 46/3. AJA.

12. Lyon's speech was reprinted as "Contributions of Judaism to the Growth of the Civilization of the World," *American Jews Annual* (1894/1895), 42, 45, 49. On the World's Parliament of Religions as a "showcase" for pluralism and "inclusion," see William R. Hutchinson, *Religious Pluralism in America: The Contentious History of a Founding Ideal* (New Haven, Conn.: Yale University Press, 2003), 132–35.

13. R. Travers Herford, "What the World Owes to Pharisees," *Menorah Journal* 5:3 (June 1919): 141, 148.

14. Felix Perles (1874–1933) was born into a well-known family of Jewish scholars. His father, Joseph Perles (1835–1894), had been rabbi to the Jewish community in Munich, and his mother, Rosalie (1839–1932), was a writer and journalist for German Jewish newspapers and periodicals. Felix was the grand rabbi of Paris in 1898 before taking the position in Koenigsberg in 1899. When he wrote this *Menorah Journal* article, Felix Perles was serving as a visiting lecturer at the newly established Jewish Institute of Religion in New York City.

15. Two years later, *Menorah Journal* assistant editor Marvin Lowenthal would bolster Perles's argument. In a piece titled "On a Jewish Humanism," Lowenthal claimed that absorbing oneself in Jewish culture would reveal that Jewish history was more than the history of a religious people. He also included law, philosophy, politics, and art in the totality of Jewish experiences. See Lowenthal, "On a Jewish Humanism," *Menorah Journal* 10:2 (April 1924).

16. Perles, "Culture and History: A Summary of Jewish Experience," *Menorah Journal* 8:5 (October 1922): 317.

17. Perles, "Culture and History," 323–24.

18. See Higham, *Strangers in the Land,* especially chapter 8, "War and Revolution."

19. Some contributions to the *Menorah Journal* celebrated Jews' influence in Europe, most notably an article about the Rothschild family written by University of Illinois historian Abram Leon Sachar. This treatment differed significantly from those that celebrated Jewish history in the United States because the success of the Rothschilds was portrayed as a triumph against great odds and antisemitism, rather than as the product of an open society. See Sachar, "The Romance of the Rothschilds," *Menorah Journal* 11:4 (August 1925); a similar sentiment informed Sachar's "The Jew Enters Parliament," *Menorah Journal* 10:4 (August–September 1924).

20. Marvin M. Lowenthal, "Minutes in Colonial Jewry," *Menorah Journal* 2:2 (April 1916): 117. On Lowenthal, see Susanne Klingenstein, "'Not the Recovery of a Grave,

but of a Cradle': The Zionist Life of Marvin Lowenthal," in Kessner, *The "Other" New York Jewish Intellectuals.*

21. Moses Hyamson, "'Golden Rule' Hillel," *Menorah Journal* 1:2 (April 1915): 91.

22. *Menorah Journal* 3:5 (December 1917): 256. Adulation of Lincoln continued in the writing of American Jewish history. In a 1929 book review, Herbert Solow mocked leading rabbis in America for comparing Lincoln to Abraham, Moses, Isaiah, and Hillel, noting that one contribution to an edited volume even speculated on Lincoln's being descended from "Hebrew parentage." See Solow, "Father Abraham," *Menorah Journal* 16:2 (February 1929): 187–88.

23. See Records of the Menorah Society. Lyman Abbot, "The Political Institutions of the Ancient Hebrews." HUD 3568.900. HUA.

24. George Alexander Kohut, "Hebrew Learning in Puritan New England," *Menorah Journal* 2:4 (October 1916): 213.

25. Kohut, "Ezra Stiles and His Friends," *Menorah Journal* 3:1 (February 1917): 37–46.

26. Straus, "The Pilgrim and the Hebrew Spirit," *Menorah Journal* 6:6 (December 1920): 306.

27. See Frederic Krome, "Creating 'Jewish History for Our Own Needs': The Evolution of Cecil Roth's Historical Vision, 1925–1935," *Modern Judaism* 21 (2001): 216–37.

28. Roth to Hurwitz, January 26, 1927. HHMA 50/3. AJA.

29. David B. Ruderman, "Cecil Roth, Historian of Italian Jewry: A Reassessment," in Myers and Ruderman, *Jewish Past Revisited,* 129–30.

30. Roth, "Jewish History for Our Own Needs," *Menorah Journal* 14:5 (May 1928): 419.

31. Roth acknowledged that Simon Dubnow was an exception. The *Menorah Journal* published a translated excerpt from Dubnow's *Weltgeschichte des jüdischen Volkes.* See Dubnow, "A Sociological Conception of Jewish History," *Menorah Journal* 14:3 (March 1928).

32. Roth, "Jewish History for Our Own Needs," 424.

33. Ibid., 426.

34. Krome correctly warns against interpreting Roth's article "*just* as a polemic against rabbinical training, rabbinical seminaries, and his own personal enemies." See Krome, "Creating 'Jewish History for Our Own Needs,'" 226. Italics in original. Scholars sympathetic with the Menorah Association were not the only ones who argued that histories of the Jews should be produced in a secular university, rather than in a seminary. On this point see Ritterband and Wechsler, *Jewish Learning in American Universities,* 139–47.

35. See Roth to Hurwitz, June 1, 1928. HHMA 50/3. AJA.

36. Roth, "Jewish History for Our Own Needs," 427, 428, 429.

37. Ibid., 433, 434.

38. See Hurwitz to Board of Governors, June 25, 1928. HHMA 15/11. AJA.

39. Solow to Roth, January 6, 1928. HHMA 50/3. AJA.

40. See Solow, "Project for an American Jewish History," n.d. HHMA 56/21. AJA.

41. Roth, "European History and Jewish History: Do Their Epochs Coincide?" *Menorah Journal* 16:4 (April 1929): 306.

42. Ibid., 297.

43. Baron would produce *A Social and Religious History of the Jews,* originally pub-

lished in three volumes in 1937; he subsequently revised the work, which expanded to eighteen volumes. Roth praised Baron's history in a review for the *Menorah Journal*. See Roth, "A Great Historical Work," *Menorah Journal* 26:2 (Spring 1938): 248–50. Roth later called Baron's *The Jewish Community: Its History and Structure to the American Revolution* "one of the major historical achievements of our day." See Roth, "Feats of Scholarship," *Menorah Journal* 31:2 (Spring 1943): 199.

44. Ritterband and Wechsler, *Jewish Learning in American Universities*, 164.

45. Liberles, *Salo Wittmayer Baron*, 8, 340. Michael Stanislawski, "Salo Wittmayer Baron: Demystifying Jewish History," *Columbia* (Winter 2005–2006): 45–48. See also Baron, "Emphases in Jewish History," *Jewish Social Studies* 1:1 (January 1939): 15–38.

46. Baron, "Ghetto and Emancipation: Shall We Revise the Traditional View?" *Menorah Journal* 14:6 (June 1928): 516. Fourteen years later, Roth would again consider the mixed consequences of emancipation for European Jewry in his "A Century and a Half of Emancipation," *Menorah Journal* 30:1 (January–March 1942): 1–12.

47. Baron, "Ghetto and Emancipation," 519, 525, 526.

48. Baron, "Nationalism and Intolerance," *Menorah Journal* 16:6 (June 1929): 503.

49. Baron, "Nationalism and Intolerance," *Menorah Journal* 17:2 (November 1929): 151, 154, 158, 155.

50. See Kohn, "The Jew Enters Western Culture," *Menorah Journal* 18:4 (April 1930); Kohn, "The Teaching of Moses Hess," *Menorah Journal* 18:5 (May 1930).

51. See biographical sketch entitled "Hans Kohn," n.d. HHMA 26/9. AJA; see also Pianko, *Zionism and the Roads Not Taken*, especially chapter 5, "From German Zionism to American Nationalism: Hans Kohn, Cultural Humanism, and the Realization of 'the Political Idea of Judaism.'"

52. See Kohn to Hurwitz, December 25, 1931. HHMA 26/9. AJA.

53. On Hess, see Avineri, *Making of Modern Zionism*, 36–46.

54. Kohn, "The Teaching of Moses Hess," *Menorah Journal* 18:5 (May 1930): 400, 406.

55. The subtitle of Kohn's April 1930 article was "Escape and Return in the Nineteenth Century."

56. Roth's lecture was reprinted as Roth, "Paradoxes of Jewish History," *Menorah Journal* 19:1 (October 1930).

57. See Roth, "The Most Persecuted People?" *Menorah Journal* 20:2 (Summer 1932).

58. Roth, "Paradoxes of Jewish History," *Menorah Journal* 19:1 (October 1930): 22.

59. See "Editorial Note," *Menorah Journal* 13:4 (August 1927): 335.

60. At Wolfson's request, the *Menorah Journal* issued a statement informing readers that the magazine was an "open forum" and that "the expression of opinions" in these columns did not represent those of the journal or the IMA. See Wolfson to Hurwitz, January 17, 1918. HHMA 62/21. AJA; and "Pomegranates," *Menorah Journal* 4:1 (February 1918): 16. In the June 1921 issue of the *Menorah Journal*, three years after the publication of "Pomegranates," the editors revealed El. Lycidas's identity as Wolfson.

61. "Pomegranates," *Menorah Journal* 4:1 (February 1918): 16. Wolfson had also suggested explaining the title with the quip: "Pomegranates, indeed, are a marvelous laxative." He then queried the editors with a pun: "Don't you think it [the quip] would increase circulation?" See Schwarz, *Wolfson of Harvard*, 61.

62. Schwarz, *Wolfson of Harvard*, 60.

63. "Pomegranates," *Menorah Journal* 4:1 (February 1918): 18.

64. Ibid.

65. "Pomegranates," *Menorah Journal* 4:2 (June 1918): 167–70.

66. Many historians have challenged the notion that place of origin—whether Germany or eastern Europe—was more important than the length of time a Jewish immigrant family or their descendants had spent in the United States. See Hasia R. Diner, *A Time for Gathering: The Second Migration, 1820–1880* (Baltimore: Johns Hopkins University Press, 1992); see also Gerald Sorin, *A Time for Building: The Third Migration, 1880–1920* (Baltimore: Johns Hopkins University Press, 1992); and Gerald Sorin, "Mutual Contempt, Mutual Benefit: The Strained Encounter between German and Eastern European Jews in America, 1880–1920," *American Jewish History* 71 (September 1978): 34–59.

67. See Scholem, "The Sleuth from Slobodka," *TLS* (November 23, 1979): 16.

68. Feuer, "Recollections of Harry Austryn Wolfson," 28.

69. Kallen to Wolfson, February 19, 1918. Kallen Papers 32/4. AJA.

70. Wolfson, "Escaping Judaism," *Menorah Journal* 7:2 (June 1921): 78.

71. Wolfson, "Escaping Judaism," *Menorah Journal* 7:3 (August 1921): 166–68.

72. Kallen to Lowenthal, April 23, 1919. Kallen Papers 19/9. AJA.

73. See Klingenstein, "'Not the Recovery of a Grave, but of a Cradle': The Zionist Life of Marvin Lowenthal"; and Ira Eisenstein, "Marvin Lowenthal: The Spirit of Menorah," *Reconstructionist* 31 (October 19, 1965): 17–24.

74. Lowenthal later explained that the 'H' in the pseudonym stood for "Helel" or "Heylel" (not to be confused with "Hillel"). "Helel Ben-Shahar" referred to the Hebrew phrase in Isaiah 14:12: "bright son of the morning." In the King James Bible, "bright son" became translated as "Lucifer." See Eisenstein, "Marvin Lowenthal: The Spirit of Menorah," 17–24.

75. Shahar, "The Adversary's Notebook," *Menorah Journal* 8:2 (April 1922): 122.

76. Ibid., 123–24.

77. Shahar, "The Adversary's Notebook," *Menorah Journal* 8:3 (June 1922): 192.

78. The first three parts of "The Jew in the European Scene" ran in the June, August, and October 1923 *Menorah Journal* issues. The final installment was published in February 1924.

79. Lowenthal, "The Jew in the European Scene," *Menorah Journal* 9:2 (June 1923): 80.

80. Lowenthal, "With Kunze and Hitler," *Menorah Journal* 9:3 (August 1923): 201.

81. Lowenthal, "Anti-Semitism in European Universities," *Nation* (November 14, 1923): 547–49.

82. Lowenthal, "The Jew in the European Scene: IV. Hunger and Strategems," *Menorah Journal* 10:1 (February 1924): 64, 66.

83. Higham, *Strangers in the Land*; Leonard Dinnerstein, *Anti-Semitism in America* (New York: Oxford University Press, 1994); Neil Baldwin, *Henry Ford and the Jews: The Mass Production of Hate* (New York: Public Affairs, 2001).

84. Nathan Isaacs, "'The International Jew,'" *Menorah Journal* 6:6 (December 1920): 357, 360.

85. See, for example, Israel S. Wechsler, "The Psychology of Anti-Semitism," *Menorah Journal* 11:2 (April 1925). On Coughlin, see Alan Brinkley, *Voices of Protest: Huey Long, Father Coughlin and the Great Depression* (New York: Alfred A. Knopf, 1982).

86. For biographical information, see the nearprint file "Elliot E. Cohen" at the AJA; Elinor Grumet, "Elliot Cohen: The Vocation of a Jewish Literary Mentor," *Studies in the American Jewish Experience* 1 (Cincinnati: American Jewish Archives, 1981); Strauss, "Staying Afloat in the Melting Pot"; Nathan Abrams, Commentary *Magazine 1945-59: A Journal of Significant Thought and Opinion* (London: Vallentine Mitchell, 2007), especially chapter 1.

87. Wald, *New York Intellectuals,* 31.

88. Fern Marja, "Commentary's Number One Editor," *New York Post Home News Magazine* (February 17, 1949).

89. Strauss, "Staying Afloat in the Melting Pot," 318.

90. Cohen, "The Promise of the American Synagogue," *Menorah Journal* 4:5 (October 1918): 280–82. The *Menorah Journal* published Cohen's long essay in three parts, and under two different titles: "The Promise of the American Synagogue: A Menorah Prize Essay," *Menorah Journal* 4:5 (October 1918); *Menorah Journal* 4:6 (December 1918); and "The Ideal Rabbi," *Menorah Journal* 5:1 (February 1919).

91. Cohen, "The Promise of the American Synagogue," 369.

92. See Kaplan, "The Future of Judaism," *Menorah Journal* 2:3 (June 1916): 170.

93. See Strauss, "Staying Afloat in the Melting Pot," 318; Wald, *New York Intellectuals,* 31.

94. Lionel Trilling, "On the Death of a Friend," *Commentary* 29 (February 1960): 93–94.

95. Norman Podhoretz, *Making It* (New York: Random House, 1967), 100.

96. See James Clifford, *The Predicament of Culture: Twentieth-Century Ethnography, Literature, and Art* (Cambridge, Mass.: Harvard University Press, 1988), especially 129–34.

97. On photomontage, see Matthew Teitelbaum, "Preface," in *Montage and Modern Life: 1919–1942,* ed. Teitelbaum (Cambridge, Mass.: MIT Press, 1992), 8. See also Sally Stein, "'Good feces make good neighbors': American Resistance to Photomontage Between the Wars," in *Montage and Modern Life: 1919–1942.* On photomontage in Weimar Germany, see Maud Lavin, *Cut with the Kitchen Knife: The Weimar Photomontages of Hannah Höch* (New Haven, Conn.: Yale University Press, 1993).

98. See also Daniel Greene, "'Israel! What a Wonderful People!': Elliot Cohen's Critique of Modern American Jewry 1924–1927," *American Jewish Archives Journal* 55:1 (2003). In 1929, Cohen introduced another recurring feature to the *Menorah Journal,* entitled "Marginal Annotations," which he wrote under the provocative pseudonym "An Elder of Zion," a reference to the notorious antisemitic text *The Protocols of the Elders of Zion.* These short episodic parables were written in his words rather than culled from already published material.

99. See *American Mercury* 1 (January 1924): 48–50.

100. See John Dos Passos, *U.S.A.* (New York: Library of America, 1996).

101. See Hannah Arendt, "Introduction," in Walter Benjamin, *Illuminations: Essays and Reflections* (New York: Schocken, 1968); Susan Buck-Morss, *The Dialectics of Seeing: Walter Benjamin and the Arcades Project* (Cambridge, Mass.: MIT Press, 1989).

102. Cohen, "Notes for a Modern History of the Jews," *Menorah Journal* 10:1 (February 1924): 82.

103. Cohen, "Notes," *Menorah Journal* 10:1 (February 1924): 82.

104. Cohen, "Notes," *Menorah Journal* 12:3 (June–July 1926): 307.

105. Ross, *The Old World and the New,* 289–90; see also Peter Levine, *From Ellis Island to Ebbets Field: Sport and the American Jewish Experience* (New York: Oxford University Press, 1992), 11.

106. See, for example, Cohen's "Notes for a Modern History of the Jews" columns from August–September 1924, February 1925, April 1925, June 1925, December 1925, February 1926, April–May 1926, and December 1926.

107. Cohen, "Notes," *Menorah Journal* 11:1 (February 1925): 74.

108. Gilman, *The Jew's Body* (New York: Routledge, 1991), 53.

109. See Cohen, "Notes," *Menorah Journal* 12:2 (April–May 1926): 194.

110. Cohen's criticism of Jews' Christmas celebrations abounds in his columns. For a typical example, see Cohen, "Notes," *Menorah Journal* 12:1 (February 1926): 79.

111. Cohen, "Notes," *Menorah Journal* 10:4 (August–September 1924): 400.

112. Horace J. Wolf to *Menorah Journal,* January 8, 1926. HHMA 62/17. AJA.

113. Nathan Isaacs to Cohen, October 27, 1931. HHMA 7/17. AJA.

114. Cohen, "The Age of Brass," *Menorah Journal* 11:5 (October 1925): 427–28.

115. Ibid., 440n.

116. Kallen, "Can Judaism Survive in the United States?" *Menorah Journal* 11:2 (April 1925): 101.

117. Ibid., 102, 103.

118. Ibid., 107, 110.

119. Kallen, "Can Judaism Survive in the United States?" *Menorah Journal* 11:6 (December 1925): 548.

120. Ibid., 552–55.

121. The relationship between the American Reform movement and Zionism defies simple categorization. As Michael A. Meyer explains, "Institutionally, classical Reform Judaism put itself on record as fundamentally opposed to political Zionism. . . . Yet it is of interest that, even in its classical phase, American Reform Judaism was by no means uniformly anti-Zionist. . . . Some Reform Jews found it easier to be cultural Zionists than political ones, though here too there were some problems." Meyer, *Response to Modernity,* 293, 294. One way to measure the change in the official position of the Reform movement is to examine the platforms written in 1885 (Pittsburgh) and 1937 (Columbus). The 1885 platform of the Reform movement declared: "We consider ourselves no longer a nation, but a religious community, and, therefore, expect neither a return to Palestine, nor a sacrificial worship under the sons of Aaron, nor the restoration of any of the laws concerning the Jewish state." The 1937 platform read: "In the rehabilitation of Palestine, the land hallowed by memories and hopes, we behold the promise of renewed life for many of our brethren. We affirm the obligation of all Jewry to aid in its upbuilding as a Jewish homeland by endeavoring to make it not only a haven of refuge for the oppressed but also a center of Jewish culture and spiritual life." The two platforms are reprinted in Meyer, *Response to Modernity,* 387–91.

122. Kallen, "Can Judaism Survive in the United States?" 557, 558.

123. Ibid., 559.

124. Israel Zangwill, *Watchman, What of the Night?* (New York: American Jewish Congress, 1923).

125. Hurwitz, "Watchmen, What of the Day?" *Menorah Journal* 12:1 (February 1926): 1–2.

126. Ibid., 10, 18.

127. Kaplan to Hurwitz, February 9, 1926. HHMA 25/5. AJA.

128. Hurwitz to Kaplan, March 3, 1926. HHMA 25/5. AJA.

129. Morgenstern to Hurwitz, April 26, 1926. HHMA 36/5. AJA.

130. For some of the many examples, see Hurwitz to Silver, May 1, 1917; December 22, 1925; and January 5, 1926. HHMA 56/1. AJA.

131. See Silver to Hurwitz, April 6, 1926. HHMA 56/2. AJA.

132. For biographical information on Silver, see Marc Lee Raphael, *Abba Hillel Silver: A Profile in American Judaism* (New York: Holmes and Meier, 1989); Mark A. Raider, Jonathan D. Sarna, and Ronald W. Zweig, eds., *Abba Hillel Silver and American Zionism* (London: Frank Cass Publishers, 1997); and Harold P. Manson, "Abba Hillel Silver—An Appreciation," in *In the Time of Harvest: Essays in Honor of Abba Hillel Silver on the Occasion of His 70th Birthday*, ed. Daniel Jeremy Silver (New York: Macmillan, 1963), 1–27.

133. Hurwitz to Silver, May 18, 1926. HHMA 56/2. AJA.

134. Copies of the undated memo are in many different files in the HHMA collection. An original handwritten copy is in HHMA 7/15. AJA.

135. Isaacs to Hurwitz, June 3, 1926; Hurwitz quoted Oko's and Wolfson's opinions in his letter to Isaacs, June 7, 1926. HHMA 21/3. AJA.

136. Silver to "Gentlemen," July 13, 1926. "Why Do the Heathen Rage?" *Jewish Tribune* (July 23, 30, August 6, 13, 1926), reprinted in *Therefore Choose Life: Selected Sermons, Addresses, and Writings of Abba Hillel Silver*, vol. 1, ed. Herbert Weiner (Cleveland and New York: World Publishing Co., 1967), 364–87.

137. Silver, "Why Do the Heathen Rage?" 365.

138. Ibid., 375.

139. Ibid., 386, 387.

140. See "Some Marginal Annotations on 'Why Do the Heathen Rage?'" HHMA 29/11. AJA.

141. Hurwitz to Herman Bernstein, editor of the *Jewish Tribune*, July 28, 1926. HHMA 56/2. AJA.

142. Clipping titled, "Reflections," no source given, July 26, 1928. HHMA 56/2. AJA.

143. Morgenstern to Hurwitz, September 29, 1926. HHMA 36/4. AJA.

144. Freehof to Hurwitz, January 20, 1927. HHMA 13/9. AJA.

145. David de Sola Pool to Hurwitz, February 4, 1928. HHMA 42/17. AJA.

6. Pluralism in Fiction

1. Fiction was just one aspect of the Menorah Association's intended renaissance of Jewish arts and culture; the *Menorah Journal* also was an important forum for in poetry and the visual arts. On visual art in the *Menorah Journal*, see Andrea Pappas, "The Picture at *Menorah Journal*: Making 'Jewish Art.'"

2. See Laurence J. Silberstein, "Others Within and Without: Rethinking Jewish Identity and Culture," in *The Other in Jewish Thought and History: Constructions of Jewish Culture and Identity*, ed. Silberstein and Robert L. Cohn (New York: New York University Press, 1994), 11–12.

3. Cohen began to work as an assistant editor at the *Menorah Journal* in April 1924 and was the managing editor from June 1925 until September 1931.

4. Halper wrote of Cohen: "He had been my literary godfather and the godfather to so many others." See *Good-bye, Union Square: A Writer's Memoir of the Thirties* (Chicago: Quadrangle Books, 1970), 275.

5. See Louis Berg, "Personal Memoir," *Commentary* 51 (April 1971): 98–102. Halper to Cohen, July 19, 1929, and Halper to Whom It May Concern, November 28, 1919. HHMA 17/10. AJA.

6. Grumet, "The Menorah Idea and the Apprenticeship of Lionel Trilling," 74.

7. Louis Harap, *Creative Awakening: The Jewish Presence in Twentieth-Century American Literature, 1900–1940s* (New York: Greenwood Press, 1987).

8. Mary Antin, *The Promised Land* (1912; reprint, Princeton, N.J.: Princeton University Press, 1969), xix.

9. Abraham Cahan, *The Rise of David Levinsky* (1917; reprint, New York: Penguin Books, 1993).

10. The *Menorah Journal* biography of Yezierska stated that she was born in 1886 in Russia. This late birth date seems unlikely. Historian Alice Kessler-Harris places her birth around 1882 in Plotsk, a shtetl in Russian Poland. See Kessler-Harris, "Introduction," to Yezierska, *Bread Givers* (1925; reprint, New York: Persea Books, 1999), xvi.

11. Yezierska, "The Lord Giveth," *Menorah Journal* 9:1 (February 1923): 37, 39. She used a similar line in her 1925 novel *Bread Givers,* adding the word "good" so the admonition reads: "Poverty is an ornament on a good Jew, like a red ribbon on a white horse." See Yezierska, *Bread Givers,* 70.

12. Yezierska, "The Lord Giveth," 40, 43, 44.

13. See Levin, "Roosevelt Road," *Menorah Journal* 10:1 (February 1924): 46–51.

14. See Lawrence Graver, *An Obsession with Anne Frank: Meyer Levin and the Diary* (Berkeley: University of California Press, 1995); Alexandra Zapruder, ed., *Salvaged Pages: Young Writers' Diaries of the Holocaust* (New Haven, Conn.: Yale University Press, 2002), 1–13.

15. Levin, "A Seder," *Menorah Journal* 10:2 (April 1924): 145.

16. See the editorial note preceding the first "Commentaries" installment, *Menorah Journal* 10:4 (August–September 1924): 401; and Editor to James Oppenheim, October 20, 1923. HHMA 7/15. AJA.

17. Cohen circular letter, October 22, 1923. HHMA 7/15. AJA.

18. Maximillian Hurwitz, "Necrologues and Noodles," *Menorah Journal* 10:4 (August–September 1924): 401.

19. Jochanan ben Jacob (pseudonym), "Jewish Contributions to Civilization," *Menorah Journal* 11:2 (April 1925): 186–89.

20. Javitz, "For Immediate Release," *Menorah Journal* 12:2 (April–May 1926): 197.

21. Ibid., 198.

22. Javitz, "O Genteel Jewish Lady!" *Menorah Journal* 12:6 (October–November 1926): 642–44.

23. See Riv-Ellen Prell, *Fighting to Become Americans: Jews, Gender, and the Anxiety of Assimilation* (Boston: Beacon Press, 1999), 13.

24. In a somewhat less effective "Commentaries" published later that year, Javitz mocked Jews' tendency to idolize Jewish sports heroes in America. See Javitz, "Rah! Rah! Israel!" *Menorah Journal* 12:5 (October–November 1926): 534–35.

25. Between 1929 and 1931, Halper also published in the *Dial,* the *New Republic,* and

the *American Mercury,* among many other magazines. See Halper, *Good-bye, Union Square;* John E. Hart, *Albert Halper* (Boston: G. K. Hall, 1980).

26. Tess Slesinger, a writer for the *Menorah Journal* and, from 1928 to 1932, the wife of one of its editors, Herbert Solow, portrayed and parodied this group of writers in her novel *The Unpossessed* (1934; reprint, New York: New York Review Books, 2002).

27. Halper, "Brothers Over a Grave," *Menorah Journal* 16:4 (April 1929): 367.

28. Halper, "Memorial," *Menorah Journal* 18:5 (May 1930): 462. "Memorial" was excerpted from Halper's unpublished novel, *Good-bye Again.* Hart, *Albert Halper,* 35.

29. Melvin P. Levy, "Assimilation," *Menorah Journal* 11:1 (February 1925): 80–82.

30. Ibid., 80–82.

31. Fearing, "Mapleton Welcomes the Stranger," *Menorah Journal* 15:5 (November 1928): 468–74.

32. Ibid., 474.

33. For more on the Reuben Cohen series, see Daniel Greene, "Reuben Cohen Comes of Age: American Jewish Youth and the Lived Experience of Cultural Pluralism in the 1920s," *American Jewish History* 95:2 (June 2009): 157–82.

34. Irwin Edman, *Richard Kane Looks at Life* (Boston: Houghton Mifflin, 1926), vii.

35. Hurwitz to Edman, February 18, 1926. HHMA 9/18. AJA.

36. Hurwitz to Edman, May 21, 1925. HHMA 9/18. AJA.

37. Philosopher and educator John Dewey advised Edman's dissertation, "Human Traits and Their Social Significance."

38. Herman J. Saatkamp Jr. and Clay Davis Spawn, "Edman, Irwin," *American National Biography,* vol. 7, ed. John A. Garraty and Mark C. Carnes (New York: Oxford University Press, 1999), 315–16; Timothy P. Cross, *An Oasis of Order: The Core Curriculum at Columbia College* (New York: Columbia College, Office of the Dean, 1995), 15.

39. On literary examples of Jews who "sound different because they are represented as being different," see Sander Gilman's "The Jewish Voice" in *The Jew's Body,* 10–37; quotation on 11.

40. Edman, "Reuben Cohen Goes to College," *Menorah Journal* 12:2 (April–May 1926): 132.

41. Ibid., 127, 128, 129.

42. Ibid., 134. The fictional Jewish cultural organization likely was a good-natured send-up of the Intercollegiate Menorah Association, though Edman took too great a liberty if he meant to suggest that the IMA harped on antisemitism, which it surely did not.

43. Ibid., 135.

44. Ibid., 135, 136, 137.

45. Edman, "Reuben Cohen Enters American Life," *Menorah Journal* 12 (June–July 1926): 247.

46. Ibid., 247.

47. Two instructive works on the notion of Jewish identity as constructed versus essential are Goldstein, *The Price of Whiteness;* and Heinze, *Jews and the American Soul.*

48. Edman, "Reuben Cohen Enters American Life," 248.

49. Ibid., 249.

50. Ibid., 247, 249.

51. Edman, "Reuben Cohen Claims His Inheritance," *Menorah Journal* 12:6 (December 1926): 576, 568.

52. Ibid., 568.

53. Ibid., 569, 571, 573.

54. Ibid., 576.

55. Edman, "Reuben Cohen Goes to Temple," *Menorah Journal* 14:6 (June 1928): 527–36.

56. Edman, "Reuben Cohen Considers Marriage—and Intermarriage," *Menorah Journal* 15:4 (October 1928): 316.

57. Edman, "Reuben Cohen Considers Anti-Semitism," *Menorah Journal* 16:1 (January 1929): 30–31.

58. Ibid., 31.

59. Henry M. Rosenthal, "Emancipated Jew: Faculty Model," *Menorah Journal* 11:2 (April 1925).

60. Hadas earned his doctorate in classics at Columbia in 1930 and became one of the world's foremost classicists, serving on the Columbia faculty until his death in 1966.

61. Rosenthal, "Emancipated Jew: Faculty Model," 182–84.

62. Rosenthal, "Theological Student: Advanced Model," *Menorah Journal* 11:5 (October 1925): 508.

63. Grumet, "The Menorah Idea and the Apprenticeship of Lionel Trilling," 103.

64. Rosenthal's articles during this period also included "A Dervish," *Menorah Journal* 12:1 (February 1926): 82–86; "To a Young Man Who Wishes to Write about Jews," *Menorah Journal* 13:2 (April 1927): 142–52; and "Inventions," *Menorah Journal* 14:1 (January 1928): 49–61. Rosenthal did not publish in the *Menorah Journal* between 1928 and 1947. In 1947, by which time he was no longer friendly with Trilling, Rosenthal joined the magazine's staff as a contributing editor, a position he held through 1962, when the magazine ceased publication.

65. On Trilling's work for the *Menorah Journal,* see Grumet, "The Menorah Idea and the Apprenticeship of Lionel Trilling"; Mark Krupnick, "The Menorah Journal Group and the Origins of Modern Jewish-American Radicalism," 56–67; Krupnick, *Lionel Trilling and the Fate of Cultural Criticism* (Evanston, Ill.: Northwestern University Press, 1986); and Thomas Bender, "Lionel Trilling and American Culture," *American Quarterly* 42:2 (June 1990): 324–47.

66. Bender, "Lionel Trilling and American Culture," 333.

67. One of Trilling's works of literary criticism, "The Changing Myth of the Jew" was accepted by the *Menorah Journal* and even was set in type in 1931, but it never was published in the magazine. It finally appeared in a 1978 issue of *Commentary* magazine. See Lionel Trilling, *Speaking of Literature and Society,* ed. Diana Trilling (Oxford: Oxford University Press, 1982), 50–76.

68. Louis Menand, "Regrets Only: Lionel Trilling and His Discontents," *New Yorker* (September 29, 2008): 86.

69. See Cynthia Ozick, "The Buried Life," *New Yorker* (October 2, 2000): 119. Thomas Bender writes, "Dewey represented for Trilling the possibilities of humanism." See Bender, "Lionel Trilling and American Culture," 334. Mark Van Doren of Columbia's English department wrote about Rosenthal and Trilling for the *Menorah*

Journal. Van Doren portrayed Rosenthal, identified only as "student A," as a viciously intelligent skeptic, while Trilling, "student F," was described as a writer with unlimited potential. See Van Doren, "Jewish Students I Have Known," *Menorah Journal* 13:3 (June 1927): 264–68.

70. Grumet, "The Menorah Idea and the Apprenticeship of Lionel Trilling," 115, 120.

71. Trilling, "Impediments," *Menorah Journal* 11:3 (June 1925): 286–90.

72. Rosenthal would later write a piece about Trilling and himself for the magazine. See Rosenthal, "Inventions."

73. Krupnick, *Lionel Trilling and the Fate of Cultural Criticism,* 26.

74. Three examples are "Chapter for a Fashionable Jewish Novel," *Menorah Journal* 12:3 (June–July 1926); "Funeral at the Club, with Lunch," *Menorah Journal* 13:4 (August 1927); and "Notes on a Departure," *Menorah Journal* 16:5 (May 1929).

75. Trilling, "Our Colonial Forefathers," *Menorah Journal* 14 (February 1928): 220. On Trilling and the outsider's gaze, see Grumet, "The Menorah Idea and the Apprenticeship of Lionel Trilling," 163.

76. Trilling, "A Light unto the Nations," *Menorah Journal* 14:4 (April 1928): 402–08.

77. Ibid.

78. Trilling, "Funeral at the Club, with Lunch," *Menorah Journal* 13:4 (August 1927): 382.

79. Ibid., 387.

80. Krupnick, *Lionel Trilling and the Fate of Cultural Criticism,* 29. Thomas H. Samet has also remarked on this quality of Trilling's early fiction in his dissertation, "The Problematic Self: Lionel Trilling and the Anxieties of the Modern" (Ph.D. diss., Brown University, 1980).

81. Trilling, "Funeral at the Club, with Lunch," 390.

82. Grumet, "The Menorah Idea and the Apprenticeship of Lionel Trilling," 134–35.

83. Trilling, "Notes on a Departure," 425.

84. In a 1932 letter, Trilling informed Hurwitz that "personal loyalty toward Elliot [Cohen]" would preclude Trilling's being involved with the *Menorah Journal* again. See Trilling to Hurwitz, September 3, 1932. HHMA 60/1. AJA. A series of anti-Zionist and politically radical articles by Herbert Solow led to a rift within the journal's editorial staff. Cohen and Solow quarreled with Hurwitz about what they perceived as Hurwitz's tendency to make safe editorial choices. On this rift, see Wald, *The New York Intellectuals,* 27–45.

85. In her 1993 memoir, Diana Trilling referred to her husband's stories for the *Menorah Journal*—specifically "Funeral at the Club, with Lunch" and "Notes on a Departure"—as "inauthentic" and "contrived to meet the specifications of a Jewish magazine." She claimed that Trilling, driven perhaps by a desire to publish, wrote what he thought the magazine's editors wanted, leading him to overemphasize his feelings of alienation in Madison. There is no evidence in the correspondence between Lionel Trilling and anyone on the *Menorah Journal* staff, however, to support Diana Trilling's contention, which came more than sixty years after these stories were first published. See Diana Trilling, *The Beginning of the Journey: The Marriage of Diana and Lionel Trilling* (New York: Harcourt Brace, 1993), 143, 380.

86. Diana Trilling, "Lionel Trilling, A Jew at Columbia," *Commentary* 67 (March 1979): 40–46; Grumet, "The Menorah Idea and the Apprenticeship of Lionel Trilling," 279n21.

87. Stanley F. Chyet, "Ludwig Lewisohn: The Years of Becoming," *American Jewish Archives Journal* 11 (1959): 129n7.

88. Ludwig Lewisohn, *Up Stream* (New York: Boni and Liveright, 1922), 77.

89. Carpenter, as quoted in Chyet, "Ludwig Lewisohn: The Years of Becoming," 134.

90. Literary critic Mark Krupnick notes that, despite Trilling's and Lewisohn's different outcomes with Columbia's English Department faculty, "in both instances the department was trying to get rid of a promising young academic because he was Jewish, and they were compounding the insult by assuring him that the decision was for his own good." Krupnick, *Lionel Trilling and the Fate of Cultural Criticism,* 32n.

91. Chyet, "Ludwig Lewisohn: The Years of Becoming," 141.

92. Lewisohn, *Up Stream.*

93. Lewisohn, *Israel* (New York: Boni and Liveright, 1925).

94. On Lewisohn and the Ohio State University Menorah Society, see Ralph Melnick, *The Life and Work of Ludwig Lewisohn,* 2 vols. (Detroit: Wayne State University Press, 1998), 198–99.

95. See Lewisohn to Hurwitz, July 15, 1931. HHMA 31/11. AJA.

96. For biographical information on Lewisohn, see Klingenstein, *Jews in the American Academy, 1900–1940,* 83–136; Stanley F. Chyet, "Ludwig Lewisohn: A Life in Zionism," in Kessner, *The "Other" New York Jewish Intellectuals,* 160–90.

97. See, for example, Hurwitz to Lewisohn, May 10, 1921. HHMA 31/11. AJA.

98. As Lewisohn traveled, he submitted contributions to the *Menorah Journal's* "Letters from Abroad" columns. He wrote from Berlin in November–December 1924, Vilna in February 1925, Tel Aviv in April 1925, Warsaw in August 1925, and Vienna in November 1927.

99. Zeitlin received similar advice as Lewisohn about the difficulty a Jew would face in gaining an academic appointment in English, but, according to historian Stanley F. Chyet: "Possessed of a good deal more *sang-froid* and a good deal less sensitivity than Lewisohn, Zeitlin naturally found the obstacles which both he and Lewisohn encountered less formidable." Chyet, "Ludwig Lewisohn: The Years of Becoming," 135.

100. Jacob Zeitlin, "The Case of Mr. Lewisohn," *Menorah Journal* 8:3 (June 1922): 189, 188, 191.

101. Lewisohn, "The Fallacies of Assimilation," *Menorah Journal* 11:5 (October 1925): 460–72. The article is an abbreviated version of the first chapter of Lewisohn's *Israel.*

102. See Lewisohn to Hurwitz, April 5, 1928; and Hurwitz to Lewisohn, May 4, 1928. HHMA 31/11. AJA. Lewisohn's novels *The Island Within* (1928; reprint, Syracuse: Syracuse University Press, 1997) and *The Case of Mr. Crump* (Paris: E. W. Titus, 1926) also drew attention during this era. *The Case of Mr. Crump* was not published in the United States until 1965.

103. Lewisohn had contributed a short article to the *Menorah Journal* in praise of Martin Buber's teaching that separating conviction and action would lead to a life of sin. See Lewisohn, "Martin Buber," *Menorah Journal* 12:1 (February 1926): 65–70.

104. Lewisohn, *Mid-Channel* (New York: Harper and Brothers, 1929), 88.

105. Ibid., 153.

106. Ibid., 255.

107. Ibid., 261.

108. Ibid., 303, 306.

Epilogue

1. For the details of this split, see Wald, *The New York Intellectuals,* 27–45; Greene, "The Crisis of Jewish Freedom," 346–68.

2. James Gilbert, *Writers and Partisans: A History of Literary Radicalism in America* (1968; reprint, New York: Columbia University Press, 1992); Abrams, Commentary *Magazine 1945–59.*

3. "Memorandum on Menorah Refugee Aid," attached to Hurwitz to A. L. Sachar, March 8, 1940. HHMA 51/4. AJA; see Hannah Arendt, "We Refugees," *Menorah Journal* 31:1 (Winter 1943): 69–77; also "The Menorah Journal: Testimony," [c. 1945]. HHMA 65/6. AJA.

4. On the later years of the *Menorah Journal,* see Lewis Fried, "The *Menorah Journal:* Yavneh in America, 1945–1950," 76–108.

5. David Lyon Hurwood, "Ave Atque Vale," *Menorah Journal* 49 (Autumn–Winter 1962), n.p.

6. Kallen, "The Promise of the Menorah Idea," 9–16.

7. Ibid., 9.

8. Kallen to Rischin, December 4, 1953. Kallen Papers. 26/4. AJA.

9. Kallen, "The Promise of the Menorah Idea," 10.

10. Ibid.

11. Ibid.

12. Ibid., 11.

13. Klingenstein, *Jews in the American Academy 1900–1940,* 39.

14. Since the 1910s, Kallen had promised a separate analysis of African Americans' cultural impact on the United States, but he never kept this promise. See Whitfield, "Introduction to the Transaction Edition," *Culture and Democracy in the United States,* 45.

15. Kallen, "The Promise of the Menorah Idea," 10.

16. Will Herberg, *Protestant, Catholic, Jew: An Essay in American Religious Sociology* (New York: Doubleday, 1955). See also Hollinger, *Postethnic America,* 98; Whitfield, "Introduction to the Transaction Edition," *Culture and Democracy in the United States,* 38–41; Kevin Michael Schultz, "The Decline of the Melting Pot: Catholics, Jews, and Pluralism in Postwar America" (Ph.D. diss., University of California, Berkeley, 2005).

17. See Gleason, *Speaking of Diversity,* 3–46.

18. Nathan Glazer and Daniel Patrick Moynihan, *Beyond the Melting Pot: The Negroes, Puerto Ricans, Jews, Italians, and Irish of New York City* (Cambridge, Mass.: MIT Press, 1963), v.

19. Kennedy and Douglas are quoted in Whitfield, "Introduction to the Transaction Edition," *Culture and Democracy in the United States,* 50.

20. Daniel T. Rodgers, *Contested Truths: Keywords in American Politics since Independence* (New York: Basic Books, 1987).

21. One important exception was Gordon, *Assimilation in American Life.*

22. Kallen, "The Promise of the Menorah Idea," 11.

23. See Kallen, *Cultural Pluralism and the American Idea.*

24. See Kallen, "Alain Locke and Cultural Pluralism," 119–27.

25. Waters, *Ethnic Options.*

26. Heinze, "Is It 'Cos I's Black? Jews and the Whiteness Problem," 8, 9, 12–13.

27. Kallen's experience provides convincing support for Heinze's claim that many historians are wrong in assuming that "immigrants worried America would take them for black unless they proved themselves white. The opposite was true." See Heinze, "Is It 'Cos I's Black? Jews and the Whiteness Problem," 13.

28. Hollinger, *Postethnic America,* 11.

29. Walzer, "Multiculturalism and the Politics of Interest," in Biale, Galchinsky, and Heschel, *Insider/Outsider,* 89.

30. Hollinger, *Postethnic America,* 92–93.

31. Kallen, "The Promise of the Menorah Idea," 14–15.

32. Ibid., 16. Italics in original.

BIBLIOGRAPHY

Archival and Manuscript Collections

Harvard University Archives, Cambridge, Massachusetts
  Menorah Society Papers, 1906–1927
  Harry A. Wolfson Papers
The Jacob Rader Marcus Center of the American Jewish Archives, Cincinnati, Ohio
  Henry Hurwitz/Menorah Association Collection
  Horace M. Kallen Papers
  Adolph S. Oko Papers
  Samuel Schulman Papers

Selected Periodicals

American Jewish Chronicle
American Jewish Year Book
Central Conference of American Rabbis, *Yearbook*
Commentary
Harper's Weekly
Menorah Bulletin
Menorah Journal
Nation
New Republic
Publications of the American Jewish Historical Society

Works Consulted

Abrams, Nathan. Commentary *Magazine 1945–59: A Journal of Significant Thought and Opinion*. London: Vallentine Mitchell, 2007.
Ahlstrom, Sydney E. *A Religious History of the American People*. New Haven, Conn.: Yale University Press, 1972.

Alexander, Michael. *Jazz Age Jews*. Princeton, N.J.: Princeton University Press, 2001.

Alter, Robert. "Epitaph for a Jewish Magazine: Notes on the 'Menorah Journal.'" *Commentary* 39 (May 1965): 51–55.

Anderson, Benedict. *Imagined Communities: Reflections on the Origins and Spread of Nationalism*. London: Verso, 1983, 1991.

Antin, Mary. *The Promised Land*. 1912. Reprint, Princeton, N.J.: Princeton University Press, 1969.

Arnessen, Eric. "Whiteness and the Historians' Imagination." *International Labor and Working-Class History* 60 (Fall 2001): 3–32.

Arnold, Matthew. *Culture and Anarchy*. Ed. Stefan Collini. Cambridge: Cambridge University Press, 1993.

Austin, William E. "The Story of the Menorah Movement." 1963. Unpublished paper located in Menorah Movement, Misc. File, The Jacob Rader Marcus Center of the American Jewish Archives.

Avineri, Shlomo. *The Making of Modern Zionism: The Intellectual Origins of the Jewish State*. New York: Basic Books, 1981.

Baeck, Leo. "Revelation and World Religion." In *The Essence of Judaism*, ed. Irving Howe. New York: Schocken, 1948.

Baldwin, Neil. *Henry Ford and the Jews: The Mass Production of Hate*. New York: Public Affairs, 2001.

Band, Arnold J. "Jewish Studies in American Liberal-Arts Colleges and Universities." *American Jewish Year Book* 67 (1966): 3–30.

Baron, Salo W. "Emphases in Jewish History." *Jewish Social Studies* 1:1 (January 1939): 15–38.

———. *History and Jewish Historians: Essays and Addresses by Salo W. Baron*. Philadelphia: Jewish Publication Society, 1964.

Barrett, James R. "Americanization from the Bottom Up: Immigration and the Remaking of the Working Class in the United States, 1880–1930." *Journal of American History* 79 (December 1992): 996–1020.

Barrett, James R., and David Roediger. "Inbetween Peoples: Race, Nationality and the 'New Immigrant' Working Class." *Journal of American Ethnic History* 16 (Spring 1997): 3–44.

Bender, Thomas. *Intellect and Public Life*. Baltimore: Johns Hopkins University Press, 1992.

———. "Lionel Trilling and American Culture." *American Quarterly* 42:2 (June 1990): 324–47.

———. *New York Intellect: A History of Intellectual Life in New York City, From 1750 to the Beginnings of Our Own Time*. Baltimore: Johns Hopkins University Press, 1987.

Bender, Thomas, and Carl E. Schorske, eds. *American Academic Culture in Transformation*. Princeton, N.J.: Princeton University Press, 1997.

Benjamin, Walter. *Illuminations: Essays and Reflections*. Ed. and with an introduction by Hannah Arendt. New York: Schocken, 1968.

Bentinck-Smith, William, and Elizabeth Stouffer. *Harvard University History of Named Chairs: Sketches of Donors and Donations*. Cambridge, Mass.: Secretary to the [Harvard] University, 1991.

Berkowitz, Michael. *The Jewish Self-Image in the West*. New York: New York University Press, 2000.

———. *Zionist Culture and West European Jewry before the First World War*. Chapel Hill: University of North Carolina Press, 1993.

Berkson, Isaac B. *Theories of Americanization: A Critical Study with Special Reference to the Jewish Group*. New York: Teachers College, Columbia University, 1920.

Berman, Lila Corwin. *Speaking of Jews: Rabbis, Intellectuals, and the Creation of an American Public Identity*. Berkeley: University of California Press, 2009.

Bertz, Inka. "Jewish Renaissance—Jewish Modernism." In *Berlin Metropolis: Jews and the New Culture 1890–1918*, ed. Emily D. Bilski. Berkeley: University of California Press, 1999.

Biale, David, Michael Galchinsky, and Susannah Heschel, eds. *Insider/Outsider: American Jews and Multiculturalism*. Berkeley: University of California Press, 1998.

Birnbaum, Pierre, and Ira Katznelson, eds. *Paths of Emancipation: Jews, States, and Citizenship*. Princeton, N.J.: Princeton University Press, 1995.

Blake, Casey. *Beloved Community: The Cultural Criticism of Randolph Bourne, Van Wyck Brooks, Waldo Frank, and Lewis Mumford*. Chapel Hill: University of North Carolina Press, 1990.

Bloom, Alexander. *Prodigal Sons: The New York Intellectuals and Their World*. New York: Oxford University Press, 1986.

Boas, Franz. "Are the Jews a Race?" *World Tomorrow* 6 (January 1923): 5–6.

Boas, Ralph Philip. "Who Shall Go to College?" *Atlantic Monthly* 130 (October 1922): 441–48.

Borowitz, Eugene B. *The Mask Jews Wear: The Self-Deception of American Jewry*. New York: Simon and Schuster, 1973.

Bourne, Randolph S. *The Radical Will: Selected Writings 1911–1918*. Ed. Olaf Hansen. New York: Urizen Books, 1977.

———. "Trans-National America." *Atlantic Monthly* 118 (July 1916): 86–97.

Brandeis, Louis D. *The Jewish Problem: How to Solve It*. New York: Zionist Essays Publication Committee, 1915.

———. *Zionism and Patriotism*. New York: Foundation of American Zionists, 1915.

Brenner, David A. *Marketing Identities: The Invention of Jewish Ethnicity in Ost und West*. Detroit: Wayne State University Press, 1998.

Brenner, Michael. *The Renaissance of Jewish Culture in Weimar Germany*. New Haven, Conn.: Yale University Press, 1996.

Brinkley, Alan. *Voices of Protest: Huey Long, Father Coughlin and the Great Depression*. New York: Alfred A. Knopf, 1982.

Brodkin, Karen. *How Jews Became White Folks and What That Says about Race in America*. New Brunswick, N.J.: Rutgers University Press, 1998.

Buck-Morss, Susan. *The Dialectics of Seeing: Walter Benjamin and the Arcades Project*. Cambridge, Mass.: MIT Press, 1989.

Burt, Robert A. *Two Jewish Justices: Outcasts in the Promised Land*. Berkeley: University of California Press, 1988.

Cahan, Abraham. *The Rise of David Levinsky*. 1917. Reprint, New York: Penguin Books, 1993.

Carlebach, Elisheva, John M. Efron, and David N. Myers, eds. *Jewish History and Jewish Memory: Essays in Honor of Yosef Hayim Yerushalmi.* Hanover, N.H.: Brandeis University Press, 1998.

Carver, Thomas Nixon. "Discussion Groups and Harvard." *Harvard Graduates' Magazine* 28 (December 1919): 263–65.

"The Cercle Francais." *Harvard Illustrated Magazine* (May 1900): 200–203.

Cheyette, Bryan, ed. *Between 'Race' and Culture: Representations of 'the Jew' in English and American Literature.* Stanford, Calif.: Stanford University Press, 1996.

Chyet, Stanley F. "Ludwig Lewisohn: The Years of Becoming." *American Jewish Archives Journal* 11 (1959): 125–47.

Clifford, James. *The Predicament of Culture: Twentieth-Century Ethnography, Literature, and Art.* Cambridge, Mass.: Harvard University Press, 1988.

Cohen, Arthur A. *The Shaping of American Higher Education.* San Francisco, Calif.: Jossey-Bass, 1998.

Cohen, George. *The Jews in the Making of America.* Boston: Stratford, 1924.

Cohen, Israel. *Jewish Life in Modern Times.* New York: Dodd, Mead and Co., 1914.

Cohen, Naomi W. *Jacob H. Schiff: A Study in American Jewish Leadership.* Hanover, N.H.: Brandeis University Press, 1999.

Conzen, Kathleen Neils. "German-Americans and the Invention of Ethnicity." In *America and the Germans: An Assessment of a Three-Hundred-Year History,* vol. 1, ed. Frank Trommler and Joseph McVeigh. Philadelphia: University of Pennsylvania Press, 1985.

———. "Phantom Landscapes of Colonization: Germans in the Making of a Pluralist America." In *The German American Encounter: Conflict and Cooperation between Two Cultures, 1800–2000,* ed. Frank Trommler and Elliott Shore. New York: Berghahn Books, 2001.

Conzen, Kathleen Neils, et al. "The Invention of Ethnicity: A Perspective from the U.S.A." *Journal of American Ethnic History* 12 (Fall 1992): 3–41.

Cooney, Terry A. *The Rise of the New York Intellectuals: Partisan Review and Its Circle.* Madison: University of Wisconsin Press, 1986.

Cremin, Lawrence A. *The Transformation of the School: Progressivism in American Education, 1876–1957.* New York: Alfred A. Knopf, 1961.

Cross, Timothy P. *An Oasis of Order: The Core Curriculum at Columbia College.* New York: Columbia College, Office of the Dean, 1995.

Cutter, William. "Jewish Studies as Self-Definition: A Review Essay." *Jewish Social Studies* 3:1 (Fall 1996): 158–76.

Daniels, Roger. *Coming to America: A History of Immigration and Ethnicity in American Life.* New York: HarperCollins, 1990.

———. *Guarding the Golden Door: American Immigration Policy and Immigrants since 1882.* New York: Hill and Wang, 2004.

Diner, Hasia R. *Lower East Side Memories: A Jewish Place in America.* Princeton, N.J.: Princeton University Press, 2000.

———. *A Time for Gathering: The Second Migration, 1820–1880.* Baltimore: Johns Hopkins University Press, 1992.

Dinnerstein, Leonard. *Anti-Semitism in America.* New York: Oxford University Press, 1994.

Dinnerstein, Leonard, and David M. Reimers. *Ethnic Americans: A History of Immigration.* New York: Harper and Row, 1988.

Dollinger, Mark. *Quest for Inclusion: Jews and Liberalism in Modern America.* Princeton, N.J.: Princeton University Press, 2000.

Dos Passos, John. *U.S.A.* 1946. Reprint, New York: Library of America, 1996.

Drachsler, Julius. *Democracy and Assimilation: The Blending of Immigrant Heritages in America.* New York: Macmillan, 1920.

———. "The Trend of Jewish Communal Life in the United States." *Jewish Social Service Quarterly* 1 (November 1924): 1–22; (February 1925): 1–20.

Du Bois, W. E. B. *The Souls of Black Folk.* 1903. Reprint, New York: Oxford University Press, 2007.

Dumenil, Lynn. *The Modern Temper: American Culture and Society in the 1920s.* New York: Hill and Wang, 1995.

Dushkin, Alexander M. *Jewish Education in New York City.* New York: Bureau of Jewish Education, 1918.

Edman, Irwin. *Richard Kane Looks at Life.* Boston: Houghton Mifflin, 1926.

Eisen, Arnold M. *The Chosen People in America: A Study in Jewish Religious Ideology.* Bloomington: Indiana University Press, 1983.

———. *Rethinking Modern Judaism: Ritual, Commandment, Community.* Chicago: University of Chicago Press, 1998.

Eisen, Arnold, and Noam Pianko, eds. "Mordecai Kaplan's *Judaism as a Civilization:* The Legacy of an American Idea." Special Issue, *Jewish Social Studies* 12:2 (Winter 2006).

Eisenstein, Ira. "Marvin Lowenthal: The Spirit of Menorah." *Reconstructionist* 31 (October 29, 1965): 17–24.

Elbogen, Ismar. "American Jewish Scholarship: A Survey." *American Jewish Year Book* 45 (1943–44): 47–65.

Endelman, Todd. "Jewish Self-Hatred in Britain and Germany." In *Two Nations: British and German Jews in Comparative Perspective,* ed. Michael Brenner, Rainer Liedtke, and David Rechter. London: Leo Baeck Institute, 1999.

Faber, Eli. *A Time for Planting: The First Migration: 1654–1820.* Baltimore: Johns Hopkins University Press, 1992.

Fass, Paula. *The Damned and the Beautiful: American Youth in the 1920s.* New York: Oxford University Press, 1977.

Feiner, Shmuel. *The Jewish Enlightenment.* Trans. Chaya Naor. Philadelphia: University of Pennsylvania Press, 2002.

Feiner, Shmuel, and David Sorkin, eds. *New Perspectives on the Haskalah.* London: Littman Library of Jewish Civilization, 2001.

Feingold, Henry L. "American Jewish History and American Jewish Survival." *American Jewish History* 71:4 (June 1982): 421–31.

———. *Bearing Witness: How America and Its Jews Responded to the Holocaust.* Syracuse, N.Y.: Syracuse University Press, 1995.

———. *A Time for Searching: Entering the Mainstream, 1920–1945.* Baltimore: Johns Hopkins University Press, 1992.

Feldstein, Janice J., ed. *Rabbi Jacob Weinstein: Advocate of the People.* New York: Ktav Publishing House, 1980.

Feuer, Lewis S. "Recollections of Harry Austryn Wolfson." *American Jewish Archives Journal* 28 (April 1976): 25–50.

Fink, Leon. *Progressive Intellectuals and the Dilemmas of Democratic Commitment.* Cambridge, Mass.: Harvard University Press, 1997.

Foner, Eric. *The Story of American Freedom.* New York: W. W. Norton, 1998.

Frank, Daniel H., ed. *A People Apart: Chosenness and Ritual in Jewish Philosophical Thought.* Albany: State University of New York Press, 1993.

Frank, Geyla. "Jews, Multiculturalism, and Boasian Anthropology." *American Anthropologist* 99 (1997): 731–45.

Frankel, Jonathan, and Steven J. Zipperstein, eds. *Assimilation and Community: The Jews in Nineteenth-Century Europe.* Cambridge: Cambridge University Press, 1992.

Freedman, Morris. "The Jewish College Student: New Model." In *Commentary on the American Scene,* ed. Elliot E. Cohen. New York: Alfred A. Knopf, 1953.

Fried, Lewis. "Creating Hebraism, Confronting Hellenism: The *Menorah Journal* and Its Struggle for the Jewish Imagination." *American Jewish Archives Journal* 53 (2001): 147–74.

———. "The *Menorah Journal:* Yavneh in America, 1945–1950." *American Jewish Archives Journal* 50 (1998): 76–108.

Friedenreich, Harriet Pass. *Female, Jewish, and Educated: The Lives of Central European University Women.* Bloomington: Indiana University Press, 2002.

Friedlaender, Israel. *Past and Present: A Collection of Jewish Essays.* Cincinnati: Ark Publishing, 1919.

Friesel, Evyatar. "Brandeis' Role in American Zionism Historically Reconsidered." *American Jewish History* 69 (September 1979): 34–59.

Fuchs, Lawrence H. *The American Kaleidoscope: Race, Ethnicity, and the Civic Culture.* Hanover, N.H.: Wesleyan University Press, 1990.

Fuchs, Richard. "The 'Hochschule für die Wissenschaft des Judentums' in the Period of Nazi Rule." *Leo Baeck Institute Year Book* 12 (1967): 3–31.

Funkenstein, Amos. *Perceptions of Jewish History.* Berkeley: University of California Press, 1993.

Gans, Herbert J. *On the Making of Americans.* Philadelphia: University of Pennsylvania Press, 1979.

Gerber, David A., ed. *Anti-Semitism in American History.* Urbana: University of Illinois Press, 1986.

Gerstle, Gary. *American Crucible: Race and Nation in the Twentieth Century.* Princeton, N.J.: Princeton University Press, 2001.

———. "Liberty, Coercion, and the Making of Americans." *Journal of American History* 84 (September 1997): 524–58.

———. "The Protean Character of American Liberalism." *American Historical Review* 99 (October 1994): 1043–73.

Gilbert, James. *Writers and Partisans: A History of Literary Radicalism in America.* 1968. Reprint, New York: Columbia University Press, 1992.

Gilman, Sander L. *Jewish Self-Hatred: Anti-Semitism and the Hidden Language of the Jews.* Baltimore: Johns Hopkins University Press, 1990.

———. *The Jew's Body.* New York: Routledge, 1991.

———. *Smart Jews: The Construction of the Image of Jewish Superior Intelligence.* Lincoln: University of Nebraska Press, 1996.

Ginsberg, Elaine K., ed. *Passing and the Fictions of Identity.* Durham, N.C.: Duke University Press, 1996.

Glatzer, Nahum N. "The Beginnings of Modern Jewish Studies." In *Studies in Nineteenth-Century Jewish Intellectual History,* ed. Alexander Altmann. Cambridge, Mass.: Harvard University Press, 1964.

Glazer, Nathan, and Daniel Patrick Moynihan. *Beyond the Melting Pot: The Negroes, Puerto Ricans, Jews, Italians, and Irish of New York City.* Cambridge, Mass.: MIT Press, 1963.

Gleason, Phillip. "American Identity and Americanization." In *Harvard Encyclopedia of American Ethnic Groups,* ed. Stephan Thernstrom. Cambridge, Mass.: Harvard University Press, 1980.

———. *Speaking of Diversity: Language and Ethnicity in Twentieth Century America.* Baltimore: Johns Hopkins University Press, 1992.

Glenn, Susan A. *Daughters of the Shtetl: Life and Labor in the Immigrant Generation.* Ithaca, N.Y.: Cornell University Press, 1990.

———. "The Vogue of Jewish Self-Hatred in Post–World War II America." *Jewish Social Studies* 12:3 (Spring/Summer 2006): 95–136.

Glick, Leonard B. "Types Distinct from Our Own: Franz Boas on Jewish Identity and Assimilation." *American Anthropologist* 84 (September 1982): 545–65.

Goldberg, Hillel. *Between Berlin and Slobodka: Jewish Transition Figures from Eastern Europe.* Hoboken, N.J.: Ktav Publishing House, 1989.

Goldscheider, Calvin, and Alan S. Zuckerman. *The Transformation of the Jews.* Chicago: University of Chicago Press, 1984.

Goldstein, Eric L. *The Price of Whiteness: Jews, Race, and American Identity.* Princeton, N.J.: Princeton University Press, 2006.

Goodman, Paul. *A History of the Jews.* New York: E. P. Dutton, 1911.

Gordon, Milton M. *Assimilation in American Life: The Role of Race, Religion, and National Origins.* New York: Oxford University Press, 1964.

Gorelick, Sherry. *City College and the Jewish Poor: Education in New York, 1880–1924.* New Brunswick, N.J.: Rutgers University Press, 1981.

Goren, Arthur A. *The American Jews.* Cambridge, Mass.: Harvard University Press, 1980.

———. "The Jewish Press." In *The Ethnic Press in the United States,* ed. Sally M. Miller. Westport, Conn.: Greenwood Press, 1987.

———. *New York Jews and the Quest for Community: The Kehillah Experiment, 1908–1922.* New York: Columbia University Press, 1970.

———. *The Politics and Public Culture of American Jews.* Bloomington: Indiana University Press, 1999.

Graver, Lawrence. *An Obsession with Anne Frank: Meyer Levin and the Diary.* Berkeley: University of California Press, 1995.

Greenberg, Cheryl Lynn. *Troubling the Waters: Black-Jewish Relations in the American Century.* Princeton, N.J.: Princeton University Press, 2006.

Greene, Daniel. "A Chosen People in a Pluralist Nation: Horace Kallen and the Jewish American Experience." *Religion and American Culture* 16:2 (2006): 161–93.

———. "The Crisis of Jewish Freedom: The Menorah Association and American Pluralism, 1906–1934." Ph.D. diss., University of Chicago, 2004.

———. "'Israel! What a Wonderful People!': Elliot Cohen's Critique of Modern American Jewry 1924–1927." *American Jewish Archives Journal* 55:1 (2003): 10–34.

———. "Reuben Cohen Comes of Age: American Jewish Youth and the Lived Experience of Cultural Pluralism in the 1920s." *American Jewish History* 95:2 (June 2009): 157–82.

Greenebaum, Gary T. "The Jewish Experience in the American College and University." Master's thesis, Hebrew Union College-Jewish Institute of Religion, 1978.

Gruber, Ruth Ellen. *Virtually Jewish: Reinventing Jewish Culture in Europe.* Berkeley: University of California Press, 2002.

Grumet, Elinor. "Elliot Cohen: The Vocation of a Jewish Literary Mentor." *Studies in the American Jewish Experience* 1 (1981): 8–25.

———. "The Menorah Idea and the Apprenticeship of Lionel Trilling." Ph.D. diss., University of Iowa, 1979.

Grunberger, Michael W., ed. *From Haven to Home: 350 Years of Jewish Life in America.* New York: George Braziller in association with the Library of Congress, 2004.

Gurock, Jeffrey S. *Orthodox Jews in America.* Bloomington: Indiana University Press, 2009.

Ha'am, Ahad. "The Jewish State and the Jewish Problem." In *The Zionist Idea: A Historical Analysis and Reader,* ed. Arthur Hertzberg. New York: Atheneum, 1959.

Halper, Albert. *Good-bye, Union Square: A Writer's Memoir of the Thirties.* Chicago: Quadrangle Books, 1970.

Halpern, Ben. *The Idea of the Jewish State.* Cambridge, Mass.: Harvard University Press, 1961.

Handlin, Oscar. *The Uprooted: The Epic Story of the Great Migrations That Made the American People.* 1951. Reprint, Boston: Little, Brown, 1973.

Hansen, Jonathan M. *The Lost Promise of American Patriotism: Debating American Identity, 1890–1920.* Chicago: University of Chicago Press, 2003.

Hapgood, Hutchins. *The Spirit of the Ghetto.* New York: Schocken, 1976.

Harap, Louis. *Creative Awakening: The Jewish Presence in Twentieth-Century American Literature, 1900–1940s.* New York: Greenwood Press, 1987.

———. "The *Menorah Journal*—A Literary Precursor." *Midstream* 30 (October 1984): 51–55.

Hart, John E. *Albert Halper.* Boston: G. K. Hall, 1980.

Hart, Mitchell B. *Social Science and the Politics of Modern Jewish Identity.* Stanford, Calif.: Stanford University Press, 2000.

Harvard Class of 1907: Twenty-fifth Anniversary Report. Norwood, Mass.: Plimpton Press, 1932.

Harvard Class of 1921: Fiftieth Anniversary Report. Cambridge, Mass.: Harvard University Printing Office, 1971.

Hattam, Victoria. *In the Shadow of Race: Jews, Latinos, and Immigrant Politics in the United States.* Chicago: University of Chicago Press, 2007.

Hawkins, Hugh. *Between Harvard and America: The Educational Leadership of Charles W. Eliot.* New York: Oxford University Press, 1972.

Heinze, Andrew R. *Adapting to Abundance: Jewish Immigrants, Mass Consumption, and the Search for American Identity.* New York: Columbia University Press, 1990.

———. "Is It 'Cos I's Black? Jews and the Whiteness Problem." Ann Arbor, Mich.: Regents of the University of Michigan, Jean & Samuel Frankel Center for Judaic Studies, 2007.

———. *Jews and the American Soul: Human Nature in the 20th Century.* Princeton, N.J.: Princeton University Press, 2004.

———. "Schizophrenia Americana: Aliens, Alienists, and the 'Personality Shift' of Twentieth-Century Culture." *American Quarterly* 55:2 (2003): 227–56.

Herberg, Will. *Protestant, Catholic, Jew: An Essay in American Religious Sociology.* New York: Doubleday, 1955.

Hertzberg, Arthur. *The Jews in America: Four Centuries of an Uneasy Encounter.* New York: Simon and Schuster, 1989, 1997.

———. *Judaism.* New York: Simon and Schuster, 1991.

Hertzberg, Arthur, and Aron Hirt-Manheimer. *Jews: The Essence and Character of a People.* San Francisco: Harper San Francisco, 1998.

Heschel, Susannah. "Revolt of the Colonized: Abraham Geiger's *Wissenschaft des Judentums* as a Challenge to Christian Hegemony in the Academy." *New German Critique* 77 (1999): 61–85.

Higham, John. "Another Look at Nativism." *Catholic Historical Review* 44 (July 1958): 147–58.

———. *Send These to Me: Jews and Other Immigrants in Urban America.* New York: Atheneum, 1975.

———. *Strangers in the Land: Patterns of American Nativism, 1860–1925.* New Brunswick, N.J.: Rutgers University Press, 1955, 1988, 1992.

"The Hillel Foundation." *B'nai B'rith News* (March 1924): 204.

Hobsbawm, Eric. *The Age of Extremes: A History of the World, 1914–1991.* New York: Pantheon Books, 1994.

Hobson, Fred. *Mencken: A Life.* Baltimore: Johns Hopkins University Press, 1995.

Hollinger, David A. "Ethnic Diversity, Cosmopolitanism and the Emergence of the American Liberal Intelligentsia." *American Quarterly* 27 (May 1975): 133–51.

———. *In the American Province: Studies in the History and Historiography of Ideas.* Bloomington: Indiana University Press, 1985.

———. *Postethnic America: Beyond Multiculturalism.* New York: Basic Books, 1995.

———. *Science, Jews, and Secular Culture: Studies in Mid-Twentieth Century American Intellectual History.* Princeton, N.J.: Princeton University Press, 1996.

Holt, Thomas C. *The Problem of Race in the Twenty-First Century.* Cambridge, Mass.: Harvard University Press, 2000.

Howe, Irving. *World of Our Fathers.* New York: Simon and Schuster, 1976.

Huggins, Nathan Irvin. *Harlem Renaissance.* New York: Oxford University Press, 1971.

Hurwitz, Henry. "The Menorah Movement," *B'nai B'rith Magazine* 40 (April 1926): 230.

———. "A Mother Remembered." *American Jewish History* 70 (September 1980): 5–21.

Hutchinson, William R. *Religious Pluralism in America: The Contentious History of a Founding Ideal.* New Haven, Conn.: Yale University Press, 2003.

Hyman, Paula E. *From Dreyfus to Vichy: The Remaking of French Jewry, 1906–1939.* New York: Columbia University Press, 1979.

———. *Gender and Assimilation in Modern Jewish History: The Roles and Representation of Women.* Seattle: University of Washington Press, 1995.

———. *The Jews of Modern France.* Berkeley: University of California Press, 1998.

Jacobson, Matthew Frye. *Barbarian Virtues: The United States Encounters Foreign Peoples at Home and Abroad, 1876–1917.* New York: Hill and Wang, 2000.

———. *Whiteness of a Different Color: European Immigrants and the Alchemy of Race.* Cambridge, Mass.: Harvard University Press, 1998.

James, William. *Essays in Pragmatism.* Ed. and with an introduction by Alburey Castell. New York: Hafner, 1948.

———. "On a Certain Blindness in Human Beings." In *Pragmatism and Other Writings,* ed. Giles Gunn. New York: Penguin Books, 2000.

Jewish Students: A Survey Dealing with the Religious, Educational, Social and Fraternal Activities among Jewish Students and Universities and Colleges. Cincinnati: Department of Synagog and School Extension, 1915.

Jewish Studies in American Colleges and Universities: A Catalogue. Washington, D.C.: B'nai B'rith Hillel Foundations, 1972.

Jick, Leon A., ed. *The Teaching of Judaica in American Universities: The Proceedings of a Colloquium.* Waltham, Mass.: Association for Jewish Studies, 1970.

Joselit, Jenna Weissman. *New York's Jewish Jews: The Orthodox Community in the Interwar Years.* Bloomington: Indiana University Press, 1990.

———. "Without Ghettoism: A History of the Intercollegiate Menorah Association 1906–1930." *American Jewish Archives Journal* 30 (1978): 133–54.

———. *The Wonders of America: Reinventing Jewish Culture, 1880–1950.* New York: Hill and Wang, 1994.

Jospe, Alfred. "Jewish College Students in the United States." *American Jewish Year Book* 65 (1964): 131–45.

———. *Jewish Studies in American Colleges and Universities: A Catalogue.* Washington, D.C.: B'nai B'rith Hillel Foundations, 1972.

Kallen, Horace M. "Alain Locke and Cultural Pluralism." *Journal of Philosophy* 54 (February 28, 1957): 119–27.

———. *Art and Freedom.* New York: Duell, Sloan and Pearce, 1942.

———. *The Book of Job as a Greek Tragedy.* New York: Moffat, Yard and Co., 1918.

———. *Cultural Pluralism and the American Idea: An Essay in Social Philosophy.* Philadelphia: University of Pennsylvania Press, 1956.

———. *Culture and Democracy in the United States.* 1924. Reprint, New Brunswick, N.J.: Transaction Publishers, 1998.

———. *The Decline and Rise of the Consumer.* New York: D. Appleton-Century, 1936.

———. "Democracy versus the Melting Pot." *Nation* 100 (February 18 and 25, 1915): 190–94, 217–20.

———. *The Education of Free Men.* New York: Farrar, Straus, 1950.

———. *Frontiers of Hope.* New York: Liveright, 1929.

———. *Indecency and the Seven Arts.* New York: Liveright, 1930.

———. *Individualism: An American Way of Life.* New York: Liveright, 1933.

———. "Introduction." *The Philosophy of William James.* New York: Modern Library, 1925.

———. *Judaism at Bay: Essays toward the Adjustment of Judaism to Modernity.* New York: Bloch, 1932.

———. "Judaism, Hebraism and Zionism." *American Hebrew* (June 24, 1910): 181–83.

———. *The League of Nations: Today and Tomorrow.* Boston: Marshall Jones, 1918.

———. *The Structure of Lasting Peace.* Boston: Marshall Jones, 1918.

———. *Utopians at Bay.* New York: Theodor Herzl Foundation, 1958.

Kaplan, Marion A. "Tradition and Transition: The Acculturation, Assimilation and Integration of Jews in Imperial Germany. A Gender Analysis." *Leo Baeck Institute Year Book* 27 (1982): 3–35.

Kaplan, Mordecai M. *Judaism as a Civilization.* 1934. Reprint, Philadelphia: Jewish Publication Society, 1994.

———. *A New Approach to the Problem of Judaism: Toward a Reconstruction of American-Jewish Life.* New York: Society for the Advancement of Judaism, 1924.

Karabel, Jerome. *The Chosen: The Hidden History of Admission and Inclusion at Harvard, Yale, and Princeton.* Boston: Houghton Mifflin, 2005.

Katkin, Wendy F., Ned Landsman, and Andrea Tyree, eds. *Beyond Pluralism: The Conception of Groups and Group Identities in America.* Urbana: University of Illinois Press, 1998.

Kaufman, David. *Shul with a Pool: The 'Synagogue-Center' in American Jewish History.* Hanover, N.H.: Brandeis University Press, 1999.

Kaufman, Matthew. "The *Menorah Journal* from 1915–1928 and Shaping American Jewish Identity: Culture, Race, and Evolutionary Sociology." Unpublished paper, York University, 2009.

Kazal, Russell A. "Revisiting Assimilation: The Rise, Fall, and Reappraisal of a Concept in American Ethnic History." *American Historical Review* 100 (April 1995): 437–71.

Keller, Morton, and Phyllis Keller. *Making Harvard Modern: The Rise of America's University.* New York: Oxford University Press, 2001.

Kennedy, David M. *Over Here: The First World War and American Society.* New York: Oxford University Press, 1980.

Kessner, Carol S., ed. *The "Other" New York Jewish Intellectuals.* New York: New York University Press, 1994.

Kirshenblatt-Gimblett, Barbara. *Destination Culture: Tourism, Museums, and Heritage.* Berkeley: University of California Press, 1998.

Kleeblatt, Norman L., and Susan Chevlowe, eds. *Painting a Place in America: Jewish Artists in New York 1900–1945.* New York: Jewish Museum, 1991.

Klingenstein, Susanne. *Jews in the American Academy 1900–1940: The Dynamics of Intellectual Assimilation.* New Haven, Conn.: Yale University Press, 1991.

Konvitz, Milton R. "Horace Meyer Kallen (1882–1974)." *American Jewish Year Book* 75 (1974–75): 55–80.

———. *Nine American Jewish Thinkers.* New Brunswick, N.J.: Transaction Publishers, 2000.

———, ed. *The Legacy of Horace M. Kallen.* Cranbury, N.J.: Associated University Presses, 1987.

Korelitz, Seth. "The Menorah Idea: From Religion to Culture, From Race to Ethnicity." *American Jewish History* 85 (March 1997): 75–100.

Korn, Bertram W. *German-Jewish Intellectual Influences of American Jewish Life, 1824–1972.* Syracuse, N.Y.: Syracuse University Press, 1972.

Kraut, Benny. *From Reform Judaism to Ethical Culture: The Religious Education of Felix Adler.* Cincinnati: Hebrew Union College Press, 1979.

Krome, Frederic. "Creating 'Jewish History for Our Own Needs': The Evolution of Cecil Roth's Historical Vision, 1925–1935." *Modern Judaism* 21 (2001): 216–37.

Krupnick, Mark. *Lionel Trilling and the Fate of Cultural Criticism.* Evanston, Ill.: Northwestern University Press, 1986.

———. "The Menorah Journal Group and the Origins of Modern Jewish Radicalism." *Studies in American Jewish Literature* 5 (Winter 1979): 56–67.

Lacquer, Walter. *A History of Zionism.* New York: Schocken, 1972.

Lasch, Christopher. *The New Radicalism in America 1889–1963: The Intellectual as a Social Type.* New York: Alfred A. Knopf, 1965.

Lavin, Maud. *Cut with the Kitchen Knife: The Weimar Photomontages of Hannah Höch.* New Haven, Conn.: Yale University Press, 1993.

Lederhandler, Eli. *Jewish Responses to Modernity.* New York: New York University Press, 1994.

Levine, David O. *The American College and the Culture of Aspiration 1915–1940.* Ithaca, N.Y.: Cornell University Press, 1986.

Levine, Peter. *From Ellis Island to Ebbets Field: Sport and the American Jewish Experience.* New York: Oxford University Press, 1992.

Levinger, Lee J. *The Jewish Student in America: A Study Made by the Research Bureau of the B'Nai B'rith Hillel Foundations.* Cincinnati: B'nai B'rith, 1937.

Lewis, David Levering. *W. E. B. Du Bois: Biography of a Race, 1868–1919.* New York: Henry Holt, 1993.

Lewisohn, Ludwig. *The Case of Mr. Crump.* Paris: E. W. Titus, 1926.

———. *The Island Within.* 1928. Reprint, Syracuse, N.Y.: Syracuse University Press, 1997.

———. *Israel.* New York: Boni and Liveright, 1925.

———. *Mid-Channel.* New York: Blue Ribbon Books, 1929.

———. *Up Stream.* New York: Boni and Liveright, 1922.

Liberles, Robert. "Postemancipation Historiography and the Jewish Historical Societies of America and England." In *Reshaping the Past: Jewish History and the Historians,* vol. 10 of *Studies in Contemporary Jewry,* ed. Jonathan Frankel. New York: Oxford University Press, 1994.

———. *Salo Wittmayer Baron: Architect of Jewish History.* New York: New York University Press, 1995.

Lipset, Seymour Martin, and Everett Carl Ladd Jr. "Jewish Academics in the United States." In *The Jew in American Society,* ed. Marshall Sklare. New York: Behrman House, 1974.

Lipset, Seymour Martin, and Earl Raab. *Jews and the New American Scene.* Cambridge, Mass.: Harvard University Press, 1995.

Locke, Alain, ed. *The New Negro: An Interpretation.* New York: Albert and Charles Boni, 1925.

Lowe, Lisa. *Immigrant Acts: On Asian American Cultural Politics.* Durham, N.C.: Duke University Press, 1996.

Ludington, Townsend. *John Dos Passos: A Twentieth Century Odyssey.* 1980. Reprint, New York: Carroll and Graf Publishers, 1998.

Lyon, David Gordon. "The Semitics Museum." *Harvard Alumni Bulletin* (February 9, 1916): 357–59.

MacLean, Nancy. *Behind the Mask of Chivalry: The Making of the Second Ku Klux Klan.* New York: Oxford University Press, 1994.

Malinovich, Nadia Donna. "Le Reveil D'Israel: Jewish Identity and Culture in France 1900–1932." Ph.D. diss., University of Michigan, 2000.

Marja, Fern. "Commentary's Number One Editor." *New York Post Home News Magazine* (February 17, 1949): n.p.

Markewich, Eve Rachel. "The Menorah Society, or Being Jewish at Harvard, 1906–11." B.A. thesis, Harvard-Radcliffe College, 1983.

McElvaine, Robert S. *The Great Depression: America 1929–1941.* New York: Times Book, 1984.

Melnick, Ralph. *The Life and Work of Ludwig Lewisohn,* 2 vols. Detroit: Wayne State University Press, 1998.

"'The Melting Pot': Will the Jew Become Merged in It and Disappear?" *American Israelite* 55 (March 4, 1909): 1.

Menand, Louis. *The Metaphysical Club: A Story of Ideas in America.* New York: Farrar, Straus and Giroux, 2001.

——. "Regrets Only: Lionel Trilling and His Discontents." *New Yorker* (September 29, 2008): 80–90.

Mendes-Flohr, Paul. *Divided Passions: Jewish Intellectuals and the Experience of Modernity.* Detroit: Wayne State University Press, 1991.

——. *German Jews: A Dual Identity.* New Haven, Conn.: Yale University Press, 1999.

——, ed. *A Land of Two Peoples: Martin Buber on Jews and Arabs.* New York: Oxford University Press, 1983.

Mendes-Flohr, Paul, and Jehuda Reinharz, eds. *The Jew in the Modern World: A Documentary History.* 2nd ed. New York: Oxford University Press, 1995.

The Menorah Movement for the Advancement of Jewish Culture and Ideals. Ann Arbor, Mich.: Intercollegiate Menorah Association, 1914.

Meyer, Michael A. *Jewish Identity in the Modern World.* Seattle: University of Washington Press, 1990.

——. *Judaism within Modernity: Essays on Jewish History and Religion.* Detroit: Wayne State University Press, 2001.

——. *Origins of the Modern Jew: Jewish Identity and European Culture in Germany, 1749–1824.* Detroit: Wayne State University Press, 1967.

——. "The Refugee Scholars Project of the Hebrew Union College." In *A Bicentennial Festschrift for Jacob Rader Marcus,* ed. Bertram Korn. Waltham, Mass.: American Jewish Historical Society and New York: Ktav Publishing House, 1976.

——. *Response to Modernity: A History of the Reform Movement in Judaism.* New York: Oxford University Press, 1988.

——. "Where Does the Modern Period of Jewish History Begin?" *Judaism* 24:3 (Summer 1975): 329–38.

——, ed. *Ideas of Jewish History.* New York: Behrman House, 1974.

Michaels, Walter Benn. *Our America: Nativism, Modernism, and Pluralism.* Durham, N.C.: Duke University Press, 1995.

Michels, Tony. *A Fire in Their Hearts: Yiddish Socialists in New York.* Cambridge, Mass.: Harvard University Press, 2005.

Miller, Larry C. "William James and Twentieth-Century Ethnic Thought." *American Quarterly* 31:4 (Autumn 1979): 533–55.

Miller, Sally M., ed. *The Ethnic Press in the United States: A Historical Analysis and Handbook*. Westport, Conn.: Greenwood Press, 1987.

Mittleman, Karen S., ed. *Creating American Jews: Historical Conversations about Identity*. Philadelphia: National Museum of American Jewish History, 1998.

Moore, Deborah Dash. *At Home in America: Second Generation New York Jews*. New York: Columbia University Press, 1981.

———. *B'nai B'rith and the Challenge of Ethnic Leadership*. Albany: State University of New York Press, 1981.

———. "Defining American Jewish Ethnicity." *Prospects* 6 (1981): 387–409.

Moore, George Foote. *History of Religions*. New York: Charles Scribner's Sons, 1919.

Morawska, Ewa. "In Defense of the Assimilation Model." *Journal of American Ethnic History* 13 (Winter 1994): 76–87.

Morison, Samuel Eliot. *Three Centuries of Harvard, 1636–1936*. Cambridge, Mass.: Harvard University Press, 1936.

Morris-Reich, Amos. *The Quest for Jewish Assimilation in Modern Social Science*. New York: Routledge, 2008.

Mosse, George L. *German Jews beyond Judaism*. Bloomington: Indiana University Press, 1985.

Myers, David N. *Re-Inventing the Jewish Past: European Jewish Intellectuals and the Zionist Return to History*. New York: Oxford University Press, 1995.

Myers, David N., and David B. Ruderman, eds. *The Jewish Past Revisited: Reflections on Modern Jewish Historians*. New Haven, Conn.: Yale University Press, 1998.

Nahshon, Edna, ed. *From the Ghetto to the Melting Pot: Israel Zangwill's Jewish Plays*. Detroit: Wayne State University Press, 2006.

Neusner, Jacob. *The Way of Torah: An Introduction to Judaism*. Belmont, Calif.: Dickenson Publishing, 1970.

Newman, Louis I. *A Jewish University in America?* New York: Bloch, 1923.

Ngai, Mae M. "The Architecture of Race in American Immigration Law: A Re-examination of the Immigration Act of 1924." *Journal of American History* 86:1 (June 1999): 67–92.

———. *Impossible Subjects: Illegal Aliens and the Making of Modern America*. Princeton, N.J.: Princeton University Press, 2004.

———. "The Strange Career of the Illegal Alien: Immigration Restriction and De-portation Policy in the United States, 1921–1965." *Law and History Review* 21:1 (Spring 2003): 69–107.

Nochlin, Linda, and Tamar Garb, eds. *The Jew in the Text: Modernity and the Construction of Identity*. London: Thames and Hudson, 1996.

Novak, David. *The Election of Israel: The Idea of the Chosen People*. Cambridge: Cambridge University Press, 1995.

Novak, Michael. *The Rise of the Unmeltable Ethnics: Politics and Culture in the Seventies*. New York: Macmillan, 1971.

Novick, Peter. *The Holocaust in American Life*. Boston: Houghton Mifflin, 1999.

———. *That Noble Dream: The "Objectivity Question" and the American Historical Profession*. New York: Cambridge University Press, 1988.

Olin, Margaret. *The Nation without Art: Examining Modern Discourses on Jewish Art*. Lincoln: University of Nebraska Press, 2001.

Oren, Dan A. *Joining the Club: A History of Jews and Yale*. 1985. Reprint, New Haven, Conn.: Yale University Press, 2000.

Øverland, Orm. *Immigrant Minds, American Identities: Making the United States Home, 1870–1930*. Urbana: University of Illinois Press, 2000.

Ozick, Cynthia. "The Buried Life." *New Yorker* (October 2, 2000): 116–27.

Pappas, Andrea. "The Picture at *Menorah Journal*: Making 'Jewish Art.'" *American Jewish History* 90 (September 2002): 205–38.

Peck, Abraham J., ed. *The German-Jewish Legacy in America, 1938–1988*. Detroit: Wayne State University Press, 1989.

Pianko, Noam. "'The True Liberalism of Zionism': Horace Kallen, Jewish Nationalism, and the Limits of American Pluralism." *American Jewish History* 94 (December 2008): 299–329.

———. *Zionism and the Roads Not Taken: Rawidowicz, Kaplan, Kohn*. Bloomington: Indiana University Press, 2010.

Pickus, Keith H. *Constructing Modern Identities: Jewish University Students in Germany 1815–1914*. Detroit: Wayne State University Press, 1999.

Podhoretz, Norman. *Making It*. New York: Random House, 1967.

Posnock, Ross. *Color and Culture: Black Writers and the Making of the Modern Intellectual*. Cambridge, Mass.: Harvard University Press, 1998.

Prell, Riv-Ellen. *Fighting to Become Americans: Jews, Gender, and the Anxiety of Assimilation*. Boston: Beacon Press, 1999.

Raider, Mark A. *The Emergence of American Zionism*. New York: New York University Press, 1998.

———. Review of *The Life and Work of Ludwig Lewisohn*, by Ralph Melnick. *AJS Review* 26:2 (November 2002): 341–47.

Raider, Mark A., Jonathan D. Sarna, and Ronald W. Zweig, eds. *Abba Hillel Silver and American Zionism*. London: Frank Cass, 1997.

Raphael, Marc Lee. *Abba Hillel Silver: A Profile in American Judaism*. New York: Holmes and Meier, 1989.

———, ed. *"Jewishness" and the World of "Difference" in the United States*. Williamsburg, Va.: College of William and Mary, 2001.

Reuben, Julie A. *The Making of the Modern University: Intellectual Transformation and the Marginalization of Morality*. Chicago: University of Chicago Press, 1996.

Rischin, Moses. *The Promised City: New York's Jews, 1870–1914*. New York: Harper and Row, 1962.

Ritterband, Paul, and Harold S. Wechsler. *Jewish Learning in American Universities: The First Century*. Bloomington: Indiana University Press, 1994.

———. "Judaica in American Colleges and Universities." In *Encyclopedia Judaica Yearbook 1977/8*. Jerusalem: Keter Publishing House, 1979.

Rodgers, Daniel T. *Contested Truths: Keywords in American Politics since Independence*. New York: Basic Books, 1987.

Rodrigue, Aron. "Rearticulations of French Jewish Identities after the Dreyfus Affair." *Jewish Social Studies* 2 (Spring/Summer 1996): 1–24.

Roediger, David R. *The Wages of Whiteness: Race and the Making of the American Working Class*. London: Verso, 2007.

———. *Working toward Whiteness: How America's Immigrants Became White: The Strange Journey from Ellis Island to the Suburbs.* New York: Basic Books, 2005.

Rogin, Michael. *Blackface, White Noise: Jewish Immigrants in the Hollywood Melting Pot.* Berkeley: University of California Press, 1996.

Rosenstock, Morton. "Are There Too Many Jews at Harvard?" In *Antisemitism in the United States,* ed. Leonard Dinnerstein. New York: Holt, Reinhart, and Winston, 1971.

Rosovsky, Nina. *The Jewish Experience at Harvard and Radcliffe.* Cambridge, Mass.: Harvard University Press, 1986.

Ross, Edward Alsworth. *The Old World in the New: The Significance of Past and Present Immigration to the American People.* New York: Century, 1913.

Roth, Cecil. *The Jewish Contribution to Civilization.* New York: Harper and Brothers, 1940.

Roth, Michael S. *The Ironist's Cage: Memory, Trauma, and the Construction of History.* New York: Columbia University Press, 1995.

Roth, Susan. "And the Youth Shall See Visions: The Jewish Experience in Champaign-Urbana and the Founding of Hillel." Master's thesis, Eastern Illinois University, 1995.

Rudy, Willis S. *The College of the City of New York: A History, 1847–1947.* New York: City College Press, 1949.

Ruppin, Arthur. *The Jews of To-day.* New York: Henry Holt, 1913.

Sachar, Howard M. *The Course of Modern Jewish History.* 1958. Reprint, New York: Dell, 1977.

———. *A History of the Jews in America.* New York: Vintage, 1992.

Samet, Thomas H. "The Problematic Self: Lionel Trilling and the Anxieties of the Modern." Ph.D. diss., Brown University, 1980.

Sanua, Marianne R. *"Here's to Our Fraternity": One Hundred Years of Zeta Beta Tau 1898–1998.* Hanover, N.H.: Zeta Beta Tau Foundation, 1998.

———. "Jewish College Fraternities in the United States, 1895–1968: An Overview." *Journal of American Ethnic History* 19 (Winter 2000): 3–42.

———. "The Non-Recognition of Jewish Fraternities: The Case of Columbia and Brown Universities." *American Jewish Archives Journal* 45 (Fall/Winter 1993): 125–45.

Sarna, Jonathan D. *American Judaism: A History.* New Haven, Conn.: Yale University Press, 2004.

———. "The Cult of Synthesis in American Jewish Culture." *Jewish Social Studies* 5 (1998/99): 52–79.

———. "From Immigrants to Ethnics: Towards a New Theory of 'Ethnicization.'" *Ethnicity* 5 (1978): 370–78.

———. *JPS: The Americanization of Jewish Culture, 1888–1988.* Philadelphia: Jewish Publication Society, 1989.

Schlissel, Lillian, ed. *The World of Randolph Bourne.* New York: E. P. Dutton, 1965.

Schmidt, Sarah. *Horace M. Kallen: Prophet of American Zionism.* Brooklyn: Carlson, 1995.

———. "The *Parushim*: A Secret Episode in American Zionist History." *American Jewish Historical Quarterly* 65 (December 1975): 121–39.

Scholem, Gershom G. "The Sleuth from Slobodka." *TLS* (November 23, 1979): 16.

Schorsch, Ismar. *From Text to Context: The Turn to History in Modern Judaism.* Hanover, N.H.: Brandeis University Press, 1994.

———. *Thoughts from 3080: Selected Address and Writings.* New York: Jewish Theological Seminary of America, 1987.

Schultz, Kevin Michael. "The Decline of the Melting Pot: Catholics, Jews, and Pluralism in Postwar America." Ph.D. diss., University of California, Berkeley, 2005.

Schwartz, Shuly Rubin. *The Emergence of Jewish Scholarship in America: The Publication of the Jewish Encyclopedia.* Cincinnati: Hebrew Union College Press, 1991.

Schwarz, Leo W. *Wolfson of Harvard: Portrait of a Scholar.* Philadelphia: Jewish Publication Society, 1978.

Segev, Tom. *One Palestine, Complete: Jews and Arabs under the British Mandate.* New York: Henry Holt, 1999.

Selig, Diana. *Americans All: The Cultural Gifts Movement.* Cambridge, Mass.: Harvard University Press, 2008.

Seltzer, Robert M., and Norman J. Cohen, eds. *The Americanization of the Jews.* New York: New York University Press, 1995.

The Semitic Museum at Harvard University. Cambridge, Mass.: Harvard University, 1903.

Shargel, Baila Round. *Practical Dreamer: Israel Friedlaender and the Shaping of American Judaism.* New York: Jewish Theological Seminary of America, 1985.

Sherwin, Byron L. *Context and Content: Higher Jewish Education in the United States.* Chicago: Spertus College of Judaica Press, 1987.

Shumsky, Neil Larry. "Zangwill's *The Melting Pot:* Ethnic Tensions on Stage." *American Quarterly* 27 (March 1975): 29–41.

Silberstein, Laurence J., and Robert L. Cohn, eds. *The Other in Jewish Thought and History: Constructions of Jewish Culture and Identity.* New York: New York University Press, 1994.

Silver, Daniel Jeremy, ed. *In The Time of Harvest: Essays in Honor of Abba Hillel Silver on the Occasion of His 70th Birthday.* New York: Macmillan, 1963.

Silverstein, Alan. *Alternatives to Assimilation: The Response of Reform Judaism to American Culture, 1840–1930.* Hanover, N.H.: Brandeis University Press, 1994.

Slade, Irving Leonard. "An Introductory Survey of Jewish Student Organizations in American Higher Education." Ph.D. diss., Columbia University, 1966.

Slesinger, Tess. *The Unpossessed.* 1934. Reprint, New York: New York Review Books, 2002.

Sleskine, Yuri. *The Jewish Century.* Princeton, N.J.: Princeton University Press, 2004.

Smith, Richard Norton. *The Harvard Century: The Making of a University to a Nation.* New York: Simon and Schuster, 1986.

Smith, Rogers M. *Civic Ideals: Conflicting Visions of Citizenship in U.S. History.* New Haven, Conn.: Yale University Press, 1997.

Solberg, Winton U. "The Early Years of the Jewish Presence at the University of Illinois." *Religion and American Culture* 2 (1992): 215–45.

Sollors, Werner. *Beyond Ethnicity: Consent and Descent in American Culture.* New York: Oxford University Press, 1986.

———. "A Critique of Pure Pluralism." In *Reconstructing American Literary History,* ed. Sacvan Bercovitch. Cambridge, Mass.: Harvard University Press, 1986.

Sorin, Gerald R. "Mutual Contempt, Mutual Benefit: The Strained Encounter between German and Eastern European Jews in America, 1880–1920." *American Jewish History* 71 (September 1978): 34–59.

———. *A Time for Building: The Third Migration, 1880–1920.* Baltimore: Johns Hopkins University Press, 1992.

———. *Tradition Transformed: The Jewish Experience in America.* Baltimore: Johns Hopkins University Press, 1997.

Sorkin, David. *The Transformation of German Jewry, 1780–1840.* New York: Oxford University Press, 1987.

Soyer, Daniel. *Jewish Immigrant Associations and American Identity in New York 1880–1939.* Cambridge, Mass.: Harvard University Press, 1997.

Stanislawski, Michael. "Salo Wittmayer Baron: Demystifying Jewish History." *Columbia* (Winter 2005–2006): 45–48.

———. *Zionism and the Fin de Siècle: Cosmopolitanism and Nationalism from Nordau to Jabotinsky.* Berkeley: University of California Press, 2001.

Stansell, Christine. *American Moderns: Bohemian New York and the Creation of a New Century.* New York: Henry Holt, 2000.

Staub, Michael E. *Torn at the Roots: The Crisis of Jewish Liberalism in Postwar America.* New York: Columbia University Press, 2002.

Stearns, Harold E. *Confessions of a Harvard Man.* Santa Barbara, Calif.: Paget Press, 1984.

Steinberg, Stephen. *The Academic Melting Pot: Catholics and Jews in American Higher Education.* New York: McGraw-Hill, 1974.

———. *The Ethnic Myth: Race, Ethnicity, and Class in America.* Boston: Beacon Press, 2001.

Stenerson, Douglas C. *Critical Essays on H. L. Mencken.* Boston: G. K. Hall, 1987.

Strauss, Lauren B. "Staying Afloat in the Melting Pot: Constructing an American Jewish Identity in the *Menorah Journal* of the 1920s." *American Jewish History* 84 (December 1996): 319–31.

Strum, Philippa, ed. *Brandeis on Democracy.* Lawrence: University Press of Kansas, 1995.

Sutcliffe, Adam. *Judaism and Enlightenment.* Cambridge: Cambridge University Press, 2003.

Synnott, Marcia Graham. "Anti-Semitism and American Universities: Did Quotas Follow Jews?" In *Anti-Semitism in American History,* ed. David Gerber. Urbana: University of Illinois Press, 1986.

———. *The Half-Opened Door: Discrimination in Admissions at Harvard, Yale, and Princeton, 1900–1970.* Westport, Conn.: Greenwood Press, 1979.

Teitelbaum, Matthew, ed. *Montage and Modern Life: 1919–1942.* Cambridge, Mass.: MIT Press, 1992.

Toll, George S. *Alpha Epsilon Pi: The First Sixty-Five Years, 1913–1978.* Fulton, Mo.: Alpha Epsilon Pi Foundation, 1980.

Toll, William. "Horace M. Kallen: Pluralism and American Jewish Identity." *American Jewish History* 85 (March 1997): 57–74.

Trilling, Diana. *The Beginning of the Journey: The Marriage of Diana and Lionel Trilling.* New York: Harcourt Brace, 1993.

Trilling, Lionel. *Speaking of Literature and Society.* Ed. Diana Trilling. Oxford: Oxford University Press, 1982.

Udelson, Joseph H. *Dreamer of the Ghetto: The Life and Works of Israel Zangwill.* Tuscaloosa: University of Alabama Press, 1990.

"Under Forty: A Symposium on American Literature and the Younger Generation of American Jews." *Contemporary Jewish Record* 7 (February 1944): 3–36.

Urofsky, Melvin I. *American Zionism: From Herzl to the Holocaust.* Lincoln: University of Nebraska Press, 1975.

———. *Louis D. Brandeis: A Life.* New York: Pantheon, 2009.

Veblen, Thorstein. "The Intellectual Pre-Eminence of Jews in Modern Europe." *Political Science Quarterly* 34 (1919): 33–42.

Vernon, Elizabeth. *Jewish Studies Courses at American Colleges and Universities.* Cambridge, Mass.: Association for Jewish Studies, 1992.

Wald, Alan. "Herbert Solow: Portrait of a New York Intellectual." In *Prospects: An Annual of American Cultural Studies,* vol. 3, ed. Jack Salzman. New York: Burt Franklin, 1977.

———. "The Menorah Group Moves Left." *Jewish Social Studies* 38 (Summer/Fall 1976): 289–320.

———. *The New York Intellectuals: The Rise and Decline of the Anti-Stalinist Left from the 1930s to the 1980s.* Chapel Hill: University of North Carolina Press, 1987.

Walzer, Michael. *What It Means to Be an American.* New York: Marsilio, 1996.

Walzer, Michael, Menachem Lorberbaum, and Noam J. Zohar, eds. *The Jewish Political Tradition, Volume II: Membership.* New Haven, Conn.: Yale University Press, 2000.

Wasserman, Henry. "The Wissenschaft des Judentums and Protestant Theology: A Review Essay." *Modern Judaism* 22 (2002): 83–98.

Waters, Mary C. *Ethnic Options: Choosing Identities in America.* Berkeley: University of California Press, 1990.

Wechsler, Harold S. *The Qualified Student: A History of Selective College Admission in America.* New York: John Wiley and Sons, 1977.

Weiner, Herbert, ed. *Therefore Choose Life: Selected Sermons, Addresses, and Writings of Abba Hillel Silver,* vol. 1. Cleveland: World Publishing, 1967.

Weinfeld, David. "What Difference Does the Difference Make? Horace Kallen, Alain Locke and Cosmopolitan Cultural Pluralism." Unpublished paper, New York University, Spring 2009.

Wenger, Beth S. *New York Jews and the Great Depression: Uncertain Promise.* New Haven, Conn.: Yale University Press, 1996.

Wertheimer, Jack, ed. *The American Synagogue: A Sanctuary Transformed.* Hanover, N.H.: Brandeis University Press, 1987.

Westbrook, Robert B. *John Dewey and American Democracy.* Ithaca, N.Y.: Cornell University Press, 1991.

Whitfield, Stephen J. *In Search of American Jewish Culture.* Hanover, N.H.: Brandeis University Press, 1999.

———. "Introduction to the Transaction Edition." In Horace M. Kallen, *Culture and Democracy in the United States.* New Brunswick, N.J.: Transaction Publishers, 1998.

Wiebe, Robert H. *The Search for Order, 1877–1920.* New York: Hill and Wang, 1966.

Wirth, Louis. *The Ghetto.* 1928. Reprint, New Brunswick, N.J.: Transaction Publishers, 1998.

Yagoda, Ben. *About Town: The* New Yorker *and the World It Made.* New York: Scribner, 2000.

Yerushalmi, Yosef Hayim. *Freud's Moses: Judaism Terminable and Interminable.* New Haven, Conn.: Yale University Press, 1991.

——. *Zakhor: Jewish History and Jewish Memory.* Seattle: University of Washington Press, 1982, 1996.

Yezierska, Anzia. *Bread Givers.* 1925. Reprint, with a foreword and revised introduction by Alice Kessler-Harris. New York: Persea Books, 1999.

Zangwill, Israel. *The Melting Pot. A Drama in Four Acts.* New York: Macmillan, 1909.

——. *Watchman, What of the Night?* New York: American Jewish Congress, 1923.

Zapruder, Alexandra, ed. *Salvaged Pages: Young Writers' Diaries of the Holocaust.* New Haven, Conn.: Yale University Press, 2002.

Zipperstein, Steven J. *Elusive Prophet: Ahad Ha'am and the Origins of Zionism.* London: Peter Halban, 1993.

INDEX

model, 11–12, 74–79, 85, 178; mission and, 70; name changing, 164; passing and, 181, 183–84; secular universities and, 15, 35–36; superficiality/fraudulence of, 143–44, 170, 175–76; whiteness and, 125–26, 183–84. *See also* Americanization movement
Association for Jewish Studies, 113

Baeck, Leo, 67
Barnard College, 199n60
Baron, Salo W., 13, 109, 116, 118, 122, 124–26, 214n86
Baruch, Bernard, 41
Baruch, S. (Adolph S. Oko), 91–94, 93
Bender, Thomas, 169, 225n69
Benderly, Samson, 98–99
Benjamin, Walter, 139
Ben-Shahar, H. (Marvin Lowenthal), 132, 219n74
Berg, Louis, 158
Berkson, Isaac B., 86–89
Biale, David, 10
Birnbaum, Pierre, 189n17
Blau, Joel, 47
B'nai B'rith Hillel Foundation. *See* Hillel Foundation
Boas, Franz, 88, 99
Boas, Ralph Philip, 57
Boston University, 37
Bourne, Randolph S., 7, 79, 83–86
Brandeis, Louis D., 7, 80–82, 131
Brandeis University, 111–12, 215n99
Brenner, Anita, 158
Brooklyn College, 110
Brown University, 37, 46
Buber, Martin, 96–97, 110, 175, 227n103
Bureau of Jewish Education, 98
Butler, Nicholas Murray, 200n69

Cahan, Abraham, 152
Carpenter, George Rice, 173
Carregal, Raphael Hayyim Isaac, 121
Casanowicz, Immanuel Moses, 210n34
CCAR (Central Conference of American Rabbis), 21, 198n38

CCNY (College of the City of New York), 40–41, 110
Central Conference of American Rabbis (CCAR), 21, 198n38
Central University of Madrid, 213n85
chosenness, 9, 67–74, 208n109
Christianity: nationalism and, 176; Protestant homogeneity in higher education, 99–100; Puritanism, 66, 121; supersession premise, 119, 208n109
Chyet, Stanley F., 227n99
Clark University, 37–38, 110
class (social class): Brandeis legal career and, 80; generational advancement and, 158–59; in higher education, 99–100; Jewish intellectualism and, 25–26; mission and, 72; old vs. new world experiences of, 152–53
Cohen, Elliot: biography, 136; on Jewish historiography, 123; on Jewish life in America, 137–42; on Jewish studies programs, 112; as *Menorah Journal* contributor/editor, 13, 115–17, 128, 137, 147–48, 151, 155–56, 168, 173, 220n98, 222nn3,4; *Menorah Journal* resignation, 177; as Menorah Summer School student, 105; photograph, 138
Cohen, Morris R., 42
College of the City of New York (CCNY), 40–41, 110
colleges. *See* higher education
Columbia University: antisemitism at, 57, 100, 226–27n90; Baron appointment, 124, 214n86; Columbia Zionist Society, 47–48; Edman fiction and, 161–62; IMA convention at, 38; Jewish enrollment, 20, 57, 200n69; Jewish studies at, 103, 109, 112, 210n34; Trilling appointment, 173
Committee on Religious Work in Universities, 21
community theory of American life, 87–88
Conzen, Kathleen Neils, 215n6
Cornell University, 44, 48, 99, 199n60, 210n34
cosmopolitanism, 84–85

Coughlin, Charles, 135
Crèvecoeur, Jean de, 74
cult of synthesis, 39–40
cultural Judaism: cultural vs. religious Judaism, 22; Hebraism and, 31, 33; as MEC objective, 102–103; Reform Judaism and, 9
cultural pluralism: chosenness and, 9, 67–74; coining of term, 64; competing models for diversity, 11–12; cosmopolitanism and, 84–85; democratic society and, 1, 32–34, 180; in Edman fiction, 161–62, 166–68; federation-of-nationalities model, 82, 85; Hebraism and, 16, 33–34, 64, 76–77, 185; intellectual development of concept, 1–2; Jewish identity and, 6–7; Jewish intellectual roots of, 10, 180; Lowell opposition to, 51, 200n80; melting pot as pluralist model, 182–83; menorah as symbol for, 22–23, 29, 31, 56, 101, 169, 178–80; orchestra metaphor for, 1, 70–71, 85, 205n31; as paradigm for American culture, 7, 181–83; Pragmatism and, 64, 76–77; race (non-white minorities) and, 9, 73–74, 181, 184, 205nn40,41, 228n14; symbiotic identity and, 32–34, 39; U.S. as accommodating environment for Jews, 9, 135; victimhood and, 184–85. See also integration; multiculturalism
Cutter, William, 113

Daniels, Roger, 191n28
Dartmouth University, 37, 57
De Haas, Jacob, 131
Delta Phi Epsilon, 199n60
democracy: cultural pluralism and, 1, 76–77, 180; Hebraism and, 32; hyphenated Americans and, 12, 82
Dewey, John: on antisemitism in the academy, 99; influence on Kallen, 7, 79, 89; influence on Trilling, 169, 225n69; Menorah Journal contributions, 83–86; Trotsky defense and, 116
Dos Passos, John, 139

double allegiance (Berkson), 88
double consciousness (Du Bois), 7–8, 36, 39–40, 176
Douglas, William O., 182
Dr. Herzl Zion Club, 146
Drachsler, Julius, 86–87, 89
Dropsie College for Hebrew and Cognate Learning, 98
Du Bois, W. E. B., 7–8, 45–46, 176, 183
dual loyalty: assimilation and, 163–64; chosenness and, 70; community theory of American life and, 88; cult of synthesis and, 39–40; cultural pluralism and, 6–7; double consciousness (Du Bois), 7–8, 36, 39–40; equality and, 180; hyphenated Americans and, 82; Zionism and, 22, 84, 163–65. See also double consciousness (Du Bois); identity (Jewish identity)
Dubnow, Simon, 118, 125, 217n31
Dushkin, Alexander M., 98–99, 102

eastern European Jews: antisemitism and, 134; immigration and, 14–15, 25–26, 120; mission discourse and, 72; resistance to assimilation, 16–17; in U.S. higher education, 17, 195n52; Wolfson on, 130
Edman, Irwin, 161–68
education (cultural heritage initiatives). See Jewish history; Jewish studies programs
Einstein, Albert, 17
Eisen, Arnold, 68
election (chosenness), 67–69
Eliot, Charles W.: biography, 18–20; as Harvard president, 18, 28, 30, 51, 193n24; influence on Kallen, 31; photograph, 19; pluralist philosophy of, 30, 51; Semitic studies programs supported by, 99
Elkus, Abram I., 41
"Emancipated Jew: Faculty Model" (Rosenthal), 168
emancipation, 6, 111, 175–76, 189n17
ethnicity. See race/ethnicity

heritage initiatives. *See* Jewish history; Jewish studies programs

Herzl, Theodor, 131–32

Hess, Moses, 127

Higham, John, 30, 205n40

higher education: academic milieu, 4; admissions quotas and, 20, 36–37, 50, 53–58, 201n101, 202n106; assimilation and, 15, 35–36; enrollment increases, 1870–1944, 17; hiring traditions, 107–108; Jewish enrollment, 18–21, 40, 49–50, 57–58, 195n52, 200nn69,74; Jewish fraternities and sororities, 45, 48–49, 112, 199nn58,60; Jewish student clubs, 14, 21, 46–48; in *Menorah Journal* fiction, 168; religious studies as discipline, 18; Semitic studies programs, 24, 94, 194n45; student recreational interests, 60–61. *See also* Jewish studies programs

Hillel Foundation, 58–61, 112, 215n99

Hirsch, Emil G., 210n34

Hitler, Adolf, 134

Hohlfeld, Alexander, 174

Hollinger, David A., 10, 79, 84–85, 184, 191n35

Holocaust studies, 113

Holt, Edwin, 66

homeland discourse, 9–10, 74

Horvitz, Aaron, 44

HUC. *See* Hebrew Union College (HUC)

Hunter College, 110, 199n60

Hurwitz, Henry: biography, 24–25; Cohen/Solow dispute with, 177; death, 178; defense of Jewish student affiliations, 55–56; German Jewish intellectual influences on, 94–97; Hillel dispute with, 59–61; IMA/HMS advocacy, 24–26, 38–39, 49, 94–97; on Jewish historiography, 123; on Jewish life in America, 145; on Jewish studies programs, 100–104, 111–12; as *Menorah Journal* contributor/editor, 13, 128, 147–48, 161, 173, 226n84; photograph, 25, 106; position on Zionism, 42, 47–48

Hurwitz, Maximillian, 156

Hurwood, David Lyon, 178

Husik, Isaac, 210n34

Hyamson, Moses, 120

hyphenated Americans, 9, 12, 82

identity (Jewish identity): affiliation/belonging as component of, 191n35, 215n6; assimilation and, 143–44, 165–66, 171–72, 175–76; cultural vs. religious Judaism, 22; descent and, 66–67, 88–90; double consciousness and, 7–8, 36, 39–40; Hebraism and, 33, 175–76; Hillel articulation of, 60–61; Jewish self-hatred, 5, 189n13; lameness/handicap of dual identity, 181, 184–85; mission and, 73, 77–78; name changing, 164; religious identity, 147–48; self-emancipation and, 6, 111, 175–76, 189n17; symbiotic identity, 32–34, 39–40; "Yidds" stereotype and, 128–31. *See also* dual loyalty

IMA. *See* Harvard Menorah Society; Intercollegiate Menorah Association (IMA)

immigration (Jewish immigration in the U.S.): absence of viable homeland (circular migration) for, 9–10, 191n28; abundance of opportunities in U.S., 9; eastern European Jewish immigration, 14–15, 16–17, 25–26, 120, 130, 219n66; gender expectations and, 152–53; immediate emancipation as model, 6; immigrants in higher education, 99–100; Jewish immigrant population, 192n8

"Impediments" (Trilling), 170

integration: chosenness and, 68–74; double allegiance and, 88; ghetto as segregated living, 125; group interaction as essential to, 85–86; Jewish studies curriculum and, 109, 111–12; Judaism/Zionism as basis for, 7, 189n18; seminary-based intellectualism, 101, 109, 111–12, 122–24, 144–46. *See also* cultural pluralism; nation

Intercollegiate Menorah Association (IMA): at Canadian universities,

197n6; competing Jewish student organizations, 35, 46–48, 196n1; cultural/secular perspective of, 43, 60–61; Dewey support for, 86; founding of, 2, 38; German Jewish intellectual influences on, 94–97; on Hebrew University, 110; Hillel dispute with, 59–60; Hurwitz and, 24–26, 38–39, 49, 94–97; Jewish studies programs and, 91–92, 97–100; lasting influence of, 63; Menorah education initiative, 100–14, 211n57, 213n85; publication of, 38–39, 203n128; Silver critique of, 147–48; social functions and, 44–45; spread nationwide, 33–34, 36–38, 61–62, 203n130; study circle initiative of, 40–41, 103–104, 212n63; Zionism and, 40–43. *See also* Harvard Menorah Society

Intercollegiate Zionist Association of America (IZAA), 47–48
intermarriage, 11, 75–76, 87, 167
Iota Alpha Pi, 199n60
Isaacs, Abram S., 210n34
Isaacs, Nathan, 102, 107, 111, 142, 147, 211n50
Israel, 113. *See also* Palestine
Israel (Lewisohn), 174–75
IZAA. *See* Intercollegiate Zionist Association of America (IZAA)

James, William: influence on Bourne, 84; influence on Kallen, 8, 16, 64–66, 78, 180; as Menorah Society influence, 29; on pluralism, 32, 65
Jastrow, Morris, 210n34
Javitz, Alexander, 157–58, 223n24
Jefferson, Thomas, 180
Jewish Chautauqua Society, 97–98
Jewish history: American historical narrative and, 120–21, 156–57, 180–81, 217n22; American Jewish Historical Society, 97–98; antisemitism theme in, 216n19; ethnic history as means to belonging, 215n6; European emancipation, 125; heritage education initia-

tives, 86–87, 89–90, 96, 165–66; Jewish historical consciousness, 115–16; as Jewish humanism, 216n15; as key to American Jewish revitalization, 143–44; "lachrymose conception" of (Baron), 125; periodization, 124; pre-eminent Jewish historical narratives, 118; seminary-based historiography, 122–24, 217nn31,34; as struggle for persistence, 125–27

Jewish Institute of Religion (JIR), 98, 108–109, 123–24, 144
Jewish intellectualism: as alternative to religious identity, 22–24, 26–27; cultural pluralism and, 2, 10; historical reference works, 97–98; IMA conception of, 4; Menorah education initiative, 100–114; Menorah Society study circles and, 40–41, 103–104; seminary-based intellectualism, 101, 109, 111–12, 122–24; Semitic studies programs, 24, 94, 99; theories of Jewish culture/civilization, 100–101. *See also* Jewish studies programs

Jewish Publication Society (JPS), 97, 103
Jewish studies programs: curriculum for, 103; Hurwitz, Henry on, 100–107; IMA support for, 91–92, 100–104; Menorah Summer School, 104–107; overview, 97–100, 210nn22,34; university faculty and, 107–114. *See also* Jewish intellectualism
Jewish Theological Seminary, 48, 98, 144
JIR. *See* Jewish Institute of Religion (JIR)
Johns Hopkins University, 47, 99, 210n34
Johnson, Lyndon B., 198n49
JPS. *See* Jewish Publication Society (JPS)
Judaism: chosenness discourse, 9, 67–74; Cohen community-based Judaism, 136–37; Hebraism as fundamental to, 33; Hillel religious initiatives, 59; immigrant Passover traditions, 154–55; influence on Puritanism, 66; *Menorah Journal* critique of American rabbinate, 142–49; old vs. new world experiences of, 152–55; re-

stereotypes (Jewish stereotypes): clannishness, 53, 56, 164; cleanliness/
dirtiness, 141; male physical weakness, 34, 141; materialism, 142;
spendthrift/miserly, 164; "Yidds," 128–
31. *See also* antisemitism
Stiles, Ezra, 121
Straus, Oscar S., 121
Straus, S. W., 105
Strauss, Lauren B., 136
supersession premise, 119, 208n109
Synnott, Marcia Graham, 195n52

Temple University, 99, 110, 210n34
"Theological Student: Advanced Model"
(Rosenthal), 168–69
Toll, William, 66
Trilling, Diana, 226n85
Trilling, Lionel: biography, 169–70,
173; Cohen influence on, 115–16, 137;
Dewey influence on, 169, 225n69; dis-
missal at Columbia, 173, 226–27n90;
fiction writing, 168, 170–73; as *Meno-
rah Journal* contributor, 13, 151, 173,
177, 226nn84,85
Trotsky, Leon, 116
Tufts University, 37
Tulane University, 99, 210n34

Union of American Hebrew Congrega-
tions (UAHC), 20–21, 27
universities. *See* higher education; *par-
ticular colleges and universities*
University of Atlanta, 49
University of California, 99, 210n34
University of Chicago, 21, 44, 57, 99–
100, 209n5, 210n34
University of Cincinnati, 42–43
University of Colorado, 38
University of Denver, 38
University of Frankfurt am Main, 110
University of Illinois, 21, 37, 49, 58–59
University of Manitoba, 197n6
University of Minnesota, 21, 33–34, 196n1
University of Missouri, 37
University of Pennsylvania, 47, 50, 99,
210n34

University of Pittsburgh, 37
University of Texas, 37
University of Toronto, 197n6
Up Stream (Lewisohn), 174–75

Van Doren, Mark, 169, 225n69
Veblen, Thorstein, 10
*Verein für Cultur und Wissenschaft der
Juden* (Society for Culture and Science
of the Jews): approach to Jewish tradition, 94–97; Hebraism and, 29; membership, 209n10; as Menorah Association influence, 5–6, 25–26, 102, 117–18;
Menorah Summer School and, 104–105
victimhood, 184–85
Villard, Oswald Garrison, 174
vocation (chosenness), 68
Voorsanger, Jacob, 210n34

Walzer, Michael, 184
Warburg, Felix, 213n79
Washington University, 37
Wechsler, Harold S., 200n69
Weinreich, Max, 214n89
Weinstein, Jacob J., 45–46, 199n49
Wendell, Barrett, 29–30, 32, 65–66, 78,
180–81
whiteness, 183–84
Whitfield, Stephen J., 182
Whitman, Walt, 180
Wilson, Woodrow, 80, 83, 120
Wirth, Louis, 100, 211n41
Wise, Stephen S., 27, 40, 60–61, 98, 108–
109, 122
*Wissenschaft des Judentums. See Verein
für Cultur und Wissenschaft der Juden*
(Society for Culture and Science of
the Jews)
Wolf, Horace J., 98, 142
Wolfson, Harry (pseud. El. Lycidas):
biography, 108–109, 213nn79,84; de-
fense of Jewish student affiliations,
55–56; as faculty committee member,
54; on Jewish history, 116–17; on Jew-
ish studies programs, 108–109, 112;
as MEC Committee member, 102; as
Menorah Journal contributor/editor, 13,

128–30, 147; photograph, *129;* "Pomegranates" series, 128–31, 218nn60,61

World War I: dual loyalty and, 38–39; Kallen pacifism and, 29; Menorah Society patriotism and, 43–44

Yahuda, Abraham Shalom, 213n85

Yale University, 18, 21, 38, 57, 121, 136, 195n52, 200n74

Yezierska, Anzia, 13, 151–52, 223nn10,11

Yiddish language and culture: as academic subject, 110, 214n89; assimilation and, 158, 162, 168, 219n66; class status and, 26; Wolfson on Yiddish culture, 128–31, 219n66

Yiddish Scientific Institute (YIVO), 110, 214n89

YIVO. *See* Yiddish Scientific Institute (YIVO)

Yugoslavia, 134

Zangwill, Israel, 11, 74–76, 145

ZBT fraternity, 48

Zeitlin, Jacob, 174–75, 227n99

Zepin, George, 27

Zionism: assimilation and, 82–83, 84; Avukah student group, 60; chosenness and, 70; dual loyalty and, 84, 163–65; European antisemitism and, 174; Hebraism and, 33–34, 74; homeland discourse, 9–10, 74, 127; humanist conception of, 127; as Menorah Society issue, 22, 40–43, 46–48, 226n84; Parushim (Zionist organization), 195n63; Reform Judaism and, 43, 146–47, 198n38, 221n121; Silver as advocate for, 146–47

Zionist Bureau, 131

Zionist Organization of America (ZOA), 47

Zunz, Leopold, 6, 29, 94–96, 105, 117

Daniel Greene is Director of the Dr. William M. Scholl Center for American History and Culture at the Newberry Library in Chicago. He also has worked as a curator and historian at the U.S. Holocaust Memorial Museum in Washington, D.C. Greene earned his Ph.D. in history at the University of Chicago.